THE MAGIC
OF WALKING

*by Aaron Sussman
and Ruth Goode*

Simon and Schuster · New York

SECOND PRINTING

LIBRARY OF CONGRESS CATALOG CARD NUMBER: 67–25376

DESIGNED BY EVE METZ

MANUFACTURED IN THE UNITED STATES OF AMERICA, BY AMERICAN BOOK–
STRATFORD PRESS, NEW YORK, N.Y.

ACKNOWLEDGMENTS

For permission to reprint the following material, thanks are due to:

Brooks Atkinson for selections from *East of the Hudson,* Alfred A. Knopf, 1928.

Estate of Rachel Carson for a selection from *The Edge of the Sea,* copyright © 1955 by Rachel L. Carson.

Doubleday & Company, Inc., for "Penang," from *Change of Weather,* copyright © 1962 by Winfield Townley Scott. This poem originally appeared in *Poetry.*

J. B. Lippincott Company for "The Art of Walking," from *Essays* by Christopher Morley, copyright 1918, 1945 by Christopher Morley.

Miss D. E. Collins for a selection from *Alarms and Discursions* by G. K. Chesterton.

Houghton Mifflin Company for selections from *The Heart of Emerson's Journals,* edited by Bliss Perry, copyright 1909, 1910, 1911, 1912, 1913 by Edward Waldo Emerson, copyright 1926 by Houghton Mifflin Company.

Norma Millay Ellis for "Departure," from *Collected Poems* of Edna St. Vincent Millay, Harper & Row, copyright 1923, 1951 by Edna St. Vincent Millay and Norma Millay Ellis.

John Kieran for "A Spring Walk." This essay originally appeared in *Collier's,* April 18, 1953.

Lin Yutang for "On Going About and Seeing Things," from *The Importance of Living,* 1937.

Estate of Donald Culross Peattie and its agent, James Brown Associates, Inc., and The New York Times Company for "The Joy of Walking," from *The New York Times Magazine,* April 5, 1942, copyright 1942 by The New York Times Company.

The Macmillan Company for "What a Lovely Walk!" from *The Private Journals of Henri Frédéric Amiel,* translated by Van Wyck Brooks and Charles Van Wyck Brooks, copyright 1935 by the Macmillan Company, renewed 1963 by Van Wyck Brooks and Charles Van Wyck Brooks.

Dodd, Mead & Company, Inc., for "Walking Down a River," from *Journey into Summer* by Edwin Way Teale, copyright © 1960 by Edwin Way Teale.

Collins-Knowlton-Wing for "To Own the Streets and Fields" by Hal Borland, published in *The New York Times Magazine,* October 6, 1946, copyright 1946 by The New York Times Company.

The American Scholar for "Is Walking the New Status Symbol?" by Joseph Wood Krutch, Volume 33, No. 4, Autumn 1964. Copyright © 1964 by the United Chapters of Phi Beta Kappa.

Harold Matson Company, Inc., for "The Pedestrian," from *The Golden Apples of the Sun,* copyright 1952 by Ray Bradbury.

The New York Times Company for "The Gentle Art of Walking" by H. I. Brock, published in *The New York Times Magazine,* June 12, 1942, copyright 1942 by The New York Times Company.

Holt, Rinehart & Winston, Inc., for "The Road Not Taken," from *The Complete Poems of Robert Frost,* copyright 1916 by Holt, Rinehart & Winston, Inc., copyright 1944 by Robert Frost.

Alfred A. Knopf for "A Morning Walk with Bashan," from *A Man and His Dog* by Thomas Mann, copyright 1936 by Alfred A. Knopf.

Atheneum Publishers for "Country Walks," from *Area Code 215* by Walter Teller, copyright © 1962 by Walter Teller.

Vladimir Nabokov for "Butterfly Walks," from *Speak, Memory, An Autobiography revisited,* G. P. Putnam's Sons, 1966. Copyright 1947, 1948, 1949, 1950, 1951 by Vladimir Nabokov; © 1951 (*Conclusive Evidence*); © 1960, 1966 (*Speak, Memory*) by Vladimir Nabokov. A version of this material originally appeared in *The New Yorker* Magazine.

To Caryl and Gerry
OUR CO-WALKERS

FOREWORD

THERE IS A VAST DIFFERENCE, Chesterton pointed out, between the eager man who wants to read a book and the tired man who wants a book to read. There is also a world of difference between the troubled man who saunters to relax and the nervous man who hurries to a date.

This book is designed to satisfy all shades of walkers and readers. There is something here for the man who reads out of curiosity as well as the man who reads for the fun of it, the one who walks because it is an effective way to get around and the one who walks because he knows no pleasanter way on earth to get from one place to another.

Take a walk, despite the colloquialism, is less an injunction to get out of here than a prescription for getting the most out of life. The more you walk, the better you feel, the more relaxed you become, the more you sense, the better you think, the less mental clutter you accumulate. And it's the uncluttered man who is the happy man.

There is something odd about walking. It is the first thing an infant wants to do and the last thing an old man wants to give up doing. But in between, we travel on wheels (above and below ground), on saddles, on ships (where we can at least walk the deck), on planes, on buses, or on trains. Yet doing it the easiest way, by shanks' mare, on foot, almost never occurs to us . . . even when we go to mail a letter. It takes a power failure or a transit strike to give us back our legs.

Walking has become the step almost no one takes.

This is a book about the joys of walking: the hows, the wheres, the whys, and the with-whats of it. The authors have brought to it a devotion to the pleasures walking provides, based on many happy years of living the lives of unhampered pedestrians. You can't do much bird-watching— or people-watching, for that matter—at sixty miles an hour, and to see anything, if you're a photographer at heart, you have to walk around it and take a good look. So both of us, and our spouses, have learned from experience that walking is best.

You pay a heavy price for the comforts and conveniences of civilization. Get into a car and you are trapped by the whims and peculiarities of the roadmakers. Want to go down toward that lovely village in the valley? The highway takes you around it. Of course, you can come back, winding your way through uncharted, washboard dirt roads that may destroy your car. But that impulse to stop and enjoy is gone. Besides, the road signs warn DO NOT STOP EXCEPT FOR EMERGENCY. And is the breathless wonder of a never-to-be-forgotten sunlit sight really an emergency? And could you explain it to a state trooper or a local policeman?

This, then, is a book by walkers for walkers and would-be walkers. As you will see from the contents, it tries to cover as much ground as one book can. We hope to persuade you, comfort you, direct you, alert you, clothe you, even feed you. And then, as though that were not enough, we shall give you a sampling of some of the best writing on walking by writers who were walkers. And there's no better kind of writing.

In the labor of love that this book has been for us, we have enjoyed help and advice from many people. We gratefully thank the following:

Mrs. Elsie Lincoln Rosner, biologist, medical journalist, and a gifted writer in her own right, whose expert editorial research was an indispensable contribution to this book, and whose pleasure in the joys of walking and its literature were an inspiration to us both.

Miss Jackie Wein, who helped in the typing of the manuscript, who tamed the sometime chaos until it began to purr like order, and who offered a few apt suggestions along the way.

Dr. Leon P. Lewithin and Dr. Isadore Rosenfeld, enthusiastic walkers, staunch believers in the medical benefits of walking, and seductive persuaders, for their help.

Paul Goodman, for a singular contribution to pedestrian comfort; Mrs. Helene Frede, for spotting a choice addition to "The Company of Walkers"; and Lawrence Markoe, for help in many ways.

Jim Buck, who took time out from dog-training and the work of his famous obedience school in New York City to teach us how to enjoy a canine walking companion.

Mrs. Lora Stowe, for her sheltering enthusiasm and her shrewd guidance as the book's editor.

Throughout these pages, but especially in the extensive task of assembling and checking "The Walking Guide" and its accompanying lists, we enjoyed the cooperation of American and foreign Government information officers, hiking clubs, nature and conservation societies, tourist agencies, travel book publishers, colleagues and friends who have walked at home and abroad. We thank them all, and in particular:

Mr. George M. Zoebelein, president of the New York–New Jersey Trail Conference, Inc.; Miss Anne Chamberlain of the Sierra Club and Mr. Kenneth N. Anglemire, chairman of its Great Lakes Chapter; Mr. Duryea Morton, director of the National Audubon Society's Department of Audubon Camps and Centers; Mr. Byron L. Ashbaugh, associate director of its Nature Centers Division; Mr. Roland Clement, staff biologist, and indeed all the headquarters staff of the Society.

Also Mr. M. Rupert Cutler, assistant executive director of the Wilderness Society; Mr. Peter L. McCandless of the executive staff of Reston, Virginia; the Appalachian Club, the Appalachian Trail Conference, and the Boy Scouts of America. All these organizations and numerous others supplied valuable information, and many individuals in their offices took time to contribute their personal assistance and encouragement, often anonymously.

AARON SUSSMAN
RUTH GOODE

CONTENTS

Fun for people-watchers. Walking by mind's eye. Those footprints behind you. Transactions with gravity.

PART III **THE COMPANY OF WALKERS** 223
A peripatetic ramble through the literature of walking,
to which is added THE WALKER'S BOOKSHELF
(389)—a reminder of some delightful books for the
armchair saunterer—as well as walking-tour and na-
ture guides for practical use.

Footprints

What attracts my attention shall have it.—EMERSON

Don't do anything. Just stand there!—ADLAI STEVENSON

The longest journey starts with just one step.—TAO TE CHING

To be a discoverer you must go looking for something.—WALTER TELLER

I have two doctors, my left leg and my right.—G. M. TREVELYAN

You never know when an adventure is going to happen.
    —CHRISTOPHER MORLEY

Every mountain means at least two valleys.—ANON

Before supper walk a little; after supper do the same.—ERASMUS

To find new things, take the path you took yesterday.—JOHN BURROUGHS

Of all exercises walking is the best.—THOMAS JEFFERSON

If an ass goes traveling, he'll not come home a horse.—THOMAS FULLER

People love bypaths.—TAO TE CHING

In every photographer, there is something of the stroller.
    —HENRI CARTIER-BRESSON

All walking is discovery. On foot we take the time to see things whole.
    —HAL BORLAND

*Everything has been thought of before, but the difficulty is to think of it
    again.*—GOETHE

Society is always taken by surprise at any new example of common sense.
    —EMERSON

I travel not to go anywhere, but to go.—R. L. STEVENSON

*It is always a silly thing to give advice, but to give good advice is ab-
    solutely fatal.*—OSCAR WILDE

*You can find plenty of people who know all the answers . . . it's the
    questions that confuse them.*—ANON

I will arise and go now.—WILLIAM BUTLER YEATS

The devil never yet asked his victims to take a walk with him.
    —JOHN BURROUGHS

It is good to collect things; it is better to take walks.—ANATOLE FRANCE

Part I

THE FIRST STEP

The why, where, and how of walking.

Chapter 1

YOU MEAN YOU *WALKED?*

Years ago, scientists were predicting the evolution of a race of men without legs, thanks to the automobile. Nowadays we know they were wrong. It is not our legs we are losing. It is our minds.

We are also losing our figures, our good looks, the use of our senses, our health—and some of us are losing our lives as a result of ills that walking could prevent or keep in check.

Walking is the exercise that needs no gym. It is the prescription without medicine, the weight control without diet, the cosmetic that is sold in no drugstore. It is the tranquilizer without a pill, the therapy without a psychoanalyst, the fountain of youth that is no legend. A walk is the vacation that does not cost a cent.

Some people know this. Some people never give up walking from the day they take their first step. There are more such people than anyone knows, because walkers tend to keep their walking private. When anyone admits that he arrived somewhere not by car, bus, subway or taxi but on his own two legs, people stare at him and exclaim, "You mean you *walked?*"

Nobody likes to be looked upon as an oddball. But the fact is that more and more people are joining the oddball club of those who would rather walk even when they can ride. And a further fact is that there is more talk about walking today, more attention paid to it in the public prints, more concern about preserving old places and creating new places where people can walk, than there has been in a quarter of a century.

The last time Americans thought very much about walking was when we were at war, and gasoline rationing had slammed the garage doors shut for any but the most necessary transportation. During the war years the magazines blossomed with articles on the joys of walking and the newspapers sprouted columns on walking trails around the cities. People could not take their cars out for a Sunday drive, and so they went walking instead. Many of them got together in hiking clubs. Some of those people are still walking, not because they must but because they found they liked it.

We are again witnessing a walking revival. City planners talk about turning urban centers into pedestrian malls, state authorities talk less about superhighways and more about state parks, and cities and states both look hopefully to Washington for money for these projects. In Washington, meanwhile, Congress is presented with proposals for new park areas, new wilderness and seashore areas, and a giant bill for the rehabilitation of our historic national trails. Some of these proposals come under the heading of wildlife sanctuaries, some are for conservation, some are for recreation—but all, in one way or another, mean more places to walk.

This time we have not a single overriding emergency, such as a world war, but a whole complex of them. We have a health emergency, a population emergency, a recreation emergency. But most intimate and oppressive to us all in our personal lives is the automobile emergency.

We are fed up with our cars. We are sick of getting stuck in traffic whether in a city street or on a highway, sitting trapped and helpless, breathing air befouled by automobile fumes, feeling tempers and tensions rise to the point of explosion. Not long ago a veteran parkway planner argued for a road along a famous island beach, on the ground that families needed this additional place to take a pleasant Sunday drive. He was greeted with derisive laughter. It is a long time since people found any pleasure in a Sunday drive.

Walkers by Necessity

It is true, of course, that people who give up the automobile as a form of recreation do not necessarily turn to walking. They may simply stay home and read the Sunday papers instead, or watch television. For most people it takes some extraordinary event to reintroduce them to the use of their legs. Suddenly the wheels stop turning, they are obliged to walk—and they discover for the first time the joy and the magic of walking.

This happened twice in seven weeks to the people of New York. The first occasion was a power failure that darkened the entire Northeast. In the metropolis it stopped the wheels of subway and commuter trains at the rush hour of a November evening, and stranded millions in the heart of the city, far from home. Thousands of them—no one knows how many—set out with grace and good spirit to walk the long avenues to upper Manhattan, and over the bridges to the Bronx, Brooklyn and Queens.

Some New Yorkers who had not walked more than a few blocks at a time since childhood walked five, ten, fifteen miles that night. Some at the end of their walk climbed many flights to their beds in apartment houses whose elevators, too, were stalled. To the surprise of everyone including the walkers, there was no epidemic of collapses, not one heart attack traceable to the unusual exertion.

The people who struggled to get home by bus, car, or taxi that night told of exhausting experiences. The people who could not get home at all were also exhausted. But the walkers did not complain. Indeed, they boasted. They were as proud of their walking achievement as mountain climbers who have conquered a perilous peak.

Most of all, they discovered that legs are a form of locomotion, and that a remarkable sense of independence and self-confidence comes with using them.

The Twelve-Day Walk

The transit strike that came several weeks later was the real test. Charter buses, car pools, taxis—everything on wheels—sat stalled for hours in the clogged streets. Those who could, walked, and counted themselves lucky.

At the end of the first week the walkers were footsore and leg-weary. People who would normally take a bus or taxi for any distance longer than four or five blocks were walking four and five miles a day. Many did not have suitable footwear, did not even know what suitable footwear was. By the second week they had learned. They had also learned that muscles strengthen, feet toughen, and walking can be a pleasure.

Morning and evening, they poured up and down the canyons of industry, in rain, cold, and biting wind. The pretty secretaries no longer teetered on high heels but went sturdily and warmly booted. And a new social phenomenon appeared. The city became divided into two classes of people, those who rode and those who walked.

The people on wheels, imprisoned for hours in the traffic jams, were exasperated. The people on foot, free to move under their own power, were exhilarated. The riders talked wearyingly about inconveniences and fatigue. But the walkers talked about their discovery of the city, its beauties, its hitherto unknown neighborhoods and unexpected turnings. A psychiatrist told of his patients who were shaking off fears and phobias on their walks. A drug company executive sounded so exuberant on the telephone that his caller asked him what new pill he was taking.

"No pill!" he retorted. "I'm walking four miles to work and four miles home every day and I feel great!"

From Boston Dr. Paul Dudley White, the cardiologist who at seventy-nine was still walking to his office, sent word to New Yorkers that the strike was the best thing that had ever happened to them. (Incidentally when Dr. White has to go somewhere by air, he pays off his cab a mile before the airport and walks to his plane from there.) A newsman, summing up the medical authorities on walking, speculated that the transit stoppage may have converted more people to walking than Dr. White and his colleagues had been able to do in a decade.

And so it may have done. Some who learned to walk during the strike went right on walking. Dwellers in Manhattan were walking one or two miles between home and work. Suburbanites were walking to their train and bus terminals. Even some whose work kept them on their feet all day, dentists and beauty operators, were walking where previously they would ride. Cabdrivers plying the midtown trade complained that people were walking to their luncheon engagements and business conferences.

Well before the twelve-day walk of 1966, New York real estate men were advertising luxury apartments in midtown with the slogan WALK TO WORK! In Chicago and other big cities, residential areas within walking range of the business center are part of the urban renewal plans. More and more, people are entertaining the revolutionary notion that a person might actually *like* to walk.

The Secret Society of Walkers

There have always been people—a few—who like to walk. Throughout the half century when the automobile has governed American life, there have been walkers. They have been a smallish, somewhat secret society, in which each one tends to keep his membership private. Walkers recognize each other by certain signs, like the signs of an underground movement, but most walkers are soloists, each a revolutionary cell unto himself.

Non-walkers sometimes note the signs and ask, "Have you been away? You look tan!" because even in midwinter the walker has an outdoor glow on his face without benefit of ultraviolet lamp. People ask how he keeps his weight down and what diet he follows. People who have not seen him for a while remark that he doesn't get any older and ask what's his secret.

Walkers do not boast of their addiction. And generally they do not proselytize, because they know from experience that everyone has to discover the magic of walking for himself.

A Psychophysical Magic

Writers have written eloquently of the joys of walking, but the magic of walking is something more than pleasure. It is a true magic, a psychophysical alchemy, which transforms the body and the mind.

The evidence for this is not merely the subjective testimony of walkers. It is laboratory-tested. Walking conserves and restores physical and psychological health. It prolongs youth, enhances beauty. All this is physiology, quite apart from the subjective enjoyments that confirmed walkers sometimes try to share with those who do not walk.

Men are warned by their doctors and their wives that they ought to walk, and yet they do not walk. Women are even more resistant, having sacrificed their feet to fashion.

Why walk, when you can ride? This now rhetorical question was first asked by prehistoric man, who answered it by taming a horse, donkey, camel, onager or water buffalo, and went on to invent the wheel. Today there remain areas on earth where most people still walk because they have not the wherewithal to ride, but these areas are shrinking away. In the Western world, walking ceased to be a necessity long ago.

As soon as walking stopped being a necessity, it became a luxury, an aristocratic privilege. Men of means and leisure went walking to hunt, fish, study nature or explore Africa. Another aristocracy adopted walking for another reason. This was the aristocracy of the intellect and the arts, the poets, novelists, composers, painters; the philosophers, sometimes the statesmen. They went walking to think, to experience, to dream.

Walk to Save Your Life

Now walking is again becoming a necessity, but of a different kind. It is not and probably never again will be a necessity for getting from one place to another. But now it is a necessity for health and well-being. Walking may save our lives.

Any exercise may be life-preserving, provided it is regular. Some people play golf, tennis, or other games every week and all year round, and some—a few—keep doing this into their middle years and beyond. Some people faithfully go to the gym and some do their calisthenics or isometrics every day at home. Some go bowling once a week; some ski regularly through the winter and a select few go mountain-climbing in summer. Many invest in stationary bicycles and a few actually use them. For those people, walking is not a necessity although it may still be a pleasure.

But the faithful exercisers are a very small minority. And even their dedication to a favorite form of muscle-flexing tends to dwindle with each passing birthday. In their forties, perhaps before, they falter. Going to the gym is for most a dreary ritual, and exercising at home is even drearier. The demands of business, career, family, edge the pleasures of sports into an ever narrower corner. Tennis and skiing are seasonal, and each year it seems more of a drag to get into condition again. Golf is also seasonal in much of the country. The golfers generally stay with the game, but long before their legs give out they are riding rather than walking over the course, because it takes less time or is just so seductively easy. And there is always the expense in time and money, to say nothing of the effort of getting to the scene of the sport, which for city dwellers is considerable.

Walking has none of these disadvantages. Anybody who is not disabled can walk, whatever his age or the state of his muscles. Its playing field is as near as the street at one's front door; it requires no equipment, no lessons with a pro, no expenditure beyond the price of an extra pair of shoes per year, if that. Walking is the cheapest exercise in time, money, and energy. It is the most accessible and the most generally available. Simple as it is, it is listed as a "best" exercise by the physical fitness experts and recommended as a health preserver and, for some of their patients, an outright life saver by the doctors.

Why, then, don't more Americans walk? Why is walking still the private and somewhat secret pleasure of a sophisticated few?

The Wheel-and-Chair Syndrome

It is our belief that people do not walk because of simple unawareness of the ease, the pleasures, and especially the benefits of walking. They take their ability to walk too utterly for granted. Only once, and that very early in life, is walking a conscious, supreme achievement, when as babies they take their first tottering steps. At that moment, bells ring, fireworks sparkle, parents telephone grandparents, aunts and uncles and cousins join in the general celebration. And that is the first and last time that they are aware of walking, throughout the whole of their lives.

The excitement lasts just about a day. Before the child or anyone else realizes it, he is not walking but running, jumping, skipping, climbing. Soon enough he is pedaling his three-wheeler, his two-wheeler, rolling on roller skates and skate boards, getting ready to go on wheels for the rest of his life. Thereafter, whenever he is not on wheels he is in a chair. Walking from then on is something he has to do to get from his chair to his car, a minor inconvenience. Some people house the car under the same roof with the chair, reducing the inconvenience still further.

To a few people, an accident or an illness may make walking significant again by threatening to take it away. When this happens, they and their doctors, as well as hospitals, philanthropic organizations and even governments invest energies, skills, treasure and endless effort to restore their ability to walk. It is an ironic fact that people never miss walking unless they are deprived of it. They cheerfully spend all their waking hours in chairs or on wheels. But they will move heaven and earth to avoid the chair and the wheels combined: the wheelchair.

No responsible person—except a physician, under special circumstances in some special cases—would tell you that if you do not walk you are headed for a wheelchair. And yet this is not such a wildly farfetched exaggeration. From one point of view, a great number of Americans are voluntarily going about in the equivalent of wheelchairs at this very moment.

The Heart Saver

Our bodies are built for use. All the body systems—muscles, joints, circulation, respiration, digestion, metabolism, waste disposal, even the nervous system—depend for their proper functioning on the sheer physical activity of the musculoskeletal structure. Man is a miraculous organism, but whether he is reading a murder mystery or plotting a course among the stars, he is still a physical organism made of glands and organs, bones and muscles. One muscle alone can end all his fabulous intellectual and emotional experiences. He will have no more thoughts or feelings if his heart fails to function.

Cardiologists like Dr. Paul Dudley White tell us repeatedly that we must move, we must exercise, we must walk. We listen—and forget. We do not relate these warnings to ourselves. Only a heart patient really absorbs the meaning of these words, because he knows his life depends upon them. The rest of us brush them aside, even though they tell us that we must embrace some form of exercise within our lives as a necessary prevention of the very ills that we most fear.

We brush aside these warnings because we are lazy, because we are ostrichlike optimists ("It can't happen to me!") but mostly because we are abysmally ignorant of the body and how it works. Walking seems too easy, too commonplace, too obvious and indeed too inexpensive a preventive of serious illness. We are accustomed to far more complex and costly prescriptions.

But it is true and proven that some amount of brisk and invigorating walking every day or every two or three days actually lowers blood pressure and pulse rate and sustains the heart muscle in healthy tone.

The Non-Dieting Diet

People, especially men, begin to worry about the added pounds creeping up on them as they progress through their thirties and forties. They know that overweight is an invitation to trouble and a known cause of shortened life. They resolve on energetic measures—dieting, workouts at the gym, reducing courses—and perhaps they carry out some of them. They lose the extra pounds, but sooner or later the weight comes creeping back again.

If they would but realize it, they could accomplish the same ends, less painfully and more permanently, by walking. But again, it seems too easy, too ordinary a method to be taken seriously. Surely, they think, reducing and weight control require a more strenuous and punishing regime.

And yet it is true and proven that walking is the non-dieting diet, the non-exercising exercise that can keep the pounds under control.

Antidote to Tension

Tension is probably the most widespread complaint that people bring to their physicians. It gives them headaches, backaches, elevated blood pressure. It keeps them awake at night or tossing in unrestful sleep. It makes them inefficient at work and irritable at home. They take expensive pills and go on expensive vacations to get rid of their tension. The pills and the vacations work, to a degree, about as well as the dieting for overweight. They win relief for a while, but the tension is always there, stealing back into muscles and nerves and tying body and mind into little knots.

Walking is the direct physiological answer to tension. Even a short brisk walk can drain away anger and anxiety, solve a problem, untangle the knots both physical and psychological. Walking as a regular part of the day or week draws off tensions before they turn into headaches and insomnia that need pills, or backaches that take expensive orthopedic skills to relieve them.

Most people do not know that walking, commonplace ordinary walking, can perform these wonders for them. Or if they have been told, they do not believe it. Yet it is a relatively simple interaction of body and mind, psychosomatic and somatopsychic, which does not require a course in physiology to understand. The mechanisms by which walking restores and preserves muscular, nervous, and emotional health are a heritage as ancient as the first man.

The Pleasure-Pain Principle

Like all human activities, walking becomes part of our lives or not, according to the pleasure-pain principle. Sigmund Freud stated it long ago: All living creatures tend to seek pleasure and avoid pain, and man is no exception. In the lower animals this principle contributes to their survival. The things that are good for them also give them pleasure, and the things that may harm them give them pain, or at least are disagreeable enough to be avoided.

Only man enjoys what may harm him and avoids what may be good for him. Only wondering, seeking, clever man invents shortcuts to save work and deprives himself of the activity that can keep him healthy. Only man goes to excesses of ease and comfort that may do him harm.

People take to walking to avoid pain—the pain of illness or of the fear of illness—only when their physicians persuade them that the danger is real and present. But they will walk if once they discover that walking gives them pleasure—the pleasure of well-being, of better looks, of peace of mind, the pleasure of new and refreshing experience for their senses and their emotions.

In our world, walking has suffered from a bad press. Recent waves of physical fitness mania have equated walking with fifty-mile hikes, which are painful in the extreme for most people even to think about. Many men take into later life an association of walking with the dreary marches of their military training. Many women complain that walking tires them, when in fact they do not walk at all. They go window-shopping, stopping and starting, standing and looking. This is an enjoyable occupation but it has no resemblance to the tireless swing of rhythmic walking.

The nature-walkers have contributed handsomely to literature but little, it must be admitted, to the allurements of walking. The vast number of Americans who live in cities and suburbs have no experience of nature to which to relate these pleasures. A naturalist's excitements, however eloquently recounted, persuade few people to go out with pocket lenses, creeping over the ground to examine ferns and mosses or the exquisite miniature structure of a wildflower.

As for bird-walkers, although their numbers are increasing at a gratifying rate, they are still eccentrics. Many suburbanites build bird-baths and birdhouses, and plant their gardens with the shrubs and flowers that birds like, and then they sit and watch the birds through the picture window. They go to great lengths to get the birds to come to them, but they will not move out of their comfortable houses to go to the birds.

Nature walking and bird walking must be experienced at first hand; they are acquired tastes. Flowers, ferns, rocks and rivers, birds and butterflies, do work their enticements, but only after one or more enjoyable exposures. An armchair naturalist may be lured out to see what he has read about, but usually the pleasure of the walk comes first, and the binoculars, cameras, butterfly nets, the naturalist's pocket lenses and the geologist's pocket hammers, come as a separate development if at all.

And not nature walking alone, but city walking or any other walking must be a direct experience. Until you have walked, the magic of walking will remain something of a mystery. Until you have known the rhythm of a good walk in your own muscles, the movement of air on your own face, the changing scenes with your own eyes, you do not know what you have been missing.

But if once you have felt the refreshment of mind and body that is the reward of a good walk, then you are on the way to making walking a pleasure that will go with you through the rest of your life.

The purpose of this book is to help you discover this pleasure.

Chapter 2

THE REDISCOVERY
OF WALKING

HUMAN BEINGS have been walking for a half-million, perhaps a million, years, depending upon what date the anthropologists set for the birth of man. Walking was born with man, and man is the only true walker among earth's creatures. Others creep, crawl, climb, swim, fly; they hop, leap, bound, gallop, and most of all they run. Man walks.

Man may run to catch his quarry or escape his enemy, but to go from one place to another he walks. He is the one persistent walker throughout the history of life on earth.

The other two characteristics that make man unique among the animals are the skill of his hands and the size of his brain, and there is reason to believe that both the brain and the hands evolved in a subtle interrelationship with the two-legged gait. Because of our history, our whole psychophysical structure has been integrated with walking, from the very birth of the human species. And the well-being of the whole man, mind and body, is still dependent upon his continuing to walk. It is *not walking* that is unnatural.

At some point in the remote past, a simian ancestor came down out of the trees to walk on the earth. The big apes are mostly terrestrial; the gorillas climb the trees only to make a nest for sleeping. But they are poor walkers. They lumber along like inefficient quadrupeds on their short legs, supporting their heavy torsos on the knuckles of one or both hands.

Lord of the Earth

Eventually a primate evolved that did indeed walk on two legs without using his hands even for knuckle-walking. He had a pelvis wide enough to hold his torso erect above his legs, and his legs had lengthened.

His fossil bones are at least 1,000,000 years old. He was apelike in some respects, but in others a man: one who walked upright. He is called a hominid, a manlike creature. Later still came *Homo sapiens,* or "knowing man," meaning us.

As a walker, man became lord of the earth even before he learned to sow a seed or make a clay pot. He was not the fastest animal nor the strongest. He could not run with the quadrupeds. But he could outwalk them. Stone Age men walked all over the continents, hunting beasts far swifter and fiercer than themselves.

Cave-dwelling men in the glacial age of Europe would walk a hundred miles on a hunt, and bring back enough meat for their families to live on through the frozen winter. Bipedal man could walk; with his two hands free he could carry his weapons and his food. And with his ingenious brain he could use the experience of the past to provide for the future. No other creature was endowed with these advantages for survival.

Conquerors Afoot

Walking thus began as a biological asset, but soon enough it became a cultural advantage. Throughout history the walkers have inherited the earth. The Israelites walked for forty years in the wilderness, but they came in the end to the land of milk and honey.

The great migrations were all made on foot. The Tatars, Mongols, and Huns rode their swift shaggy ponies across Asia and much of Europe, and for a while they conquered, but the men who came and stayed were the ones who came on foot, bringing their gods and tools and household arts—and their families. Only the walkers, advancing at the pace of the slowest among them, could bring the old men with the wisdom of the past, the women and children with the promise of the future. The men on horseback have been the conquerors of history, but the men afoot have been the thinkers, the dreamers, the organizers and founders of civilizations.

Even the conquerors made their conquests with men afoot. The Roman legionary, walking 21 miles a day with his pack on his back, marched the length and breadth of Europe, Britain, North Africa and much of the Middle East, and held it all for the Caesars. Hannibal had elephants and brilliant cavalry troops but he did not conquer Rome. The people who took Europe from the loosening grasp of the Caesars were the immigrant

Teutonic tribes, walking from the east in search of a new home. The chiefs and the warriors rode out to raid, besiege, and pillage the seats of power, but the farmers and their families followed on foot, taking possession of the land.

To See the World

In the Middle Ages, walking became the way to adventure. On pilgrimages and on the Crusades the kings and the captains rode, but the men—and on one Crusade the children—walked in their thousands to a seaport, voyaged across the waters and disembarked to walk again. Were the pilgrims moved by religious fervor or did they merely long to escape from their walled towns into a more exciting world? No one can say. Despite the hazards of the medieval roads, there were always adventurous men walking—minstrels, troubadours, wandering scholars, jugglers and acrobats, rascally poets like François Villon escaping the jailer's torture and the hangman's noose. A respectable burgher rode in fear with a retinue of men-at-arms, but a man whose only property was a song, a trick, and a ready wit went merrily on foot to see the world.

For some centuries longer, walking continued to be the one means of travel available to everyone. Johann Sebastian Bach as a lad walked from Lüneberg to Hamburg on his holidays from choir school, to hear the renowned Buxtehude play the organ.

Then suddenly, after half a million years, people stopped walking. Public coaches began to travel the roads from city to city, and people began to ride in them. This revolution dates from a time less than two hundred years ago. The historian Thomas Macaulay mourned that people no longer saw the country, now that they were traveling by coach. Some decades later came the railroads, making walking even less popular (and Alexandre Dumas the elder, scorning to ride the trains, now declared that the only way to see the country was by coach). Later still, within living memory, Mr. Henry Ford dreamed of putting every man behind the wheel of his own automobile, and that is where we are today.

Who Were the Walkers?

Through all this the walkers continued to walk, but now they walked wholly by choice, and they were few and highly select. What kind of people would walk when they could ride? Henry David Thoreau, the greatest of American walkers, ranked walkers as a class apart, "a fourth estate outside of Church, State, and People." The critic and essayist John Ruskin rose at six, walked six miles, and worked six hours every day. The poet Coleridge walked his ten miles daily, and worked out the scheme of "The Rime of the Ancient Mariner" on a walking tour with Wordsworth.

Wordsworth was a formidable walker who at the age of twenty walked 350 miles in the first two weeks of a European holiday, and went on to explore Switzerland, Italy, and Savoy, all on foot. At home he habitually walked 14 miles a day; his friends estimated that he must have walked 185,000 miles in the English Lake Country which inspired so much of his poetry. According to his sister Dorothy, a small stooped woman who was nevertheless a great walker herself, Wordsworth at sixty was as fit as when he tramped across the Alps forty years before.

Shakespeare's contemporary Ben Jonson, playwright and poet, was a great walker; so was delicate Keats, and so was elegant Shelley, who often walked the 32 miles to London when he was a student at Oxford. When Shelley eloped to France with Mary Wollstonecraft, accompanied by her stepsister, they could not afford a coach, and so they set out blithely to walk to Switzerland, the two pretty young ladies in their silk dresses with a little donkey to carry their luggage. They walked 100 miles in six days, until Shelley sprained his ankle and they had to hire a carriage to take them the rest of the way.

Thomas de Quincey, frail, sickly, addicted to opium, walked from boyhood all through his life. In his last years he walked the 7 miles between his home and Edinburgh at night, carrying a lantern, and at the age of sixty-three he made the trip on foot in the rain to meet the great American, Emerson. He believed that his health depended on walking, and he may have been right. For a period, when he was afflicted with a liver disorder, he walked around his garden, a distance of 44 yards, 440 times a day, in ninety days a distance of 1,000 miles. In his better years he was a walking companion to Wordsworth, and to the tall, handsome Edinburgh professor of moral philosophy, John Wilson, who strode the hills like a Viking beside the small, shrinking De Quincey. But De Quincey kept up with the pace.

Portly Samuel Johnson enjoyed walking in eighteenth-century London and went on walking trips with Boswell and with his friends the Thrales. Prim, satiric Jane Austen was a walker, and she made walkers of her favorite heroines in her novels. George Borrow set out to walk and write as a youth, joined the Gypsies and tinkers on the road for some seven years, and eventually walked back to London—112 miles in twenty-seven hours—got a job distributing Bibles, married and became a respectable citizen. But he still took long walks daily and went on walking tours, and at the age of fifty-one he could walk 34 miles in a day and cover the last mile in ten minutes. In his seventies, a hardy old man living in Maine, he would break the ice on a wintry morning to bathe.

Robert Louis Stevenson, Thomas Carlyle, Sir Walter Scott, Charles Dickens were all walkers. It has been said that the great English literature of the eighteenth and nineteenth centuries was all born afoot. The same might be said of philosophy. Aristotle, discoursing as he strolled with his students, founded the philosophic school called Peripatetic. Kant walked for an hour every afternoon, no matter what the weather.

Rousseau wrote of his walks, "Never have I thought so much, never have I realized my own existence so much, have been so much alive." George Trevelyan, who reclaimed history as a form of literature and wrote the classic *Short History of England,* said of walking, "I never knew a man go for an honest day's walk for whatever distance, great or small . . . and not have his reward in the repossession of his soul."

In this spirit Abraham Lincoln used to walk to a hilltop outside Springfield and stride around it for hours. As Adlai Stevenson told it, Lincoln walking about on the hilltop found that thoughts came to him as they never could do when people and problems were crowding in upon him. Stevenson, when he was Governor of Illinois, would walk out to that same hill and stay there, walking and thinking, sometimes for the better part of a day.

Throughout the centuries men have been aware, as Lincoln was, of the deficit they suffered when they were giving out more than they were taking in. They walked to replenish the deficit, and to store up spiritual and intellectual treasure against the demands of their daily lives, whether as poets, philosphers, statesmen—or simply as human beings concerned with using to the full their human potentialities.

Headline Walkers

Walking has also been a sport and a stunt. An eighteenth-century gentleman named Foster Powell, correctly clad in frilled shirt, long waistcoat, full-skirted coat, wig and three-cornered hat, walked the 402 miles from London to York and back again in five days and eighteen hours. A more athletically clad champion named George Wilson set himself to walk 50 miles a day for ten consecutive days and completed his 500 miles in eleven. An early nineteenth-century gentleman, a Captain Robert Barclay, walked 1,000 miles in a thousand consecutive hours. Somewhat more recently a Peruvian Boy Scout walked from Buenos Aires to New York, a distance of 18,000 miles, in two years.

When normal walking became too commonplace to attract attention, a stunt-minded Englishman named Plennie Wingo walked 3,926 miles around Europe and the United States, backward. An Austrian taxi driver tried walking on his hands from Vienna to Graz but gave up after 40 miles on account of blisters.

Among the marathon walkers there were some enthusiasts who enjoyed walking for its own sake. One such was Edward Payson Weston, who first won public notice as a youth of twenty-two when he walked from Boston to Washington, D.C., to see Lincoln inaugurated. He was a puny lad who went to work for the Boston *Herald* as an office boy; lacking impressive brawn, he made an asset of his small wiry stature by being the quickest to run an errand. When he was promoted to reporter, his speed and stamina as a walker made him a notable newshound in the days before telephones and automobiles.

Weston became a doughty propagandist for the healthful effects of walking, and eventually made a career of long-distance marathons, winning medals and going on lecture tours all over the United States and Europe. But he continued to be an amateur of walking for health and pleasure, and his lectures were lively accounts of the adventures of the road. At seventy-one he capped his career by walking from New York to San Francisco in a hundred and five days and back from Los Angeles to New York in seventy-six days; a few years later he celebrated his 100,000th mile. He was walking in the city street when a taxi struck and crippled him, ending his pedestrian career at the age of eighty-eight.

Another newspaperman-walker was the famous editor of *The New York Times,* Dr. John H. Finley, who once each year walked the 36-mile perimeter of Manhattan. An appreciative city named its East River promenade in his honor; it is a pretty walk with a river view, but it is only eight blocks long, scarcely a warm-up for a walker like Dr. Finley. Still, it is the only known civic memorial a man has ever earned simply by walking.

Why the Walkers Walk

True walkers, including Dr. Finley, do not walk to make records or to win monuments. They walk for no reason but to enjoy the pleasure of walking. This may be the purely physical enjoyment of stretching muscles, expanding lungs, and the rhythmic relaxation from crown to toe in man's most natural exercise. Or it may be the psychological release of walking away from desk, telephone, automobile errands, shopping lists, the sheer dailiness of daily life, and enjoying the most available, least expensive of vacations, whether for an hour, an afternoon, or a weekend.

It may be the esthetic and adventurous pleasure of seeing what one never can see except on foot, whether the course is along city streets, country roads, or wilderness trails. Any walk may be a blend of all these pleasures.

One celebrated pair of walkers, Thomas and Catherine Storie, set out to walk systematically the length of every street of a city. They began with their home town, New York, in the 1920's, and up to a few years ago they were still walking, having covered some 20,000 miles of pavement within weekend distance of home during the year and in foreign parts on their vacations. Another walking couple, the John David Gills, set out on a conventional vacation trip to Europe following Mr. Gill's retirement. They spent four years walking the Continent, and came back to continue walking over the United States. They found it was the only way they could really see the world and the people in it.

Sometimes a true walker will take a headline-catching walk to make a point. This is what Supreme Court Justice William O. Douglas, a walker of the purest dedication to enjoyment, did in 1954 when he led a 180-mile walk the entire length of the Chesapeake and Ohio Canal from Cumberland, Maryland, to Washington, D.C. Justice Douglas did this in answer to an editorial in the Washington *Post* proposing the construction of a scenic parkway along the historic route. He invited the editorial writers to walk it with him, and see at first hand what they were proposing to tamper with.

One of the *Post* writers and some dozens of enthusiasts set out, but only the hardy jurist and eight companions stayed the course. Still, the newspaper was persuaded to change its opinion, and recommended altering the parkway plan so as not to encroach on the most beautiful and unspoiled sections of the canal. Thanks to Justice Douglas, the C and O Canal is still one of the fine non-strenuous, semi-wilderness walks remaining within reach of city dwellers in the continuous megalopolis of the Eastern seaboard.

Justice Douglas was in the news again more recently, when he and a party of walking companions, caught in a sudden downpour, came at last dripping and squishing into an eating place and tried to buy hot coffee, only to be thrown out as tramps by the indignant mistress of the establishment. Ever since people took to riding in stagecoaches, the world has been inclined to look upon those who preferred to walk as something less than respectable.

The poets found it to be so in nineteenth-century England, when they were often refused bed and board at an inn. Shelley and his friends recommended wearing sober black like a clergyman—since the clergy's respectability was beyond question and so was the clergy's slenderness of purse that made coach fare a luxury.

The Los Angeles police have an impressive record of halting notable walkers—the late Aldous Huxley, the popular nutritionist Gayelord Hauser, the science fiction writer Ray Bradbury—with the demand that they identify themselves as responsible citizens or spend the night in jail as vagrants. There must be something wrong with a man who will walk when he can afford to ride!

During its long decline, walking has been a private pleasure known to relatively few. But the signs are many that walking is on the way to becoming popular again, that people are beginning to rediscover the art and the magic of walking. More people are walking the wilderness trails in the national parks each year. More people in the public eye are confessing an addiction to daily walks, like the television newscaster Robert Trout, who a dozen years ago began walking five miles a day but only recently dared to admit it without the fear that he would be considered an eccentric.

People are walking at home, and on vacations away from home. Recently the news pages displayed a photograph of an American woman walking in Europe with a pedometer dangling from her belt (the same pedometer, incidentally, that we recommend in Chapter 11). The pedometer is new but her explorations afoot are not. Even on a fast three-week trip she clocked 153 miles, 51 miles a week. She has a friend, male, who quite casually walks 14 miles in a day's exploring around Copenhagen, 15 miles in Brussels, 21.5 miles in London.

This woman walks, she says, because it is a way to make friends. People are friendly to a walker. Asking directions, waiting on a curb for the traffic signal to change, or just walking, has led to shared codfish cakes in Portugal, an invitation to breakfast in Yugoslavia, a country picnic in Hungary. Walking brings adventures and experiences we can never have when we tour by bus or car.

Walking has a further, unexpected reward: It keeps the weight down. We will stuff ourselves regardless on the *haute cuisine* in France, the *pasta* in Italy, the pastries in Denmark, and moan through dreary diets for months afterward at home. On our travels we are resigned to eating now and paying later. But we can eat now and *not* pay later, so long as we walk.

So it appears that walkers are not eccentrics, but simply people who have discovered a secret. We propose now to disclose their secret.

Chapter 3

ENGINEER'S DELIGHT

"WALKING," says Dr. Paul Dudley White, "is as natural as breathing." Dr. White, who knows his physiology, may be taken to mean this not as an expression of his known enthusiasm for walking but as a statement of literal fact.

For it is a literal fact. The mechanics of walking are built into the human body in much the same way as the mechanics of respiration, and both are triumphs of mechanical engineering. For sheer efficiency, which means getting best performance at least energy cost, these nature-built mechanisms surpass anything devised by man.

As a locomotor device, the bony structure of the human body is an engineer's delight. It is not built for speed, to be sure. But for carrying its own weight from one point to another on the earth's surface it is an evolutionary wonder. The body is built poorly for sitting, only a little better for standing, but for walking it is unrivaled.

In plan it is so simple that a child can draw it in a stick figure: a single upright for the spine; two crossbars balanced on it horizontally from which swing a pair each of arms and legs; a knob at the top for a head. But on examination, certain subtleties appear. The spine is not a straight vertical rod but a jointed and double-curved spring. The legs also have springy joints at knees and ankles and springlike arches in the feet, and they swing from the hips on ball-and-socket joints. The crossbar supports for the appendages, furthermore, are not fixed rigidly on the spine but can swing and pivot. At every point the structure is flexible, mobile, clearly built as a dynamic rather than a static support.

The distribution of weight, too, is subtle and at first glance rather puzzling. The bony dome of the skull, the bony shoulder girdle and the arms swinging from it all add up to a top-heavy construction. Can this be efficient?

We're Not Built for Sitting

It is very far from efficient for sitting, especially for sitting at a desk, a workbench, or a machine. When we must sit at our work, the topheavy head and shoulders are constantly pulled forward by the force of gravity, and the flexible S-curved spine is hard put to keep its shape against the steady distorting pull. The muscles that are placed to hold all these movable parts in their proper relation to one another are under unrelieved tension. The consequences are, at the very least, fatigue, irritability, vague psychological and emotional discomfort growing out of unidentified physical stress. When sitting is a way of life—as it is for most of us in our world—the consequences come in a progression of stiff necks, headaches, gastric distress, and the lower back pain that is currently the most common undiagnosed and often undiagnosable complaint.

When we sit at our ease, not working, the effects are somewhat less disruptive to the musculoskeletal system but perhaps more serious for other systems, for example the cardiovascular. We will have more to say about this. Still, even when we are at ease, even with head and spine leaning backward and supported against the clutch of gravity, sitting for long periods is a physiological stress no matter how well constructed the chair may be—and few are shaped to comfort the human body. Sitting at the movies can actually hurt!

Your favorite chair, in which you may spend many hours of the week reading, conversing, watching television and occasionally dozing, may be beautifully designed to go with the decor of the living room, and it certainly feels wonderful when you sink into it. It may even be well built for sitting. But after an hour or two it might just as well be the Iron Maiden for its effect on your body systems.

Of course you are unaware of being tortured. The body is remarkably patient; it can adapt to all sorts of conditions and respond to all sorts of demands, however stressful. Also, some of the effects are cumulative and do not make themselves felt for a long long time. There is no question that we sit through our sedentary lives at our peril, unless we understand and use the necessary antidote of regular exercise. Such as walking, for instance.

Nor for Standing

Standing is a little better than sitting. When we stand erect and in good posture, the top-heavy torso is properly supported over the pelvic girdle and the weight is efficiently distributed above the twin supports of the legs. Ideally, that would result in little engineering stress on the structure. But the ideal would require us to stand absolutely still, like a stone statue.

The fact is that even when we consciously try, we cannot stand wholly still. The most perfectly trained parade troops, even an honor guard standing at attention on a ceremonial occasion, cannot stand entirely still. Within that apparently unmoving body there is constant motion. The lungs inflate and deflate, the heart pumps, the blood pushes along its circulatory route.

When we are standing still, there is enough movement within the body to tilt the top-heavy head and shoulders off dead center, and however still we stand we are actually swaying. As in sitting, certain muscles are constantly contracting to restore the structure's equilibrium. At the same time, there is not enough muscular action to push the return flow of the blood against gravity from the feet up. What happens to the circulation is evident when healthy young soldiers kept too long at attention keel over in a dead faint.

Luckily, people are not often obliged to stand still. When they must stand—at a counter, on a line, in a crowd—they are far from still. They shift, wriggle, turn, stretch, stand on one foot and then the other, and sooner or later they look around for a pillar, pole, rail, or wall against which to lean. Almost no one likes to stand. Almost everyone finds standing more fatiguing than walking.

Physiologically speaking, we would all be far better off if we could do all our talking, thinking, reading, music-listening, television-watching, even our work, neither sitting nor standing but lying down. Or better yet, walking.

Design for Walking

Walking, the human design comes into its own. Form blends with function and the result is harmony—and perfect performance. The body is built for action, and the action for which it is specifically built is walking.

Consider what happens to the body structure when we walk. The flexible spine yields and springs back with each stride; the springlike forms of the arched feet dissipate the impact of weight meeting surface as effectively as any fluid suspension designed by General Motors engineers.

And see what use is made of the body's peculiar distribution of weight. The top-heavy torso now reveals its true value in two-legged locomotion: The forward pull of its weight becomes the motive power for its progress. With each stride we are falling forward, and one or the other leg is swinging out on its ball-and-socket hip joint to catch us.

In terms of its mechanics, walking is nothing more than a series of stumbles caught in the nick of time, a continuous, rhythmic loss and recovery of balance. Gravitation, no less, is the force that we harness to our service when we walk. If we need any proof of this, we have only to remember that when the astronauts go "walking" weightless in space, they need a little jet-propulsion gadget to move them—*because they do not have the help of gravity.*

A Symphony of Muscles

Walking is a muscular symphony. More than half of the body's muscular equipment has as its primary function nothing else than loco-motion—which in man means walking. All the foot, leg, and hip muscles and much of the back musculature are involved in the sheer mechanics of walking. Add to this the tendency of the abdominal muscles to contract and support their share of the weight—for it is a normal reflex of the muscles, when stretched, to tighten up, and the weight of the viscera pressing against the abdominal wall sparks this reflex. Add further the increased action of the diaphragm and rib muscles in breathing—for any activity, even the mild activity of walking, deepens the breathing.

Add still further the almost automatic action of arm and shoulder muscles swinging with the stride. Add the action of shoulder and neck muscles in holding the head erect and looking up, down, and around, and the eye muscles focusing nearby on the ground and farther off at the surroundings. Sooner or later in walking we are using all our muscles except the jaw muscles. And if we have a companion we are using those, too, in conversation.

Yet all of this is unconscious, and without effort. We are not aware of this automatically conducted symphony of muscular action. It is possible to make hard work of walking, but a person who is not actually disabled must fairly dislocate himself to do so—except, of course, if he is grossly overweight.

Doing What Comes Naturally

For walking is indeed as natural to the human body as breathing. No more than a few days after the child has taken his first step, he has mastered the coordination necessary for walking, and barring unusual circumstances, he need never again be conscious of it for the rest of his life. We have to learn how to swim, to skate, to ski; we have to make a conscious effort to run, jump, or climb. But to walk, all we have to do is put one foot before the other. From that point on, the body's singular structure takes over.

And when we hit our stride—the step that is just the right length for our height and length of leg, the speed that is just right for our weight and muscular strength—then something miraculous happens. We become unconscious of weight, of locomotion; we are aware only of rhythm. It is a sensation akin to swimming, in which the water bears our weight. In the right rhythm of walking, the body's weight does in fact float, borne along in a perfect balance between gravitational force and the momentum of forward motion. We do not seem to be carrying our weight at all.

That is walking. To hit your stride is to discover a new sensation, the sensation of moving as effortlessly as the deer bounds, the horse gallops, the fish swims and the bird flies.

Chapter 4

WHY WALKING IS GOOD MEDICINE

FOR ALL ITS economy of muscle and energy, walking is endorsed by medical and health authorities for an astonishing variety of benefits. It is listed as:

A "best" exercise (by physical fitness experts)

A preventive of heart and circulatory disorders (by cardiologists)

A first-rate weight controller (by obesity experts)

A preventive and a remedy for respiratory disorders (by chest specialists)

An aid to digestion and elimination

An aid to sleep

An antidote to tensions whether physical, nervous, psychological, emotional

A partial protection, at least, against the damaging effects of heavy smoking on the heart, circulatory, and respiratory systems. Heavy smokers find that walking also cuts down their smoking, at the very least by removing the temptation to smoke while they are enjoying a good walk, probably also by relieving some of the tensions that lead to heavy smoking. At the smoking clinics, clients seeking to give up cigarettes are advised, "Take a drink of water and take a walk."

So it is overwhelmingly evident that, according to the experts, walking can be a prime preventive and even a cure for a long list of common nuisance ailments and some of the more serious ones.

This is puzzling. It is even hard to believe. We think of exercise as being effective only if it is strenuous and somewhat punishing. Men, in particular, have the impression that unless they come sweating from tennis, squash, handball, or a workout on the rowing machine, nothing they can do will be of any use. They will be doomed to flabby muscles, wheezing on the stairs, and a cushion of fat at the beltline where it can be seen, probably also in the heart and arteries where it cannot be seen but is more to be feared.

People think of bicycling, rowing, mountain-climbing, 50-mile-hiking as exercise, but not walking. Walking is so ordinary. How can walking, so mild, so far from strenuous, achieve so many desirable effects?

The answer to this puzzle is that walking is one of the natural functions of the human body. The erect posture and bipedal gait were an early and essential part of human evolution. And so other essential functions developed along with walking, became integrated with it, became to some extent dependent upon it.

The Circulation Story

The circulatory system is a particularly good example of how an essential function is integrated with walking. The circulation of a quadruped, a horse or a lion, has little to contend with in gravity. The great muscles of shoulder and haunch are almost on a level with the heart. So is the head, with its guiding brain. So are the lungs, viscera, glands, the sexual and reproductive organs. All the major systems are in a nearly horizontal plane with the heart.

Contrast this with the human structure. The blood must be pumped straight upward to the brain. The abdominal organs and the legs present no problem on the outward flow of the circulation, since gravity is on the favorable side. But how is the blood to come back?

We tend to forget that the system is indeed circulatory. Once every minute, the same five quarts of fluid go out and return to the heart. They go out laden with oxygen, nutrients, enzymes, hormones to be distributed, and they return equally laden with waste products to be disposed of. Every one of the body's thirty trillion cells depends upon this continuous transport for its life and health.

The sheer magnitude of this vital traffic system is staggering. In an adult of average size, the blood makes a circuit of some 60,000 to 100,000 miles of circulatory "roads" once every minute, a movement of 72,000 quarts of fluid every twenty-four hours.

The heart is a powerful pump, but fortunately it does not have to move this fabulous freight entirely unaided. The arteries are also equipped with muscle. Their walls propel the flow along with minute but regular rhythmic contractions.

The return flow is another matter. The veins have valves that prevent backflow, but they are without the power of muscular contractions to pump the blood along. Some part of the heart and arterial pumping power carries on to the veins, simply from the pressure of arterial flow behind. And from regions above the heart, gravity does part of the work.

But from everything below, the abdominal organs and the legs and feet, what is there to help overcome both the loss of pressure and the pull of gravity? How could man survive, and even thrive, with such a problem presented to the circulatory system by his erect posture?

The Second Heart

Probably man could not have survived except for a second mechanism that is also built into his evolution as an upright, two-legged species. And that is the mechanism of walking, which in effect constitutes a second heart.

The muscles of feet, calves, thighs, of buttocks and abdomen, all work when we walk. So does the diaphragm, the powerful muscle that forms the floor of the chest and is part of our breathing apparatus. However moderately they may work in the act of walking, all these muscles nevertheless work. And as they rhythmically contract and release, they squeeze the veins, pressing the blood along. Since the venal valves prevent the blood from flowing backward, it goes in the only direction possible. It goes upward, against gravity. As we walk, our muscles literally milk the blood back to the heart.

The Heart Pays the Penalty

When we settle for a sedentary life, and fail to give the circulation this extra muscular push upward, the blood tends to pool in the belly and especially in the feet. The rate of the return flow slows down, and its volume decreases. The heart must work harder, must keep the decreased supply of blood moving faster, to keep the life-giving oxygen and the removal of wastes up to the needs of the organs.

When we stand too still too long, the blood collects in the veins of belly, legs, and feet, and the upper body and the brain are deprived. That is why those healthy youths on the parade ground faint away. When we sit too much and too long, all our organs are chronically shortchanged by a transport system that is too sluggish in bringing and taking away, and the heart rate and blood pressure rise in an effort to counteract the stasis, or slackening, of the blood flow.

But when we walk, the muscles take over their proper share of the work. The circulation speeds up. *And the heart rate and blood pressure go down.*

This has been shown by actual measurement. In people whose pulse was habitually accelerated and whose blood pressure was habitually elevated, a regime of regular walking—not necessarily very far or very fast—brought their resting pulse rate and blood pressure down to normal levels.

Walking the Patient

The surgeons know the importance of getting a patient up and walking within hours after an operation. Early ambulation, as they call it, became standard procedure after World War II. Uncomfortable, even painful, though it may be, the nurses arrive on the dot and get the patient on his feet and walking, willy-nilly, if only a step or two the first time. And every day he must walk a little more. The ostensible purpose is to prevent a clot, or embolus, from forming and breaking off to cause the blockage of a blood vessel. This is reason enough, to be sure. But early ambulation has shown its value in so many ways that the surgeons no longer talk very much about embolisms. The rapid improvement in circulation, muscle tone, digestion and elimination, and healing—to say nothing of the patient's morale—has resulted in much more rapid convalescence on all levels.

Doctors recognize the more subtle and complex improvements that result from walking, even though they cannot always measure them. And they are in no doubt about the value of the muscular assistance that walking gives to the heart. To quote Dr. White again, "Although the heart is, of course, the main agent in maintaining the circulation of the blood, the aid it receives from these other structures is considerable and may indeed on occasion mean the difference between good health and physical unfitness."

Recently Dr. White remarked that 4 miles of walking a day, or an equivalent amount of exercise in some other form, is the minimum if the heart is to have the help it needs from the large muscles. A 4-mile walk sounds like more than most of us can fit into the working day. But in reality it is not a 4-mile walk that we need, because we already do some walking, although not pleasure-walking, in the course of the day. Even sedentary workers average about a mile and a half, going to and from the office by their normal transportation means, going to lunch, going about within the premises where they work. And they could do even better, if instead of picking up the inter-office phone to consult a colleague they picked themselves up and walked down the hall to his office.

One of us tested this by wearing his pedometer through an average working day. At the day's end, not counting his walk to and from work, he had clocked 2½ miles, all within the office except for luncheon around the corner and one visit to a client nearby. So it appears that to meet Dr. White's minimum, most of us need to add only 2 miles—two twenty-minute walks—to our normal daily round.

The Price of Affluence

This, then, is how walking protects the heart, by a mechanism simpler than a child's water pistol, yet utterly effective in the grand pattern of man's evolution as an erect biped in defiance of gravity. For 500,-000 years it worked—until this century, or perhaps only the past several decades of this century, when a great many human beings stopped walking. They stopped walking because they were living in the most favored environment man as a species has ever known. And unwittingly they deprived the cardiovascular system of one of its strongest supports.

Not all people, even in the West, have stopped walking. Some walk by vocation. Sales clerks, housewives, waiters and bartenders walk between eight and ten miles a day at their work. People like these, whose work keeps them on their feet and moving, do not have to walk for their hearts' sake. But they may have to walk for other benefits, perhaps equally or nearly equally important to their health.

One of these benefits is weight control. Some years ago, when worry about overweight was just arriving at its place of preeminence in the American consciousness, someone computed how many flights of stairs one would have to climb to work off the calories in a single chocolate bar or a wedge of apple pie. Merely to read about that number of stairs made people pant. The point was indelibly made, and of course it is true. Neither walking nor indeed any other form of exercise can take off excess weight by itself. Exercise helps. But to get rid of pounds it is necessary to diet.

Overweight? Or Underwalked?

Walking will not reduce you. But walking will keep your weight at the level where you and your doctor want it kept. For those who have suffered through a reducing regime of stark diet and strenuous exercise, walking will keep the pounds from coming back. And for those who would like to avoid that torment, walking will keep the pounds from coming on.

A brisk walk uses up about 300 calories an hour. This does not seem like very much of an expenditure. But as a method of weight control, for most people it is quite enough. Because for most of us, this expenditure of a few hundred calories has a direct relationship to the way in which we gain weight.

Most people do not gain weight suddenly. They discover it suddenly, but they actually gain it very slowly. A man who gains a fifth of a pound a week does not see it on his bathroom scale. But if he gains that fifth of a pound week after week, at the end of a year he will have gained ten pounds.

That is the way most of us gain our excess pounds. Some few people gain weight because of a glandular disorder, and some few because of psychological problems, but both these groups are very small minorities in the overweight class. Most people gain slowly, a little each week, over the years, because they consistently take in as food a little more than they expend as energy.

For years the Health Department of New York City has conducted a highly successful obesity clinic, and the finding is that most people are overweight either because they are hearty eaters by family tradition or because their way of life has become increasingly sedentary and they have not cut down their food intake. Wherever they begin, both kinds of overweight people end with the same unbalanced equation. They are taking in more supplies than they are using up, and are carrying around with them a million or so little storage warehouses in which the excess supplies are put away in the concentrated form of fatty tissue.

People who were never aware of overweight in their twenties begin to notice it in their thirties and forties. They are not eating any more than before. They may even be eating less than in their growing, athletic teens and their dating and dancing twenties. But no matter how modestly they are eating, they will gain if they are eating as little as one more slice of toast a day than their bodies need for their normal daily activity.

Meanwhile, their daily activities change. The family moves from the old suburban house to a new split-level ranch house or perhaps an apartment—and there go the stairs. They buy a second car—and there goes the walk to the bus stop or the station. The salesman is promoted to sales manager, or the inspector rises to the rank of supervisor, or the outside man moves to an inside, executive job. And instead of being up and down and about all day, he is planted at a desk.

Walking and Appetite Control

It is also true that with added responsibility in his new job come added pressures, added tensions, and he may be eating more, or more often, because eating does relax tensions both physical and psychological. Eating is as intimately tied to the workings of body and mind as walking.

And this is where the brisk daily walk enters the picture. The walk can relax the tense muscles and racing mind as effectively as the snack or the drink, indeed more effectively, because walking directly engages the muscles and the nerves. And the walk takes off the weight that the snack or the drink would put on. In fact, if the tense executive takes a walk, he can probably take a drink, too, and not gain weight.

Exercise is supposed to increase the appetite, and so destroy its effectiveness as a weight control. Walking does not increase the appetite. A 50-mile hike may well render the hiker ravenous, but the effect of a normal brisk walk of a mile or two has been measured, and it does not make the walker hungry. The Harvard nutritionist and obesity specialist, Dr. Jean Mayer, who has studied overweight in mice and men, had this to say: "If you don't walk at all, you may well become a little *less* hungry if you start walking for an hour a day. If you are already active and increase your activity, your appetite will go up, but not so much that you won't profit from the activity."

More and more, the doctors who worry about our overweight are convinced that *output,* not *intake,* is the crucial factor. The specialists voice this opinion in remarks like these: "I do not believe that obesity is a nutrition problem. I think it is a physical activity problem." And "We just don't walk more than ten steps any more if we can avoid it. The result of all this inactivity is going to overcome us. It could be as destructive as The Bomb."

And in *Lancet,* England's great medical journal, the case is put with customary English terseness: "In obesity, sloth may be more important than gluttony."

Habitual walkers are characteristically not overweight. Habitual walkers tend on the whole to be moderate eaters. Habitual walkers rarely have to be warned by their physicians that they ought to go on a diet.

And it is also an observable truth that overweight people are almost never spontaneously moved to take a walk.

Which comes first, the overweight or the underwalking? Like the question of the chicken and the egg, this one may never be answered. But it is not the important question. The important question has already been answered: As long as we walk, we are not likely to be overweight.

Chapter 5

PSYCHOLOGICAL MAGIC

WALKING also does something for the mind. Setting out on a walk is setting out on a psychological holiday.

"Something happens to the walker," wrote a famous one, the naturalist Donald Culross Peattie. "While you are walking you cannot be reached by telephone or telegraph, and you cannot reach anybody. . . . You cannot put out a hand, as you do even in an automobile, and twiddle the radio and so let in the war and the stock market, a flood of soda-pop and chewing-gum spiels, and all the quizzes and jazzes that wrangle on the innocent airs. You cannot play bridge or consult an astrologer, bet on a horse or go to a movie. In the compensation for these keen deprivations, walking offers you health, happiness and an escape from civilization's many madnesses."

A walk is an escape, not only from the larger world and its madnesses but from one's own immediate world: the desk and the papers on it; the household and its clamoring tasks; correspondence, conferences, contracts, shopping lists; children, parents, spouse. We need escape even from our nearest and dearest occasionally, and for a walk we have the choice of companionship or solitude.

It does not matter whether the walker's destination is near or far, or whether he has a destination at all. He may be walking for a day, for many days, or for less than an hour. While he is walking he is a free spirit, as separate from his ordinary world as if he were on a plane, a train, a ship at sea.

A Private Ship on a Private Sea

A man walking is even freer than he would be on any of these, for he may choose his route at will. He may stop, change direction, or return as he came—and whenever he likes. He may note the passing scene or not, invite communication with others or not, as he pleases. He may be sociable and observant or he may walk enclosed within himself, insulated from distraction as though in a glass bubble. He is his own pilot, sailing his private ship on his private sea.

The psychology of walking is the psychology of vacation, but with a significant difference. When we go on vacation, our well-wishers send us off with the parting admonition, "Don't think about a thing—leave your worries behind. Just enjoy yourself!" When we go walking, we may do just that. We may simply close the door and walk away from whatever is troubling us, and find the release of not thinking, not worrying, not seeking solutions and weighing decisions. Any walk, long or short, can be that kind of vacation.

But it can be another kind. A walk can be the kind of vacation on which we take our troubles along. Because on a walk, as walkers know, we will solve, resolve, or shed our troubles along the way. There are walks on which we have nothing in our pockets but our hands. And there are other walks on which we carry a load of frustration, indignation, irritation, a towering temper or a bottomless discouragement. We may set out with a problem or perplexity of a very specific kind, and be confident that we will come back either with a solution or in a better frame of mind to find one.

The Vacation with a Difference

Almost everyone at some time or other has experienced that vacation with a difference, the walk that clears the mind, dissipates destructive emotions, and points the way to a productive course of action. Almost everyone at some time has gone out for a walk in low spirits and has come back with his spirits lifted, the clinging mists of boredom dispelled, the shadowy anxieties dispersed.

A walk can do all this. It can bring us back with our energies renewed, our zest for living restored.

The physicians know it. "Action absorbs anxiety," as one of them tersely tells us. They know it not only from subjective evidence, hearing people say they feel better after a walk, but also from objective evidence, the tests that confirm it.

Dr. Flanders Dunbar, the psychiatrist, recorded such measurements in her classic psychosomatic studies. For example, a man of forty-five at the end of an upsetting analytic session showed a rise in his blood pressure from 150 to a thundering 200. That was at eleven-thirty in the morning. Some hours later, still disturbed and with his blood pressure still elevated, he went out and walked for two hours. When he came back from his walk, his blood pressure was back to its normal, peaceful 150.

The clue to all this is in the word *psychosomatic*. As everyone knows nowadays, this means the effect of the mind, psyche, on the body, soma. We read the word and think at once of illness, the harmful effect that the mind can have on the body, because it was in the discovery of how many ills the body suffers as a result of unresolved psychological and emotional difficulties that the word first came into our everyday language.

But psychosomatic effects are not only harmful. They can also be helpful and even curative. When we take a treatment or a medicine in which we have confidence, it helps faster and better than when we are suspicious of it. Even a few reassuring words from a trusted physician can alleviate pain by alleviating fear and tension. Many women give birth to their babies without any anesthetic and with little or no pain, because they have prepared for the task not only physically but also emotionally and intellectually. They understand the physiological mechanism of this natural function and are not afraid. The word *psychosomatic* has its positive as well as its negative aspect.

The Power of Body over Mind

The same is true of the other side of the coin, the somatopsychic. If the mind has power over the body, the body also has great and subtle powers over the mind. Physicians are familiar with some kinds of abnormal behavior that resemble mental illness, which stem not from the mind but from certain glandular disorders and nutritional deficiency diseases. Psychologists today tell us what good teachers always knew: that an underfed or poorly nourished child can behave and even test like a child of below-normal intelligence. The same is true of a child who does not have enough exercise, or enough rest.

Mountain climbers know that at high altitudes they may behave irrationally or recklessly; so may skin divers when they go too deep or stay down too long. Boisterous laughter and unprovoked pugnacity are symptoms of altitude sickness, which is a condition not of the mind but of insufficient oxygen in the blood. Traffic experts tell us that they can expect normally peace-loving, law-abiding motorists to shout insults at each other out of their car windows, even get out and swing at each other, when the weather is right for it. The right weather is a day of high humidity, which affects the mind and the personality by way of its effect on the body.

The untoward effects of soma over psyche, body over mind, are familiar enough. But we rarely credit the body with its positive powers over the mind, its ability to calm excessive feelings, brighten attitudes, lighten the entire color and tone of our thinking. Yet this is what the body can do for us when we give it the chance to exert its powers in its most natural, inborn action, the action of walking.

The Body's Own Speech Organs

Walking does this by the sheer effortless rhythm of coordinated muscles working in harmony. In our brainy world we have downgraded our muscles. We imagine that only professional athletes, prizefighters and ballplayers need to think about their muscles. But our muscles not only account for the major part of our body weight and circulation; they are also the other half of the nerve link between body and mind.

Every time we think an anxious thought, every time we experience a painful emotion, our muscles respond. They are the organs of the body's language. If we cannot sleep at night, it is because our mind's anxieties communicate tension to our muscles, and our muscles' tensions respond and intensify the anxieties of the mind.

When we walk, we make a frontal attack by way of the muscles on whatever is disturbing the mind. The first thing that happens is that the muscles smooth out. The muscular tensions that originated in disturbing and anxious thoughts are dissipated as the muscles rhythmically contract and relax, doing their natural work of locomotion.

The next thing that happens is that the nerve ends in these muscles— all those hundreds of thousands of sensitive receivers attached to the muscle fibers—send back to the reflex centers and thence to the central nervous system the soothing message that all is well, all is working as it is built to work. And the nervous system smooths out.

Finally these reassuring messages rise to the top of the tree, the conscious mind that resides in the highly evolved cerebral cortex. And the conscious mind, the I that is our knowing self, is also calmed and quieted.

When All Systems Are "GO"

In this schematic diagram many details have been omitted. There is the breathing that becomes, in walking, deeper and more regular, the circulation that responds to the summons of the working muscles and is stirred from sluggishness to smooth and even flow.

In the body all these changes are noted; nothing goes unobserved by the alert nervous system. It has a sensory branch, the proprioceptive nerves, whose sole function is to keep headquarters informed of the state of affairs throughout the body's realm. As in the muscles, all the proprioceptive nerve ends in organs and blood vessels send back their messages that all is in order, all is working. As the astronauts say, all systems are "go." The space explorers invented the language but the human body has the mechanism, built in from the beginning.

The Feedback

We cannot doubt that the reordering effect of walking on the body systems has this beneficent effect on the mind. The trouble may well have begun in the mind, a genuine trouble, not to be dismissed as imaginary. But mind and body are closely intertwined, and their communications are swift and interpenetrating. Every disturbing wave, wherever it originates, sends its ripples of alarm throughout the entire system, and the wave returns from the farthest tendrils of the nervous system, in the skin and muscles, to wash back again on the center.

The psychologists of the cybernetics school, who take their metaphors from modern physics and electronics, would call this a reverberating cycle. They talk of the psyche sending out its disturbance through the body systems and then receiving it again as a feedback. If the body can absorb and discharge the voltage harmlessly, well and good. But if the pattern is repeated and if eventually it becomes chronic, then mind and body both are trapped in endlessly reverberating cycles of anxiety and tension, tension and anxiety, and there is no way out unless somehow we can reach in, turn the right switch, and change either the psychic or the physical current.

Turning the Right Switch

To change the psychic state, really to change it and not merely interrupt it for a while with some superficial distraction, is not easy. It requires either a great effort of will, or some fortuitous change in circumstances which usually are not in our control.

But to change the physical state is relatively easy. Indeed, for a person in ordinary health and normal conditions of living, nothing could be easier. He can break the reverberating cycle and change the feedback from tension to calm, from distress to reassurance, just by taking a walk.

Then the muscles drain off anger, drain off anxiety. By their rhythmic action they dissipate the physical responses to psychological disturbance, and restore the body systems to normal. This happens quite apart from any esthetic or intellectual pleasures we may enjoy on our walk although, to be sure, these also add to the recovery of our equilibrium.

If the disturbance stems from some real and current problem, the walk by itself may not solve the problem. But it will surely clear away the attendant physical and emotional storm that can only confuse us, and will leave us free to focus calmly on the problem and its wisest solution.

The Answer to Stress

Anyone who has not experienced the psychological magic of walking tends to discount it. When walkers talk eloquently about the sights and smells of the country that we are deprived of when we drive, of the aspects of streets and people in the city that we never see unless we are afoot, the non-walker remains unmoved. Even when his doctor tells him to take a walk and relax, he will say, at least to himself, that he can do as well by going to a movie, playing some bridge, sitting in his easy chair and watching television.

He is thinking of distraction, and distraction can be found in any of a thousand ways. But none of them can give him profound psychological release. Not even golf, the diversion of choice for overwound executives, can give him this. Entertainments, games, a change of scene—all can divert him from his stresses for a time, but none can give him the instant antidote for stress that he will have by simply going for a walk.

In the modern world we no longer have to hunt for our food or fight ravening animals for our lives. We who live in the fortunate Western lands rarely have to endure hunger, cold, exhaustion, or any severe physical stress. What we do endure, although we are not often conscious of it, is psychological stress. Dr. Hans Kraus, the great backache specialist, wrote of this in a book for physicians on hypokinetic disease—that is, disease resulting from too little physical activity.

He pointed out that the modern city dweller is subject to continuous tension-producing stimuli—to traffic, telephones, competition, high-pressure work, the sheer tension of crowding in streets, buses, subways, apartment dwellings. Animals in zoos get heart attacks from crowding, as the Philadelphia Zoo keepers revealed not long ago.

These are not physical but psychological stresses. They produce psychological effects but they also, as we know, produce physical ones. We may not notice the stress. We may not be aware of the psychological tensions that show themselves in shortness of patience, quickness of temper, in irritability, diffuse anxiety, difficulty in making ordinary decisions.

What we do notice is the backache, the headache, the insomnia, the persistent fatigue, the accelerated pulse, the elevated blood pressure, the stomach upsets—all the many and varied *physical* ills for which the doctor tells us he can find no physical cause.

Dr. Hans Selye, the scientist who put the word *stress* into our medical language, conducted an experiment in which he subjected ten sedentary laboratory rats to a stressful course of blinding lights, deafening noise, electric shocks—and in a month his ten rats were dead. Then he took ten more rats, gave them a course of exercise on the treadmill until they were in prime muscular condition, and subjected them to the same stresses. After a month they were well and thriving.

The stresses that killed his sedentary rats were all, in rat or human terms, psychological. The sedentary rats gave up and died of them, but the well-exercised rats could take them all.

This famous Selye experiment is a graphic illustration of how significantly the body's muscular equipment functions in coping with the mind's stresses. This is the very somatopsychic effect that we have been exploring. Unfortunately, as Dr. Kraus and others have observed, the people who live in modern cities, and are most steadily exposed to intense psychological stresses, are also the ones who have least opportunity to make use of the body's restorative capabilities.

City dwellers do not chop wood, dig gardens, prune orchard trees or harvest their fruit. They have little opportunity to use their muscles in work or play except during their two or more weeks of summer vacation. Even suburbanites enjoy only seasonal activity. Many are the strained suburban backs from winter snow-shoveling and spring planting.

The vacation weeks or weekends of games and swimming, the seasonal challenges of snowstorms and garden care, are not the answer to stress. Even a reasonably regular program of golf, tennis, or bowling is not the answer. Games are fine for the spirits but they have little value for the muscles and the circulation.

Why Games Won't Do It

In the physical fitness research laboratory at the University of Illinois, teams of investigators explored the effects of games. They charted the action, and found that in all games the action is intermittent, starting and stopping—a burst of energy and then a wait. The bowler swings a ball for 2.5 seconds and gets about one minute of actual muscular work per game. Golf is a succession of pause, swing, walk—or, more often, ride—to the next pause, swing, and so on, with a good deal of standing and waiting for the party ahead to get on, as well as for one's own partner or partners. Tennis is all starting and stopping; so is handball.

No game has the essential, tension-releasing pattern of continuous, vigorous, rhythmic motion.

First on the List: Walking

Dr. Thomas Kirk Cureton, Jr., the director of the laboratory and one of the consultants to the President's Council on Physical Fitness, put the evangelist Billy Graham on a regime that began with walking a mile every day. Among his famous published cases is one of a university professor, fifty-nine years old, whose restorative regime included walking to and from his office, a distance of two miles, five days a week, and golf or a long hike every weekend.

Dr. Cureton has had forty years of testing and training people and has published some ten books on physical fitness. His list of preferred exercises includes only those that give continuous rhythmic action, such as swimming, rowing, skiing, skating, jogging. *And first on his list is walking.*

So if the city dweller is imprisoned in his reverberating cycle of stress and tension, and ends up with either a psychological or a physical hypokinetic disease, he has only himself to blame. He may not get much swimming, rowing, skiing or skating, and jogging may make him look like an oddball on the city or suburban street.

But he can always walk. He may set out on his walk with his mind in knots and every nerve jumping, but he will come back a whole man.

Chapter 6

A BEGINNER'S RECIPE FOR WALKING

LET US say that you are a non-walker reading this book, and that we have nearly converted you. You would like to try transforming yourself into a walker. How to begin?

We asked this question of a friend of ours, a grown man and father of four, who is a walker, and he said, "Well, as nearly as I can remember, I put my hands on the edge of my playpen, pulled myself up, and . . ." Meaning that none of us needs to be told how to walk. We all learned long ago.

True. But we did not learn to become walkers. Children are not ordinarily walkers. They walk when they must, to get to where they are going. They do not walk for walking's sake.

Walking in this sense is an acquired taste, an adult and sophisticated taste, like a taste for oysters, caviar, wines. Children prefer hamburger and Coke. They have to grow up to the refined pleasures.

And the same with walking. The mechanics are nothing; you can walk as well as the next fellow. But no matter what your motivation, whether you walk because a book or a friend or your spouse recommended it, or your doctor prescribed it, you will go on walking only if you enjoy it. However much you may enjoy oysters, you want them fresh, iced, and attractively served. An unpleasant experience with oysters may spoil your taste for them for years, maybe for life. Again, the same with walking.

So it is worth while to begin in the pleasantest way. Much of what we will say now we have already said in other pages and contexts, but we will put it all together, in a Beginner's Recipe for Walking.

The Ingredients

Take (as the recipes say) a comfortable pair of shoes. In a man's wardrobe any daytime pair will do for a beginning, but a woman may have to hunt through the closet for shoes low in the heel and broad in the toe.

Take comfortable clothes, suitable for the season, light rather than heavy. Again, a man is ordinarily dressed for a first try at walking, but a woman will have to look in her wardrobe for a wide enough skirt or, better yet, slacks. What you wear depends on where you walk; look at Chapter 11, "Walking Comfort," for more on clothes and shoes. There is no doubt that dressing especially for a walk puts us in the right frame of mind for good walking, but we also want to fit walking into our daily lives, and we will not do that if we insist on too many special trimmings.

And here is a negative: *Do not take your dog.* That is, not unless he (or she) is trained as a walking companion. An animal pulling or dragging on a leash, or running free and into trouble, is no pleasure on a walk. If your dog is young enough, take it to an obedience school. When it has passed the course, both of you will enjoy your walks together. (See "The Companionable Dog" in Chapter 10.)

Take a time. Any time that you can fit into your daily round is a good time for walking. If you have only twenty minutes, you can walk a mile.

Take a place. Any place will do that is pleasant. Look for places convenient to your daily tasks and customary ways. If you go to an office or job, find a part of the route that you can walk. Walk to the train if you commute. Walk to the second or third bus stop or subway station from your house; get off, as Paul Dudley White does, a stop or two before your usual one. Park your car ten blocks farther away and walk the half mile to and from it. Walk ten blocks to and from lunch. Go out and walk after dinner, before you sit down to the television, a book, or the work you brought home in your attaché case.

Walk your wife to the neighborhood movie. Instead of getting out the car, walk her to visit friends in the neighborhood—but carry her shoe tote for her, with the high heels inside it. One man we know flatly refuses to take his wife to the theater or the opera (they live in the city) unless she takes walking shoes for the trip home. He is working up to walking her there, too, if she is ever able to be ready early enough. He is not an unreasonable man, merely firm about taking every opportunity for a walk.

Special for Suburban Wives

For home-staying wives it is, surprisingly, harder than for their husbands to find a time and a place for a daily walk. Our middle-period suburbs were diabolically designed to discourage walking (although not the older suburbs, nor the very newest: see "Walks Everywhere," Chapter 12). The suburban mother of a family, moreover, gets little enough time to sit down. If the proposal that she ought to take a walk is not met with a flying skillet, it is only because she is too tired to throw it.

But we will dare to make the proposal, and she can let fly with this book, since we are out of range. It is no coincidence that the mothers of young families are so often tense, distracted, discontented. A best seller of some seasons ago was devoted to their "Problem," with a capital P, misguidedly, we thought. The child-rearing years are relatively only a brief period in her life, but they are hard. It is no easy matter to be the ever-ready handmaiden to children, husband, school, car, and a houseful of appliances, every one of which means that instead of hiring the work done she does it herself (when did women who could afford not to, do their own laundry?). With a dayworker perhaps once a week to clean, a baby-sitter now and then, a husband commuting, women raise families today just about single-handed.

If, reader, you are such a young mother, take our word for it that nobody, but nobody, needs the rhythmic release of a walk at some time in your day more than you do. You need it to take you out of the clamoring household, smooth out the nervous system jangled by a thousand conflicting signals, let out the muscles that are tense with the stop-and-go push buttons of a relentless timetable. You need it to freshen your senses, restore your perspective, take you off the edge, give you back your love for your children, for your husband, for being alive. You will not be wasting your time, that most precious commodity, when you walk. You can use it for thinking (or not-thinking) your way out of the latest child problem, school problem, any problem. And it is not wasting time to use it just for yourself, to experience the relief of going at your own pace for a brief holiday, you who are forever adapting your pace to the demands and needs of others.

The question is, when will you walk? You can take your break between marketing and errands, park the car at a likely spot and enjoy your twenty-minute holiday. There is surely a park or its equivalent along your way, or try the local nature center (see "The Open-Space Contagion" in Chapter 13, and the Walking Guide for your locality). You can leave your husband in charge after dinner and take your walk before the children's bedtime. If there is no other time, the baby's outing may be your walking hour. It will not be a brisk walk. There is no speed limit on baby buggies or strollers, but unless the pavement where you walk is smoother than most, a three-mile-an-hour pace will be bumpy for the passenger. So it will be a slower walk than we would recommend, but it still need not be an uninvigorating saunter. It can be rhythmic and swinging, at a fair and steady pace, even with the stroller to push.

The daily walk for suburban wives is a double-dividend proposal. It is a psychological life saver for you and it may be a physical life saver for your husband. He may not need the walk more than you do, but he surely needs it as much. You and he both know it, and probably you have told him so, but—to adapt a Chinese proverb—a good example is worth a thousand words. Furthermore, if you fail to walk your mile or so every day, how are you going to be in shape for those days off, when you can distribute the children among their friends and get off by yourselves for a Sunday walk of three, four, maybe five miles in the country?

Distance

Walk a modest distance at first. If you walk a mile out, you have to walk a mile back, and that's two miles. Walking in the city, you have the streets to tell you how far you have gone, but in the country you can go farther than you realize and the return trip can take you past your fatigue point. Even the shoes that were so comfortable can pinch and chafe on the way back. As you walk day by day, your limit stretches. Your watch will tell you how long you have walked but not how far, unless you know your rate of speed. So add this ingredient to the recipe:

Take a pedometer. (See "About Pedometers," in Chapter 11, for a reliable kind to buy.) Set it to your stride and register the distance of your walk while you measure the time by your watch. You will be walking farther and farther without fatigue, and with pedometer and watch you can readily see after each walk where your fatigue point is. Use your pedometer as a safety device, until you are a seasoned walker who can go for miles without tiring.

Comfortably dressed and shod, a person in ordinary health can walk a mile without fatigue. At three miles an hour, a brisk but not strenuous pace for most people, that's a twenty-minute walk. After you have walked a mile a day for a week, and enjoyed it, you will be looking for ways to steal twenty minutes more for another mile. The time will soon come when five miles (one hour and forty minutes) is your weekend treat, and the daily mile or two miles is a walk you hardly even notice. Then you'll be combing through our Walking Guide for places to take a walking vacation.

Pace

Until you find your natural stride and rhythm, the pace is important. It may even be the clue to making yourself a walker.

Set off at a good pace. Step out with the longest stride that is comfortable; let your arms swing and your muscles stretch. Make this *walking* walk feel different from the other kinds of walking that you do, whether tense and hurrying, stop-and-start window-shopping, or casual strolling. Strike a rhythm and keep to it. Lengthen your customary stride; stretch it consciously just a little. Read "The Custom-Built Pace" in Chapter 8, and when you go out to walk, give yourself a chance to find yours.

Breathing

If, instead, you find yourself puffing, slow down. But *not to a saunter,* for nothing is so tiring as a slow, unrhythmic walk. Keep the rhythm; keep the swing. Slow down, but stretch your stride, loosen up, let the rhythm take you. You are not catching a train.

Except for not getting out of breath, you need pay no particular attention to your breathing. You may feel like taking a few deep breaths as you set out, just because it feels good (and it shakes off muscular tensions, too), but conscious deep breathing is not part of walking. Over-breathing can make some people dizzy. Your breathing will naturally deepen as you walk. Let it take care of itself.

How It Feels

Feel yourself tall, feel yourself floating, feel the tensions running out at your fingertips and your toes. Feel the motion in your calves, thighs, shoulders. Don't push; let it flow.

Then forget yourself. Look around, see what you can see. Let your muscles take over your body; let your senses take over your mind. Let yourself go; lose yourself (but keep a corner of your eye alert to traffic and traffic lights). You are doing the most natural thing in the world, the thing your body is built for: you're walking.

Later on, when walking is part of your way of life, you will be using your walk for other purposes besides the simple pleasure of released motion. You will use it for solving problems, dissipating anxieties, turning off the feedback of unproductive emotions and nagging worries. But you will never lose the ability to make your walk a simple, direct pleasure, the kind of pleasure that you can enjoy at a moment's notice, all your life long. Once you have learned this pleasure, and found a way to fit it into your daily life like eating and sleeping, you will never give it up.

Chapter 7

THE SCIENCE AND
ART OF WALKING

LIKE ANY OTHER sophisticated enjoyment, walking is both science and art. One is entitled to ask a confirmed walker: How far do you walk? How fast do you walk? Or even, How do you walk?

The way we carry our bodies when we walk is as personal and individual as anything can be. Walking style begins with standing style, or posture. When it comes to posture, everyone has some resentments left over from childhood and adolescence. One of the privileges of being grown up is that nobody is going to tell us to stand up straight.

Neither will this book.

It is true that people who habitually hold themselves badly while standing are likely to carry themselves badly also in their habitual walk. Habitual posture, whether standing, sitting, or walking, expresses the individual. And because walking is dynamic, it is even more expressive than either sitting or standing. It is a most articulate body language. So we are going to talk not about standing well, as the posture experts do, but about walking well.

A Walking Style

Someone once said that if you stood on the corner of Fifth Avenue and 42nd Street in New York you would see the whole world go by. An observant philosopher could also tell what the world was like, from the way the people walked. Indeed he could learn as much about the human condition if he stood on the corner of Main and Elm in any American town, or its equivalent abroad. People everywhere reveal themselves by the way they walk.

Europeans say they can tell an American at a distance by his walk. We can return the compliment: A perceptive American can spot a European by his walk, and can distinguish between a visitor from the British Isles and one from the Continent. A sharp eye can pick out national and regional walking styles, just as a sharp ear can pick out their accents.

But what is far more striking is the way in which a walking style reveals the individual. The noted photographer of celebrities Philippe Halsman used to make his subjects jump, and he would photograph the jump (at 1/1000th of a second) to reveal the individual's personality. World-famous statesmen, actresses, best-selling authors, and even publishers, willingly or not, all jumped for him. He need not have put them to all that trouble. He would have had as revealing a record if he had photographed them merely walking.

The Step That Unmasks the Self

We walk differently at different times, and the way we walk at any given moment expresses our state of mind and emotion at that moment, our content or discontent, our drive and purposefulness or our timidity, languor, indifference, despair. A walking style unmasks the feelings in all their nuances.

But it unmasks much more. It expresses our whole physical and psychological history. A habitual walking style reveals with great accuracy the individual's deepest attitudes toward the world and toward himself, attitudes of which he himself may be unaware. To those who have eyes to see and empathy to feel with him, his walk tells what he is and what he has been. A good physician, whether he is a medical doctor or a psychiatrist, learns a great deal from the way his patient walks into the office.

Our walk records our history in some ways obvious even to the layman's eye. A person may still walk on his heels, as if he were pushing an expanded waistline ahead of him, even though he has long since struggled with and conquered his excess weight. He has changed his clothes to fit his new figure, but not his walk.

A grown woman may still waddle like the chubby adolescent she once was. Or she may still slump and slouch like the self-conscious teen-ager who shot up suddenly and felt embarrassingly tall and well-developed among her peers.

A man may make a great show of self-confidence in his speech and gestures, but his walk may give him away if he does not really believe his own performance. A woman may be potentially beautiful, but if she does not believe she is attractive she shows it in her walk, and no one else will believe in her attractiveness either.

She Walks in Beauty

Conversely, a woman who accepts herself as an attractive person also walks like one, and people look at her with pleasure and think of her as beautiful. A romantic example of this was the Duchess of Alba, whom Goya made immortal in his paintings. When we look closely at her in his portraits, we see that her eyes were too close together and her mouth too small for true beauty, and recently it was discovered that she suffered from spinal tuberculosis and undoubtedly she should have walked with a limp.

Yet somehow in her walk she overcame her disability. No one knew of it in her lifetime, and the marvelous style with which she carried herself gave her the enduring reputation of having been a great beauty. And so she was, because her walking style made her one.

There are lovely and unlovely walking styles, and it is easy to tag the unlovely ones with appropriate labels. There is the gorilla, or great-ape, walk, in which the head and upper torso lumber heavily ahead and the whole structure seems about to crash to the ground at every step. This is a normal walking style for the great apes, which reach forward with their long arms and knuckle-walk on the equivalent of three or four legs. But for human beings it is a grotesque distortion of the proud upright posture.

There is the rabbit or rubber-ball walk, a bouncy progress in which the walker rises straight up on the toes and moves ahead by parabolas instead of a straight line. Likewise the jumping-jack walk, in which the body goes down and up in a knee bend at every step.

There is the mechanical-toy walk, in which the walker holds every joint stiff from head to toe and flails the arms to provide forward momentum. And the turtle walk, with the head pulled in between hunched shoulders and a rounded back like a turtle's shell.

Fun for People-Watchers

Confirmed people-watchers take malicious pleasure in adding to this list. But we walk for our own pleasure, not theirs. A person with a poor walking style can have little joy in walking.

And the converse is also true. A walker, one who pursues the joys of walking, invariably has a good walking style—or else he develops one. The fact is that anyone who is not physically handicapped can overcome his old, inefficient habits of locomotion if he simply sets out to walk, and keeps on walking.

The change comes almost automatically, almost without trying. It comes because walking is in itself the one natural method for setting the body's engineering in order.

It is astonishing how far the single conscious act of lengthening the stride can go in correcting faulty walking habits. With the longer stride, the whole structure begins to swing into natural performance. The body's own engineering takes over, with all its subtle mechanisms for carrying and distributing its own weight.

Try it and see. You will find that once the leg swings freely an inch or two ahead of where it formerly has stopped, the hips slide into place under the torso, the belly muscles tighten, the spine straightens and toughens as the supporting network of back muscles takes hold. Shoulders loosen and hang easily from the shoulder girdle, arms swing of their own weight with the body's rhythm, and the head comes up to its normal proud position on the erect body.

This may not happen with the first half-dozen blocks, perhaps not within the first mile. The habit patterns of years are not likely to vanish in a few minutes. But if we keep walking, the body's own walking mechanisms will take over. (Caution to women walkers: This experiment will be fruitless unless you change your high heels for low and your narrow skirt for one with enough width or, better yet, slacks.)

Walking by Mind's Eye

We can actually think ourselves into good walking style by getting into our minds an image of the structure in motion. In walking, as in all other voluntary motion, we do not consciously direct each muscle. We would probably fall on our faces if we had to do this consciously every time we took a step. Fortunately the brain is departmentalized. The top conscious level has only to give the order to walk, and lower levels activate and coordinate the muscle combinations to carry it out. They get the right muscles working together, in the right order and with the right intensity of contractions, so that the movement is smoothly and efficiently executed.

In addition, these centers take their action on the basis of information received from the senses by way of the top-level centers of perception and interpretation. A step, or any movement, is governed by the visual information on whether the walking surface is level, rising, descending, whether there is a curb up or down or a hole or obstacle to sidestep. Walking is an enormously complex activity involving many muscles large and small, as well as nerves and sensory information, all of which are blended and graded to transport the body safely from one point to another. And we do it without giving it a thought.

The conscious mind contributes the command and the guiding sensory information. It also carries a kind of picture or *Gestalt* of the entire movement. To improve our walking style and make the most of the body's built-in walking capabilities, we do not have to take the complicated pattern apart, piece by piece. We only need to establish an improved mental image, a more natural, efficient *Gestalt*.

To put it with primer simplicity, we need to *see* ourselves walking better, not in the mirror but in the mind's eye. When we also *feel* ourselves walking with that easy efficient gait, we have just about got it made. Anyone who remembers learning a physical skill—skating, or skiing, or working to improve a golf stroke, perhaps—will recognize this experience. The pro tells you how to do it; he shows you how. You watch him, listen to him, try, perhaps over and over again. Then suddenly you feel yourself and see yourself doing it. It is like the light bulb going on in the comic strip—you've got it. You may lose it again and again but at least you know what you are trying for. You know it in your mind's eye and in your muscles and nerves.

A good walking style comes in the same way, except that it comes far more easily, because unlike golf or tennis or skiing, unlike even swimming, walking is the natural form of locomotion of the human body, the form for which it is built.

Those Footprints Behind You

One important aspect of good walking style—and one that can be consciously corrected—is the way the walker places his feet. Duck waddle, pigeon-toed step, tightrope walk—is your footwork one of these? If you don't know, look behind you at your footprints in the wet sand the next time you are at the beach. Walk across the bedroom rug with wet feet, if the rug can take it. Or just stop in the middle of walking, look down, and see which way your toes point.

Or look at your hands. The Australian F. Matthias Alexander discovered that this was one of the keys to correct posture and good health. Alexander, as a young actor, kept losing his voice, but he could get no help from doctors and decided to help himself. He sat down before an improvised arrangement of mirrors, watched himself carry out actions, and learned some surprising facts about the body in motion. For one thing, he discovered that what you order your body to do is not necessarily what the body does. When he tried to raise his head, the resulting action felt right, but in the mirror he saw that he had not moved his head *up* but had tipped it *back*.

One of his most striking observations was that people who walk with their toes turned out also stand with their hands turned out, instead of letting them hang naturally with the thumbs against their sides. This led him to the principles of integrated behavior and conditioned reflexes, which he later taught to such men as John Dewey, Bernard Shaw, the actors Sir Henry Irving and Robert Donat, James Harvey Robinson, and Aldous Huxley. Huxley wrote about Alexander in his novel *Eyeless in Gaza* and also in the book of essays *Ends and Means*.

The duck waddle, with toes pointed outward, is a characteristic walk of ballerinas. Their feet are tough enough to stand it, but for the rest of us it is a sure way to break down arches and much else besides. Turned-out toes mean turned-out ankles, knees, hip joints, usually also buttocks thrust out behind and an exaggerated incurve of the lower spine, which in a horse we call a swayback. With this often goes a forward thrust of the abdomen, sagging abdominal muscles, and lower back strain. It would be hard to say where this series of distortions began—probably not with the toes. But turning the toes in the right direction goes far toward putting the whole structure back into natural alignment.

Besides all the other maladjustments that go with them, the turned-out toes themselves impose a shortened, constricted step that can never yield a natural walking stride. With the many unnatural stresses it imposes on the body structure, the duck waddle can never be an efficient walking style, and a waddle-walk of any distance is bound to be fatiguing.

The pigeon-toed walk is less damaging to the foot structure, but it puts an unnecessary stress on ankle and knee joints and it also inhibits a free walking stride. The cure for both these unnatural gaits is to get the toes pointing neither in nor out but the same way the body is going.

The tightrope walker places one foot directly in front of the other. This is a good test of balance (or of sobriety), but it is not efficient footwork for walking, even though the toes point straight ahead.

It is worth remembering the simple fact that our legs are attached to the hips not at the same joint but separately and side by side. We can stand with our feet together, and they are still side by side. We stand more comfortably with our feet slightly apart, or with one foot bearing most of the weight and the other a little ahead or behind, but never in a straight line. The center of gravity may be closer to one foot or the other but it is always somewhere between them.

When we walk, the center of gravity is no longer static but moving, and in an easy natural gait it moves steadily forward in a nearly straight line. It swings a little to one side and the other as the corresponding foot steps forward, but the opposite arm also swings forward and keeps the body's weight from shifting too far off the center line. The swing to left and right is more apparent than real, because the torso swivels more than it leans. You can see this easily in the shoulder motion of a tall, long-legged person going at a good pace.

A good walking stride on a level surface could be diagramed as two parallel lines, one line for each foot, with a third line running between them. Each foot steps on its own line, but the inner edge of each foot touches the center line. A good walker does not waddle from side to side, but neither does he walk the center line as he would a tightrope. Each foot has its own side of the path. And the toes point neither in nor out, but straight ahead.

A lengthened stride can help to correct inefficient footwork in the same way that it helps to rectify other distortions of natural walking style. The duck waddle and the pigeon-toed step tend to disappear when we consciously stretch our stride. So does the tightrope walk. When the leg is released from old habit tensions and allowed to swing freely forward, it is likely to end with the foot placed on the ground as it naturally should be.

Transactions with Gravity

To describe walking as a successive loss and recovery of balance is mechanically accurate, but it gives us the image of a herky-jerky gait that is nothing at all like the smooth flow of natural walking style. Our mind's-eye picture is closer to the fact when we see it as a continuous ripple of motion flowing up and down through muscles and joints, from head to toes and back, without a break anywhere along the line.

The motion is smooth because the successive transactions with gravity are bridged by forward momentum. The body moves flexibly, but all at once. To take a step, it tilts slightly forward, but not head and shoulders first, or abdomen first, or bent at the hips to push the torso ahead. It tilts forward by bending slightly at the ankles. Try it. Shift from an erect standing position to walking position in slow motion, and you will see that it is your ankles that tilt you forward, or rather the ankle of the standing foot, because the other is already lifting to take your weight in a forward step. The knee of the standing leg does not bend, but rather straightens, at the same time as the heel lifts and the foot muscles push off from the toe. The knee of the forward leg does bend, to lift and again to take the weight as it lands.

In a good walking style, the body tilts forward just far enough to keep the center of gravity moving forward in the right mechanical relation to the individual's natural length of stride. We don't need a slide rule to figure this out, fortunately, because if we give it a chance the body figures it out pretty much for itself.

Once the body finds its proper angle, it does not jerk forward and back with each stride. It keeps the angle unaltered within the fluid forward motion, as long as it is going along at the same pace and the ground is level.

Going up or down hill changes the angle, because the ground angle has changed and with it the center of gravity. Going downhill, we have to lean back from the ankles, and if the going is steep we tend to crouch and take shorter steps, in a general ingathering of our weight over the center for balance and control. We also tend to put the foot down with the toe instead of the heel first, on a really steep grade, for better traction and protection against slipping.

Going uphill, we have to lean forward, and here we may inadvertently break the smooth body line and bend forward from the hips. This feels comfortable but it is poor mechanics, because it shifts the weight of the top-heavy torso from the pelvis, where it belongs, to the muscles of the lower back, and a long uphill climb can end in tired back muscles and even a backache. The body still carries its weight best in a fairly straight line to the ankles, even when it is tilted quite far forward. If the bend continues to be in the ankles, the added work of going uphill falls on the thigh and buttocks muscles, which are well able to take it.

People construct their mind's-eye image of the body in good walking style in various ways. Some think of it in stick figures, tilted at an angle to the walking surface. Some prefer the image of a figure suspended on a string, being pulled forward as if by an invisible hand. Some think of the body in blocks, head and torso balanced on the foundation of the hips, keeping the same relative alignment over the moving legs. Some people simply think of the best walker they know, and try to imagine themselves walking the same way.

It hardly matters what form your mind's-eye image takes, so long as it puts you on the road. Once there, you begin to feel your way to your own most comfortable, efficient, and therefore tireless walking style.

The way the body's weight is distributed, the way its bony structure is articulated, and the way the natural laws of gravity and momentum operate—all these are on the side of your finding your natural stride, your individual walking style, and your own enjoyable, untiring pace.

Chapter 8

HOW FAST? HOW FAR?

ONE OF the agreeable surprises of becoming a walker is that you can walk faster and farther than you think, and with complete comfort. If you are of average height you can walk three miles in an hour, and at the end of the hour you will not be more than pleasantly tired.

Most people do not know how fast they walk. The only ones who make a point of walking speed are army sergeants, athletic coaches, and commuters who have to catch a train. People speed up when they are in a hurry, but when they set out for a walk they go at the speed that has become habitual to them. Until they become walkers, they do not discover that a different speed, usually a faster one, can add to the pleasure and diminish the fatigue of walking.

Army sergeants have a timetable. They are obliged to get a company of men from one point to another in a specific time, and for this they have to get everybody to walk at the same rate of speed. Athletic coaches, talking as physical fitness experts, recommend fast walking as a wholesome exercise. Pinned down, they define fast walking as three and a half to four miles an hour, which for most people is painfully fast. Some physical education specialists seem to talk about walking as though it had to be punishing to do any good, as though they really wish we would do push-ups or go to the gym instead.

Obviously if a man is walking for exercise he gets more exercise if he walks faster. In terms of muscular work, it takes more foot-pounds of energy per minute to move a given weight, in this case his own, from here to there in less time. But if he reads an article that tells him he has to walk fast to get any benefit out of his walk, and if he finds that walking fast is disagreeable—that it makes him pant, or feel pushed and tense—then he will sit down and watch television instead. And that's a pity, because even an ambling walk is better for the health of both his body and his mind than no walk at all.

It is even more of a pity because if he can once discover his true walking pace, he will find that he enjoys walking. And his true walking pace is likely to be faster than he thinks, although not so fast as those overambitious athletic coaches recommend, and certainly not too fast for comfort. His own best pace is by definition a comfortable one for him.

Faster Is Easier

To the non-walker's surprise, he finds that it is easier, less tiring, more agreeable in every way, to walk fast than slow. Strolling, sauntering, ambling, whatever you call it, has its charms. But a really satisfying walk, one in which the walking is a pleasure in itself, is a walk sustained at the fastest pace that is right for the particular walker—right for his height, weight, length of leg, not to mention temperament.

Earlier in these pages we remarked that each individual has his natural pace, and that once he discovers it he will walk as easily as the fish swims or the bird flies. Most people do not walk at the pace that is right and natural for them. They have never discovered what that pace is. They walk at a habitual pace, and that is not necessarily their natural pace. It is merely the pace at which, over the years, they have become accustomed to walk, for a great variety of reasons which are usually irrelevant to walking.

Women, for instance, walk as they do because of the width of their skirts and the height of their heels, which are imposed on them arbitrarily by fashion and taste and have nothing to do with their physical structure. Custom puts men into clothes more suitable for walking, but not many men enjoy their advantage. Men as well as women are beset by psychological tensions that tighten nerves and muscles and hold a short leash on every body movement.

Men as well as women tend to walk with a short stiff stride almost as though their legs were in a cast from hip to toe. Habits born of tension negate the marvelous resiliency of a structure ideally engineered for walking.

Every step we take is a transaction between our body weight and the earth's gravity. The faster we walk, the smoother are these successive transactions. When we walk too slowly, we have to make a new arrangement with gravity at each step, practically from a standstill. But when we walk at a good pace, the momentum of each stride carries over into the next. When we walk faster rather than slower, we have the law of inertia on our side. Once a mass gets moving it tends to keep moving, and that goes for the human body as for any other mass.

So faster is easier, a matter of simple mechanics. But speeding up our habitual pace by moving the legs faster is just putting more effort into the job. We end up panting, having spent more foot-pounds for more speed but not for more ease in walking.

Faster is easier only at the pace that is right and natural for each of us. How to discover it?

The Custom-Built Pace

To find your own custom-built pace you don't need a computer nor yet a slide rule. Posture—meaning the way your body carries its weight—enters into it, but we will come to that later. The first step is simplicity itself. Just make the step longer.

Lengthen your stride. Even if you have only a block or two to walk, swing your front foot a little farther ahead than you habitually do. Try it consciously for a block or two, until the pace begins to feel rhythmical and easy.

Merely lengthening your stride has already speeded up your walking pace, because you are covering more distance at the same speed and with no additional expenditure of energy.

But lengthening your stride does more than merely speed up your walking at no extra cost. It loosens up those tense, taut muscles, puts other, neglected muscles to work, and gives you increasingly the benefit of the body's flexible engineering.

The longer stride brings hip, knee and ankle joints into action, and the springiness of the foot. It brings thigh and calf and toe muscles into play. When you take your longer stride, you are not merely lifting your foot behind you and planting it down ahead of you as if it were a dead weight, a wooden leg without a joint. You are pushing off with it behind, swinging it forward from the hip, coming down on it with knee and ankle limber and flexible, and with a sustained forward motion that carries over into the next stride. You have made a new deal with gravity, with a continuous forward momentum that literally takes some of the weight off your feet.

And that is worth repeating: A longer stride, at a faster walking pace, takes over part of the weight-moving job. It makes less work for the muscles and puts less weight on the feet.

Precisely how long any individual's stride should be—and how fast, consequently, he may comfortably walk—depends upon how he is built. Mainly it depends on his height and length of leg. Mayor John Lindsay, walking to City Hall each morning during New York's transit strike, went at a pace of four miles an hour and left a trail of exhausted newsmen along his route. Mayor Lindsay is six feet three inches tall. President Johnson has similarly outwalked the correspondents in his peripatetic press conferences around the White House rose garden. President Johnson is six feet four inches tall.

Former President Truman on his morning constitutionals set a brisk pace, and some of the newsmen found themselves out of breath. But they were trying to interview him as they walked, and the ones who were out of breath were probably non-walkers. Nobody timed Harry Truman, but he very likely walked not much faster than three miles an hour.

The Comfortable 3 m.p.h.

Three miles an hour is the generally accepted average because it suits the average male height. It is the United States Army pace for long hikes, and it is the pace that most men find comfortable for a longish walk, although many can of course go faster if they need to.

Since women have a shorter average height, the assumption must be that their best average pace is something less than three miles an hour. Yet most good women walkers, wearing the right shoes and either a walking skirt or slacks, can let out their stride and do three miles an hour without feeling pushed, even on a long walk. They can do this although they may be inches shorter than the average man, say five feet three or four. At five feet and an inch or two, a woman might find it hard to keep the average pace, because there is a limit to her stride and she must move her legs that much faster to make up the difference.

The average length of stride for a man is two feet from the toe of the back foot to the toe of the front one. The number of steps per minute for a brisk walking pace, according to the United States Army, is 106. This of course has to do not with height or length of leg, but with temperament and energies. On a crisp day an energetic fellow may enjoy his walk at 110 steps per minute or even more. People who like to keep statistics on their walking can do it with the aid of a wristwatch and a pedometer.

The number of steps a walker takes per minute, or the number of miles he covers per hour, is no measure of his enjoyment. Nor is it a guarantee that he has hit his natural walking stride, the easy rhythmic pace that makes walking a pleasure in itself and can take him for miles without fatigue.

That he discovers only by experiment. He discovers it by lengthening his stride, again and again if necessary, until he has stretched the habit-formed, tension-dictated kinks out of muscles and joints.

When he has found it, he will know it unmistakably. And again and again, as he sets out for home after a tense day, he will find himself beginning with the short, stiff-legged walk of old habit until his legs remember and begin to reach. And then he is off and swinging as though he had not a care in the world.

Women can do this, too. But women have to find their natural stride in spite of fashion. This is not so difficult as it may sound, however. Intelligent women have always found what they want in any fashion era, no matter how anti-walking the skirts and heels may be. We will come to this strategy in a later chapter on the subject of how walkers like to dress.

How Far Is a Mile?

Distance is as full of illusion as a magician's bag. A mile sounds like a long way, but a twenty-minute walk is a pleasant prospect. Yet at the average walking pace of three miles an hour, a mile on level ground is precisely a twenty-minute walk.

A mile is an exact measure, 5,280 feet. At an average man's walking stride of 2 feet per step it will take him 2,640 steps to go the distance. And if he slogs through it counting his steps, it will be a very long mile indeed. But if he goes along interested in what he is seeing, thinking, or talking about with a companion, a mile will be hardly any distance at all.

Anyone in ordinary health and wearing comfortable shoes can walk a mile or a couple of miles and not know it. The authors and their spouses have tried this experiment numerous times with friends who are not walkers. Walker and friend set out together with the implicit understanding that they will board a bus or taxi, or some equivalent conveyance, at whatever point they feel like it. Almost without exception, they arrive at their destination on foot, without the question of taking a bus or a taxi ever arising. The non-walker's action is typically one of surprise that he or she has actually covered so much distance. A mile and a half, two miles, without ever feeling it? They would hardly have thought it possible.

One of the authors made the more difficult experiment of telling his subject in advance just how far she was going to walk. To be sure, the poor girl had little alternative to walking if she wanted to get home at all. This was during New York's transit strike, when even a shared ride was next to impossible to get at the end of the business day.

It was January, already dark, bleakly cold, far from ideal for a walk. When they set out she was sure she could never make it. When she was deposited at her apartment house door forty minutes later, she was astonished to discover that she could go right on walking if she had to. She also confessed that in normal times the ride home, standing up in a slow, crowded, rush-hour bus, took almost as long and was not half so rewarding.

Walking by Segments

This non-walker's companion had made the two miles go by painlessly, by tricks that every experienced walker knows. Walkers use these devices when walking is only incidentally for pleasure, exercise and health; when its primary purpose is transportation, for example on the daily journey between home and work.

The walk to work—or, if that is too far, to the bus or subway or commuter's railway station—is too familiar a walk to promise many surprises. It is also a walk we take without regard to the weather. When the weather is truly forbidding we may seek other transportation, but ordinary inclemencies like rain, snow, or cold or warm weather do not stop a habitual walker unless they are extreme.

A walker starts on such a walk the way you would start on the job of painting a wall. The wall in its whole extent is formidable; divide it into segments and it is child's play. Each segment is only a little bit more to do, and soon the entire wall is finished. A walker thinks of his regular walk in the same way, by segments. He walks from home to the crossing where he must wait for the light, from there to the shopping center, from there to the house of a walking companion who ordinarily makes the same train, and on to the first newsstand where he buys his paper, to the turning from which he can see the clock on the station, and so to the station.

That's a suburban walk. A city walk may be broken up by neighborhoods. A city walker may decide he will walk to the second bus stop from his house, or the third. Or he will get off the bus or subway and walk the last half mile because it is the nicest part. Whatever the walk, it is shorter when you think of it by segments.

When the Long Way Is Shorter

A walk may also lend itself to variety. It is a rare walk that does not offer two or more different routes between the same two points. A park may lie within range of the walk, in certain seasons worth taking the longer way round. To walk past someone's garden in bloom may be inviting enough for a detour from the direct route. On a wintry day the walker takes the sunny, sheltered route; on a summer day he chooses the shady street, the breezy avenue. Such variations make the walk not only more agreeable as we go but psychologically shorter, even though they may add a few steps to its physical length.

Company shortens a walk. But there is a hidden hazard here, for it has to be the right company. Many a walk is unpleasantly drawn out by a companion who walks too slowly, who stops and dawdles at shopwindows of interest to the companion but not to the walker, or who is merely not one's preference in companionship. A chance acquaintance met en route may add interest to the walk or he may not. A skill that the walker must develop in self-defense is how to disengage himself tactfully from an unwanted companion.

This is why, unless he knows his potential companion, the walker's preference is often his own company. When he is on his own, he can choose his route, his pace and, most important, the content of his mind. He may use the walk for many purposes besides merely getting to where he is going. He may use it to stretch muscles long confined in static sitting at a desk, to stretch thoughts that have concentrated all day on problems of his work. Or he may take his work along on his walk, and deal with something he has to solve in the coming day or has failed to solve in the day just past. A walk may be to think, or to not-think. Either way, the walk need never be too long.

It must be admitted that some walks tax the walker's ingenuity to the utmost. These are mostly involuntary walks, for example the obligatory marches of military training. On a 15- or 20-mile hike with full pack and at an enforced pace, what psychological invention can shorten the miles and forestall boredom and fatigue?

The psychoanalyst Allan Fromme told us how he did it, when as a newly minted Ph.D. he served his time in the infantry. Before the march, he would clip a book or several books out of his G.I. Bible (no one in his right mind would tote the whole volume) and stuff the sheaves of thin paper under his helmet. When the going became wearisome, he would pull out a sheaf, read, ponder, commit to memory. If he had the breath to spare, he might declaim aloud the thunder of Jeremiah, the cynicism of Proverbs, the wonder of the Gospels, the poetry of the Psalms. He diverted and edified his companions as well as himself. And he found that the rolling King James rhythms made remarkably fine marching music.

Short Miles and Long Ones

A country mile is not the same as a city mile. A city mile is twenty city blocks, but a country mile is any distance the man you ask may think of as far, or not very far. If he says, oh, a couple of miles, he may mean two miles, two and a half, or possibly four or five.

Mile for mile, city walking is more fatiguing than country walking. There are the steps up and down for the curb, the stops for traffic lights, the detours around strollers, baby carriages, children, which break the stride. And 2,640 steps on a mile of city pavement mean 2,640 jolts, compared with the shock-absorber surface of a dirt road or a woodland trail.

But a country mile may be psychologically longer. Unless you are walking a familiar road whose landmarks you know, you never know as you are walking just how much of the distance is behind you. In the city, you have only to look at the street signs and you know how far you have come, and how far you have still to go.

In Switzerland, where walking is a traditional enjoyment, mileage markers are set up along the trails so that a walker knows just how far he is from the next village and the good beer, the *Würstchen* or cheese. But Americans have markers to tell them where they are only when they are behind the wheel of an automobile.

In the city, furthermore, when you have had enough walking you can generally find a bus, or perhaps a taxi. In the country you may not have any choice but to go on walking. Thumbing a ride is not always feasible, and it may be farther than you thought to the place where you left your car. So a mile is long or short, depending on how many you have bargained for.

What it comes down to is that a country walk of any substantial distance is the better for a little advance planning. A walk is an adventure but it need not be all that adventurous. Anyone has a right to know how far it is to lunch. And anyone with common sense will not undertake a walk that is too far out of the range of his past experience. A tenderfoot who has never walked more than ten city blocks at a stretch has no business joining an experienced group of walkers for a 20-mile hike.

Although walking is the most natural of exercises, it is still an exercise. Until you have walked your five or ten miles, a 20-mile walk is not for you. Unused muscles begin to complain, so do misused feet, and the miles become longer and longer. No walk can be simultaneously an endurance test and a pleasure. A walk in unfamiliar country is like a swim in the ocean: You have to come back the same way you went out, and it is a good idea to have something left for the return trip.

Since the length of a mile is as much in the mind as in the muscles, a walk for which one is reasonably conditioned is never long if it is beautiful or otherwise interesting. On some walks the return is as pleasant as the going, with views that you could not have seen on the way out unless you walked backward or had eyes in the back of your head.

You can also plan your route so as to walk out and ride back, or ride out and walk back. Group walks are often laid out with public or prearranged private transportation either going or coming.

Most continuously interesting is a roundabout walk, which goes out by one route and comes back by another. Experienced walkers plan their walks this way as a matter of course in country that they know, but even in unfamiliar territory it can be done handily with a U.S. Geological Survey map.

Walking with a Map

Mapping roundabouts in farm country is one of the great walking pleasures. A map of old, long-settled land shows just about every cowpath and woodlot road. With moderate circumspection and the courtesy of stopping to ask permission at the farmhouse before crossing private land, one can roam with freedom over pastures, through woods, along quiet shaded lanes, climbing over or ducking under a fence now and then, being mindful each time to close a gate one has opened or replace bars one has removed.

The scale of the Government's survey map gives distances, and the contour lines show elevations. To avoid the unpleasant surprise of too steep a climb or too precipitous a descent, it is necessary only to avoid a route on which the contour lines come too close together on the map.

A man and his wife, experienced walkers but somewhat out of condition, spent a non-strenuous week of country walking in one lovely valley in central Vermont. The time they chose was October, at the peak of the autumnal color. In Vermont, with its hillsides massed with sugar maples, this is about the most dazzlingly beautiful display in the world. Vermonters themselves thrill to it each year. They will respond to your enthusiasm with an equal glow: "Yes, isn't it fine!" But they add, reminding you that you are in New England, "Too bad you couldn't be here last week—it was even finer!"

The pair of visitors had never seen this valley except from the windows of their car, passing through; afoot it was terra incognita. But it was interlaced with hard-packed dirt roads, the best kind of walking, which beckoned them off the highway past fields and tree-framed farmhouses and across century-old covered bridges. On the first morning out, with sandwiches in their pockets, they yielded to the invitation of one such road, parked their car on its grassy bank, and began walking.

At the end of the day, over a good dinner, they totted up the sum of the experience. They had enjoyed delights and discoveries, and with some attention to the sun and the shape of the hills they had never actually been lost. But they had trusted to luck to find them a roundabout, with the consequence that they had walked too far, climbed too much, and plodded the last of their twelve miles back to their car along the automobile highway, which is not a walker's choice.

That evening they borrowed the innkeeper's survey map, and for the rest of their stay they plotted their walks in advance. They walked a different roundabout every day that week, never once retracing their route, never encountering too steep a climb, never having to walk on a highway. They carried a sandwich and a thirst-quenching piece of fruit, which they ate when they were hungry, sitting on a rock or a fence in the pleasant October sun. They looked at hills, fields, trees, birds, cows, farmers at work. They discovered hidden streams, beautiful old barns, peaceful villages they would never see from a car. They walked between six and eight leisurely miles a day, got back to their inn in ample time for a hot bath and a good dinner, and slept like babes each night.

It was a perfect week for lazy walkers, one they will never forget. Nor will they forget the moral, which is that when you set out for country walking, provide yourself with a map from the U.S. Geological Survey in Washington, since not every innkeeper can be counted on to have one.

It is wise to have a city map, too, unless you know the city in which you are walking like the palm of your hand.

Chapter 9

THE WORLD AT
THREE MILES AN HOUR

FASTER AND FASTER WE GO. Within living memory we have accelerated from the speed of a horse-drawn vehicle to the 500 miles per hour of a jet, and before long we will be going faster than the speed of sound. We already have instant communication, and we soon will have nearly instant transportation. In our everyday lives we normally see the world going by at a mile a minute outside our car windows.

All this speed is supposed to give us a sense of power. Instead, it gives many of us a feeling of helplessness, of being caught on a supercharged treadmill beyond our control. It may not be a coincidence that our Age of Anxiety is also the age of speed.

The man who enjoys the profoundest sense of power is not necessarily the man behind the wheel of a high-powered car. It may be the man who can step off the racing treadmill now and then, and get about on his own two legs. There is a remarkable experience of power in being able to turn the world's speed back to the rate of three miles an hour whenever we choose to do so.

Three miles an hour restores our humanity to us. It gives us back our identity, our awareness of ourselves as individual human beings instead of bodies on a vehicle being carried from here to there with the greatest possible efficiency, like so many crates of vegetables.

Three miles an hour makes us people. Compare the behavior of a man driving his car with the manners of the same man walking. Driving, he may or may not be courteous, considerate, reasonable. Walking, he almost invariably is. The behavior of ordinarily decent people behind the wheels of their cars is not only on record with the traffic police. It is a phenomenon we have all had occasion to observe at first hand.

Overwinding Our Biological Clock

When we travel to distant places at high speeds, we can only be filled with wonder and gratitude for the human capabilities that have made it possible for us to span continents and oceans so swiftly. To go from San Francisco to New York before lunch and have tea in London the same day; to breakfast in New York and dine in Moscow or Cairo—surely this is nothing short of marvelous. But we pay an enormous price, psychologically and also, it now appears, physically as well.

The psychological cost is something of which many people have long been aware. Jet travelers have confessed to a feeling of confusion and disorientation on arriving, wherever it may be. They know they have traveled from where they were to where they are, but they have had no sense of the going, the being in transit. They have had no threshold on which to compose themselves for receiving unfamiliar and often exotic impressions.

Recently the medical profession has expressed concern about the physical effects of high-speed travel over long distances. They tell us that our malaise is not only psychological, but is due also to actual physical causes, to a disruption of the biological time by which our body systems function.

Diplomats, executives in industry, professional people whose work takes them across the world and back within a few days or weeks, even the jet plane crews themselves, are found to be suffering from this jet sickness, this disorganization of body time. The body operates on a twenty-four-hour schedule, with a rise and fall of its metabolic rate that matches the succession of day and night. Every tiny biochemical change within us is tuned to this rise and fall of the metabolic curve. Every time we cross a time zone, not only our watches but our biological clocks as well must be reset.

When we make the change little by little, an hour at a time, the body resets itself with relative ease. But when we leap in a few hours from morning to evening, midday to midnight, the disruption is sudden and severe. And if we make these giant steps in rapid succession, the effects can throw the whole delicate clockwork into chaotic disorder.

This is what happens, the physicians now tell us, to people who must frequently travel long distances at jet speeds. The flight itself is a dream of comfort, and the actual flying time passes smoothly enough. But the body time is another matter. A traveler from the Soviet Union recently figured that from the time she was awakened in her Moscow hotel to the time she went to bed in her New York apartment, her watch showed the passage only of morning to evening, but her body had lived through twenty-eight hours of biological time.

To travel at such speeds on professional or business errands may be unavoidable. But the pleasures of travel are something else again. We cannot snatch them as we fly, like the brass rings on a merry-go-round. This is true whether we make our vacation journeys by jet plane or high-speed automobile.

To travel at high speed is not to savor new scenes. It is hardly more than a way of collecting fragments, like the shards of pottery out of which archeologists reconstruct ancient civilizations. Like the snapshots and the souvenirs, the memories of a whirlwind trip by plane or car are only symbols of travel, not the experience of travel itself.

Our high-speed facilities get us to far more—and more distant—places in the time we have to spend. But once we are there, the car or plane has served its purpose. To experience the new place, whether city, countryside, or scenic wilderness, we must get out and walk.

The World in Scale

In a world in which we are constantly confronted with the immensities of the universe, in which men are catapulted into space and soon will land on the moon, we need more than ever a way to restore our environment to human scale. The artists and architects of the Middle Ages understood this. They reared their soaring cathedrals to the glory of God, and designed their façades with lofty, massive doors. But the great doors were opened only on great occasions. Set low and small in the façade of the grandest cathedral there is always a door of human size. Through it the worshipers go in and out every day, and feel themselves men and women, humble but nevertheless human and worthy of addressing their prayers to heaven.

Ever since people took to riding on wheels, the poets and philosophers have been telling us that to see the world we must go on foot. Walking restores the world to human scale. It puts us humanly in touch with our environment, both man-made and natural. Like the giant Antaeus, whom

Hercules could not subdue until he held him overhead and away from his Mother Earth, we all need to touch earth from time to time, to feel ourselves man-size and woman-size in relation to our surroundings.

Walking gives us back the human sense of distances and perspectives. It gives us back the human sense of time that is measured in moments. When we walk we experience each step in space and each moment in time. We are aware of the passing sights and sounds and people, of the passing thoughts within our own minds, of the motion and rhythm of our bodies. Proportions and relationships are reaffirmed for us when we walk.

The Senses Regained

Walking gives us back our senses. We see, hear, smell the world as we never can when we ride. No matter what the vehicle, it is the vehicle that is moving, not ourselves. We are trapped inside its fixed environment, and once we have taken in its sensory aspects—mainly in terms of comfort or discomfort—we turn off our perceptions and either go to sleep or open a magazine and begin dozing awake.

But when we walk, the environment changes every moment and our senses are continuously being alerted. Around each corner of a city block, around each bend in a country road, there is something new to greet the eyes, the ears, the nose. Even the same walk, the one we may take every day, is never the same from one day to another, from one week and season to another.

This is true not only in the country, but anywhere at all. In New York City, a group of executives meets every weekday morning to walk from their homes in Brooklyn Heights to their offices in downtown Manhattan. Their way takes them through quiet streets of old brownstones, one of the oldest neighborhoods in the city, then up and over the Brooklyn Bridge with its cathedral arches supporting the weblike drapery of cables, then down into the tight skyscraper canyons of the financial district.

On their daily route they see, hear, smell the city in all its seasonal changes, under bright and cloudy skies. Only the most inclement weather stops them—suitably dressed, they can walk with pleasure in spring rains, autumn drizzles, the sunlight of a summer morning or a soft winter snowfall. The river waters roll by below their feet, sullen or sparkling. Tugboats chug past, shoving and hauling their variously laden barges; on a shrouded morning, foghorns hoot and moan. The famous skyline of lower Manhattan rises before them, glittering in sun, afloat in mist, against a backdrop of sky never twice the same.

The Camera of the Mind

Granted this is a more dramatic walk than most of us can take every day. Yet every city neighborhood however prosaic, every country path however familiar, has its daily, its moment-to-moment variety. Even if everything else remains the same, nevertheless the hour passes, the sun rises higher in the sky or it declines, and the light in which we see the world is different from what it was only a few moments before.

As the light changes, the shadows change, color values change; the forms and faces of buildings, trees, and people become subtly modified. And all our sensory perceptions—so inextricably twined together— register the changes. Sounds and smells and the very feel of the air on the skin also seem to vary with the varying light.

For example, a man went walking in a Minnesota city on a November afternoon, and this is what he saw:

On a small city lake a thousand Canada geese were resting.

On a miniature stone bridge, five city kids were dangling lines into a stream with little water and certainly no fish, enjoying small-boy small talk while they pursued the illusion of fishing.

Farther on, two blooming teen-age girls ran by, blouses open at the throat, hair flying and haloed in the low, pale sunlight. They were running because they felt like it, and giggling as they ran. The rivulet of their giggles trailed behind as they ran out of sight.

Behind tall, gaunt November trees the declining sun poised on the brink of a slaty cloud crevasse. Just before it toppled, the geese in swirls of powerful wing thrusts swept up from the lake and paraded, a succession of honking, V-shaped formations, across the last cold rays of sunlight.

The sun gone, the light turned lifeless and bleak. The five young fishermen plodded homeward with nothing but hooks on their lines. The two girls went by, walking now, buttoned up and subdued. The geese fluttered back to the lake.

These were the sights Bill Ward saw, taking an ordinary walk in his familiar home city on a slightly milder than ordinary November afternoon. As it happens, Bill is a photographer and he had his camera with him, being a convinced member of the school of photography that believes you get your good pictures only on foot—in his own words, "A photographer must walk if he is to be a photographer at all."

He got some excellent pictures. But even if he had not had his camera to record them, they would be his forever, on the indelible film of his mind. The camera of the brain records all such moments, and records them, moreover, in their full orchestration, with the accompanying sounds and scents, most of all with the accompanying emotions.

A Walk for Every Taste

There are walks for all seasons and for every taste and mood. The walker-writer H. I. Brock divided walkers into two kinds, those who walk to be walking and those who walk to look at things. People who begin walking for exercise, he observed, come to fall in love with it for its own sake. They clock their mileage, accumulate "centuries" or hundred-mile credits, and talk about walking the way horsy folk talk about riding. The other kind of walkers, whom he made no secret of preferring, go walking like explorers. They enjoy the scenery whether of woods, pastures, nature wild or tamed in city parks, or the habitations of people packed together in city streets. He admitted that some manage to combine a passion for walking as exercise with the curiosity of the sightseer.

The sports-writer turned naturalist, John Kieran, once listed no fewer than eight kinds of walking, from the escape walk, a sheer bursting out of the wheeled city, to a winter walk as a test of strength in competition with the elements. The professor and literary critic turned naturalist, Joseph Wood Krutch, did not try to classify walks but contented himself with asserting that he who goes afoot gets the best no matter where he walks, because the best is mainly made up of little things, the miniature beauties and excitements that we experience only when we are moving at a foot pace.

The newspaperman-philosopher-naturalist of *The New York Times,* Hal Borland, declared that walkers acquire a peculiar ownership of roads, streets, fields, and parks by virtue of personal discovery and intimate knowledge. And another walker-writer, the Londoner H. F. Ellis, declared that he walks best who walks alone, savoring every moment of what he sees, feels, and thinks, without the distraction of conversation.

As many walkers as one consults, so many "best" kinds of walking will one discover. And the reason for these many divergent opinions is that walking is by definition the freest, most individualistic of human activities. A man riding in any kind of conveyance must go where the vehicle or the road takes him, at the speed and with the companions chosen for him, usually by circumstance and not by himself. A man walking is his own man, and he can go as he pleases, where he pleases, with whom he pleases or with only himself for company.

Even a man driving his own car rarely enjoys such freedom of choice as he can have whenever he elects to go on his own two legs. The walker discovers that however constricted his environment may seem—by traffic, time schedules, and the sheer number of his fellow inhabitants—once he is afoot the world is wide indeed and in it are walks for every man's desire.

On the Wild Side

Vigorous walkers like Justice Douglas take to the trails and the mountains. They set out for walks many days long, with packs on their backs and untamed nature as companion and sometimes adversary. Justice Douglas talks of hikes, not walks, and his hikes are sometimes on snowshoes across wild country and through wild weather.

This is walking as the highest kind of sport, for sportsmen with stamina and specialized skills. They are also walks taken advisedly with companions of equal capabilities, since they embody a degree of danger in coping with the elements and the rigors of the trail. For those with the muscle and the skills, there is probably no more exhilarating sport than a really wild wilderness walk.

But wilderness walking is not necessarily so strenuous. Each year hundreds of thousands of Americans drive to our magnificent national parks, take pictures of each other against the scenery, and drive away again. They do not know how much they are cheated, because right at their feet as they stand admiring the view are trails that can lead them on walks of discovery, refreshment, and beauty, compared to which the scene they have admired is hardly better than a picture postcard.

In Yosemite—to take a single example—there are three trail walks mapped long ago by the naturalist and explorer John Muir, who so loved the splendor of the coastal range, its forests and especially its towering redwoods. Muir's practiced legs could cover these trails in half the time it would take most of us in our automobile-softened generation, so changed are we Americans in the half century since he lived. But to walk any of the three trails one way—and downhill—takes only a comfortable day.

The trails are graded according to their difficulty. The shortest, the Four-Mile Trail, which is really close to five miles, is a steep descent and requires lug-soled boots and some mountaineering skill. The other two, while longer, are relatively gentle and can be negotiated in sneakers. The walker carries only his lunch and a light waterproof parka against sudden showers at some seasons. Transport is arranged to bring walkers back to their lodgings.

Surely this is wilderness walking made easy—as it has to be for most of us to enjoy it. And the rewards are incalculable. No one who has not experienced it can imagine the enchantment of a day spent intimately with untamed Nature at her most superb, as Yosemite and our other great national parks have preserved her for us. Within our own boundaries, from the Sierras to the Great Smokies, from the northern lake country to the Southwest's canyons and deserts, we have such riches of wilderness beauty as few other lands can match, and a great part of it is within the range of an average healthy walker.

Yosemite has a special season of magic besides, when for some two weeks in the spring the valley bursts into bloom and puts on a breath-taking display of wildflowers. To walk in Yosemite when the valley floor is thus magically carpeted is a pleasure beyond price. But for this it is necessary to plan and reserve lodgings well ahead, because half the city of San Francisco drives or flies to see Yosemite in bloom.

Philip Wylie wrote a few years ago rebuking his fellow Americans for using the automobile not as a way of "getting to life" but as a way of life. He began by rebuking himself, when he found that he was taking the car to mail some letters. The way to the post office was a distance of 281 steps, across a brook, past a blacksmith's shop and down a shady street, and he was not even in a hurry.

Wylie observed that most of the people he knew did not dare approach Nature any more. They saw the natural world as a menace. They found their security in a steel river thundering along a cement street, did their meditating while waiting for the traffic light to turn green. He was shocked to discover, while writing a book for young men about to do their military service, that not one American male in fifty knows how to walk or live out of doors.

This may still be so, even though every year more thousands of Americans are visiting the national parks. The question is not whether they go but whether, once there, they get out of their cars to see—truly see and savor—the grandeurs they traveled so far to enjoy.

They need not learn woodsmanship and camping skills. They can approach the wilderness in easy stages, as a tenderfoot should. But if they do not walk at all, they will go away cheated of experiences they would cherish their whole lives long. The same automobile that made it possible for them to go there will have denied them their pleasure, simply because they have forgotten that, once there, they can get out and walk.

Nature on a Leash

Tamed nature is less challenging than the wild but it is more accessible. Within reach of the most urban or suburban American is a day-long walk in country or woodland, along a lake or an ocean shore. Or at the very least there is an hour's walk in a city park.

We do not have to go far to find Nature gentled to man's hand. She coexists peacefully with us even in the heart of the metropolis. The sharp bird-watcher's eye has spotted the sparrow hawk, a swift little falcon, catching its lunch on the wing, far above the heads of office workers going to their lunch on the streets of downtown Mahattan. Even the less bird-conscious walker has the company of wild geese, swans, and bright-plumaged ducks that come from distant woodlands, marshes and salt-water bays to winter in comfort on the man-made lakes of a city park. Native and exotic trees, shrubs, and sometimes wildflowers in season gladden the park walker's way.

Some parks are wild woodlands within the city. A famous wild park is Rock Creek Park in Washington, D.C., where Louis J. Hallé, Jr., got up with the sun every morning through one long, lovely season to walk and watch the spring come in. His record of nature reawakening to beauty, in the heart of the nation's capital, is *Spring in Washington,* published a few years ago.

John Kieran is a city naturalist. He calls his walking window-shopping (as does Joseph Wood Krutch in his book *Grand Canyon*) because he is forever stopping to put his binoculars on a bird or his pocket lens on a moss, or he may slow his pace to avoid disturbing frogs chorusing on a pond or a painted turtle sunbathing on a rock. He holds all or nearly all this converse with nature within the city limits, and he has found nature in the city so plentiful and so varied that he wrote a book entitled *The Natural History of New York City.*

In the city or anywhere, a walk with Nature on a leash is an intimate personal experience, happy when pursued in solitude and more than doubled in pleasure when it is shared with a good companion. It is the nicest kind of walk to take with a child, especially a child of the magic years between seven and eleven when energies are high and curiosity is at its exuberant flood tide. No matter if the child is the better naturalist— there is no shame in learning from children. On the other hand, any adult who discreetly shares his joy in walking and his enthusiasm for nature with a child is giving that boy or girl a priceless heritage of pleasure for a long lifetime ahead.

Pavement Walking

Walking along the city streets is also a walk with nature, human nature. One city man enjoys his walk to work because it takes him through his neighborhood at the hour when the children are going to school. He says his morning encounter with youngsters of many ages, running, bumping, bouncing along the street like so many lively rubber balls, sends him off to his day's work energized, reminded that it is good to be alive.

Another city man likes to take his long walk on a weekend, and he walks by choice in the foreign neighborhoods of his city. On a Saturday or Sunday afternoon the shops are open and the streets are full of life— children playing, men gossiping, women shopping. His ears rejoice in the sounds of a foreign language, his nostrils drink in the fragrances of foreign dishes cooking, and he calls his walk his weekly trip abroad.

And a third city man keeps walking around his city—of which he is a native and a lifelong resident—to see what his fellow citizens have been doing to it. He visits old landmarks to see if they are still there, explores new and rehabilitated neighborhoods to discover what kind of job the urban renewers have done and how the people are living with it. He knows his city as only a walker knows it, and he claims he never goes out to walk without discovering something new.

A city walker has choices of what he walks to see. He may enjoy people, or he may enjoy the works of people, the monuments, public buildings, habitations. Some cities offer riverbanks, harbors, lakeshores, canals, all beautiful for walking. Some have bridges and walkways over the bridges, and some—a few—still have ferries, so that a voyage may be combined with the walk. Some have hills with views from their tops, and some are level, less exciting but also less strenuous.

San Francisco is one of the great cities of the world for walking, with all its hills. *Herb Caen's Guide to San Francisco* quotes an admiring visitor who expressed his love for the hilly city: "When you get tired of walking around you can lean against it." Even San Franciscans would rather ride than walk up the steep side of Nob Hill, but some walk up sideways like skiers climbing uphill and at least one indomitable citizen goes up backward. Yet even hilly San Francisco has many miles of beautiful walking on level ground, and its fond citizens know how to walk and enjoy their city. Whether it is thanks to their hills or their invigorating air, they are trim and full of vitality and they walk along at a smart pace. One rarely sees a languid San Franciscan, or an overweight one.

In an unfamiliar or a foreign city, the only way to savor it is to walk its streets and squares. American tourists are willing to sit with endless patience in a sight-seeing bus, being told what to see without ever really seeing it. But how many of them, on the "free" day of a guided tour, take the opportunity to see, hear, smell the city they have come so far to experience, by going out into its streets on foot?

No one who has walked across Waterloo Bridge in a drizzle can ever lose the sense of London as it really is, the London of Londoners, gray, shrouded, its storied towers drifting in fog, its stones dripping with legend as well as damp. No one who has walked the *quais* and boulevards of Paris, who has lost himself in the Trastevere alleys of Rome, who has strolled and stood and strolled and stood again before the rough stone bastions of Florence or the graceful palazzi of Venice, will ever forget what he has seen and felt in those cities. The bus-tour tourist comes home with a jumble of unfocused impressions—too many, gathered too fast— and often he has to look at the snapshots he has brought back to remember where he has been. But the tourist who manages at least one walk in the city knows beyond question where he has been, and what he has experienced there.

Anyone will admit that some cities are more interesting than others, and that cities away from home are most interesting of all. But every city, at home or abroad, has something of its own to show. Every city has people and their works and ways of living. And only the walker, the explorer on his own two legs, truly knows the city.

Walking to Think—and Not-Think

Not every walk is a voyage of exploration. Or rather, not every walker walks to explore the world around him. He may walk to explore his own inner world.

Some of the world's greatest thinkers have walked to do their thinking. Einstein puzzled out many secrets of the universe on his walks around Princeton. Freud did not only his thinking but much of his discussing and teaching while walking through the streets of Vienna at breakneck speed, so that his colleagues and disciples had hard work to keep up with the pace of his legs as well as of his mind.

The thinking walk has a long and distinguished history. The humanist philosopher Erasmus, in the sixteenth century, counseled his disciples, "Before supper walk a little; after supper do the same." Dr. Samuel Johnson protested that he hated the country, and yet he went on long walking trips and—according to Boswell—gave voice to some of his best thoughts while striding through the English countryside.

All these thinking walkers did not really explain why they walked to think. Why should walking stimulate good thinking? Would it not be more rational to do one's thinking sitting down in a closed, quiet room, without distraction?

Perhaps it would be more rational. But have you ever tried it? How long was it before you got up and began pacing? Or got your hat and went out for a walk? Or, if you did continue sitting, how far did you get with your thinking before you found the sofa too tempting and ended up taking a nap?

The human organism is not rational. It is natural, nature-evolved and nature-built, and it is not so very far removed from the organisms of other animals. And the other animals show us why, apart from a few exceptional members of our species, human beings cannot do their thinking sitting still. When animals are not on the prowl for food or a mate, or on the run from danger—in other words, when they have no survival business to attend to—what do they do? They sleep, or at least they doze.

Dr. Nathaniel Kleitman, the famous sleep expert, distinguished between the "wakefulness of necessity" and the "wakefulness of choice."

Man and the other animals share the wakefulness of necessity, since we must all attend to our survival and a few other basic needs; lions and lambs, mice and men, we must all gain our living. But only man is wakeful by choice. Man stays awake to talk, go to a movie, read, play games, and think.

A man can stay awake, more or less, for all these sedentary activities but one. When it comes to thinking, even the great human brain cannot overcome the built-in mechanisms of the inherited animal organism. Our biological history determines that when the muscles are sufficiently relaxed, the brain goes to sleep.

Wakefulness can be described as a constant dialogue between the muscles and the brain. We fall asleep sometimes when we are reading, not necessarily because we are tired but because the book or the magazine is just not stimulating enough to start the circuit of lively messages flowing from the brain to the muscles, and from the muscles back to the brain. A man may sit still and think if he is agitated enough by what he is thinking about—if he is dealing with a pressing business or personal problem, for example. But then the emotions aroused by his thoughts, whether of anxiety or pleasurable excitement, are stimulus enough to keep his muscles alertly tensing and sending their feedback of alertness to the brain.

It is part of our biological inheritance that we respond as a whole, body and mind, to any stimulus, and if the stimulus is lacking, we go to sleep. When thinking is accompanied by strong feelings, then the feelings are the stimulus. But pure thinking, in that cerebral region that physiologists call the New Brain, is simply not enough stimulation for most people most of the time. Like healthy animals, they go to sleep.

When we walk, the muscles are all functioning. When we walk well and easily, the muscles function smoothly and without calling undue attention to themselves, without distracting the thinking cerebrum. But they are in action, and their action keeps the brain awake. Walking, we are wide-awake and we can think.

Walking, we can think more clearly, even about a problem infused with strong feelings. This is because, as we noted in an earlier chapter, the muscular activity drains off the emotion and leaves the mind free to think. As one doctor puts it, "Action absorbs anxiety." At the same time, as one walker demanded, who ever thought deep thoughts while doing push-ups in front of an open window? The action that helps thinking is the steady, swinging, rhythmic action of walking.

The Not-Think Mechanism

More magical even than the thinking walk is the walk for not-thinking. This is the walk in which a problem to be solved or a decision to be made goes along with the walker, but not in his conscious mind. It is put aside, tucked away, left to cool.

Often the not-thinking walk is the one from which you will come back with a solution ready to hand. Walkers have discovered this marvelous phenomenon for themselves. But it is not new. It is an example of the Zen doctrine of no-mind, and it is a simple and yet effective way to tap the intuitive wisdom of the mind's unconscious levels.

When we walk, the natural, rhythmic, muscular action takes over the body, and the mind can fly free, unhampered. In the Zen method, we are told to empty the mind deliberately, and give the unconscious a chance to take over.

The rhythmic act of walking is a powerful lever to unlock the deeper levels of the mind. You can test it for yourself by following these three steps.

First, *state the problem*. You need not do this orally or in writing, although that sometimes helps. The purpose is to understand clearly what your problem is.

Second, *forget it*. Put it out of your mind. Think of anything else—or of nothing, which is harder. You are deliberately creating a vacuum, a void, in your conscious mind, and inviting the normally buried unconscious (or preconscious, as this part of the unconscious is often called) to fill it.

Third, *wait*. Don't force the solution. Fretting will not help. Wait it out. The solution will come, at the most surprising time and often in the strangest way.

It is at step number two that walking makes its contribution to this process. Once you have put the question, take a walk. A walk is the effortless way to not-think. It is also the perfect way to stave off the impulse to fret, to push, to panic, while you are waiting for an answer.

It worked for one of us, not long ago, in a most dramatic way. A telephone call from a client brought the announcement that an important project, one that had taken a good deal of preparation and had only just been started, was on the point of being jettisoned by a management committee. Would the author of the project like an opportunity to be heard? The decision would be delayed until he had had his say, if he could come at once.

He set out on foot, the idea of taking a taxi barely occurring to him. The twenty-block walk produced only a consciousness of having been allowed a last word before the hanging. The no-mind that entered that committee room would have delighted the great Zen teacher D. T. Suzuki—it was truly empty. There was a touch of anger, some sadness, but no shred of an idea about how to check the panic gripping the committee. Then, at the invitation to speak, these words came out, surprising the speaker as much as his hearers:

"I'll say just this. Did you ever hear of anyone successfully jumping halfway across a chasm? That's what you're trying to do."

The committee went into private session, did some further talking, and finally voted not to abandon the project. (And a good thing, too, as it turned out.)

What had happened on that walk? The conscious mind had not come up with an answer. The conscious mind had not supplied that startling statement which gave the committee pause. It could have come only from the mind beneath the conscious level, which had been freed to function by the walk.

A writer we know swears that he does more of his writing on his walk than at his desk. When he comes to a stubborn point, he leaves it in his typewriter and walks away from it, right out of the house. He may walk for ten minutes, or he may walk for an hour. He does not walk fretting about the unfinished paragraph in his typewriter. He just walks, and enjoys it. When he comes back, the obstacle has melted away; his fingers fly right past the blocking point. The hour he spent walking is more than paid for by the productiveness of the hours that follow.

Wrestling head-on with a problem sometimes produces the answer, and sometimes produces only a nervous sweat. Try walking. If you perspire on your walk, it will be healthy perspiration, and if you come back without a solution, at least you've had a walk!

All Kinds of Walks

So we see that people often walk with their thinking minds turned inward, or turned off. Or they may walk with only their proprioceptive senses turned on, those senses tuned to the body's own sensations of vigor, warmth, rhythm, speed of movement. This is the athletic walk, and it can be a great delight.

And finally there is the social walk, in which conversation and companionship are the central pleasure. Some walkers walk only alone, and some carry this preference for solitude even to long walking tours. Isobel Wylie Hutchinson, a famous walking tourist as well as botanist, novelist, and poet, began walking her way through historic and beautiful places in 1924, with a walk in the Outer Hebrides. She walked over Iceland (260 miles in the course of a fortnight's visit), through the castle country of Scotland, from Edinburgh to London, from Innsbruck over the Austrian Alps to Venice. Possibly she walked alone by choice, or perhaps no companion could keep pace with this hardy Scotswoman. But most long walks, and many short ones, especially the rambles of exploration, are the better for a good companion. And sometimes the companion is more important than the exploration.

Almost any kind of walk can include something of the others—athleticism and thoughtfulness, conversation and observation. Any walk, in the end, is what the walker chooses to make of it. Your walk is your own creation.

Chapter 10

THE WALKING MAN'S PLEASURES

SOME WALKERS do not walk for walking's sake at all. They walk because only their legs can take them to nature, to the enjoyment of their own particular nature enthusiasm.

What do people get out of such enthusiasms?

Jim Buck, the famous dog trainer whom we asked about walking with a dog, put it precisely when he talked of enjoying his dog companion. He described his pleasure in watching a handsome healthy animal in motion. On a deeper level, there is the pleasure of experiencing the walk through the dog. Walking with a dog, one enjoys in one's own muscles, kinesthetically, the muscular action of the animal's well-conditioned body. One enjoys in empathy with his senses the excitement of following a scent with quivering nose, of stopping still and alert with pricked-up ears at an interesting sound.

What Jim Buck enjoys in a dog as walking companion can be said of any aspect of nature as a companion. With only a little alteration, his experience of dog nature describes the experiences of all nature enthusiasts, whatever their persuasion—the bird-watchers, the rock chippers, the shell gatherers, those who look at trees, stoop over wildflowers or creep about among mosses and lichens, those who trace geologic history in the shapes of hills and those who measure a river's age by its meanderings. Whether they enjoy their chosen segment of nature esthetically, scientifically, or as a game of which the end result is a score of some kind—a collection of specimens, photographs, or sightings as with the bird-golfers —they still experience the extension of the senses and of the self that is like a dip in the fountain of life.

The more mechanized and man-made our environment, the more intensely we need this renewing communication with mother earth. There is a disturbing phenomenon, called the break-off phenomenon, known to fliers whose testing and exploring in the upper atmosphere sometimes take them too far from the earth's surface for too long a time. They suffer a loss of reality, even a loss of their own identity. Theirs is an acute disturbance that may last minutes or hours. For the rest of us, whose lives are spent closer to the ground, the break-off phenomenon is not so dramatic but it is more pervasive. We live with a hovering uneasiness, a diffuse anxiety.

We may not know its origin but we grope for its anodyne. We put trees in our city streets, plants in building lobbies, pots of greenery in our offices and homes. People clamor for more park space, for green belts around towns; they endure hours of daily commuting to live in a house with a bit of a garden.

The Never-Failing Spring of Refreshment

The nature enthusiasts are luckier. They do not have to grope; they have found their way, not merely to an escape but to a positive gain in body and mind. They know a source where refreshment and renewal are never-failing.

It does not matter whether their source is dog nature, bird or flower or plant nature, or the nature of the earth itself, its rocks and hills, rivers and seas. Whatever their taste, they all follow one path to its enjoyment—a footpath. They may ride to the bird sanctuary, the woodland, the river road, but once there, they get out and walk. The pleasures of nature are accessible only to people afoot.

People do not always know what first sent them walking on a nature quest. Most often a nature enthusiasm has its obscure origin in some scarcely remembered experience of childhood. A country childhood would seem an obvious beginning, but if a census were taken, it would be no surprise to find that the city-bred outnumber the country-bred among the nature enthusiasts.

People discover a particular love in nature even without a childhood history; we know, because we have asked. A man under doctor's orders to walk began looking at trees along his suburban route, merely to pass the time, and found fascination in them at a season when most people find them least interesting—in winter, when they were leafless and bare. Parents on vacation in the country buy a book to answer the young child's questions: "What's that flower's name?" A young woman who had often had birds at a feeder pointed out to her through a window, and seen nothing to interest her, was captivated when two friends stood dripping in a wood on a rainy day, binoculars glued to their eyeballs, watching and listening while an oriole poured song from his golden throat at the top of a willow tree. Another bird-watcher discovered birds through his camera, and produced a famous and beautiful book of hummingbird pictures.

Sometimes a book can plant the seed of an interest (we hope the following pages may do it for some reader). When the seed sprouts, however small it may seem, it is worth cultivating. The rewards are beyond measure.

The Companionable Dog

A dog trainer defined nature pleasure for us in terms of dog pleasure. In an unexpected way he also laid down a second principle: Whatever our nature pleasure may be, we enjoy it in proportion to how much we put into it.

A great many people love dogs, and almost as many own dogs, some as watchdogs, hunting dogs or working dogs of one kind or another, and many more as pets. In the suburbs almost every family has a dog; in the cities it only seems so. Hunting dogs and watchdogs are usually trained to the profession if they are to work at it. Family dogs are of course house-broken, and there their training usually ends. Walking them is a necessity, usually delegated to the youngest responsible member of the family. It is almost never regarded as an opportunity for pleasure, and neither dog nor master is educated for the enjoyment of it.

As a household animal the dog goes back to prehistory; as a hunting assistant he has several thousand years of tradition behind him. His history as a walking companion is as old as the history of walking for pleasure, a relatively recent development but old enough to be classic.

If a dog is to be a good walking companion, he must know what is expected of him, and that is a matter of training. The great naturalist Konrad Lorenz, in his book *Man Meets Dog* (which should be in every dog owner's hands), loves dogs—indeed he loves all animals, and fills his house with them. He acknowledges that training the dog is necessarily strict and may on occasion be severe. But he points out also that training enriches the dog's life, because a well-trained dog can accompany his master almost anywhere. So to Jim Buck's two pleasures of walking with a dog we can add one more, which is specific to the pleasure of enjoying dog nature. That is the pleasure a master justly takes in the correct behavior of his well-trained dog.

A well-trained dog is not regimented. He still behaves according to his dog nature and his individual nature. But he behaves well, and earns his master's confidence. In his canine terms he undoubtedly also enjoys confidence in his master, and the mutual confidence enhances the pleasure of both dog and man.

Anyone who lives in a city has seen both well- and ill-trained, or untrained, dogs, and the difference is impressive. Even on a leash, as he must be by law in most cities and many suburbs, the educated dog shows his superiority. He walks circumspectly, does not strain on the leash, does not molest strangers. His behavior in an encounter with an untrained, excitable fellow dog is a lesson in dignity.

Walking in the country, with a dog off the leash, and not trained to come on call or to heel when commanded, can be a nuisance to the neighbors and a source of pain to his master. He is also exposed to danger, and that is something no dog owner would willfully incur for his dog.

Perhaps because the need has grown in our overpopulated automobile world, dog-training or obedience schools have sprung up everywhere. In a good school, not only the dog but everyone in the family goes to school, down to the youngest ambulatory member and even the baby-sitter. If the dog has to know what is expected of him, his human companion must know every bit as much as the dog knows, and how to act on it besides.

The enjoyment of a dog as a walking companion begins with the kind of dog he is. Dogs that have been bred for hunting (Afghans, setters, pointers) or as watchdogs (Dobermanns, boxers) or as pampered lap-dogs (Pekingese and most toy dogs) are not ordinarily ideal as walking companions. But the individual puppy has his individual traits which may matter more than his breed, and if he is not responsive and intelligent to begin with, the effort of training him may never have a satisfactory outcome. (Says Jim Buck: Trade him in for a brighter pup.)

Whether in city or country, it is up to the master to interpret signs of danger ahead, and avoid them. A farmer's dog is bound to resent intrusion on his property; one keeps one's dog close at heel, passing the farmhouse and barns, or one makes a detour. In the city, a dog off the leash, or one on too long a leash or out of control, is also a potential danger and a warning to cross with one's own dog to the other side of the street.

Dog owners give themselves and their dogs a bad name, especially with walkers, by failing to take them to the curb for their excretory functions. American dog owners are not the only offenders. One of the authors, walking in a suburb of immaculate Amsterdam, was horrified when a Dutch lady just ahead permitted her toy poodle to jump up on a speckless wall around a manicured private lawn and leave his canine calling card there. A city-dwelling dog can easily learn to respect sidewalks and crossings where pedestrians must tread. If he fails to do so, it is not the dog that is ill-mannered but his master.

Anyone who loves his dog will want him to be no nuisance but a joy, and a well-trained dog is the most joyful of walking companions. Thomas Mann wrote eloquently of this pleasure in his little book of essays, *A Man and His Dog.* He described the pure delight of the morning walk, with the dog's exuberant pleasure enhancing the man's, putting an added sparkle into the fresh sights and scents of the beginning day. Mann's dog Bashan loved to leap across a certain low fence, and for his master's pleasure he leaped back and forth, again and again, extending himself in beauty and grace and coming back each time for his reward of extravagant praise. Mann wrote, "Drawing in deep breaths of the morning air, you believe in your freedom and in your worth, though you ought to be aware, and at heart *are* aware, that the world is holding its snares ready to entangle you in them. . . . You are . . . the right royal lord of that mad hunter yonder who is just making another jump across the fence out of sheer joy. . . ." What is there to compare with a walking man's pleasure in his dog companion?

The Birds

From dog to bird is not too long a leap for the imagination. Many people smile at bird-watchers. But behind their smiles they wonder: What do the birders see, what do they feel, that rouses them from their warm beds in the chill and drizzle of an early spring morning at the start of the migration season? What lures them to tramp through parkland, marsh-land, woodland in search of birds? A puzzled bystander asked one of them, "What do you do, take pictures?" And at the answer, "No, we just look," he was even more puzzled.

Some birders carry cameras, but they are few. Most carry only their binoculars, perhaps a copy of the indispensable *Field Guide* of Roger

Tory Peterson, perhaps also a pencil and a pocket notebook to jot down identifications. They go to see and hear, to experience the birds, to name them with their species names. They go in the migration seasons to welcome the birds back in spring and bid them goodbye in the fall. They go to see how the birds are faring, to renew old acquaintanceships and make new ones, to wish them well.

But mostly the birders go to enjoy the beauty of the wild things and to share, by the magical empathy of the senses, the free and lovely flight, the swell of song, the busy occupations of feeding and nest-building, of rearing the young and teaching them to fly.

No moment is as heart-lifting as welcoming the birds back in the spring. They arrive in their bright spring dress, singly, in pairs, in clouds, and the birder in imagination becomes possessed of all the far lands over which the little navigators of the air have journeyed. This small, pansy-yellow warbler has just flown in from Central America, and that cigar-brown chimney swift only last week was wheeling over the Amazon forests as he now wheels over our city housetops. Watching the birds, Louis J. Hallé, Jr., who in his non-birding life is a member of the State Department, wrote in his delicious book, *Spring in Washington,* "It is as if I had the power to revolve this globe under my feet like a plaything."

Like any other collection of human beings, birders have their individual preferences. Some will not look twice at a commonplace bird—a robin or a house sparrow—but hurry on to spot the unusual finch or grosbeak, the hard-to-identify warbler. Roger Baldwin called them bird-golfers, the people who get pleasure from bettering their score of sightings each year and practicing one-upmanship on their fellow players.

Others take their deepest enjoyment in the bird itself, however familiar. Seeing a robin drilling in the moist earth, they will stop and wait to learn whether he gets the worm. They will glimpse that great underwater swimmer, the cormorant, as he dives, and will wait until he surfaces yards away, to share his triumph if he has caught the little fish. In years of bird-watching, they may have seen hundreds of swallows darting over the lake for insects, thousands of terns plunging head foremost into the sea for a fishy morsel, dozens of hawks cruising against the sky. Yet they stop again and watch, entranced with the agile skill and powerful motion, sharing by an extension of their own senses the very sensations of the bird.

For that matter, even the most single-minded scorekeeper cannot suppress a gasp of pleasure on seeing the spring's first scarlet tanager, with the velvet black of his wings folded against his royally glowing body. Nor can the most determined bird-golfer resist the flicker's showy plumage or the dazzling geometry of the black-and-white warbler; the elegance of a cedar waxwing erect on a telephone wire, flaunting his little crest; the heraldic outline of a heron on a high branch with his long neck outstretched, silhouetted against the sky. None of these is a rare bird, but every one of them is an endearing or a dramatic sight.

Dedicated birders will walk where walking itself is no pleasure. They will slog through swamp and salt marsh, crawl over dunes in a biting sea wind, steal through woods and stand unmoving, letting gnats and mosquitoes eat them alive, just to glimpse a shy creature or hear his unearthly music.

But they also have more accessible bird haunts; some indeed are sybaritically easy walking. Up the East Coast from Washington, D.C., and in other cities that chance to be on the flyways, the birders in spring and fall have only to walk in the park to see the birds. In the heart of Central Park in New York is an area less than a half-mile square, perhaps five acres all together, called the Ramble, an unmanicured woodland with winding paths where birds come from everywhere on their journey between winter and summer, and birders come from everywhere to see them. In the weeks between mid-April and mid-May a good birder can see a hundred species—birds of wood and field, marsh birds and shore birds—and they are too busy feeding, and replenishing their strength for the rest of their journey, to be shy. On a busy morning in the Ramble the sound of bird voices caroling and calling is enough to drown out the city roundabout; the air shimmers with their music.

With such an addition to one's walking pleasure so readily accessible, it is sheer wastefulness not to sample it. There is nothing difficult about beginning bird-watching, no effort of study or acquired skill. All one needs is eyes and ears and a willingness to use them. After one has begun to see and hear birds, the next step may be to buy binoculars to see them better, and a field guide—Peterson's is the time-tested classic—in which to look at their pictures and discover their names. A little more experience, and the novice birder wants to know their families, their habits, what they eat and where they live; he will find this in the text.

For the ear-minded who like to recognize a bird by his call, there are hi-fi recordings to play on the phonograph once in a while. At some point a bird walk or a series of them with a leader may become attractive—one learns a great deal that enhances further solitary expeditions. And later still a birding vacation beckons, at one of the Audubon Society's camps, or a weekend at one of the famous migration gathering places in the fall where birders share their pleasure with each other.

To enjoy the birds in one's own city park or suburban greenery costs no effort; to see them in the wild in their own habitat, nesting and rearing their young, takes a little investment of energy. Bird sanctuaries are everywhere now, and wherever there are trails and country walks there are also birds. The birder's pleasure goes with him wherever he goes, on weekends, summer and winter holidays, even around the world. The birds are everywhere, and one meets old friends in a London park, new ones on the Caribbean or the Nile.

There are other small creatures in nature besides the birds, and other enthusiasts who take pleasure in them; butterflies and moths, beetles, lizards, snakes also have their buffs. These enthusiasms are somewhat more specialized, although no less pleasurable to their devotees. The natural history museum in any city can usually guide the would-be amateur.

The Green Kingdom

A woman walker in a northern city regularly makes an expedition every spring to the center of the city park, just to see a certain tree. It is an exotic from the Southwest, an Osage orange, but she began visiting it long before she knew its origin or its name, just to see how it weathered the northern winter. She loved it for the beauty of its high, upreaching branches and especially of its bark, of the color of old gold, deeply and regularly ridged. She was also concerned for it because of its age. She eventually learned its name and habitat from one of the park gardeners, and she still visits it faithfully each spring.

There are people who love trees and shrubs and flowers with a kind of generalized affection, without ever having to know the names of any of them. They wonder, even, whether the need to name things is not rather pedantic and stuffy. But the namers are not necessarily pedantic (although some are) or showing off. They are only following the natural aptitude of the human mind, which is given to summing up in a word—in this case, a species name—all the qualities of an object, a person, an experience. The name of a beloved tree or shrub or wildflower evokes for us all its aspects. Once she learned its name, the woman who was having a love affair with her tree in the park had only to think "Osage orange" to evoke in an instant all its beauty and the feeling she had for it.

Oliver Wendell Holmes talked of his "tree wives," the great old trees around New England on which he had placed his wedding ring, by which he meant the 30-foot tape measure with which he had measured their girth. He especially loved the American elm, but he called anyone a goose who expected him to discourse on *Ulmus americana* in scientific terms. He wrote of trees as he saw and loved them, not as specimens but as living individuals, "holding their green sunshades over our heads, talking to us with their hundred thousand whispering tongues, looking down on us with that sweet meekness which belongs to huge, but limited organisms . . . while Nature dresses and undresses them, like so many full-sized, but under-witted children."

To add a love and knowledge of trees to one's walking pleasures is the simplest of pursuits. Trees are almost everywhere, except in the benighted real estate developments where every touch of nature has been bulldozed away. City parks worthy of the name proudly display many exotic species along with the native ones. To the tree lover every species has its characteristic beauty and design, its own way of spreading its limbs, its own habit of budding and leafing, its peculiar coloring in spring and fall. The evergreens are a separate love in themselves, as varied as the deciduous trees.

A walking man's pleasure in the green kingdom of the plants may stop here, with the visual enjoyment of their forms. Or he may pursue it with book and pocket lens, learning more facts and discovering more beauty as he goes. The most familiar leaf, the most commonplace blossom or grass, shows complexities of structure under the lens that cannot be imagined. It is a revelation like the pattern of a snowflake.

Wildflowers have a magical appeal; they talk of elves and fairies. People also fall in love with ferns, with mosses. They find a joy in minute plant forms like the joy in exquisite jewels. Once they are ensnared in this addiction, they become even more indifferent to comfort than the most addicted bird-watchers. They clamber over rocks and fells, trudge through desert and barren in the search for their miniature beauties. We may marvel at their absorption but we cannot scorn it. What they are worshiping, in this self-forgetful ritualistic search, is life itself, and its power to grow and adapt even to the most inhospitable environment.

No general book such as this one can guide these specialist walkers. Even a lover of wildflowers must find his own way to the shy hepatica and dogtooth violet in the spring woods, the single wood lily lifting its red cup, the tiny orchis and the scarlet pimpernel, so much more modest than its name, in the open pasture. We can say only that these are also the walker's pleasures, because only on foot can they be discovered and enjoyed.

Collectors' Walks

Certain keys off Florida and certain islands in the Gulf of Mexico have become shell collectors' paradises. Any beach along our limitless coasts and some lakeshores have become the Edens of driftwood collectors. Certain rugged rocky regions where geological dramas have unfolded are the magnets of rock and mineral collectors.

Collecting, in whatever kingdom of nature, is also a walker's pleasure. The collector in pursuit of a wanted specimen does not count the miles; he takes no note of weary legs or—if his hobby is rocks—of the growing weight of his pack. Every item is precious and worth the effort.

A glamorous specialty of some collectors is the search for semiprecious stones. It is a sub-branch of the mineralogy collection, but it has a place of its own with amateurs who care little for the science but are entranced with the specimens, which are often dazzlingly beautiful. Opal, topaz, chalcedony, jade, coral—their names alone are alluring.

In the western mountains of both the United States and Canada, in the Southwest, and in Mexico there are areas where these treasures lie waiting for the collector. Some are in national or state parks; the Petrified Forest is one such place, but only for admiring (there are penalties for "collecting"). The natural history museums and the mineralogy hobby journals are sources of guidance to this glamorous collecting interest.

The Companionship of Science

A distinguished biology professor, afield in search of fossil specimens, came upon a crack in the earth, a narrow deep ravine cut in the sandstone by some ancient mountain torrent. He worked his way to the bottom of the crack, which was scarcely body-width and cut through some ten million years of earth history, while above him the sky narrowed to a thin blue slit and became ever more distant.

He hoped to find a bone or two; what he encountered was an early mammal skull staring out at him, of a creature that had not lived to see the birth of man. As he patiently chipped at its stone matrix, he slipped backward in daydream to that time of the earth before men walked on it. So enthralled was he in his dream of a younger earth that when at last he collected his specimen and his tools and climbed upward again through the geologic eras, he was not sure it was a horse, which he had left grazing at the top, that he would see.

It might have been Eohippus, a dawn horse, no bigger than a dog, that waited for him, or it might have been a dinosaur. Professor Loren Eiseley did not say, in the marvelous account of his adventure that opens his book of adventures in evolution, *The Immense Journey,* in which, as one of the scientist-poets of our time, he shares his imaginative experience with us.

Ours is a great time of science fiction which looks ahead into a fantasy world of human, or perhaps Martian, creation. But we also have, fortunately, our science poets, the eloquent natural scientists who share with us a past and present that is not man-made but nature-made. They show us the world that holds our first experience of beauty, as it has done since men painted running animals on the walls of their caves or cupped their hands in a cool spring to drink.

The science of earth and life makes a thrilling walking companion. Rachel Carson wrote of this in *The Edge of the Sea,* when she guided us along the beach.

"When we go down to the low-tide line," she wrote, "we enter a world that is as old as the earth itself—the primeval meeting place of the elements of earth and water, a place of compromise and conflict and eternal change. For us as living creatures it has special meaning as an area in or near which some entity that could be distinguished as Life first drifted in shallow waters—reproducing, evolving, yielding that endlessly varied stream of living things that has surged through time and space to occupy the earth."

We do not need to be scientists to add this dimension to our walks. We have the scientist poets, the Eiseleys and Carsons, and before them the Muirs, Audubons, and all who preceded them in a long tradition of great literature, to point the way.

They show us how to read the sands and the rocks, the story of a field or a forest. They show us on the hills and in the valleys the tiny fingers of sculpturing rains or the great grinding footprints of an Ice Age. On our walks we can both enjoy the beauty of a landscape and see behind it the long and fascinating history from which it grew; we can see it being sculptured and painted through the geologic eras until this moment when we can drink it in.

It takes, actually, very little to open this further door in our mind's eye. A professor of geology in a famous Massachusetts women's college used to put on a little show for his students in the introductory course. On their first field trip, he did not set them chipping rock samples or looking at outcrops to distinguish igneous from sedimentary. Instead, he led them to the edge of the river and showed them a slab of rock there, on which were imprinted from ages long gone two huge footprints of a dinosaur and a further pair of tiny ones with the sweep of a tail still showing behind, a smaller lizard, which had sat down. Then at a breakneck pace he led his young ladies uphill until, panting, they caught up with him at the top and found him standing with his foot on a rounded outcrop of rock. This, he told them, was the core of an extinct volcano.

All this was in the gentle Connecticut Valley, in the heart of civilized, long-tamed New England. It was a revelation to those young ladies, of the earthshaking dramas of nature that had once convulsed the serene landscape around them. Even though not one in the whole class took the professor's advanced course, they never forgot that afternoon when he folded back for them the curtain of earth time.

When we travel to foreign parts, some of us use the weeks beforehand to read about places we are going to see, partly to feed our anticipations and partly because we have learned—if we are experienced travelers—that the more we take with us of art and social history the more we will enjoy our travel experiences. The same is true of our smaller journeys, our walks around and about the places where we live and where we vacation, familiar though they are. A little knowledge—of the history of this small segment of earth, of its plant and animal life, resident and migrant—can fill our walks with imaginative riches.

Walking with Weather and Seasons

People who walk only when the weather is fine and mild do not know what they miss. They deprive themselves of the enchantment of mist and fog, the soft splash of spring rain, the velvet touch of snow, the wild challenge of cold and wind, the languor of summer heat.

People walk everywhere on the earth, in the tropics and in the arctic, but there can be no question about it: The best walking is in the temperate zones of the world, where the weather is never the same for two days in succession and where the majestic march of the seasons marks with its preludes and its dramatic peaks the cycle of the year. Even the unseasonable days—the autumn days that are not crisp but languorous as summer, the winter days that do not bite but give soft and watery promise of spring—even these are special, reminding us by their very inappropriateness of the grandeur of the earth's seasonal round.

Brooks Atkinson, the dean of drama critics who was always at heart a naturalist, once took a cabin in the hills of Greene County, New York, for weekend relaxation. He wrote of the seasons, "Although we hastily regard them as a thing apart from ourselves, we are really united to them closely. Not merely because they bring the harvest upon which we depend, or because they fertilize the soil with falling leaves and store the mountains with the water we need in spring and summer; but because as natural beings we are drawn into their movement, emotionally and physically."

And he wrote, "Each season was bright with beauty. I felt no melancholy about autumn. After the leaves had fallen, clean and crackling under foot, the woods were full of light, the views widened through the bare branches, the evergreens bathed the eye more soothingly than ever and the structural design of the deciduous trees was revealed as perfect symmetry. . . . The nipping air foretold, not so much the death of Nature, as the coming of a glorious season in which every field and hill would be newly transfigured."

Of a winter walk he said, "The outdoors was glorious. Conscious of the tingling cold, I felt a kinship with everything—with the crusted snow, the sparkling ledges on Bear Mountain, the restless, hidden lake, the muffled brook flowing under huge covers of glittering ice." He spoke of birds, winter residents and wanderers from even farther north, and he added, "The winter season was self-sufficient—a complete state, an entity. I could hardly remember when the lake was open. Winter dominated every sense; I could not add to it, take away from it or withhold myself. I could not play truant by dreaming of balmier days. Every sensation seemed complete and final, and beyond human equivocation."

When spring came, liberating the frozen country, turning sharp etchings to hazy soft pastels and filling the air with birds, the excitement of the earth's renewal mounted to ecstasy. All this, the heart-stirring cycle of the seasons, has gone on through centuries and millennia, since long before a sophisticated urban gentleman journeyed each weekend to watch it, from a great metropolis only fifty-odd miles away. It goes on still, in every meadow and valley, on every hillside and the margin of every lake, river, and streamlet in our wide land, and even in our city parks. It is still there, for all of us to see, hear, smell, to know with our senses and our minds. In our belt of the globe we are the more alive for the swinging sun and tilting earth that give us our weather and our seasons.

It is one more of the many pleasures, unpredictable and endlessly changing, that are especially reserved for those who walk.

Chapter 11

WALKING COMFORT

WHEN Isobel Wylie Hutchinson, some decades ago, made her famous pedestrian sight-seeing trips of hundreds of miles over Scotland, England, Iceland, and parts of Europe, she wore no special costume. The Scottish novelist-botanist-poet walked her many miles in ordinary clothes that made her inconspicuous and discreet on a country lane, an Alpine village square, a provincial town street or the avenue of a great city. She observed everything but was herself unobserved.

Mrs. Hutchinson's experience underlines the noteworthy truth about walking, that among active sports it is the only one requiring no peculiar equipment, not even peculiar dress. Easy clothes and good shoes are all a walker needs, with some weather protection when indicated.

All the rest is trimming, some of it practical, some merely decorative, when ordinary walking is in question. Wilderness and rough country walking take on some of the aspects of other sports—hunting, fishing, camping, mountain-climbing—and share some of their special needs. Shoes—what kind, for what kind of feet and what kind of walks—are worthy of special attention, as are the feet themselves if we are to enjoy our walking no matter where. From experienced walkers we also learn what kind of ordinary clothing is more than ordinarily comfortable on a walk, how to provide against the weather, what to carry and how to carry it without converting oneself into a beast of burden.

Urb and Suburb

The walk to the office, to lunch, even to dinner and the theater, presents no quandaries of wardrobe to a man. His ordinary city clothes and city shoes are walk-worthy.

For a woman there is a dilemma, but it is readily resolved. A woman who elects to walk can adjust her wardrobe to this preference. She can do this no matter what the current fashion, without looking unfashionable and dowdy, eccentric, or inappropriately dressed.

Women are forever making such adjustments within the range of fashion for any given season. They shop for their clothes with a mind full of individual requirements in color, design, durability, price, purpose, and personal taste. The woman walker simply adds one more requirement to her list: Her everyday town clothes must also be comfortable for walking.

She will not have to wear slacks and a kerchief to the office. If she wears hats, she buys close-fitting ones, or has a brimmed hat made secure with a pair of small combs in the inner band that will hold it against a breeze. If skirts are narrow, she gets hers with a kick pleat or slit, or has one put in by the neighborhood tailor at little expense.

Providentially, at the very moment that this is being written, a "walking suit" has come into the shops. It is high-style but it is indeed designed for walking, with a skirt wide enough to give knee space for a good stride, and a coat long enough to be warm but not too long for unimpeded motion. Unfathomable are the ways of fashion designers, and we do not propose to inquire into this timely phenomenon, only to welcome it and to hope that it will make walking ever more inviting to women.

Shoe fashions took this agreeable direction long before. Some years ago, when style dictated only stiletto heels, many women were hard put to find shoes in which they could walk. The determined ones were reduced to wearing country oxfords, also known as old-lady shoes, to work and keeping a high-heeled pair in the office desk. Others simply gave up walking during the business week. Many feet were damaged in that period (as well as many wood and linoleum floors, which became hopelessly pitted) and many girls and young women never learned the pleasure of breaking up the long working day with a brisk walk during lunch hour.

But fashion does right itself, given a few seasons, and women are no longer asked to wear what Southern ladies call "sittin' shoes" for walking in the city. When the delightful and sensible fashion came in of wearing boots for winter warmth, and eventually for their own dashing style, it also became fashionable to carry a pair of shoes along for indoor comfort, for dancing, or just for looks with the kind of dress one was wearing under the outdoor wrap. The shoe tote is now a normal accessory in the feminine wardrobe.

Low-heeled and flat-heeled shoes have followed the boot fashion into the shops, and women walkers now have a wide choice of footwear that is both comfortable and stylish. A point to remember is that even though the heel is right, a thin sole does not make for comfortable walking on city pavements. The healthy and well-muscled human foot can take a good deal of pounding, but it can hardly withstand the hard impact of concrete on every step, and foot fatigue is the price, if not also calluses and weakened metatarsal arches. Many women find that metatarsal pads help to make their city shoes more walkable. Some use cushioning insoles. The neighborhood shoemaker can put in either. Some shoes, fashionably slender and thin-soled on the outside, are fitted by their manufacturer with inner cushioning, a genuine boon to the city woman walker.

Shoes that are molded to the individual foot, such as the widely advertised Murray Space Shoes, can make walking comfortable even for damaged feet, and some walkers, men and women, enjoy them even if their feet are not in trouble. They have advantages that few standard shoe lasts can provide, such as shaped cushioning for the sole and ample space for the toes, which should be able to move and contribute muscularly to the action of every step. They can be heavy, however, and consequently fatiguing. Since these shoes represent a substantial investment, it is probably wise to experiment first with a lightweight version.

Once women are out of the formal business world, walking clothes and walking shoes create no difficulties for them. Young mothers long ago took to slacks and flats in the suburbs and residential neighborhoods when they went out with the baby buggy or the stroller, and now they even have pants suits, very chic. Walking on a weekend morning or afternoon, anyone may follow the same go-as-you-please fashion. Whatever is comfortable is right, whether you are walking in town or country.

Women walking in city or suburban clothes have one further nuisance to solve, the handbag. Carried by its strap, it immobilizes one arm and unbalances a good swinging stride. The shoulder bag, forever slipping down unless the shoulder it hangs from is elevated, is even more of an interference, unless it has a long enough strap to cross over to the opposite shoulder. This in turn may interfere with the hang of a coat or a suit jacket. Perhaps the answer is a sporran, which a Scotsman hangs from his belt down the front of his kilt. If it does not bother an energetic Scot, it would probably be comfortable for a walking woman, and it could be both practical and chic. Up to this writing, no perfect solution of the handbag problem has been discovered, however, and it is every woman for herself.

For most adventurous walking, when urban or suburban correctness is not involved, all these questions have a variety of cheerful answers. Outer wear, weather wear, protective wear for rough going, footwear, and the art of pocketry—we will take them up in order.

The Laminated Wardrobe

In some climates, regions, seasons, and on some kinds of days especially in fall and spring, one needs to be dressed for cold, warm, rainy and sunny weather, all in the course of the same walk. It is also true that when we start out walking it may be chilly, but walking itself will warm us up. Knowledgeable walkers deal with this contingency by dressing so that they can peel themselves like an onion when required. Unlike the onion, they can also resume layers as needed—when the sun ducks under clouds, for example, or a chill wind comes up in the afternoon, or even just to sit down and rest, eat, or look at the scenery.

Clothing in layers, or the laminated wardrobe, answers all these requirements. An extra-heavy shirt or a heavy jacket becomes burdensome when we warm up or the sun comes out. The laminated wardrobe provides combinations of shirt, sleeveless sweater or vest, long-sleeved sweater, and lightweight windbreaker, which can be put together for any degree of heat and cold short of arctic or tropical extremes. Each item as discarded is also readily portable, hung on the strap that already carries binoculars, camera or whatever equipment goes along on the walk, or else tied by its sleeves around the waist.

Trousers, slacks or shorts are not so adjustable en route, but underclothing that adjusts itself is the thermal variety, of cotton knit with large air spaces so that it provides warmth or coolness depending on what goes on over it. Under a thin shirt it is cool; under a windbreaker that keeps body heat contained, the thermal undershirt is warm. Slim, warmth-conserving underpants are available to walkers as they are to skiers, for whom they have been principally developed. For walking, as for skiing, nothing should be tight or binding. Comfort depends on unimpeded circulation no less than on freedom of movement. And on a long walk the body's own uncomplaining sheath, the skin, must also be comfortable. Clothing should fit so that it nowhere lumps or chafes. Indeed the ideal clothing on a walk never calls attention to itself at all.

The Secret of Keeping Warm

A basic principle of comfort, of which surprisingly many people are unaware, is that you can keep your whole body warm with far less clothing if you wear gloves on your hands, cover your head and neck, and keep your thighs warm. If the extremities are warm, the whole body is warm even with relatively light protection. The explanation is simple: The blood has to circulate to the very ends of fingertips, toes, and the roots of the hair, and at every surface that is exposed it loses heat.

People will pile warm clothing around their shoulders, and forgot entirely that arms and hands, neck and head, and the legs from hip to ankle are rapidly dissipating heat all the time they are clutching their coats together at the bosom. City and suburban dwellers are especially innocent about this, since they are ducking into shelter every few minutes, from house or office into a conveyance, and from a conveyance into house or office. In the ordinary course of their lives they rarely stay out long enough to get cold. There has also been a great vogue for some years of going bareheaded. Women wear hats for fashion's sake or to keep their hair from blowing; men, not at all.

That's all very well, until we go out for a day's walking in brisk weather. Then we discover that even with a warm jacket and perhaps a sweater underneath we may still be chilly. And if we put on heavier outer clothing we feel too bulky to walk with enjoyment. But with a hat or kerchief on the head, a scarf tucked in around the neck, warm sleeves and gloves and, for thin people especially, a pair of close-fitting ski drawers keeping the thighs warm under trousers or slacks, the torso can make do with little more than a windbreaker to keep off the chill. The advantage is double, because when we are lightly clad we can walk more energetically, and be rewarded with the pleasure of good exercise as well as the enjoyment of the walk.

Anyone who goes out to walk does well to take note of the temperature before setting out, so that he can dress accordingly. If there is a wind, count on feeling about ten degrees colder than the thermometer indicates, and dress according to the adjusted expectation. Wind is a chiller; it blows heat from the body's exposed surfaces far faster than the heat would dissipate by itself.

And of Keeping Cool

For warm-weather walking, light-colored clothes are actually cooler than dark ones, not only psychologically but in physical fact as well. The light colors reflect the heat along with the light waves, while dark colors absorb both heat and light. If the day is sunny as well as warm, a brimmed hat keeps both the head and the face cool by shading them; a good hat also shades the back of the neck. It should have ventilating perforations, and if it also has a high crown it will be even cooler, in the same way that a well-ventilated attic helps to keep the house cool in summer, by providing a layer of circulating air as insulation.

Sunglasses

The question of sunglasses arises; they are now widely considered essential outdoor wear. This is a vogue which many, if not most, ophthalmologists deplore, on the ground that the eyes are equipped by nature to deal with all the normal variations of sun and shade and need the exercise to keep their fine muscles in tone.

For snow, beach, or desert walking, even the most austere eye specialist would suggest protection against the unremitting glare of reflected sunlight. Snowy fields on a brilliant day call particularly for good glasses such as skiers wear. But under ordinary walking conditions most people can discard their sunglasses as merely an acquired habit, and feel no discomfort. Even in bright sun, a brimmed hat generally provides enough shade to keep the eyes comfortable and prevent squinting.

The Walking Stick

An old vogue that seems to be enjoying a revival is the walking stick. At the famous Uncle Sam Umbrella Shop in New York City, where canes as well as umbrellas are handcrafted, repaired, and made to many an eccentric order, sales of canes began increasing a few years ago, and both men and women were the purchasers.

The days are past when a city gentleman swung along the avenue to the brisk rhythm of his Malacca or ebony cane, or a countryman stopped to cut himself a stout stick of ash before setting off down the road. Nowadays one cannot even find a grandfather from whom to learn the art of walking with a walking stick.

It is an art we could all learn with ease, and to our profit. The swing of the stick on level ground enhances the rhythm of walking like a marching tune; it encourages the proud posture and free-swinging stride of a good walking style. And when the road goes up hill and down dale, or over rough ground, the stick can be useful indeed. There is no question that a friendly and well-handled cane adds to the pleasure of the walk and alleviates its fatigues. Our walking ancestors did not carry their sticks merely for show.

The walking stick can also help to carry things. Sword canes were once a valued defense weapon, and some canes of the lusty past concealed guns, poker dice, whiskey flasks. A fisherman's custom-made cane was a telescoped fishing rod, with a handle that held bait and a compartment for fishhooks. A walker's stick might be similarly designed to hold a roll of maps, a compass in its handle, perhaps even a pocket for lunch and a change of socks. Why not, after all?

Rough-Weather Wear

If many people deny themselves a walk because they do not know how to keep warm in cold weather or cool when it is warm, even more miss the pleasure of walking in rain or snow. Weather wear in the past may have been awkward and cumbersome enough to take the pleasure out of bad-weather walking, but nowadays the waterproof and water-repellent fabrics are of great variety, light in weight, and lend themselves to tailoring in comfortable, practical garments that are smart as well.

A threat of precipitation need not deter anyone from a walk if he has a lightweight waterproof parka with a hood, which he can sling through a carrying strap on his back. A three-quarter-length parka with hood weighs less than one pound. If it is already raining or snowing, and promises to go on doing so, there are rain suits, jacket and pants, for both men and women. The famous Maine sportsmen's outfitter, L. L. Bean (this address and others in the "Shopping Guide"), has ladies' rain suits in nylon coated with neoprene, the pullover shirt with a zipper closing and a hood with a drawstring; both the shirt and the pants have drawstrings at the waist, and the color is an alluring "space blue." The whole outfit weighs 24 ounces, or just a pound and a half. Their men's rain suit of the same material and similar design comes in olive green. They also have a men's rain suit of vinyl-coated cotton for rougher wear and greater warmth, which is about one pound heavier all told, in bright, highly visible yellow.

Protective Wear

Nature-walkers, like huntsmen and fishermen, often find themselves in places that are favorites also of the insect world. Walkers, like sportsmen, have to share the world's most beautiful woods at the loveliest seasons with mean, biting black flies, and a walk along lake, river, seashore, or on the most fascinating marshlands, can be a trying ordeal of mosquitoes and gnats. Sportsmen equip themselves with a head net of nylon. Sportsmen also carry an all-purpose oversize cotton bandanna which can be knotted around the neck or draped from under a hat like an Arab's headcloth, to keep off insects or to forestall a painful sunburn on the back of the neck.

To expose large areas of bare skin on a long walk is no wiser in summer than at other seasons. Once the sun begins to climb above the equator, after the spring equinox, its rays rapidly gain in power, and a walk even on a warm Memorial Day weekend can result in unpleasant consequences for bare shoulders, upper arms and back. It is one thing to sunbathe lying on a beach or garden chair, when we can control the exposure, and quite another to be a mile or several miles from home, in T-shirt or sleeveless sunback top, with nothing to shield winter-white skin from the constant assault of the sun.

The sunbather can turn as on a spit, but the walker gets the sun always on the same parts of his anatomy as long as the sun is high. An experienced walker even in warm weather wears a thin shirt that covers the arms at least to the elbow and a collar that can be turned up in back. A head covering is also advisable, if only for protection against the fatigue of continuous brilliant sunlight. For the fair-skinned, forehead and nose can benefit from special protection. A cool, light, wide-brimmed straw hat such as Caribbean fishermen wear, with a cord to tie under the chin, is by all odds the pleasantest of walking sunshades.

Woodland and cross-country walking can be scratchy, thorny, brambly —and there are always insect enemies, to say nothing of the poison ivy-oak-sumac family. For this kind of walking, shorts are obviously not practical. Thin cotton slacks and socks above the ankle are adequate against insects and poison plants but not against brambles. For these, levis or corduroys are necessary, although warm; on a summer walk we must expect some healthy sweat. In colder weather, whipcord is protective and also warmer. A good pair of shooting pants is usually made of all-wool whipcord and is resistant to brambles and briers.

Pocket and Pack

The easiest way to carry things without a sense of encumbrance is in pockets, and good walking clothes have ample pockets for storing lunch, maps, even the minimum toilet kit and change of underthings and socks for an overnight jaunt. Some favorites of sportsmen, all well-pocketed, are the warden's jacket and the longer bush coat. This latter can be worn with a belt, which is convenient to hang things from, such as an extra sweater. Sportsmen's jackets are also usually windproof and water-repellent. The classic English hacking coat has pockets like an overnight bag, to carry either weekend necessities or a complete nature library in paperbacks. For warm-weather walking, a fisherman's vest has many small pockets, but lunch, toilet kit and the rest must go in a shoulder-strap pouch or a light knapsack or rucksack, whichever form of portage one prefers.

Pouches and knapsacks are available in variety; size and design are optional, but a good one should be durable, weatherproof, and as light in weight as possible. A short, wide rucksack is most comfortable when carried high on the back; a larger one, lower—a tall sack tends to sway as you walk. Heavy objects should be packed at the bottom and on the inner side, against the back, to stabilize the sack. Straps are best when broad and flat, easy to adjust, and padded if the sack is heavy, or even if it is not—to spare the collarbones. A well-fitted, well-packed rucksack should not restrict shoulder freedom or bind so tightly that it hampers circulation. On a strenuous tramp or on a warm day, a sack is almost bound to make for a sweaty back. There is a type of carrier built on a frame, such as the Bergan, that leaves an air space between the load and the carrier's back, but it holds less for its size and weight, costs more, and tends to throw the walker's balance backward.

There are, of course, packs for wilderness walkers who will carry on their backs everything they need—sleeping and cooking equipment and the food itself. Backpacking is a specialty of experienced outdoorsmen and we will not try to cover it here. (Look in the Shopping Guide and the Walking Guide checklist for more on this.)

Of all forms of locomotion, walking is the one for traveling light, since our own two feet must carry the weight of all we take. Yet the bird lover will not go without his binoculars—which add to walking pleasure even for non-birders, bringing distant views close for identification and enjoyment. And the camera buff must have his camera and accessories.

Glasses and cameras are easily portable in shoulder-strap carrying cases; the point is simply not to take one's heaviest equipment on a long walk. A good all-purpose size for binoculars, not too heavy on a lady bird-watcher's shoulder, is 7 x 35; the greater the magnification and the wider the lens, the heavier, of course, are the glasses.

A Note on Cameras

To the walker, a camera is merely a device to make visual notes, something to help him remember what he has seen. It should be light in weight; otherwise carrying it may become a burden. It should be compact and uncomplicated, so that it does not require too much attention. And it should always be at the ready, to capture what Henri Cartier-Bresson so happily termed "the decisive moment."

The ideal camera, sad to say, does not exist.

If it did, it would be a weightless wonder that could give us sharp and correctly exposed color slides, or negatives from which we could make good color or monochrome prints of any reasonable size, without fuss and without having to cash in all our stocks and bonds.

But if you are willing to compromise, there are cameras that almost fill the bill. If you already have an easily portable camera that you are used to, one which produces sharp pictures, take it along; your problem is solved. If you want to get a new one, these are some of the factors to consider:

1. FILM SIZE AND AVAILABILITY.   Your camera should take film that is stocked almost everywhere, sells fast and therefore does not get stale on the dealer's shelf. Among these are the 12-exposure 120 roll film, the 35-mm. sprocket film in both 20- and 36-exposure cartridges, and the Kodapak film cartridges used in the *Instamatic* cameras.

2. CAMERA TYPE.   You have a wide variety of choice, from the twin-lens roll-film reflexes like the *Rolleiflex*, the single-lens roll-film reflexes like the *Hasselblad* and the new *Rollei SL66*, the 35-mm.

range-finder cameras like the *Leica M3,* the 35-mm. single-lens reflexes like the *Leicaflex* and the *Nikon F,* the 35-mm. zone-focusing cameras like the *Olympus,* the *Tenax,* the *Minoltina P,* the *Rollei 35,* and the *Fujica Compact 35,* to, finally, the *Polaroid Land* cameras that deliver finished prints in 10 seconds and color prints in 60 seconds.

There are smaller and lighter cameras, like the *Minox,* the *Minolta 16MG,* and the *Yashica 16EE* and *Half 17,* but these may present technical problems in developing and printing.

3. WEIGHT.   Most cameras and accessories come in their own cases, so keep in mind that the total weight has to be carried. If the camera does not provide a built-in exposure meter, you may have to lug one along, and that means another 5 to 8 ounces, or more. To give you an idea of weight ranges, here is a list of some currently available cameras and how they tip the scales: *Minox B,* 2½ oz.; *Minox IIIS,* 3¼ oz., including its built-in exposure meter; *Tessina,* 5 oz.; *Minolta 16MG,* 5½ oz.; *Yashica 16EE,* 11 oz.; *Minoltina P,* 14 oz.; *Rollei 35,* 14 oz.; *Olympus Pen S,* 14.1 oz.; *Yashica Half 17,* 16 oz.; *Fujica Compact 35,* 16 oz.; *Olympus Pen 4,* 1.14 lbs.; *Leica M3,* 2½ lbs.; *Polaroid 100,* 2½ lbs.; *Rolleiflex F3.5,* 3¼ lbs.; *Rolleiflex F2.8,* 4 lbs. Camera fashions and models change rapidly; these are listed for comparison only. Other cameras similar in type will probably be available even if these are not.

Remember that every advantage is countered by a disadvantage. If the camera "has everything," it is probably bulky, complicated, delicate, and expensive. If you want to travel light, be prepared to give up something.

If we had to recommend one camera as the walker's ideal recording eye, the one that would stand out is the Minoltina P. It weighs a mere 14 ounces, uses the easily available 35-mm. film, is only slightly larger than a pack of cigarettes, and is comfortable to handle and easy to use. It has its own light meter, which matches two needles, one automatic and one manual, to get perfect exposure. The top shutter speed is 1/250 of a second, fast enough for almost any purpose. The lens is an excellent semi-wide-angle, with a tremendous depth of focus, which means that you get superbly sharp pictures by simple zone focusing. And finally, the best thing about this little gem of a camera is its price, under $50. If you decide to get one, shop around among the stores for the best buys (*with* a case); the prices vary.

All of these cameras use black-and-white film such as Panatomic X, Plus X, and Tri-X, as well as color film, like Kodachrome, Ektachrome, Dynachrome 25, and Anscochrome to make transparencies; or Kodacolor, which produces negatives, from which you can make color prints (or even black-and-white prints by using Panalure, the special paper manufactured for this purpose). Polacolor is for use in Polaroid Land cameras only.

As for filters, you need at most two, and only if you are bent on shooting in color as well as in black-and-white. For color, the essential one is a pink skylight filter to warm up the shadow areas, which tend to go blue. For black-and-white film you will want only a medium (K^2) yellow filter to bring out the clouds against a darkened blue sky. If there is no sun and no blue sky, the filter will not help.

Exposure meters are built into most of the newer cameras. If yours does not have one, and you want to avoid carrying this extra piece of equipment, just follow the instructions packed with your film. You won't go wrong.

Leave the tripod and the extra lenses at home. The professional touch they may add to your pictures is not worth the weight they add on your back. The point is to travel light.

Remember, you are going for a *walk*.

Taking Pictures Without a Camera

The camera was invented by a lazy artist who wanted to remember permanently everything he saw. The machine he devised has been improved so much in the past hundred years that we are now able to get a finished print in black-and-white in ten seconds and a print in color in a minute.

The chemists and the engineers hurry on to eliminate people from processes, but some of us are beginning to rebel against extinction via automation, to cherish our human capabilities. More wonderful by far than all their metal and glass gadgets is the perfect camera built into the human body, the eye.

This remarkable instrument puts the newest, the most ingenious camera to shame. It really has everything: a lens, a focusing mechanism, a meter, a negative, a positive, and a cybernetic recording device known as the brain.

It is convenient to have a button to push that does all the work of photography, just as it is convenient to have wheels that take us from place to place. But Emerson reminds us that we pay for everything we get. Surrounded by atoms and computers that promise to do everything for us, we begin to look back wistfully to that sunny afternoon in the long and dusty history of man when he could sit down at the side of a brook or a lake and just look around.

Some years ago, when George Macy, the originator of the Limited Editions Book Club, was planning a trip abroad, he asked one of us to recommend a basic assembly of photographic equipment that would include everything essential but would not be too cumbersome. An ideal *cameravaria* was duly put together for him. When he returned, he was asked:

"How'd you make out, George?"

"Fine, fine—thanks so much for your help."

"When do we see some of your pictures?"

An embarrassed pause. Then, "I have a confession to make. In the hotel in Cairo I was preparing my camera bag when I suddenly had the ridiculous notion that I had had a choice and muffed it. I had gone to Egypt to see the Pyramids, but I wasn't going to be allowed to see them. My camera would, and later my friends might, but I would not. I put your bag of marvels on the chair in the hotel room and walked out to see the Pyramids with my own two eyes.

"What I saw I shall never forget, and it was done without buttons, *f* stops, or shutter speeds. I thought about it all the way home, and I have no shame. Can you see why it was the only thing to do?"

And that's how George Macy joined the distinguished company of rebels who prefer to take their pictures *without* a camera.

The writer Henry Miller told Peter Gowland, the photographer of lovely women, "I prefer to carry the image in my mind, even if it becomes slightly blurred in time. . . . Too many people indiscriminately shoot pictures, particularly of famous spots. They point their cameras at the Eiffel Tower and think they've seen it. It would be better if they left their cameras at home and depended on their own memories. Really look at what they see, let it sink in."

Another was Yousuf Karsh, one of the world's great portrait photographers. He made a memorable trip to Helsinki in 1949 to photograph Sibelius, and ended his account of it with the surprising words, "Some pictures are better left in memory alone."

What had happened he describes movingly in *Portraits of Greatness.*

"When Sibelius said goodbye a barefoot, tow-headed boy of five years appeared from nowhere, the composer's great-grandson, and stood before the old man with his hands clasped as if in worship. The sun poured over the profile of these two, the very young and the very old, destiny yet ahead and destiny fulfilled. Nothing could have done justice to the flaxen hair of the child, to the gentleness of the aged man. . . ." And so even Karsh took one of the finest pictures of his career without a camera.

About Pedometers

A pedometer is not merely a gadget for recording the length of your daily, weekend, or vacation walks. It is a valuable safety precaution, particularly for beginning walkers or walkers who are out of condition. Your pedometer can save you from walking so far that you come slogging, staggering, limping back. Especially in the country, where there are no street signs to tell you how far you have come, your pedometer can keep you from unwittingly walking beyond your fatigue point. If four miles is the distance you can walk with comfort and pleasure, your pedometer tells you when you have reached the two-mile halfway point and it is time to turn back.

The pedometer can do other jobs for you. With the help of your watch—or a stopwatch, if you have one—it will tell you the rate at which you are traveling, a useful piece of information when you are planning a walk that happens to be limited by time. And when you are walking in unfamiliar country, your pedometer and a map can tell you how far or near you are to a point you want to reach, a place to stop for refreshment, or where you left your car.

In order to perform these useful services for you, the pedometer must first be adjusted to your own individual length of stride. The ease with which this is done, and the accuracy with which it stays done, depends upon the kind of pedometer you buy. Prices range between five and ten dollars, but what you get for your money seems to have little relation to the price or the country of origin.

We have tested a number of models. Two, made in Germany, have a stem-winding knob to adjust the mechanism to your stride, a ring that clamps around this stem, and a belt hook attached to the ring. The pedometer registers up to 25 miles. Adjusting the mechanism is easy enough, but the protecting ring pops off whenever you stoop to pick up a stone or tie a shoelace, and the movement of the body in walking tends to turn the stem and change the adjustment. The same walk on two different days may register mysteriously either 1.5 miles or 6 miles. We had to rate this kind unsatisfactory.

The pedometer we hang on our own belt is a far more dependable mechanism and no more expensive. The belt hook clips securely to the stem and yet rotates freely; the pace-length regulator, inside the instrument, has a fast-slow dial that is adjusted by moving it a few clicks either way. The pedometer registers up to 100 miles on a small dial, 10 miles on a large one, and its face is upside down as it hangs so that you need only flip it up to see how far you have walked. To reset to zero for each new walk, you move a hand-set screw with a gentle twisting pressure of a finger. This screw sits well into a hollow of the case and is not affected by the motion of your body or your clothes—a beautiful bit of engineering.

The one we have is the New Haven Pedometer, model 230; the distributor, according to the guarantee form, is: Pedometer Corporation, 96 Monroe Street, Newark, New Jersey 07105. Or you can buy it, as we did, from a mail-order house (see the Shopping Guide).

The Well-Shod Walker

On a long day's walk it can be a comfort to have an extra pair of socks along, stuffed into one of those ample pockets we recommended a few pages back. And this brings us to the crucial part of the walker's wardrobe, the part he puts on his feet.

The debate goes on about what constitutes the best shoe for walking. Should it be firm, solid, thick-soled, supporting to arches—and thus inevitably on the heavy side? Or should it be light, flexible, giving the freest motion to the foot and toe muscles and leaving the question of support mainly to the structure of the foot itself?

It can be argued that the human foot evolved for walking, and is as capable of its job in a state of nature as the hoof and the paw. Yet man is always improving on nature. Traditionally he shoes his horse and even himself. The American Indian, a notable walker until the Spaniards introduced him to the horse, perfected protective footwear for himself, the lightweight, flexible moccasin. Even prehistoric man, that great hunter who went only on foot, must early have learned to cover his feet against cold and injury, as he did his body, with animal skins. People do, of course, go barefoot in many parts of the world, but rarely by choice.

In the end there are two schools of walkers on the subject of shoes, those who like their feet sturdily shod and those who look for the least possible shoe because at heart they long to go barefoot. The sturdy-shoe school wear their solid footgear for all ordinary walking, whether on city streets or country meadows. The barefoot boys and girls kick off their hard-soled shoes the moment they get into the country, and go walking over hill and dale in sneakers.

The people who are trained to worry about our feet, the orthopedic physicians and the podiatrist foot specialists, also seem to separate into two schools, some insisting that support is an essential in a walking shoe and some outspokenly recommending light sneakers for tame-country walking. For wilderness walking there is of course no disagreement: Where the going is rough, the feet, and possibly also the ankles and calves, must have full protection against injury and in some areas against enemies in nature such as snakes.

Sportsmen's outfitters, who are in business to sell outdoor footwear and who understandably prefer to keep their customers through the years by selling satisfactory goods, have found a variety of compromises. Designers and manufacturers have striven to combine sturdiness and lightness, and with both traditional and modern materials they have added water resistance, non-slipping soles, sweat-proofing, fleece linings for cold-weather walking, all within a minimum weight allowance. The famous Maine Guide shoe, for instance, an ankle-high laced boot for both men and women, has a waterproof sole and a water-resistant leather top, and it weighs under three pounds—in one catalogue, 2 pounds 12 ounces. (For where to buy, see the "Shopping Guide" list of mail-order suppliers.)

A fisherman's shoe, made for men, with three eyelets and a moccasin toe, comes about to the ankle. The English desert boot, with a seamless toe and two eyelets, is about the same height and is made for both men and women; despite its glamorous desert appellation it was actually developed for use in the South African bush.

An eight-inch boot with moccasin toe, for rough country walking, weighs only 2 pounds 6 ounces for the pair. A seven-incher, somewhat heavier, has a notch at each side of the laced front so that it will not pinch across the front of the ankle, a welcome feature when the going is largely uphill.

A hiker's (and canoer's) version of the sneaker is an ankle-height canvas shoe with crepe-rubber sole and heel molded to the upper, which will keep the foot dry when it sinks into wet ground nearly an inch, and can get soaking wet—if you have to wade across a stream—without harm; the pair weighs only 1 pound 14 ounces.

Any good walking shoe has certain species characteristics. It has a wide flat heel, a broad rounded toe and a straight line along the inner edge from toe to heel. It gives ample room to the toes but grips the heel so that it does not slide up and down on each step and make chafes or blisters. It does not squeeze or pinch anywhere. It has a tongue to keep out pebbles, twigs, sand and grit. For any but the tamest country walking it has firm toe and heel counters for protection against injury, and nonskid heel and sole (neoprene, ridged rubber, possibly even cleats) to prevent slipping on steep slopes, rocks, or wet grass. Mountain climbers of course have their special cleated soles. If the shoe has laces, the laces should not cut; some are provided with outside hooks instead of eyelets. An inner sole, of hair or felt, provides additional cushioning and sweat absorption.

Some waterproofing, at least where the sole joins the upper, is to be desired. It is too bad to take just two steps on mushy ground and walk the rest of the way with wet feet. The good shoe is also reasonably flexible, and as light as can be, consistent with good construction and adequate protection.

As for fit, an Army sergeant, grizzled with long service, told his wartime rookie platoon to break in their good G.I. shoes in this surprising fashion: Put them on, socks and all, lace them up, and go sit with your feet in a tub of warm water for an hour or until they are thoroughly wet through. Then wear them that way for the rest of the day, letting them dry on the feet. One of his pupils, who reported this to the present writers, swore that not one tenderfoot draftee in his outfit ever had a blister. The same technique for breaking in ski boots is passed on to skiers by a leading ski magazine.

Some serious walkers have their walking shoes made to order, usually in London.

The Great Sock Mystery

Why socks should present perplexities is not clear, but if there are two shoe schools there are probably a dozen schools of thought on socks. Justice Douglas, a formidable walker by any standards, leads a host of experts on the subject: For serious walking they advise two pairs of socks, a thin inner pair, usually of cotton—but some walkers prefer silk—and a thick outer pair of textured cotton or wool. The inner pair acts as a second skin and takes the friction, of which there is bound to be some on a long walk even in the best-fitting shoe. The outer pair acts as both cushioning agent and sweat absorber.

Nylon of the thin silklike texture of women's hose is not advised because it is nonabsorbent and tends to bind around the toes after a while; it is not so flexible a fiber as either silk or good long-staple cotton, also known as lisle. Some women walkers, whose toes object to the nylon sheath, buy their nylons with cotton toes.

For the outer, thicker sock, some walkers like a textured blend of nylon with either cotton or wool. They find that the combination provides the cushioning and absorptiveness of the natural fiber and the quick-drying advantage of the synthetic. Nylon also adds warmth, making cotton socks warmer than they might otherwise be for cold weather but also less cool for warm-weather walking.

Socks for walking should of course be free from any seams or bumps that might irritate. And they must be a particularly good fit, loose enough not to bind the toes but not so loose as to lump. The outer sock should be larger; if wool, a quarter-inch longer than the foot after shrinking. And it is self-evident that the walking shoes must be long and wide enough to accommodate the walking socks.

For winter walking, knee-high socks are now available for men, as they have always been for women. They are a most agreeable comfort under trousers or slacks when the temperature falls low and especially when the wind blows.

Tender Care for Tender Feet

W. C. Fields used to complain that if he said he had hurt his foot he got sympathy, but if he said his feet hurt all he got was a laugh.

Undamaged feet, well-socked and well-shod, should not hurt even after a long day of walking. They are entitled to be tired, along with the rest of the body, but they should not hurt. Long standing makes aching feet; so does starting and stopping. But a day of walking with a good rhythmic stride should end only with a general healthy muscular fatigue, of the feet as well as the whole body.

However, few of us grow up with undamaged feet. According to public health authorities, 80 per cent of Americans have some sort of foot disability in the course of their adult lives, and podiatrists say that one out of two children have foot trouble. One out of ten young men was rejected for military service in World War II because of bad feet.

Walkers probably have better than average feet, partly because the exercise of walking is good for feet—and for body posture, musculature, and weight, all of which affect the feet—and partly because they pay more attention both to their feet and to the shoes they put on them. Women in general suffer more foot troubles than men, in a ratio of about five to one, but women walkers rarely complain of their feet. They may even wear high heels, although not for walking; high heels cause no permanent damage if they are worn no longer than four or five hours a day, two or three times a week, and this would seem to take care of the partying, dancing, and dining-out hours when high heels contribute to the festive feeling. Apart from the high heels and pointed toes that ruin women's feet, overweight, poor posture and lack of exercise are probably the major factors contributing to most people's foot troubles. Less sitting and more walking would go a long way toward curing their weight, posture, and foot aches simultaneously.

Damaged feet, whatever the cause, have to be most carefully shod if they are not to interfere with walking pleasure. A heavy person needs a heavy, sturdy shoe; a person with tender or callused feet needs a cushioning sole and soft, flexible leather for his shoe. More serious damage, of the order of bunions, hammertoes, fallen metatarsal arches or flat feet, should probably have the benefit of custom-made or molded shoes for walking. Arch supports, if they are needed, should be prescribed by a foot specialist, and corns, calluses and ingrown toenails should be treated by one.

Tired feet, like a tired body, are comforted at the end of a long day's walking by a good soaking in warm, not hot, water. If the skin is tender, hot water will only make it more so. A cool rinse, careful drying, a dusting of talcum powder and a rest with the feet elevated generally relieves the ache of fatigue, and a night's sleep is usually enough to repair the fatigue itself, and ready the feet for the next day's walk.

Feet that are out of condition, indeed legs and even back and shoulder muscles, may rebel at setting out again the next morning. The feet may feel stiff and somewhat swollen if the first day's walking has been long and hard. Any athlete knows that when he has been inactive for a period he must break in again with measured exertion, sipping rather than gulping his pleasure at first. Walking is so mild that it is rarely ranked as exertion, but we must not be deceived. Walking uses every muscle, and even a few hours of walking can make unused mucles tired and stiff.

Muscles do strengthen, however, and feet do toughen. Getting into condition for the long day's walk, or a weekend or week's walking trip, is easier than for most other active pleasures. Swimming, incidentally, is a good conditioning exercise for walking.

Rest and Refreshment

An enjoyable walk is not an endurance test nor yet a race. It allows for rest and it allows for refreshment. A walk is all the better if it is well-paced and comfortably managed.

The Army calls a halt for five minutes of rest every hour. Walkers out for pleasure may not care to measure their rest by the clock, but on a day's walk a rest at midmorning and midafternoon, as well as at lunchtime, can extend the energies and forestall fatigue. An enthusiastic walking physician points out that rest periods are adjustable to the weather, the strenuousness of the walk, and the walker's condition. Steep grades and heavy packs call for more frequent rests.

The walker who sets a steady pace and rhythm that he can maintain throughout the walk probably covers the ground with the least expenditure of energy. "But," says the doctor, "he may not have the most fun." People who like to take pictures, enjoy the view, look at trees or birds, or indulge in whatever their special enthusiasms may be, are willing to go at a brisk pace when they are going so that they can stop oftener and longer.

The same good doctor reminds us to eat more often and less heavily on a walk; four or five light meals are better than three heavy ones. He suggests a lunch of fruit, meat or cheese, bread, and something sweet, and recommends nuts and honey rather than raisins and chocolate which are not easily digestible. Water should be taken in small quantities as needed to quench thirst. Sun-parched lips or a cold-parched throat can be mistaken for thirst. On a wilderness walk, he advises adding a little salt to snow or rain water, which are lacking in minerals, at the rate of a level teaspoonful to a pint. Salt can be important in hot dry weather, when there is a good deal of water and salt loss through the skin, and indeed at any time when there is much sweating. (People on salt-free or low-salt diets should consult their doctors on this.) An alcoholic drink may seem a quick way to revive waning strength but it is illusory—it actually weakens rather than strengthens. Both alcohol and tobacco increase the dangers of exposure to cold.

The relaxing drink, the good dinner, and the long pleasant smoke are best saved for the end of the walk, when they are most enjoyable.

Chapter 12

WALKS EVERYWHERE

"THE AUTO'S APPETITE FOR SPACE IS HORRENDOUS," wrote Mitchell Gordon in his book of a recent season, *Sick Cities,* and went on to point out that when the 41,000-mile interstate highway system, which was legislated by Congress ten years ago, is completed, it will occupy more land than the state of Rhode Island.

Since Rhode Island is our Tom Thumb among the states, this prognosis does not seem so dark—until we remember the many thousands of miles of state highways, the "improved" county roads widened at the sacrifice of their ancient bordering trees, and especially the automobile's voracious subsidiary services. Across the United States, every town announces itself for miles in advance with filling stations, accessory shops, repair shops, garages, parking lots, motor restaurants, motor lodges, billboard allurements, used-car lots, finally the automobile graveyard where the car itself comes at last to lie, unhonored even with a decent burial. Los Angeles has already given two thirds of its downtown area to the automobile, half to roads and highways, the rest to car services.

From such a world it is no wonder that many of us long to escape and roam on foot, far from the automobile and its ubiquitous, apparently irreversible consequences. But where to flee?

Between the Traffic Lanes

The true story is told of three ladies of Houston, Texas, whose children had grown up and who had moved with their husbands from their large houses into apartments in the city's fashionable new hotel. All three were gaining weight and suffering other discomforts resulting from lack of exercise, and the doctor to whom they all went ordered them to take a daily walk. The three friends dutifully set out each morning for their walk. Since much of newly built Houston has dispensed with sidewalks altogether, the ladies walked down the mall dividing inflowing from outflowing traffic on the main avenue, then along the edge of the medical center grounds bordering the same boulevard, and then back again to their hotel by the same extraordinary route.

Are we all doomed to do our walking on a mall between boiling traffic lanes? Is there nowhere left, nearer home than the wilderness, where we can walk and enjoy it, whether or not we are under doctors' orders?

Surprisingly, there is. And, in fact, with a few such exceptions as the disadvantaged ladies of Houston, almost everyone can find walks at or near his front door. There are still pleasant everyday walks in cities and suburbs, and longer walks across countrysides, on hilltops and in valleys, along beaches and riverbanks. And the promise is that there will be not less but more walking space in the years ahead.

Walking in Los Angeles

Almost everywhere that people live there are, even now, places where they can walk. There are walks even in Los Angeles, that string of gasoline-perfumed villages along the freeways on what was once a lovely lip of golden California between the mountains and the sea. Even there, the late Aldous Huxley found places to walk uninvaded by the automobile, and his wife Laura knew hillsides where she picked armloads of wildflowers untainted by gasoline fumes. Once, to be sure, Huxley led his band of nature pilgrims—film stars, Hindu mystics, and fellow writers— on an all-day walk and picnic, only to be evicted by police from what turned out to be private land. It made a funny story to tell afterward—the Indian ladies in saris, the Hollywood celebrities in hobo or Gypsyish costumes, with their tall, gaunt shepherd stalking ahead—but it was not, after all, so very funny if one loved to walk.

From his youth, Huxley was addicted to long-striding, wide-ranging conversational walks. He could have lived anywhere in the world, but he chose the southern California city as his permanent home. So have many others, intellectuals and artists, to whom walking is an indispensable adjunct to the thoughtful and creative life. If they can find walks in Los Angeles, the rest of us can find them almost anywhere.

The best places to find walks for every day are not the middle-aged, automobile-built cities like Los Angeles and Houston, or the middle-aged suburban developments where every natural feature has been bulldozed away and people are expected to step from house door to car door and never set foot on the ground. The best places are the old cities with their parks, the old suburbs with their tree-shaded sidewalks, or the very newest cities and suburbs, where wheeled traffic is purposefully excluded from walkways and the citizen's right to go afoot in safety and serenity is respected from the first by the planners.

New Cities

One such planner, the Greek architect and designer Constantinos Doxiadis, labors to restore to human beings the cities they have built, which now largely belong to cars instead of people. He has been building and rebuilding in Cincinnati, Louisville, and Eastwick, a large industrial-residential community on the edge of Philadelphia which holds some 20,000 families, or about 60,000 people. In his city planning, high-speed roads swiftly carry people and goods, but motor traffic only creeps into the sectors where people live. In these living sectors, or neighborhoods, the streets are all dead-end, and the automobile is tolerated but not dominating. It is a world for people on foot, for children playing, house-wives marketing, walkers walking. Mr. Doxiadis, who is an Athenian, talks of renewing "the age-old romance between man and his buildings." That is the kind of talk a city walker understands.

An American original, which has won much enthusiasm and will surely influence planning in the future, is Reston, Virginia, eighteen miles from Washington, D.C., built on ten and a half square miles of country land. It is the creation of Robert E. Simon, Jr., whose father was one of the first "garden city" planners and involved with Radburn, New Jersey. Of its 7,100 acres, 42 per cent will be open space—parkland, playgrounds, 80 acres of water. Some 60 per cent of the land is in a stand of hardwood forest, and trees are part of Reston's precious resources, not to be bull-dozed out of existence but to be kept and tended. More than 100 acres have already been set aside as a bird sanctuary.

The first of Reston's seven cluster villages, Lake Anne, is already built and lived in. Every facility is within walking distance. Sidewalks abandon the edge of the automobile road and wind beside the lake, through the woods, along the six golf courses. They do not cross a busy street but go under it, through an underpass. People walk in Reston because it is so inviting. Some moved there because they wanted a place to live where they could walk.

These will be—let us insist that they shall be—the dwelling places of the years ahead, the city neighborhoods where the sidewalks dominate and the traffic in the street creeps quietly by on sufferance, the country-town suburbs where people can take their everyday walks among trees and beside water.

Right now, there are old, civilized cities that still give us walking like this.

Old Cities

Millions of us live in such old, civilized cities, and can find agreeable everyday walks with only a little effort. The great lakes and great rivers of America are dotted with cities on their shores, and however careless the cities have been about their waterfronts—and careless they have been, indeed—there are stretches somewhere in all of them that make good walking. Minneapolis and St. Paul have miles of beautiful walking along the Mississippi; Chicago has its Lake Shore Drive; San Francisco has its Embarcadero. New York has its riverside walk along the Hudson, its Battery Park along upper New York Bay, its Esplanade along the Brooklyn Heights waterfront with its dazzling view of lower Manhattan. Cities on rivers and bays also have bridges, short bridges and long ones, which make grand walking.

Civilized old cities also have their big beautiful parks. San Francisco has its spreading green Golden Gate Park, Philadelphia its lush Fairmount Park. In New York City, Brooklyn has its Prospect Park, the Bronx has its Van Cortlandt Park, Manhattan has its Central Park. In all the old cities, a park is no little languishing square of dusty greenery but a fine expanse, fit for hours of walking. The city fathers of a century ago understood these things, and laid firm hands on acres of farm- and woodland for the enjoyment of future generations.

Such parks are justly famous. On a crowded New York City bus, one wet snowy evening during the rush hour, a young serviceman on leave in the city stared out of the window. The bus was running along Central Park South. He gazed, and suddenly announced to the bus in general, "Why, that must be Central Park. I've got to walk there!"

The parks in old, civilized cities are full of surprises. In the middle of Central Park there is a reservoir, still in use for water storage at this writing and a haven for gulls and migratory ducks. Around it runs a cinder track about five feet wide; it is kept neatly raked and is always interesting, edged with the park's many varieties of trees and shrubs that blossom in season, with the city's skyline of high-rise apartments catching 'the sunlight, and with the bridle path below providing a parade of horses and riders and sometimes the excitement of a runaway. The reservoir path is a microcosm of city dwellers walking for exercise, pleasure, or a combination of the two. The perimeter is 1⅝ miles, and many walkers habitually do two or three circuits at a clip.

Some people amble around the Central Park reservoir, but most really walk and occasionally they break into a jog, the athlete's conditioner. Mrs. Jacqueline Kennedy, when she is in New York, is one of those who really walk. Another habitual reservoir walker, who encounters her often, met her the day after a recent Christmas. She was jogging along, with young Caroline riding after her on her new Christmas bicycle, and behind them the inevitable Secret Service man, also on a bicycle, his trench coat trailing on the cinders, trying to steer with one hand while he read his *New York Times* propped on the handlebars.

Washington, D.C., is a very special city, and not only because it is the national capital. It is a walker's city if ever there was one. Its most striking inhabitants are not its statesmen, politicians, and millions of government workers, but its stately trees, two million of them in the city's 790 parks, another 350,000 lining its public thoroughfares and un-counted thousands bending above private lawns and gardens.

Washington's bird population matches its tree population. Each year from February on, even while the trees are winter-bare, Washington's resident birds begin to sing, and for two months the travelers arrive in winged waves. First come the seashore birds and water fowl. For days, all through March, the city's skies and waters are hosts to thousands of ducks, geese, herons, and the lawn around the Washington Monument is thick with gulls. After them come the field and woodland birds, the finches, thrushes, warblers in their many-colored plumage, making their many kinds of music.

Many of Washington's birds are only dropping in on their way north, but a great number make the city their summer home. Nesting density around Washington is three times as great as in the average woodland. And everywhere the city explodes into bloom with its thousands of public and private gardens, spring bulbs yielding to summer flower borders, forsythia and cherry blossoms giving way to azalea, redbud, rhodo-dendron in an unbroken progression of flowering trees and shrubs.

Washington has probably the most wonderful walking of any city in the world. There is the walk from the Capitol along the reflecting pool to the

Washington Monument on its green hill, and on to the Lincoln Memorial, where one can sit down to rest at the feet of the great meditating figure or gaze from the terrace to the Jefferson Monument across the Potomac. There are pavement walks through public squares and past public buildings on wide avenues, or on the small quiet streets of small, old, very beautiful houses in Georgetown. There is a walk through the public gardens of Dumbarton Oaks, ending in the miniature museum designed by Philip Johnson, a cluster of glass bubbles through which the garden outside is the setting for the pre-Columbian collection displayed within.

On Theodore Roosevelt Island in the Potomac there are 3½ miles of trails. And beginning from Georgetown, for a short or longer walk, there is the towpath of the Chesapeake and Ohio Canal, one of the great and justly famous walks of the eastern seaboard. Washingtonians have no excuse for not making walking a part of their lives. As for the rest of us, a visit to the capital in the spring can be one of the memorable walking vacations of anyone's year.

Granted that Washington, New York, and San Francisco are special cities with special walking joys for their citizens and visiting walkers. But it is also true that across the country, north, south, along the coasts and all the way between, there are big and little American cities where the pedestrian still keeps his ancient rights and the walker can find his unique pleasures. Any town or city with a modicum of tradition behind it can be a walker's happy home in its pleasant seasons.

Many museums and historical associations conduct historical walks in their cities, and museums and conservation societies lead nature and bird walks in parks and nearby sanctuaries. A walker can do worse than go on such a walk, if only to spy out places where he can walk again on his own. For determined solo walkers, inquiry at one of these sources is bound to yield good walking information.

Sunday Walks

We call them Sunday walks but they can as well be Saturday or holiday walks, or weekday walks for those who have or can manage weekday leisure. They are the all-day walks that take us out of our clock-dominated working world into a world fresh to the senses and the spirit. They can be city walks, but usually for our day-long walk we want to break out into the hills and woods and along the shores.

From a car window, the Atlantic seaboard is an unrelieved man-made and man-littered megalopolis from Boston to Washington, where it seems no walker could find a place to set down his feet. But all along the shore, and often not far off the screaming superhighway and its restless roadscape, are daylong walks where human feet have walked not to despoil but only to make a path, and hands have tampered only to mark a trail where others might follow and enjoy. Once we discover these places, we no longer resent the highway, but feel a grudging gratitude toward the road builders that enable us to be off the pavements and on a footpath in an hour or less. Some knowledgeable city dwellers avoid coping with the highway traffic, which can be strangling on weekends and holidays especially, and take a train or bus for what may be a 50-mile run, more or less, to the starting point of an agreeable walk. A one-day round trip can often be bought at an excursion rate.

The spreading metropolitan areas around major cities make it a longish jump to a pleasant day of walking on one's own in the country. Around New York, rural roads are at least 60 and in some directions more than 70 miles away. Even that is not too far for early risers who like to find their own country walks.

Smaller cities have the country closer at hand. All over New England, and in the farm states of the South and the Middle West, city people can drive out of town and be on a country dirt road in little time.

Winter weather, except at its most severe, need be no deterrent. Today there is a lively revival of cross-country skiing, and walkers who are also skiers can enjoy long treks over the snow. Walkers who are not skiers need not be deprived, either. The use of snowshoes is an old way of walking on snow; they are not so stylish as skis, perhaps, but they have their honorable tradition and they have the great advantage of not requiring training in their use. Nobody needs lessons in walking on snowshoes. The utter tyro can put them on and walk, a little awkwardly at first but with adequate skill in half an hour or less. The skier goes faster but the man on snowshoes enjoys the same exhilarating air and dazzling views and more time in which to savor them.

Trails for Sunday Walking

Paradoxically, although the country is ever more distant for dwellers in a metropolis, woodland walking is nearly at their door, thanks to state and county park preservation, and the private but public-spirited recreation and conservation enthusiasts. Within the radius of metropolitan New York there are at least 400 miles of trails, of varying grades of strenuousness, that are used and to a large extent maintained by walking clubs and Scout groups organized in the New York–New Jersey Trail Conference. The trails are well marked and accessible to anyone who wants to walk them, with his own choice of companions or as a member of a club. The famous Palisades walk begins at the New Jersey end of the George Washington Bridge and goes 13 miles north atop this famous line of cliffs along the Hudson's west bank. A river path at the foot of the cliffs offers a variant for the return. A walker can choose his own terminal point at one of four places where it is possible to climb down the cliff to the river path, at the end of which a rock stairway gets him back to the top, and the bridge.

New Yorkers also have within easy reach the famous bird-watcher's haunts of Sheepshead Bay, the New Jersey wetlands, many stretches of beach, mountain, and woodland preserves. Similarly, Chicagoans have at the end of a half-hour journey from the Loop the 47,000 acres of the Cook County Forest Preserve, a walking paradise of woods, meadows, marshes, lakes and ponds, relatively unspoiled sanctuaries for a great variety of wildlife.

Overcrowded, over-highwayed though it is, the Atlantic seaboard has, in every part, an equivalent wealth of accessible, beautiful trails. The Appalachian Trail is a walker's royal road, four feet wide, winding some 2,000 miles from Maine to Georgia across fourteen states, eight national forests and two fabulously beautiful national parks. Along it are countless places where one-day walkers can find a stretch that meets their specifications for distance, challenge, nature interest, and scenic splendor. To the south, Florida marks its seaside and riverbank trails for walkers and naturalists in some half-dozen parks and sanctuaries spotted throughout the state.

The West Coast has a walker's highroad to match the East's, half as wide as the Appalachian but about 350 miles longer, the Pacific Crest Trail that runs from the Mexican to the Canadian border. Even mountain walks can be taken the easy way, from the top down and with transportation for the return, as is often done on the John Muir trails in Yosemite; details of this, as an example of wilderness walking made easy, are given in Chapter 9.

The Pacific states have their unmatched trail riches, as even Pacific

Coasters often do not realize. Within metropolitan San Francisco are 50 miles of gentle trails above Berkeley, in Tilden Park, and hundreds of trails weave over and around Mount Tamalpais, north of the city in Marin County. Southward are the breathtaking views of the Big Sur. Northward in Washington, circling around Mount Rainier, is the Wonderland Trail, 95 miles of footpath skirting the feet of glaciers, crossing crystalline streams and flower-strewn alpine meadows. The trail at full length is a week's vigorous hiking, but relatively non-strenuous stretches can be enjoyed on a day's walk. Olympic National Park has long hikes into the highlands for the hardy, shorter walks in thickly grown woodlands rich with interest for the amateur naturalist, and beach trails for the beauty of seascapes and the pleasure of collecting sea treasures.

On the Continent's Edge

Beach walking has its special excitements for both body and mind, and the knowledgeable beach walker enjoys it as much in off seasons as on sunny summer days, perhaps even more. Thoreau thought the best season for walking the beach was the fall, when the air is bracing and transparent and the sky and sea have a limitless clarity. He loved to walk the beach even when it was storming; he called autumn the beginning of the thoughtful days. No doubt he also loved the solitude of the autumnal walk, when vacationers had gone and he walked alone at the edge of the continent. Addicted walkers like him would share his preference.

Dwellers near the three great American coasts and their many offshore islands have unrivaled beach walking within their reach. People still persist in linking beach and ocean with summer, swimming and sunning. But for walking, the beach has no off season. It is good all the year around, unwalkable only in high winds and punishing storms. Now that the Federal Government is spreading its protection over our most beautiful beaches and declaring them national seashores, more people may discover them for walking.

Thoreau's famous beach walk was the 30 miles of the Great Outer Beach of Cape Cod, from Nauset Light to Provincetown. Part of Cape Cod is now a national seashore; so is Fire Island, the splinter of dazzling white shore that lies between Long Island and the sea for 30 miles or more. So is Cape Hatteras.

The beach walker is a privileged character. He may walk across a private beach that lies along his way without trespassing, so long as he walks below the high-tide line. Below high tide the land belongs to all men, or perhaps only to the sea. An old Massachusetts law gives any man the right of way across private beach or land if he is carrying a fishing rod (or a gun) and is presumably in pursuit of food for his family. Other states may have similar laws.

But the beach walker must also be ready for rugged going. A mile on sand is the work of two miles on firm ground. And a beach is not one long unbroken sweep of sand. There are stretches in the bays where the sea has torn away the sand and left a field of large round cobblestones or perhaps sharp rocks, and there are fingers of land thrusting seaward where huge boulders have piled up and must be clambered over. There are narrow margins where a scramble up the cliff is the only way to avoid wet feet, and the top of the cliff may be inhospitably grown with brambles and poison ivy. The caressing sand may welcome bare feet, but it is well to sling socks and shoes over the shoulder and to wear jeans or hardy pants that one can roll up or down over the calves.

Canal Walking

Another unexploited site for the Sunday, or all-day, walk is the canal towpath. The Chesapeake and Ohio Canal walk from Washington has had all the attention. But there are many old canals across the country, and many of them still have walkable towpaths or sections of towpaths. An obvious advantage of towpaths is that they are neither up nor down hill but mostly level, and another advantage is that they go sweetly along the edge of water for their whole extent, usually past fields and meadows and woodland, with overhanging trees and the peace of old countrysides.

Many old towpaths have become overgrown for part of their length. Canals were dug in the pre-automobile era when water transport was cheaper than the only alternative of the time, the railroad. Walkers could do worse than to rediscover their local canals and towpaths, and start a movement for their rehabilitation.

Historic Trails

Ours is a time that has become sharply conscious of the need for reclaiming our country's beauty. For walkers, this has the special meaning of saving and reclaiming beautiful places to walk. President Johnson's message to Congress in 1965 on natural beauty had the specific result of an Administration bill presented early in 1967, the National Trails Bill, providing funds for the reclamation of four great American trails.

Behind the bill is a 155-page report, collaboratively prepared by the departments of Interior and Agriculture, proposing a nationwide system of great trails. The report called for Federal encouragement—meaning money—to state, county, and municipal governments to set about making local trails of their old towpaths, railroad rights-of-way, and park systems.

"Walking, hiking and bicycling are simple pleasures within the economic reach of virtually all citizens," says the report. And it adds that walking ranks *second only to driving* for pleasure among Americans.

The report points to the Appalachian, the Pacific Crest, and the Continental Divide trails as needing Federal attention. It also lists for reclamation the great historic trails: the Chisholm Trail from San Antonio, Texas, to Abilene, Kansas; the Lewis and Clark Trail from St. Louis, Missouri, 4,600 miles to the Pacific shore of Oregon; the Natchez Trace from Nashville, Tennessee, to Natchez, Mississippi; the Oregon Trail, the Sante Fe Trail, and a great trail called the North Country, running from the Appalachian in Vermont some 3,200 miles westward across six states to join the Lewis and Clark in North Dakota. And high on the roll of trails that are a national resource to be saved is the Potomac Heritage Trail, which extends 825 miles—surprisingly, for a little river that is large only in history—from the Potomac's mouth to its sources in Pennsylvania and West Virginia.

The Administration's 1967 National Trails Bill specified funds for the first three great trails we have mentioned, plus the Potomac Heritage Trail; the others, hopefully, will come later. How soon, and how generously, Congress acts on such bills depends in the end on how persistently we who want them keep urging, begging, reminding, nagging our Senators and Representatives to vote for them.

Trail walks are like accordions; they can be extended or compressed. A trail may stretch for hundreds and even thousands of miles, but all we want of it on a given weekend or holiday may be a day's good walking. When we have two days, or a week, or a walking vacation to spend, we can explore its facilities and enjoy its hospitality for a more extended time. A growing custom is to stop and explore a trail, to spend a day walking in the course of an automobile trip. *Life* magazine, a bellwether of popular taste, has recently been listing walking trails as part of the pleasure of automobile vacationing.

Walks Abroad

A vacation in distant lands is a star-studded opportunity for walking pleasures of a special sort. Travelers of the past would eagerly set out to walk in a foreign city the very morning after they arrived, knowing it was the only way to discover and enjoy its special character. It is also traditional to walk a foreign countryside, as English travelers of the last century loved to do.

In the British Isles, the Scandinavian countries, in Switzerland, Germany, Austria, every mountain, forest, lakeshore and river valley is carved with trails well marked for the people of the country. A visitor is welcome to share the trails and there are walking clubs eager to give information and advice.

Northern Europeans are walkers by choice and custom. Southern Europeans are not. That does not mean that their lands are not walkable, only that walking there is not organized for ease and accessibility. In Italy, Spain, Greece, and on the islands off their coasts, one must do one's own choosing and exploring. Some of the most interesting walking in the world is likely to be through age-old countrysides that the automobile has not yet invaded, but it will not necessarily be the easiest or most comfortable walking, and there may not be a cozy inn with a hot bath, a sumptuous meal, and a good bed at the end of the walk.

Walking in the ancient lands is walking with history. The footprints of past greatness are everywhere; the present is bone-poor, but away from the cities and the tourist haunts it is often lyrically beautiful. In Greece one walks amid the splendor of broken marble, but also along goat tracks over rugged hills where people have gone on foot between the villages for twenty-five centuries, much as they still do.

In Italy the temptation is strong to ride from town to town and do all one's walking in their streets. But there is walking among scenes straight out of the Renaissance, away from the automobile highways, where olive groves and vineyards climb the Tuscan hills and the busy farmyards with their stone barns abut on the very road.

In these lands, including Spain, which are little accustomed to walking visitors, a day's exploring on foot in the country is best done from a base in town, where information and amenities are both available.

Some knowledge of the language is also advisable. And a further caution about climate: The northern lands are for walking vacations in full summer, the European heartland is comfortable from late spring well into fall, but the ancient lands of the Mediterranean littoral are for spring and fall walking only.

Scandinavian Walking

There is great and, for Americans, largely undiscovered walking in the Scandinavian countries. On Norway's coast from Bergen south to Stavanger are the stupendous fjords that people take the North Cape cruises to see from a luxury liner's deck, but walkers can enjoy them more intimately—if one can talk of intimacy with a fjord—from the wooded summits. There are walks among the hills and lakes just inland, and in the coast towns themselves, old North Sea fishing and maritime ports whose quays are lined with mercantile houses of another century, whose squares are filled with flowers and lively open markets in the brisk bright air, smelling of pine forest and briny sea in the northland summer. Eastward toward Sweden's border are Norway's mountains, for more rugged walking tours.

Sweden is more than half forest, and at its heart is a magnificent lake district through which the Göta Canal runs from Göteborg on the Kattegat almost to Stockholm on the Baltic. It is a steamship canal, hence there are no towpaths for walking, but there are parklike walks along its banks in the cities and towns through which it passes. Stockholm itself is a city built on islands of the Baltic archipelago, which has some 24,000 of them. Almost everywhere in the northern capitals it is possible to walk in woodlands and along shores.

Finland, like the Scandinavian peninsula, has its dark wild forests and its islanded shoreline; from Helsinki east and west along the Gulf of Finland, the offshore waters sparkle with little islands like stars in the Milky Way. Six pretty towns besides Helsinki are strung on Finland's shores and inland waters, and the interior is a labyrinth of lakes. The Finns are walkers as well as fishermen and huntsmen. A walker's adventure would be to take one of the tourist planes to Lapland and spend an hour or so walking the tundra under the midnight sun.

Denmark is less northern and more European; instead of dark forest there is green open farmland, and the walking is through gently rolling country and along a coast dotted with fishing villages, on sandy roads marked with the wheels of farmers' carts. Denmark's woodlands are not the wild mountain forests of the north but the carefully tended woods of old, nurtured farm country, as in France. Denmark is a land made up of one large peninsula and a cluster of islands girdled and threaded by the sea. Nowhere is one at a loss in Denmark to find country walking, beach walking, bridges to cross and ferries to ride to further walks, and all, or almost all, within sight or smell of the sea.

Europe's Heartland

Germany has famous walking tours in the Black Forest and the Bavarian Alps, and also rather less known and perhaps more interesting Rhineland walks. France has the château and river country of the Loire, the historical riches of Provence, the perfume-flower vales above the Riviera, the rugged country around Carcassonne at the foot of the Pyrenees, and shorelands on the north, west, and south. But the French do not advertise walking for walking's sake. They offer practical walks. Aside from museums and château visits, which entail much going about on foot, their single advertised walking tour is a mushroom hunt, with a qualified leader, in which the walkers learn to identify some of the 5,000 mushroom varieties of France. *Voilà.*

Switzerland has its Alpine trails; so have Germany and Austria, and even Italy and France have Alpine corners. We want to say a special word for mountain walking. If the walker wants to leave climbing to the climbers, and if he takes the trouble to pick his spots, he need not take on any strenuous work. He will walk not the peaks but the valleys.

Valley walking among the high peaks has its own delights. The air is as bracing, the refreshments at the inn are as agreeable, as they are for the mountain climbers. The views, while less dramatic, are splendid enough. And the valley walker has the friendly nearness of fields and farms, shady woodlands, lakes and mountain streams, all along his way.

Walking, British Style

England and Scotland are the paradise of walkers; Wales and Ireland are only less known. Wherever we may set foot, some eighteenth-century essayist or nineteenth-century poet walked there before us. When Thomas Gray, whose "Elegy Written in a Country Churchyard" we all read in school, walked the Lake Country in 1769, after a long day's walking he found the inn's best bedroom dark and damp, and went sturdily on for another 14 miles to Kendal and another inn that pleased him more, before he stopped for the night.

But he saw splendid hills, lakes that sparkled in sun and turned black in shadow, Druid circles of stone, serene villages and flamboyant sunsets. He ate fresh-caught trout and partridge, sometimes oaten cakes with fresh sweet butter or fell-fattened young mutton that had the savor of venison, and he drank good country-brewed ale.

Less hardy modern walkers may not make so thorough an exploration of the lakes as Gray did, and they will be guaranteed a good deal more comfort in today's inns. They can have as memorable an experience by staying in an agreeable hostelry, sufficiently modernized in facilities and accessible to good walks, and do their exploring a day at a time.

They may see, as Gray did from the parsonage where he arrived one evening just before sunset, "a picture, that if I could transmitt to you, & fix it in all the softness of its living colours, would fairly sell for a thousand pounds. This is the sweetest scene I can yet discover in point of pastoral beauty."

Or they may walk, as he did, alone down to the nearby lake after sunset and see "the solemn colouring of night draw on, the last gleam of sunshine fading away on the hill-tops, the deep serene of the waters, & the long shadows of the mountains thrown across them, till they nearly touch'd the hithermost shore. At distance heard the murmur of many waterfalls not audible in the day-time. Wish'd for the Moon, but she was *dark to me & silent, hid in her vacant interlunar cave.*"

That was Gray's evening in the lake country. It might easily be ours.

There are walks in every part of England, of every kind, in gentle country and rugged. One can follow the Thames away from London, walk out from Oxford in the charming towns of the Cotswold Hills, explore the Cornish coast. One can walk in striking, scenic Derbyshire, which Jane

Austen's Elizabeth Bennett admired so much, and where she came to live at last as the happy wife of the man who was so proud and against whom she was so prejudiced. One can walk in the North Country, famous in song and story, where the Roman legionaires built their wall across Britain's narrow waist to keep back the Scottish raiders, a wall that still stands. One can walk the moors or the wild Welsh hills. In Scotland walkers walk in the highlands and the lowlands, and they walk their way through the picturesque Hebrides, taking a ferry from one beautiful island to the next.

Many people today tour England, Scotland, and Wales by car, and many also go to Ireland, taking the back lanes and stopping at country inns along the way. Anywhere on such a leisurely jaunt they might stop and spend a day walking in the inviting country roundabout, returning to dinner at the inn the same night.

Lodgings in the Castle

Enterprising innkeepers in England, Scotland, and several countries of Europe have converted great old castles and châteaux into hostelries. Since these are set on their own spacious grounds, and traditionally on sites noteworthy for their scenery and the beauty of their surrounding country—for their royal or noble builders would choose only the finest spot on their lands for building—in their twentieth-century conversion they make a glamorous base for walking explorations in their vicinity.

Some castle hotels are modernized to the point of princely luxury, for example the Tower of Cala Piccola, about 100 miles north of Rome on the Tyrrhenian Sea. The Saracens built the tower in the thirteenth century. It is now a restaurant, and around it are secluded individual cottages also looking out over the sea. Rates at such places may begin at $20 per day.

Also in Italy, somewhat more modest but probably not less comfortable, with a private bath for each of its thirty-two rooms, is the Villa San Michele, a fifteenth-century Franciscan monastery for which Michelangelo is said to have designed the façade and loggia. Its situation, just outside of Florence, makes it a base for walking in the Tuscan hills.

Germany has many hotels whose names begin with *Schloss,* meaning castle, and some of them have a proper claim to the title. Castle Kronberg was the royal retreat of the nineteenth-century dowager empress who was Queen Victoria's eldest daughter, and although it is neither medieval nor Renaissance, it is royally situated and designed and it once entertained many of Europe's royal heads. It is now an undisguised luxury hotel with an 18-hole golf course, some 10 miles from historic Frankfurt.

Interesting to walkers are two more modest castle hostelries in the Rhine valley, the Schloss Reinhartshausen in the vineyard region above Wiesbaden, and the 700-year-old Burg Reichenstein, down the Rhine from Mainz; this latter is surprisingly inexpensive. Two miles south of Bonn, on the Rhine in Bad Godesberg and within sight of the Siebengebirge and Eifel Hills, is the Godesberg Hotel, built around a sixteenth-century watchtower and offering considerable luxury.

In France the castle hotel may be a Renaissance manor house on the Loire, like Le Prieuré at Chênehutte-les-Tuffeaux. Or it may be a medieval castle with towers and crenelated walls like the Château de Mercuès on the road to Biarritz, overlooking the lovely Lot River valley and in the neighborhood of the prehistoric caves of Lascaux. Still another is the Château de Coudrée, in Haute-Savoie between Geneva and Evian, with mountain and lakeside walking in reach. It should be mentioned that none of these is an inexpensive country inn.

England and Scotland also have their castle hostelries. Lochnaw Castle, on its own loch, dates from the fifteenth century, has room for only ten guests at modest weekly rates, and sits in a 90-acre forest of ancient beech trees. Sundrum Castle, southeast of Prestwick, is an eighteenth-century baronial mansion on a wooded hillside, with 160 acres of its own where there are shooting and salmon-fishing as well as walking; this one would be a rather sumptuous base for a walking holiday.

Great Cities

Finally there are the cities, all of them very old, very civilized, and grand for walking. The tourist offices nowadays take cognizance of walkers and issue special information pamphlets for them. London is full of walks: the guidebooks suggest many. With map in hand, even a first-time visitor can find grand walks in the City, along the Embankment, in the twisting byways off Fleet Street, around Mayfair, across Waterloo Bridge. Edinburgh has its famous Royal Mile.

Venice is all walking, back of the canals and over the bridges. Florence is a walker's city, but preferably during the midday hours when Florentines go home to lunch and the walker can have the narrow sidewalks, the Lungarno and all the bridges to himself. Rome, Paris, Amsterdam, Brussels, Copenhagen—yes, and Leningrad and Moscow—a walker's guide to Europe must include them all.

This chapter has been a mere appetite-whetter, a smörgåsbord of walking at home and abroad. In the back pages of this book, carefully assembled from many sources and classified by regions and countries, is what we believe to be the only complete "Walking Guide" in print. It covers the United States, including Alaska and Hawaii, and also the Virgin Islands. It crosses the border to Canada and the Atlantic to the British Isles and Europe, with the names and addresses of sources for further information.

We suggest you take a look at the Walking Guide now for a new place to walk in your neighborhood this Sunday. And take a longer look before you plan your next vacation, wherever it may be.

Chapter 13

A WALK INTO THE FUTURE

THE SCIENTIFIC SOOTHSAYERS see in their crystal ball a future world so overpopulated that it will have standing room only for the human race. Despite these dire predictions—or more likely because of them—the future of walking and walkers is brighter today than it has been for fifty years.

The rebellion is growing against the unplanned and uncontrolled urban sprawl that is eating up the countryside, against the automobile and its tentacles of superhighways and attendant services that are devouring what the sprawl has left, against the desecration of lands, waters, and the very air we breathe by shortsighted industrial and housing developers, by litterers on a mammoth scale, and by sheer neglect.

People everywhere and on all levels, as public servants and private citizens, are bestirring themselves to rescue or reclaim some part of our natural environment for human enjoyment. Conservation has become a popular stand for candidates for elective office.

It is not only the fear of loss that has moved so many to join in the salvaging of our natural heritage. They are moved also by their own belated awakening to the beauties and pleasures of the out-of-doors. With the increasing leisure of an automated working world, with the better health and longer years of vigor that come with good living, good eating, and good medicine, people are enjoying extra energies and experiencing the quickening desire to use these energies in active pursuits.

We are late in coming to the rescue of our environment. But happily we are not too late. We have only to scan the recent record of plans, proposals, and projects already in work, to see how much we can still save. The controversies are many and often sharp, the costs promise to be high and in some cases—in the salvaging of the cities, for example—they will probably be staggering. But the values at stake are at last recognized, not by a few lonely conservationists crying prophetically in the wilderness, but by people whose voices are generally heeded.

For example:

"Man is more than a motorist racing from here to there on a six-lane highway at seventy miles an hour. . . . Man is also a walker, a cyclist, a passenger. Man needs to see green hills, to hear water tumbling in a brook, to watch birds in flight—and what price can be put upon these values that superhighways often impair or destroy? Man, too, is a good neighbor with a decent respect for the other man's rights as well as his own convenience. . . ."

And this:

"It is time to build highways for the complete man. Money and speed are not the highest values. If more tax dollars have to be spent to build roads on longer and more circuitous routes in order to spare nature and neighborhoods, let the dollars be spent."

Who said that? Not a naturalist or a poet, not a hiking enthusiast, nor yet the spokesman of a conservationist minority. It was said by *The New York Times,* in a pair of editorials headed "Highways vs. People," which on two successive days thundered against the 41,000-mile-highway program administrators who are slicing their way across the land with no regard to how they maim it. The country's principal newspaper considered this issue so important that its first statement led the editorial page that day, and the protest continued with a second blast on the next.

No one would accuse the *Times* of fuzzy-mindedness about money, especially the tax dollar. But there it is: To spare nature and neighborhoods, let the dollars be spent.

This particular utterance was provoked by a cost-accounting approach to a stretch of highway in Westchester County, part of the system paid for mainly by Federal funds and administered mainly by the states. Such local battles are more and more breaking into the national headlines. The fight of a handful of citizens to keep an automobile road off a beach ended with Fire Island's becoming a National Seashore. A proposal for an automobile bridge from the mainland to another island, Martha's Vineyard, was nationally jeered into oblivion. A utilities company's project for a power station on Storm King Mountain on the Hudson and an interstate dam project on the Colorado River become issues that are publicly fought over for months and even years.

The engineers, who for so long have been treated with worshipful humility, find themselves on the defensive. When a utilities company is obliged to declare itself a friend of the fish, as a spokesman for one of them recently did, then the millennium must not be far off.

Victories for Walkers

All such victories are triumphs for walkers. Every project to save a natural treasure results in more walkways and more beautiful ones. No matter who else benefits—fishermen, huntsmen, nature amateurs, boating buffs, bicyclists, nearby home and property owners—the walkers are bound to benefit.

In the cities the rescue projects are outspokenly pro-pedestrian, if not aggressively anti-automobile. A recent proposal—also in New York, as it happens—is for a second-story pedestrian arcade to be built along Sixth Avenue, a street of small shops recently invaded by giant office buildings, whose sidewalks are already too narrow for its swelling population. Foreseeably, the suggested walkway would link Herald Square, the shopping center at 34th Street, with the green oasis of Bryant Park at 42nd and Rockefeller Center at 50th, for a stroll that could end in Central Park at 59th. Such a passage, elevated above the turmoil of a major northbound traffic artery, in the nostalgic phrase of its sponsors "would help make New York livable for people who can remember the pleasures of going for a walk."

We mentioned in an earlier chapter ("Walks Everywhere," Chapter 12) the bill presented to Congress by the Department of the Interior for a National Trails network. Already in progress is a Department of Commerce study of bits and pieces of real estate, some abandoned and some that have never been developed, that can be turned into walking trails and bicycle paths.

Old towpaths, along canals no longer used as traffic arteries, are among these interesting "parcels." And a new lot of parcels, also of the right shape for walkers, includes the many rights-of-way being abandoned by the declining railroads.

Bequests of the Iron Horse

The railroad strips run through countrysides and hamlets, over streams and rivers; they follow pleasant valleys and are graded to make easy climbing over hills. The right-of-way may be from 45 to 150 feet wide; tracks and ties are removed by the railroad company and sold for other uses.

What is left is a dirt or cinder lane, sometimes wide, sometimes narrower but never less than a locomotive's width, laid on a roadbed solid enough to withstand weather erosion and the weight of railroad rolling stock. Trestles will need walking surfaces laid, and some of the old bridges will need strengthening and repair. But the basis for a wonderful new lot of trails is there.

This unforeseen bequest, from a utility dying of the competition of automobiles, trucks, buses, and planes, was called to Congressional attention at a recent session by Representative Henry S. Reuss of Wisconsin. He pointed out that since 1918, when railroads were enjoying their heyday, some 40,000 miles of rights-of-way have gone out of railroading service and much of this valuable roadway has never been converted to any other use. In the last half-dozen years alone, 8,200 miles have been stripped and left in idleness, and the shrinking and merging of the railways are releasing these lands at an accelerating rate. Representative Reuss prompted the inclusion of railway strips as potential trails in the Commerce Department's study of unused lands, which was originally conceived as a study for roads and scenic parkways.

It is an enticing picture: the transformation of these roads, which were once cut across the wide land for rumbling, roaring steam locomotives, into a lacing of beauty and wholesome pleasure for a country no longer vacant and fresh under the sky but suffocating with crowded cities and industrial morasses. And it is no vision, but a practical proposal. Federal aid is available to the extent of $90,000,000 a year for communities to buy and develop such lands, under the Land and Water Conservation Act.

One such project is already being developed by citizen groups of metropolitan Chicago, where 268 social agencies have united in a common front to reclaim the environment, and have won foundation support for their Open Lands Project. Their goal is to convert the right-of-way of the defunct Chicago-Aurora and Elgin Railway into a green trail running through three counties, to be called the Prairie Path.

American walkers have long envied Great Britain and the countries of northern Europe, whose more leisurely progress has kept unspoiled countless lovely miles of lanes and byways. Now the prodigal course of American development may be reversing itself, and giving back to us for our pleasure the roadways of the dead or dying iron horse.

The Rescue of the Rivers

The reclamation of the rivers from urban and industrial pollution holds a similar bright promise. The people of New York State were suddenly awakened to the ruined beauty of their Hudson, one of the world's grandest rivers. It took the heroic persistence of a nature- and sports-loving minority, and a walking tour by Secretary of the Interior Udall with the full press entourage of a Cabinet member, to open their eyes. The Secretary similarly called attention to the Connecticut River in its idyllic pastoral valley, threading its way southward through the heart of New England, and equally through America's early history. Mr. Udall referred to a number of interesting projects for that valley. (Secretary Udall, for walkers, is by way of being a national resource all by himself.)

Progressing westward, as did the pioneers, the reclamation movement has prompted a stupendous plan for the rescue of the entire Ohio River basin, thousands of miles of small and large waterways including the great river itself to where it empties into the Mississippi. The proposal speaks mainly of giving the streams back to the people for pleasure-boating, but we can be sure that for every waterway that is restored to beauty, there will also be walking paths restored along the shores.

Minnesotans are embattled to defend their St. Croix River, one of the last of the wild rivers and a source of weekend delight to thousands in boats and afoot, which has been threatened by an industrial project. As with the New Yorkers and the battle of Storm King Mountain, the price of natural beauty, like the price of liberty, is eternal vigilance.

A footnote from the arid Southwest is that even dry rivers can be converted to good use. The little California city of Pico Rivera is flanked by two such dry channels, which are occasionally used to carry off water from Los Angeles' reservoir system. By arrangement with the parent city, Pico Rivera has been empowered to turn its dry riverbeds over to walkers and cyclists, under certain restrictions in the interest of safety.

The Open-Space Contagion

The most hopeful aspect of the beneficent open-space contagion is the way it is spreading on the local level. The headlines do not give national attention to these citizen victories. But they are probably more significant than the grander projects, if only because they are closer to the daily lives—and the daily and Sunday walks—of most of us.

All across the country, communities have become alarmed at the rate at which housing developments, shopping centers, highways and airports are gobbling up the land—according to one estimate, more than a million acres a year. Citizens have been casting anxious eyes about the town and county precincts, looking for lands to save for the public use. And they are buying (or inviting gifts of) old farms, family estates, neglected ponds, riverbanks, marshlands, as sanctuaries and community nature-study centers.

Their express purpose is to give their pavement-bound, automobile-enslaved children a place to learn about green growing things and the small wild creatures living among them. That in itself would be an adequate purpose. But always, where there is a nature preserve, there are trails. And usually the rest of us may be permitted to walk there, whether or not we walk to see the birds and bees, the wildflowers and the trees.

Some communities have old, established centers of this kind. Several of the National Audubon Society's sanctuaries are not wilderness areas but nature centers within metropolitan areas, with markers identifying plants along their trails, such as the well-known ones at Greenwich, Connecticut, and Wellfleet, Massachusetts.

What is striking is the accelerated rate at which such centers, intensely and proudly local, have been springing up in the past ten years. In one recent three-year period, no fewer than 170 were established, with the encouragement of the Audubon Society's special Nature Centers Division but initiated for the most part by interested citizens on the spot.

Some are under the auspices of educational institutions, like the Connecticut Arboretum which is attached to Connecticut College; or of local park authorities, like the Bayard Cutting Arboretum maintained by the Long Island Park Commission; or of museums, as in the case of the Museum and Nature Center of Stamford, Connecticut. Sometimes a private citizen who loves both nature and children has turned his own acres into a preserve, and has remained to share his lore with the children of his community's schools. And one center is uniquely sponsored by stamp collectors, the Bert Hoover Arboretum in Wildwood, New Jersey, a memorial to a famous philatelist.

No one knows precisely how many such locally originated centers there are today. No definitive list exists, although the Audubon people are in the process of assembling one. But one fact is undisputed: They are growing at a gratifying rate.

The Easements Device

Another cheering development is the legal device of easements, by which communities can buy or accept the gift of public privileges on private lands without disturbing the owner's right of possession. Citizens of Monterey, California, pioneered an "open space" law that enables city and county governments either to buy properties outright or to take such easements, in order to preserve the pastoral character of the land against buildings, roads, or other development. In Monterey County a number of owners voluntarily gave easements on their land; and thousands of magnificent acres, including portions of the Big Sur shoreline, were opened to the public, to remain unspoiled in perpetuity.

Other states have adopted similar laws. Wisconsin gained scenic easements at relatively small expenditure to preserve the Great River Road along the Mississippi. New York State obtained easements for fishermen along miles of private trout streams, which presumably any walker could share by investing in a rod and a fishing license. Massachusetts, Maryland, and Connecticut also have open-space laws of which communities can avail themselves to gain and keep unspoiled land for walking and other outdoor enjoyments.

Phoenix, Arizona, has planned for the future to the extent of 75,000 acres on the city's periphery, as a bank of public lands for coming generations. Canada's capital city of Ottawa began its open-space planning as long ago as the turn of the century, buying undeveloped lands and leasing them back to their owners with the restriction that they should remain unchanged. Recently the city bought a semicircular stretch of 37,000 acres of farm- and woodland on its southern side; it will eventually own 75,000 acres of parkland across the Ottawa River on its north.

Up to a few years ago (as Secretary Udall observes in his book *The Quiet Crisis*) hardly anyone would have taken seriously the suggestion that swamps might help to save the cities. For centuries a swamp was considered a noxious area that had to be drained and filled. Today, with modern disease controls, we can afford to enjoy the wetlands, with all their variety of plant and wildlife and their often mysterious beauty. In the past several years, three major cities—Washington, D.C., Madison,

Wisconsin, and Philadelphia—and a number of New Jersey communities have taken over large tracts of swamp and marshlands as permanent nature sanctuaries. The Federal Government has done the same on Cape Cod National Seashore, with the Atlantic White Cedar Swamp, Small's Swamp, Red Maple Swamp, and Nauset Marsh.

Beauty at Bargain Prices

In July of 1966, the Department of the Interior announced the first dozen grants to cities to develop trails within their own confines, for those whom the Secretary described as "the forgotten outdoorsmen," the hikers and bikers. Some of the trails will also include bridle paths.

These grants come on the initiative of the cities, and are matched by state funds to cover maintenance personnel and facilities for the trail users' convenience. Twenty-four cities applied for the grants in this first wave; the twelve chosen had their projects ready to be put in work.

The total for the lot is $367,436, barely a mist on the bucket that dips up money from the Federal well. And this is what it will buy for city-bound walkers:

In Atlanta, a system of walking and bicycling trails connecting three city parks.

In Phoenix, hiking and riding trails around the city.

In San Francisco, trails through Belmont and Menlo parks in San Mateo County.

In Detroit, a circular hike and bike trail on Belle Isle, 3 miles from the city's downtown center.

In Milwaukee, 4 miles of trails along Lake Michigan.

In Denver, hike and bike trails within the city limits.

In Omaha, 19 miles of bikeway over railroad rights-of-way and dike embankments as well as along city streets. If Omaha walkers are men and not mice, they will see to it that a little extra width is measured out for a footpath. Similarly, Chicago walkers may well bestir themselves for a footpath along their city's projected bikeways, especially the 19-mile stretch along Lake Michigan. Philadelphia's grant is for paved bicycle paths in Fairmount Park, which is already a paradise for walkers.

In Arlington County, on the edge of the District of Columbia, hiking and biking trails near enough for Washingtonians to enjoy.

In New York, the reclamation of old, overgrown trails in beautiful Inwood Park, on a bluff overlooking the Hudson in the northern corner of Manhattan Island.

In Seattle, perhaps the most imaginative walk of all, a waterfront trail along the Lake Washington Ship Canal, which runs from the magnificent lake in the heart of Seattle to Puget Sound. The part to be built with Federal funds is a cedar-plank trail across a freshwater cattail marsh.

The Seattle project is the most expensive, taking a $45,000 slice of the Federal grants and matching funds from a trust administered by the University of Washington. The others range all the way down to $15,000, which is no money at all in present-day Government expenditures.

Surely this is beauty at bargain prices. What a vista for the future this opens to city dwellers' eyes, of neglected places that can be turned into pleasant walks! Every city, every town, has such forgotten spots—hillsides overgrown with weeds, riverbanks, pond and lake shores, railroad and interurban trolley lines that have long since been left to the brambles, waterfronts and harbor stretches where old piers are rotting away, empty lands that have become dumping grounds.

On Martha's Vineyard recent visitors noted that bulldozers were busy on an automobile dump, digging a grave where the ugly, rusting mound of wreckage could at last be buried. If towns and cities everywhere were merely to take over their acres of similar eyesores, inter the corpses at last and give the land back to nature, soon enough they would be covered with a decent shroud of green growth, and in a few years they could be converted to pleasant walking places, with footpaths winding among wildflowers, shrubs, and saplings that would one day be trees. Sun, rain, and earth will perform the transformation if they are given the chance. Visitors to English towns torn by bombs saw, just after the war, how quickly the wildflowers spread their softening touch over the rubble.

In announcing his department's grants, Mr. Udall expressed the hope that these first awards would bring a flood of community applications. To walkers everywhere this is a challenge, and it gives new purpose to their walks. Now they can walk not only for their immediate pleasure but for the future as well: to discover in their cities the places where beauty can be reclaimed or newly created for walks in the years ahead.

When they discover a likely spot for a walking trail, their local newspapers, radio stations, recreation agencies, even the city fathers themselves, will lend an ear. The pressure is on all these wielders of power—and the money for bargain-price improvement is available. Nothing sharpens an elected official's hearing so effectively as the possibility of bringing Federal or state money into town.

A professional criterion for healthy community development is that there should be 20 acres of park for every 1,000 of a community's population. At the present rate of population growth, this means that communities across the nation should be acquiring an aggregate of 40,000 acres of open space every year, at an estimated cost of $150,000,000. This does not sound like a bargain. But it just so happens that $150,000,000 is the price of 10 miles of elevated automobile expressway.

Which purchase makes for better cities?

Recapturing the Streets

And finally we have the promise that the city streets themselves will be given back to the walkers. In some cities this is already happening. The tide of the automobile seems to have burst through the bearable limit in strangled traffic and suffocating fumes. Cities great and small have been experimenting with shutting off certain busy streets to cars; sometimes, as recently in Rome, it doesn't work, but sometimes, as in Detroit and Fort Worth, and in a new commercial and shopping center of Stockholm, it does.

New York was recently presented with its Planning Commission's design for reclaiming its most renowned—and what should be its handsomest—area, the toe of Manhattan that points like a ballet dancer's into the upper bay and parts the waters of the Hudson and East rivers. On this historic bit of bedrock rise the towers of the financial district, the skyline known around the world. It also embraces the shops of ship chandlers, fish and produce markets, the winding streets of Chinatown; and it abuts on the graceful, traditional City Hall in its miniature park. From its curving shore can be seen the looping spans of great bridges, the bay dotted with islands and afloat with ocean liners, freighters stained with the brine of seven seas, tugboats, barges, ferries; inland, the vistas of its canyoned streets open briefly for two lovely old churches and the lichened gravestones in their churchyards.

It is one of the world's most glamorous stretches of urban real estate, as well as the most expensive. But the winding seventeenth- and eighteenth-century streets are choked with the twentieth-century torrent of traffic and pedestrians, and the great waterfront is an eyesore of decayed neighborhoods and rotting piers, with here and there a block of small, historic, once-elegant buildings in the last stages of neglect.

The City Planning Commission proposes to reclaim all this ruined beauty, rehabilitating the toe around its entire shoreline and removing the usual automotive traffic from its core to a few arterial streets. The hard-pressed pedestrian will not merely be rescued; he will be restored to joy going to and from his office, about his errands and for a stroll at lunch-time, along arcades of shops and restaurants, with miniature, open-sided "intra-buses" to give him rapid transit if he needs it. Or he will be able to walk to one of the plazas that will replace the rotting piers at the shore, and on walkways that will connect them along both riverfronts to meet at Battery Park on the tip.

The plan will encounter many obstacles, and will very likely suffer pruning of its ideal design. When and if it is accepted, the first step in its first stage will be to turn some of its famous streets over to the pedes-trians.

For Washington, D.C., a plan of monumental grandeur has been developed, which will cost $500,000,000, take forty years, and eventually restore to dignity the ceremonial boulevard that runs from the White House to the Capitol.

The late President Kennedy, riding down Pennsylvania Avenue on his Inauguration Day, was struck by the seediness into which much of it had fallen, and lost no time appointing a commission to look into its rehabili-tation. This plan is the result, a twentieth-century version of the splendid vistas that the princes of an older Europe once commanded in the planning of their capital cities.

The aspect interesting to walkers is the separation of pedestrian from vehicular areas; in this plan it is done by layers. The cars with their roadways and parking spaces are relegated to the under layer, out of sight where walkers generally prefer to have them. Above are fountained plazas, galleried shopping streets, outdoor cafés, pedestrian malls. The whole aspect of the avenue is of a boulevard deep in trees, with sidewalks laid in tiers for walking and watching parades. The grand vista ends before the White House in a National Square comparable to the Place de la Concorde in Paris, but without the Place's scrambled traffic. It will be a square with no traffic at all, a pedestrian's delight of shops, cafés, benches and balustrades, with unobstructed views of one of the world's truly beautiful cities.

Future Fantasies, Present Promises

Some designers have taken off into the future in fantasies more chilling than reassuring to the human spirit. Le Corbusier, in his Ville Radieuse, envisioned a city that would house its inhabitants in towering apartment blocks within tidy, parklike settings, with squares for sitting and strolling and bridges for street crossing—but little linear provision for a walker who really wants to stretch his legs. "Corbu" is said to have been in love with cars and provided handsomely for them in his cities. On the whole, his provision for people appears to be almost painfully static and restricting.

A Japanese design for the city of the future calls for giant apartment buildings and pedestrian bridges leading from one to another of them, ten stories above the ground, which is reserved for cars. Several designers have toyed with the idea of putting the cars on top, on traffic arteries running along a continuous line of roofs. On the ground between the endless towering walls of uniform cliff dwellings, the people have a grid of pedestrian walkways, presumably planted with trees and greenery and sweetened, no doubt, by plazas, playgrounds, and custom-made recreation facilities. As one observer commented, walking in such a city would be like walking in a continuous backyard laid at the bottom of a well.

Still another forecast of man's future in an overpopulated world has us taking our walks on the bottom of the sea, presumably equipped with aqualungs. Or more likely the whole street, even the whole city, will be enclosed in a giant diving bell.

If it comes to that, some of us will be glad we will not be here to see it. Meanwhile there are more modest city developments in which we can be glad to be alive; one such is Philadelphia's Greenway walks. The city that was one of the most civilized of the thirteen colonies and the cradle of the nation's birth, Philadelphia has also pioneered its own answer to city blight, with its quiet rehabilitation of old neighborhoods. The Greenway is a system of landscaped walks to and from landmarks and historic places. Some are lushly planted promenades, a kind of pedestrian parkway. Some are no more than pleasant walks through neighborhoods that have been or are in process of being restored, such as the very old section called Society Hill.

Hopefully this is the pattern that our cities will take, that they are now beginning to take, a pattern of recovering for today's and future walkers the charming little streets of a more serene past, and of creating new walking on malls and pedestrian ways separate from the arteries of automobile traffic. Among the old cities that are leading the way, Philadelphia has already restored a network of such streets in the heart of downtown, with colonial houses that were formerly the servants' quarters of the mansions fronting on the avenues.

Georgetown, in Washington, is such a restoration. New Orleans still has its Pirates' Alley, and many small streets in the Vieux Carré. San Antonio has put together a continuous pattern of walks along the San Antonio River that winds through the center of town. The long, narrow way was once intended as a storm sewer; instead, the city fathers farsightedly laid it out as a linear garden looping through the town, where people may walk undisturbed by the traffic of a thriving automobile-age city.

Indeed this is the most appealing solution, and to walkers the most immediate and practical, to our urban dilemma. One planner, Ian Nairn, sketched it out for us in his recent and provocative book, *The American Landscape: A Critical View,* alive with photographs and infused with a genuine love of the city as an organic entity, a social and esthetic human creation. (We recommend the book, Random House, 1965, as an inspiration to city walkers.)

Nairn foresees a pattern of pedestrian walkways laid like an irregular, wayward carpet over the pattern of big buildings and traffic lanes. He would not try to exclude the traffic. A city without cars, he says, is dull, is not really a city. But he would take existing passageways, the pedestrian shortcuts and alleys that have survived in every city, the plazas and open spaces that are coming into being around the feet of giant commercial structures and high-rise apartment buildings. He would weave these together into walkways that have only an occasional, incidental relationship with the gridiron order of streets and avenues and the regimented stop-and-go of automobile traffic.

It would be a pattern like that of Venice, whose people walk in and out on footways and bridges, in a network that here and there may follow a canal by happenstance but does not cling to it. Indeed in Venice it is hardly ever possible to walk along a canal, as we walk along an avenue, since the buildings along the canals mostly rise straight up from the water and there is no sidewalk at all. Venice grew that way; other cities have the potential to develop something like it. Says this imaginative British architect, "There are plenty of hooks on which to hang such a system, and once begun it would easily spread because it makes economic sense as well as townscape sense."

Proposed: a PPP of Walkers

This is another do-it-yourself proposal for walkers, like the beauty at bargain prices that we talked of earlier. Just as on our walks we can seek out sites for green spots to be reclaimed or created in our city, so we can go walking in search of the existing hooks, the shortcuts and the alleyways, and we can trace out the possible links that could be woven into a walker's network through the high-density, traffic-filled heart of town.

We can sow a crop of Pedestrian Planning and Promotion committees —PPP's—to spring up in all our cities. We can raise a fresh and practical, if innocent, voice among the sophisticated planners with their fanciful, astronomically costly, and not necessarily inviting plans.

Our PPP policy would be to use less money and more shoe leather, less fantasy about what might be done and more imagination about what can in fact be done with what we already have. And while the dreamers dream up their blueprints of future cities that we may never be able to afford, we who literally have our feet on the ground can be modestly piecing together walkways that will make our cities once more bearable and perhaps—who knows?—even beautiful to walk in.

The suburbs of the future are also hopeful; we have already looked in on a model "new town" (Reston, Virginia, in Chapter 12). The Netherlands is the most densely populated country in the world (12,500,000 people, crammed into 15,800 square miles, a ratio of 951 per square mile compared with 54 per square mile in the United States). Their country is an almost continuous "ring city" comparable to the 400-mile stretch of nearly unrelieved urban and suburban communities from Boston to Washington. But the Dutch planners want no such continuous megalopolis. They will keep the center of the ring a green heart, and they will have green zones of at least a mile between one community and the next, making a chain of cities and towns separated by suburbs, farm communities, green zones, and parks.

England has not succeeded too well with its artificially created "new towns" to drain off population from London, but the green-belt system is being maintained against building encroachments. An American proposal is to establish rings of self-sufficient towns around the great cities, as a way of containing metropolitan sprawl and providing a livable environment within commuting distance of the cities. Most of the proposals for new versions of the suburbs depend upon a plan for high-speed mass transportation to take the place of private automobiles—as indeed do most of the proposals for reclaiming the cities. There can be no doubt that fast, efficient, comfortable mass transportation into and within the city is on the way.

And in the meantime, while we wait for these plans and proposals to curb the automobile and give the cities back to the people, we walkers can be productively busy, doing our peripatetic homework for the PPP. We can be getting up our own modest plans and proposals for bargain beauty spots and walkways, for which Federal money is already waiting in the Department of the Interior's open hand. Innocent amateurs we may be, but about one reality we are, as citizens, thoroughly sophisticated. We know that a politician is always attentive to a proposition that will bring money into town, especially if the money goes where the voters can see and enjoy it.

So the signs are promising. If even part of the promise is fulfilled in the next decades, the world will already be a pleasanter place to be walking in, to be alive in. And future generations will be able to say of us what Shakespeare had Marc Antony say of Julius Caesar to the citizens of Rome:

> . . . he hath left you all his walks,
> His private arbours and new-planted orchards,
> On this side Tiber; he hath left them you,
> And to your heirs forever; common pleasures,
> To walk abroad and recreate yourselves.

Part II

THE WALKING GUIDE

Where the walks are—the finest trails both here and abroad— and a SHOPPING GUIDE for your pedestrian comfort and convenience.

WHERE THE WALKS ARE

A WALK MAY BE an hour's stroll in a nearby park or nature pre-serve, or a camping, backpacking trip of many days behind an experi-enced guide. This Walking Guide embraces walks of both kinds and all degrees between, at home and abroad, with information sources for more. The last section, a Shopping Guide, lists reputable mail order companies whose catalogues offer clothing and gear for walking comfort.

Traditionally, the walker has found his own way and to some extent he still must do so. We have no AWA, or American Walkers' Association, like the AAA for automobile travelers, where we may learn what walks there are, where they begin and end, what their condition is at the mo-ment, where we may eat and sleep on the way. Yet walks are both vanish-ing and appearing even faster than automobile roads.

The old go-as-you-please country rambles are harder to find among the developments and superhighway networks, although many unspoiled enclaves still remain even in the most densely populated metropolitan areas. Meanwhile, more and more beautiful walks are being rediscovered or freshly carved in park and forest lands, along national seashores, in preserves and sanctuaries ranging from a few to many thousands of acres.

Some of the finest walks, and the most accessible to the city and sub-urban dwellers who form the majority of walkers, are in the fast-growing nature centers which communities have established, often on old estate and farm lands snatched by a hairbreadth from the bulldozers. We have included as many of these as we could find information for. Walk-seekers should not be put off by the word "Junior" in nature center titles. Funds for land acquisition and development often come from a community's education budget.

Also included, where we could learn of them, are county and munic-ipal park systems, but many more are only newly established or just being developed.

There are, besides, old hill country, river, and lakeshore paths, old canal towpaths, and the local sections of the great trails such as the Appalachian, Pacific Crest, Oregon, Sante Fe, the North Country stretching from Vermont to North Dakota, the Lewis and Clark Trail from St. Louis to the Pacific. All the great trails have their branching, connecting local trails. Many are still walkable, maintained by local clubs and interstate trail conservationists. Many are beautiful without being either too wild or too strenuous for Sunday walkers.

Such nearby walkers' paradises can be discovered only by local inquiry from:

State, county, and municipal park administrators.
Local branches of national or regional organizations.
Local hiking clubs.
Your daily newspaper, which may regularly print the group walks of the weekend, and generally has an outdoor editor whose files list the clubs and where they walk.
The Chamber of Commerce of the state, principal city, or resort area where you want to take a walking vacation, which can usually suggest local information sources as well as lodgings en route.

The headquarters addresses of helpful national and regional organizations—and also, most valuable and apparently least known, the United States Government agencies that give specific help to walk-seekers—are appended at the end of this Guide.

Walks in the United States [BY REGIONS]

Northeast: the New England States

COUNTRY WALKING, FREE-STYLE. Dirt roads lead off the paved highways in all New England's old farmlands. Pick your spot; your only indispensable guides are a U.S. Geological Survey map of the area and the state's Chamber of Commerce list of local hostelries. For your map, write—specifying the area you're interested in—to:

The Geological Survey
18th and F Sts. N.W.
Washington, D.C. 20405.

Investigate the ski country (but avoid highly developed summer resort areas) for spring, summer, and especially autumn walking. For example:

New Hampshire: Franconia and other White Mountain ski resorts
Vermont: Warren, in the Sugar Bush valley; Peacham
Massachusetts and Connecticut: the west Berkshire and Taconic hill
country, off Route 41

GREAT TRAILS (*Note:* Conditions on the great trails change season-
ally. Get the latest information.)

The Appalachian Trail (New England section) begins at Mt. Katah-
din, Maine, runs southwest to the White Mountains in New Hampshire,
crosses the Connecticut River into Vermont and the Green Mountains, then
south through western Massachusetts and Connecticut to the Housatonic
Valley and the New York line. Some portions make pleasant Sunday walking.
Trails in the White Mountain National Forest section are steep and rugged.
Be prepared for sudden changes in the weather and for poison ivy; stay at
low elevations in winter. For trail guides, maps, access points, accommoda-
dations, write to:

The Appalachian Mountain Club
5 Joy St.
Boston, Mass. 02108.

For the national forest sections of the trail, write to:

Forest Supervisor
White Mt. National Forest
Laconia, N.H. 03246

Forest Supervisor
Green Mt. National Forest
Rutland, Vt. 05701

The Long Trail runs from Canada to Massachusetts, meets the
Appalachian Trail at Route 4 in Vermont. For trail information:

Green Mountain Club
108 Merchants Row
Rutland, Vt. 05701.

PARKLAND TRAILS

Maine:

ACADIA NATIONAL PARK, on Mt. Desert Island, southeast of Bangor.
The island is nearly divided by Somes Sound, each half roughly 10 by 5 miles
in extent, all of it a walker's paradise with 100 miles of woodland trails,
mountain walks and gentle slopes, spectacular views of the rocky coasts and
islands of Frenchman Bay. Many pleasant lodgings in Bar Harbor and other
towns on the island.

TODD WILDLIFE SANCTUARY, a spruce-clad island in Muscongus Bay. Walks also on the mainland around Damariscotta, amid forests, lakes, streams, marshes, and on other islands in the bay.

Vacation note: Todd Sanctuary is the site of the Audubon Camp in Maine (others are in Wisconsin, Wyoming, and one in Connecticut mainly for nature study teachers and group leaders). For an invigorating walking and wildlife vacation under National Audubon Society auspices, write for information to:

> Audubon Camp Dept.
> 613 Riversville Road
> Greenwich, Conn. 06833

Massachusetts:

CAPE COD NATIONAL SEASHORE has these marked trails:

> Small's Swamp Trail, in Truro
> Pilgrim Heights Trail, also in Truro
> White Cedar Swamp Trail, in Wellfleet
> Red Maple Swamp Trail, in Eastham

The Cape Cod Magazine Guide publishes a weekly list of all the guided walks on the Cape during the summer.

Those who prefer solo exploration should provide themselves with the National Park Service's large handsome map of the Cape, which indicates the trails. Send 15¢ with your order to:

> Superintendent of Documents
> U.S. Government Printing Office
> Washington, D.C. 20402

Also on Cape Cod:

WELLFLEET BAY WILDLIFE SANCTUARY, between Eastham and Wellfleet. A self-guided nature walk on a numbered trail with an accompanying booklet. More than 250 bird species have been recorded here.

BOTANIC TRAILS of the Historical Society of Old Yarmouth. Yarmouth Port, on Route 6A. Guided and self-guided walks.

Elsewhere in Massachusetts:

ARCADIA WILDLIFE SANCTUARY, in Easthampton

PLEASANT VALLEY SANCTUARY and trailside museum, in Lenox

DRUMLIN FARM NATURE CENTER, in South Lincoln

TRAILSIDE MUSEUM, in Forest Park, Springfield

See also: *Massachusetts–Rhode Island Trail Guide,* published by the Appalachian Mountain Club, 1964.

Connecticut:

Good walking in these Audubon and other sanctuaries.

ROY AND MARGOT LARSEN AUDUBON SANCTUARY, Fairfield. 110 acres. Walk books for self-guided tours.

MID–FAIRFIELD COUNTY YOUTH MUSEUM, WESTPORT.

GREENWICH AUDUBON CENTER, 613 Riverville Road. 430 acres, including a 127-acre wildflower sanctuary.

PEQUOT-SEPOS WILDLIFE SANCTUARY, on Pequot-Sepos Road, Mystic.

NEW CANAAN NATURE CENTER, on Oenoke Avenue. 41 acres of ponds and marshes, also a weather station.

WEST ROCK NATURE RECREATION CENTER, New Haven.

CONNECTICUT ARBORETUM, New London, at Connecticut College. 350 acres, including a wildflower preserve.

THAMES SCIENCE CENTER, 622 William Street, New London.

SHARON AUDUBON CENTER, on Route 4. 526 wooded acres; has a stream with beavers, otters, deer.

STAMFORD MUSEUM AND NATURE CENTER, on High Ridge off Scofieldtown Road. Trails, zoo, children's farm.

Note: For further walking in Connecticut, consult *The Connecticut Walk Book;* also *The New York Walk Book,* which covers western Connecticut.

The Appalachian Trail passes through the Housatonic Valley, wandering back and forth across the Connecticut–New York state line. See *The Connecticut Walk Book,* third edition, 1946, and the *Guide to the Appala-*

chian Trail in New England, 1942, which describes the trail on its route down from Massachusetts to the New York–Connecticut line.

For more rugged walking, the Taconic Mountains, an elevated forested region including the western Berkshires, where the Massachusetts, Connecticut and New York boundaries meet. A chapter on walking in this area is in *The New York Walk Book.*

Middle Atlantic States

WILDERNESS WALKS. The middle states of the East Coast, despite the high density of their population, have vast state forests preserved in perpetuity as wild forest lands. New York has some 2,000,000 acres of Adirondack state forest; another state forest in the Catskills has more than 200,000. New Jersey, although small, has more than 22,000 acres in the Lebanon state forest, more than 12,000 in Stokes, more than 9,000 in Bass River. Pennsylvania can match these, and it has besides the Allegheny National Forest in its northwestern corner. In addition, all these states have state and county parks, some that equal in wildness even the forest lands. For wilderness walks in forest and parklands not mentioned here, consult the forestry and park departments of the states.

NEARBY WILDERNESS. Some of the wildest as well as the mildest of walks are within, or in easy reach of, the most metropolitan metropolis of all, the City of New York. Some will be noted below; the *New York Walk Book* covers them in detail, with maps, from western Connecticut to New Jersey. To update its information, especially for specific walks, consult:

> The New York–New Jersey Trail Conference
> G.P.O. Box 2250
> New York, N.Y. 10001

GREAT TRAILS

The Appalachian Trail here runs southwest from Kent, Connecticut, to cross the state line. In New York it passes through FAHNESTOCK STATE PARK in Putnam County, crosses the Hudson on the Bear Mountain Bridge, goes westward through HARRIMAN STATE PARK, then south, paralleling the west shore of Greenwood Lake, then west again to the state line. At HIGH POINT STATE PARK it swings south to follow the Delaware River on a high ridge, passing through STOKES STATE FOREST and the DELAWARE WATER GAP NATIONAL RECREATION AREA (still in planning). At the Delaware Water Gap it crosses into Pennsylvania. For trail information on this portion consult:

> The New York–New Jersey Trail Conference
> G.P.O. Box 2250
> New York, N.Y. 10001

and from Pennsylvania south:

> The Appalachian Trail Conference
> 1916 Sunderland Place N.W.
> Washington, D.C. 20036

The Finger Lakes Trail (under reconstruction) goes from ALLE-GHENY STATE PARK in northwest Pennsylvania to meet the Appalachian Trail near the Massachusetts-Connecticut border. A major branch of the Finger Lakes Trail, from near its western Pennsylvania end, points northward to Niagara Falls, to connect with the Bruce Trail. Information: The Finger Lakes Trail Conference (see Checklist, page 199).

The Bruce Trail (under construction) connects Niagara Falls to Tobermory on the Bruce Peninsula, which extends between Georgian Bay and Lake Huron.

The Long Path (like the Long Trail of Vermont; see Northeast section of the Guide) is being extended through New York to make a continuous trail from the George Washington Bridge to Whiteface Mountain in the Adirondacks. Information: the New York–New Jersey Trail Conference.

Hearts Content Trails, in the ALLEGHENY NATIONAL FOREST, 10 miles from Warren, Pennsylvania, through a fabulously beautiful forest of trees more than 200 years old.

Delaware and Raritan Canal towpath, 58 miles with its feeder (22 miles) following the Delaware River from above Raven Rock to Trenton, New Jersey. Access also at Princeton, Bound Brook, New Brunswick, and other points. Towpath is overgrown in portions but the intrepid walker can scramble to a parallel road. Mind the poison ivy. Lovely unspoiled stretches with scenic and historical charms. Route touches WASHINGTON CROSSING STATE PARK (see Pennsylvania, below).

PARKLAND TRAILS

Hudson River: The PALISADES INTERSTATE PARK, jointly tended by New York and New Jersey, is one of the finest stretches of unspoiled walking in an urban-suburban area anywhere. Wise men, both public and private, have conserved much of the west bank of the Hudson River for some thousands of acres and many miles of splendid river shore. The Palisades path stretches along 13 miles of gentle trail on the crest of the Palisades northward from the George Washington Bridge, with four points where the walker can climb down the cliff and walk back along the riverbank, determining the length of his own walk. Northward, the HARRIMAN and BEAR MOUNTAIN sections add some 75 square miles covered by a network of trails. Woodland picnic grounds, accommodations at Bear Mountain Inn under Park Commission auspices. Also ice skating and skiing in season. Trailside museum and nature center. Easy access from New York City by car, bus, boat. For current trail information:

Palisades Interstate Park, Administration **Headquarters**,
Bear Mountain, N.Y. 10911

or: 30 Rockefeller Plaza
New York, N.Y. 10020

New York: WARD POUNDRIDGE RESERVATION, **on** Route 121 near Cross River. A Westchester County preserve of 5,500 acres with some 50 miles of trails, picnic and camping sites, an arboretum, lovely woods and meadows, plus a museum.

WILLIAM S. CLOUGH PRESERVE, on Farm-to-Market Road, Brewster. 60 wooded acres.

SHELDRAKE RIVER TRACT, on Rockland Avenue, Mamaroneck. A 54-acre tract.

WEINBERG NATURE CENTER, Scarsdale. 8 acres of nature walks.

LAKE MOHONK MOUNTAIN HOUSE, New Paltz, N.Y. 12561. Also THE LAKE MINNEWASKA MOUNTAIN HOUSES, Lake Minnewaska, N.Y. 12561. Accommodations for walking vacations on many miles of trails on two vast estates in the Shawangunk Mountains, Ulster County. Both establishments are open all year; both follow the walk-and-carriage road traditions of the founding Smiley family.

Long Island: BAYARD CUTTING ARBORETUM, in Oakdale, 50 miles from New York City. A rhododendron walk, and wildflower, cypress, birdwatchers' walks.

TACKAPAUSHA PRESERVE, at Seaford, a Nassau County nature preserve. 65 acres along Seaford Creek, with about 5½ miles of trails among native trees, shrubs, herbaceous plants, and two lakes with aquatic and swamp plants.

New York City: For guided historical walks, the Museum of the City of New York, 103rd Street and Fifth Avenue. For guided nature and bird walks, the American Museum of Natural History, 77th Street and Central Park West. Many hiking clubs have weekend and Sunday walking trips.

CENTRAL PARK, 59th Street to 110th Street, Fifth Avenue to Central Park West. Beautiful walking in any direction. To discover the Ramble, start from the Bethesda Fountain plaza (outdoor café) off the 72nd Street drive, follow the lakeshore left and cross the bridge.

FORT WASHINGTON, FORT TRYON, and INWOOD HILL parks and THE CLOISTERS, on the upper western rim of Manhattan Island, overlooking the

Hudson (Fifth Avenue bus, or Independent Subway, to Washington Heights). From Jeffrey's Hook, a large rock in FORT WASHINGTON PARK, the view extends up the Hudson to the Tappan Zee. INWOOD HILL PARK has Indian caves. THE CLOISTERS has garden walks and a medieval herb garden especially beautiful for spring walking.

BRONX PARK, world-famous, 2½ miles of walking through a great zoo, botanic garden, woodland, hemlock grove, rose garden, formal gardens. (Broadway–Lenox Avenue IRT subway, or Lexington Avenue IRT subway and change at 145th Street.)

VAN CORTLANDT PARK, north of Manhattan. Rocky, rolling, unspoiled woodland 1½ miles each way, following Tibbetts Brook. (Broadway–Seventh Avenue IRT subway to 242nd Street.)

PROSPECT PARK, Brooklyn. Like Central Park, an Olmsted masterpiece. Splendid trees rival those in arboretums. Famous botanic garden contains a jewellike Japanese garden. (From Manhattan, both IRT and BMT subway lines.)

New Jersey: large county parks in Essex, Union, Bergen, Morris counties. New Jersey conservation efforts have preserved shore and marshland walks; unusual flora and birds, rare frogs and snakes are to be seen in the pine barrens of South Jersey: cedar swamps, cranberry bogs. BASS RIVER STATE FOREST, where maps and trail information can be obtained, is a good starting point.

WATCHUNG RESERVATION, in Union County. Trailside Nature and Science Center at Coles Avenue and New Providence Road, Mountainside. Fern, herb, wildflower gardens, a zoo, 2,000 acres of woodland walks.

JENNY JUMP STATE FOREST, in Warren County. Follows the ridge of Jenny Jump Mountain. Highest elevation only 1,100 feet but views are magnificent, extend to Delaware Water Gap. Many glacier-transported limestone boulders along the trails.

DRYDEN KUSER NATURAL AREA, north of High Point. Trails through 200 acres of hemlock, white pine, black spruce; a varied population of plants, birds, wildlife.

STONY FORD AUDUBON CENTER, Princeton. At Pretty Brook Road.

BERT HOOVER ARBORETUM, Wildwood. Established by stamp collectors in honor of a famous philatelist.

Pennsylvania: WASHINGTON CROSSING STATE PARK, Bucks County (Route 32). Has the justly famous Washington Crossing Nature Center and State Wildflower Preserve.

SCHUYLKILL NATURE CENTER, in Fairmount Park, Philadelphia (Roxborough, the Smith-Meigs property). A good objective for walks in Philadelphia's famous park.

PRESQUE ISLE STATE PARK, unique sandy peninsula reaching 7 miles into Lake Erie, backed by a stand of giant oaks. Miles of beach and woodland hiking trails, with a swim in clean lake water after your walk. Colored pebbles for collectors, 280 bird species.

PYMATUNING STATE PARK, on Route 322, Pennsylvania's 18½-mile dam-built lake (for flood control), with a shoreline 71 miles long. Conservation and bird refuge. In migration season, up to 70,000 ducks in a single day, more than 5,000 swans, nearly 300 species of wild waterfowl, marsh, shore, and woodland birds visit here.

MONTGOMERY COUNTY AUDUBON WILDLIFE SANCTUARY, Audubon's own first home in the United States turned into a sanctuary; his house, Mill Grove, built in 1762, restored, with a collection of his paintings and prints. Walking trails wind among 350 species of flowering plants; 159 bird species.

LAUREL HIGHLANDS, winter ski and summer vacation resort region, good for walking in off seasons. In Somerset County, which is Amish country. For nearby accommodations write to:

Laurel Hill State Park
R.D. #4
Somerset, Pa. 15501

Southern States

NATIONAL PARKS AND MONUMENTS of all varieties, historical, scenic, and nature preserve, abound in the Southern states. Almost any of them offers good walking: The historic mansions usually have gardens; the battlegrounds and military cemeteries cover acres of historic ground and are usually well maintained. The National Park Service, Department of the Interior, has a pamphlet locating and concisely describing them all. Write for: *The National Park System, Eastern United States.* (There is a similar pamphlet for the Western United States.)

For our purpose, the Guide lists here only those with sizable walking areas of natural beauty.

Note: A "national monument" is a natural feature reserved by the government as public property. Its value may be scenic, historic, prehistoric or scientific. Its size varies from the 2-acre Fort Sumter, S.C., to the 2,697,500-acre Katmai in Alaska.

GREAT TRAILS

The Appalachian Trail has some of its finest reaches in the southern Appalachians, readily accessible for Sunday walkers in some parts (SHENANDOAH NATIONAL PARK) where the trail parallels or crisscrosses the Skyline Drive for 94 miles; remote and challenging in others (the GEORGE WASHINGTON and the JEFFERSON NATIONAL FORESTS) where it crosses 4,000-foot peaks, traverses valleys, runs along rugged ridges. It passes through forests marked by naked trunks of American chestnuts, great trees killed by the blight; over the "balds," rounded grass-clad mountaintops; through rhododendron thickets in North Carolina (PISGAH NATIONAL FOREST) and Tennessee (CHEROKEE NATIONAL FOREST). It continues through GREAT SMOKY NATIONAL PARK and NANTAHALA NATIONAL FOREST, ends on Springer Mountain near Mt. Oglethorpe, Georgia. In places the trail may be overgrown, especially after the Southern summer. For current trail information on the southern leg of the trail, also on its many beautiful side trails:

> The Appalachian Trail Conference
> 1916 Sunderland Place N.W.
> Washington, D.C. 20036

Historic trails have been restored by Boy Scout chapters. The national headquarters (Boy Scouts of America, New Brunswick, N.J.) can direct inquiries to the local chapters for maps and train information. Among B.S.A.–approved trails in the South:

Kennesaw Mountain Trail, Georgia.

Shiloh Trail, a 14-mile stretch beginning at Shiloh, near Pittsburgh Landing, Tennessee.

PARKLAND TRAILS

Maryland: CHESAPEAKE AND OHIO CANAL NATIONAL MONUMENT. The celebrated towpath walk here runs under Federal auspices along the north bank of the Potomac River from Seneca to Cumberland, Maryland. Administration offices: 479 North Potomac St., Hagerstown, Md. 21720

Washington, D.C.: ROCK CREEK PARK NATURE CENTER, on Glover Road. Rock Creek Park, a wild gorge running across the city, is full of beautiful walks.

THEODORE ROOSEVELT ISLAND, in the Potomac, opposite Georgetown. 3½ miles of pleasant trails. Ferry to the island runs weekends in summer from foot of Wisconsin Avenue.

CHESAPEAKE AND OHIO CANAL towpath begins at Georgetown.

DUMBARTON OAKS, Georgetown. Historic mansion's grounds provide lovely garden walks.

Virginia: SHENANDOAH NATIONAL PARK. The Blue Ridge Mountains, with splendid vistas of the Shenandoah Valley, Allegheny Mountains, the Piedmont of Virginia, noble forests and a paradise of wildflowers; 207 miles of trails are mostly gentle. Naturalist talks, guided and self-guided nature walks. Access is from many points on the Skyline Drive. The park is accessible almost the year round, but most facilities are closed in winter and early spring. Accommodations in lodges and cabins of:

> Virginia Sky-Line Company, Inc.
> Luray, Va. 22835

Also in club cabins of:

> Potomac Appalachian Trail Club
> 1916 Sunderland Place N.W.
> Washington, D.C. 20036

Virginia, Kentucky, Tennessee: CUMBERLAND GAP NATIONAL HISTORICAL PARK. Follows a key pass on the Wilderness Road first blazed by Daniel Boone. Access is at administration headquarters on U.S. 25-E, between Middlesboro, Kentucky, and Cumberland Gap, Tennessee, or from U.S. 58 in Virginia.

North Carolina, Tennessee: GREAT SMOKY MOUNTAINS NATIONAL PARK. This famous park conserves one of the earth's oldest and most beautiful uplands, cradle of Eastern American plant life. Luxuriant growth often reaches giant size; wildlife is also abundant and varied. Contains Clingman's Dome, second highest peak in the East, but many of the 653 miles of trails are gentle slopes; the Appalachian Trail runs through for 70 miles. Access and park headquarters are two miles south of Gatlinburg, Tennessee; access is also from Asheville, North Carolina, Knoxville, Tennessee, and numerous other points. Hotel and tourist accomodations abound in the vicinity. Appealing to walkers is a lodge with cabins near the top of Mt. LeConte, reached only by trail. For information:

> LeConte Lodge
> Gatlinburg, Tenn. 37738

For park and trail information, consult the park administration, address also Gatlinburg, Tenn.

North Carolina: CAPE HATTERAS NATIONAL SEASHORE. An 80-mile stretch for beach walking and beachcombing, also Buxton Woods Nature Trail. Access and information at Bodie Island Lighthouse, Cape Hatteras Lighthouse, Ocracoke village.

JOYCE KILMER MEMORIAL FOREST, near Tapoco. 4-mile Middle Trail circles through a wilderness area of giant poplars and huge ferns along the banks of clear streams.

CHILDREN'S NATURE MUSEUM, Charlotte. 1658 Sterling Road. Walks.

GREENSBORO JUNIOR MUSEUM, Greensboro. 4301 Lawndale Drive. Walks.

Florida: EVERGLADES NATIONAL PARK, the country's largest sub-tropical wilderness. Mangrove forests, open Everglades prairies, fresh and saltwater wildlife and rare and beautiful birds. Access is via U.S. 1 and Florida 27, 40 miles southwest of Miami. Park headquarters are at Flamingo, also marina, restaurant, picnic area, campground, and accommodations at Flamingo Lodge:

Everglades Park Co.
3660 Coral Way,
Miami, Fla. 33145

Tourist accommodations also in the park's vicinity. Naturalist programs and guided trips. Caution: One can still get lost in the Everglades. Consult a park ranger before venturing off marked trails.

CORKSCREW SWAMP SANCTUARY, near Fort Myers. A National Audubon Society preserve, 6,080 acres of virgin bald cypress, hidden lakes and ponds, Big Cypress Nature Center. Trails on raised boardwalks traverse this area rich in exotic vegetation, birds and wildlife.

MYAKKA RIVER PARK, 17 miles east of Sarasota. Deer, raccoons, and great flocks of birds can be seen from the trail.

HIGHLAND HAMMOCK PARK, west of Sebring. Catwalk trail through swampy habitat of alligators and turtles.

HILLSBOROUGH RIVER PARK, northwest of Tampa. River trail winds through woods of huge oaks, cedars and cypresses.

Middle West

THE VAST HEARTLAND of the United States has every variety of walking—farmland, wilderness, forested lakes, great and little rivers. It has the Dakota Badlands, strange and beautiful in their unique way to Eastern eyes. Metropolitan park systems are often richly developed within the cities and on their outskirts. Some of the best walks are not in parks or preserves but must be locally investigated. Too many are unprotected and their existence is threatened even while we write of them. The Guide does its best with some large and small protected areas below.

The Middle West will have, one day in the future, one of the country's great trails, the rehabilitated North Country Trail. Portions of it may even now be walkable and known to walkers in its vicinity.

GREAT TRAILS

The North Country Trail, to be rehabilitated and to some extent rerouted to go through existing national and state forests and parks. It leaves the Appalachian Trail near Lake Champlain in Vermont, swings southwest to pass Albany on the west and continues along New York's southern tier near the Pensylvania line, to cut across northwestern Pennsylvania, into Ohio. Its course then goes to south-central Ohio, turns northwest again through that state to the western shore of the Michigan peninsula, crosses to the upper Michigan peninsula, and goes on through northern Wisconsin, Minnesota, and North Dakota to join the Lewis and Clark Trail.

PARKLAND TRAILS

Ohio: HUNTINGTON PARK RESERVATION, in Bay Village. In the park is the Lake Erie Junior Nature and Science Center, 28728 Wolf Road.

BLACKLOCK WOODS NATURE CENTER, in Columbus. 1000 Aullwood Road. Also, AULLWOOD CHILDREN'S FARM, 9101 Fredericks Road.

THE NATURE CENTER, in Secor Park, Toledo.

Indiana: INDIANA DUNES STATE PARK, on the southern tip of Lake Michigan. 3½ square miles of walks and recreation in this protected portion of the famous Indiana dunes.

Illinois: COOK COUNTY FOREST PRESERVE, 30 minutes by car from downtown Chicago in the River Forest vicinity. A longitudinal parkland, 47,000 acres of semiwild sanctuary where walkers may see minks, muskrats, foxes, sometimes wild turkeys. Several nature centers within the preserve have marked trails. For trail information:

> Superintendent of Conservation
> 536 North Harlem Ave.
> River Forest, Ill. 60305

ILLINOIS PRAIRIE PATH, on the roadbed of the defunct Chicago, Aurora and Elgin Railroad.

SAUK TRAIL, on the south side of Chicago.

ILLINOIS-MICHIGAN CANAL towpath, starting at Channahon, Illinois.

ILLINOIS BEACH STATE PARK. (All these walks in Illinois, and several in Wisconsin, so marked, are recommended by the Great Lakes Chapter of the Sierra Club.)

Michigan: ISLE ROYALE NATIONAL PARK, on Isle Royale, largest island in Lake Superior, and numerous smaller islands. Forested and wild, habitat of a great moose herd, also the site of pre-Columbian copper mines. The park is open June 21 to September 5. Access is by boat from Houghton or Copper Harbor, Michigan, or Grand Portage, Minnesota; charter-plane service also from Houghton. Two lodges are operated by:

National Park Concessions, Inc.
Isle Royale National Park,
Rock Harbor, Mich. 49940

Park administration: 87 North Ripley St., Houghton, Mich. 49932

W. K. KELLOGG BIRD SANCTUARY, in Hickory Corners.

NANKIN MILLS NATURE CENTER, in Garden City. 33175 Ann Arbor Trail.

KALAMAZOO NATURE CENTER, 7000 North Westhedge, Kalamazoo.

PHIL DE GRAAF'S LODGE, on Trout Lake. For a wildlife and walking vacation. Naturalist in residence.

Wisconsin: KETTLE MORAINE STATE FOREST. Recommended by the Sierra Club, Great Lakes Chapter, are the glacial trail in the north of the state forest and the hiking trails in its southern part.

AUDUBON CAMP, in Hunt Hill Sanctuary on Devil's Lake, near Spooner. A walking and canoeing nature vacation amid forests, bogs, lakes, meadows. For information:

Audubon Camp Dept.
613 Riversville Road
Greenwich, Conn. 06833

Minnesota: GRAND PORTAGE NATIONAL MONUMENT, about 35 miles from Grand Marais. The park proper embraces a 9-mile portage on a main route used by Indians, explorers, fur trappers of the past. A good start on walking in the northern Minnesota country.

North Dakota: THEODORE ROOSEVELT NATIONAL MEMORIAL PARK, part of the great conservation President's Elkhorn Ranch, in the Badlands along the Little Missouri River. Walks and self-guided nature trails through a scenic fantasy created by erosion. Mail: Box 7, Medora, N. Dak. 58645.

South Dakota: BADLANDS NATIONAL MONUMENT, another and perhaps more spectacular portion of this remarkable country, in brilliant colors.
The eroded sedimentary rock reveals ancient animal fossils. Accommodations
(cabins):

Cedar Pass Lodge
Interior, S. Dak. 57750

For trail information: Box 72, Interior, S. Dak. 57750

WIND CAVE NATIONAL PARK, in the Black Hills. Besides beautiful
rock formations in the cave, the park has 28,000 acres of rolling woodlands
and meadows where the buffalo roam, the antelope are at home on the range
and prairie dogs live in their colonies, all under Government protection.

Southwest

Naturalists, geologists, anthropologists love this country and know
their way around it. They ride and drive over the long distances but eventually they go afoot. Others need guided parties for walking trips of any
extent. Nature centers and state parks are good starting places. National
parks and monuments are numerous, provide good trails within their boundaries, and have park rangers to protect the innocent walker against the
hazards of difficult terrain, sudden and violent weather changes, going thirsty
and losing his way. All this is also true of the Mountain States, next on our
list. The Guide therefore stays within the supervised preserves, some of them
undeservedly little known.

Arkansas: HOT SPRINGS NATIONAL PARK. To take or not take the
waters is optional. For walkers there are scenic and nature trails along lakes
and streams, naturalist talks and walks. If advance information is wanted:
Box 1219, Hot Springs National Park, Ark. 71901

Arizona: GRAND CANYON NATIONAL PARK. Embraces the most
spectacular portion. The South Rim is accessible the year round, the North
Rim from May to October. Walking trails on the rims, also into the gorge:

The Kaibab Trail, for the hardy hiker, a 14-mile round trip from the
South Rim to the Phantom River Ranch 4,400 feet below.

The Grand Canyon Nature Trail, less strenuous by far; a leaflet available
at Park Headquarters gives information on wildlife and points of interest
for a self-guided walk.

There are also guided walks, ranger talks. Accommodations, on the South
Rim:

Fred Harvey,
Grand Canyon, Ariz. 86023

On the North Rim:

> Utah Parks Co.
> Cedar City, Utah 84720

Note: Accommodations are in great demand. Make your reservations three or four months ahead.

CHIRICAHUA NATIONAL MONUMENT, Dos Cabezas. Unusual rock shapes and strata reveal nearly a billion years of earth's history. Lodge accommodations within the park: Silver Spur Ranch, Dos Cabezas. Light housekeeping one mile from park headquarters: Faraway Ranch, Dos Cabezas.

CORONADO NATIONAL MEMORIAL, Hereford. The route by which Coronado made his famous expedition north to present Kansas in 1540–42. Self-guided trail trip. Information by mail: Star Route, Hereford, Ariz. 85615.

ORGAN PIPE CACTUS NATIONAL MONUMENT, Ajo. Sonora desert, unspoiled, with bold desert scenery, rare and unusual plant and wildlife. Walks. Information by mail: Box 38, Ajo, Ariz. 85321.

SAGUARO NATIONAL MONUMENT, near Tucson. Cactus forest of giant saguaro. Nature trails, hiking, self-guided geology tour. Information by mail: Route 8, Box 350, Tucson, Ariz. 85702.

ARIZONA–SONORA DESERT MUSEUM, Tucson. Walks.

New Mexico: AZTEC RUINS NATIONAL MONUMENT, Aztec. Archeologic walks among ruins of a twelfth-century Indian town. Mail: Route 1, Box 101, Aztec, N. Mex. 87410.

BANDELIER NATIONAL MONUMENT, Santa Fe. Canyon country and cliff and pueblo ruins. Guided and self-guided trips to ruins, on nature trails, also back-country walks. Accommodations:

> Frijoles Canyon Lodge
> Santa Fe, N. Mex. 87501

CAPULIN MOUNTAIN NATIONAL MONUMENT, Capulin. Geologic and nature trail walks around the crater rim of a spectacular volcanic cinder cone. Mail: Box 94, Capulin, N. Mex. 88414.

GHOST RANCH MUSEUM, Abiquiu. Walks.

Oklahoma: PLATT NATIONAL PARK, Sulphur. Cold mineral springs, geologic and nature interests. Camping and picnic grounds. Self-guided walks. Swimming. Mail: Box 379, Sulphur, Okla. 73086.

Texas: BIG BEND NATIONAL PARK, within the Big Bend of the Rio Grande River. Said to be the wildest of the national parks; some parts are still unexplored. Sharp mountains, deep canyons, unique blend of Mexican and North American plant and animal life. Year-round campsites and trails along which may be seen deer, pronghorns, peccaries, beaver. For birders, this is the only nesting place within the United States of the Colima warbler. Mail: Big Bend National Park, Tex. 79834.

Mountain States

In the Big Sky country, walking becomes a sport of a high order. Indians and mountain men slipped cannily through the passes with an eye to swift travel and a nose for weather; the pioneer wagon trains made hard going of it. Today, wilderness walkers go into the high wild country in companies, led by skilled guides and themselves skilled and able at backpacking, mountaineering, camping, and rugged high-altitude walking. Local clubs and two nationally known outdoor and conservation societies, the Sierra Club and the Wilderness Society, conduct such excursions regularly during the summer months. They are for the hardy outdoorsman.

But the rest of us, ordinary walkers for pleasure, are not thereby barred from the extraordinary experiences of mountain wilderness, the snow-topped peaks, dazzling lakes, streams tumbling through wild gorges, the dark forests, the heart-stirring vistas, the mountain meadows carpeted with wildflowers, the voices of birds and glimpses of animals whose home this is, the brilliant sun and exhilarating air. We can have it all, with no special competence or muscle, only average good health.

There are pack-animal trips, on which mules or burros transport the camp equipment and campers' duffels, and the walker carries only his lunch and variable-weather wear. There are "base camp" excursions, daily trips which bring the walkers back to the same camp each night.

Some Sierra Club and Wilderness Society trips are specifically planned for the whole family, children and all. The Audubon Camp of the West, in a Wyoming valley of 7,500-foot elevation, has a permanent lodge and comfortable facilities, and is prepared to take campers from the age of eighteen to past seventy.

And always there are the great national parks, with trails for a few hours or many days of magnificent walking, and with lodges and campgrounds for staying a while.

ORGANIZED WALKS

The Sierra Club, organized well over half a century ago to protect and enjoy the Sierra Nevada, now extends its trips into the Rockies and even the Utah and Arizona desert country. Sierra Club trips fall into these categories:

The High Trip, traditional with the club, roving to successive campsites near timberline, usually above 9,000 feet, on trails that may go to 11,000 or 12,000. Commissary crew does most of the camp work; pack animals carry equipment and campers' personal duffel (limited to 30 pounds). A day's walk between camps is 5 to 15 miles; two- or three-day layovers allow for nearby exploration, nature interests, rest. Complement per trip is about 100 people in all.

The High-Light Trip, more strenuous, half as many people, pack mules and small crew; trippers do much of the camp work. A 20-pound limit on personal duffel. Hikes between camps are 8 to 14 miles through more rugged country. Past High-Light trips have been to the Tetons in Wyoming, the Sawtooth Mountains in Idaho, Rainbow Bridge in Arizona, Escalante Canyon in Utah, as well as the Cascades and Olympics in the coast range.

Knapsack Trips, for experienced backpackers. Parties of 20 carry all they need and do all camp chores themselves. Some of these, called Leisure Trips, cover less ground and have more layover time. Others are rigorous cross-country hikes and climbs.

Base Camp Trip, probably the least demanding, is a stay at a base camp a day's hike from a road end. Mules carry all equipment and provisions; horses are available for riding into camp if preferred. Cook and crew provide meals (reputedly excellent camp food) and camp chores are minimal. Mountaineer and naturalist leaders conduct hikes, climbs, overnight knapsack trips. High camps within a few hours' comfortable walk are provisioned and equipped for cooking, hold 10 to 15 people for overnight stays and further exploration; trippers carry their sleeping gear and clothing changes to these. *The Base Camp trip is recommended for families.*

Wilderness Threshold Camp offers back-country vacations *for families down to one-year-olds,* younger by permission. Mules carry the loads, the family hikes into camp. Campsites when possible are located on lakes or streams, nice for the children. Each family camps as a unit, does its own chores. Camp leaders have their own children with them. A grand way to introduce the children to the wilderness arts and pleasures.

Burro Trips add the novelty of charming, often unpredictable four-legged companions. The tripper learns to catch, load, and lead his animal. Travel occupies about half the days, the others are layover time spent climbing and exploring.

Family Burro Trips, separately organized, take children of five or older, or old enough to walk five or six miles, sleep in a sleeping bag, eat camp food. Two or three burros are assigned to each family. Some trips have central commissaries with families taking turns at cooking for all. Camp moves usually on alternate days, covers relatively short distances. The Sierra people require that both parents come on these trips, one to handle the burros.

River Trips take least effort, yet provide walking in places that might not be otherwise accessible, and the riding is along miles of stunning cliffs and canyons. Some trips permit individuals to paddle their own canoes, kayaks or foldboats. Most are floating trips on large rubber rafts guided by skilled boatmen. Swimming skill is not required, only dog-paddling, a willingness to get wet occasionally, and no fear of the water. Life jackets are provided and wearing them is required. The day's travel usually ends in early afternoon, leaving time for walking explorations (or fishing, swimming, being lazy). River-running trips are scheduled for various settings, from high-mountain forests to warm desert country.

For more information on these tempting excursions:

> Sierra Club
> 1050 Mills Tower
> 220 Bush St.
> San Francisco, Calif. 94104

The Wilderness Society specializes in riding trips into the high country (horseback skill not required) but also leads backpacking trips for experienced wilderness walkers, and hiking trips for non-backpackers.

Wilderness Hiking Trips require no carrying. An outfitter transports camping and personal gear, provides meals and tents. These are relatively low-cost (nonprofit) vacations for entire families in mountain wilderness settings, mainly the Rockies although recently one has been in New Hampshire, with good trails and comfortable walking distances. For information:

> The Wilderness Society
> Western Regional Office
> 2422 South Downing St.
> Denver, Colo. 80209

The Audubon Camp of the West is in the Wind River Mountains of western Wyoming, in a valley with a sweeping view of majestic peaks, lakes, and the sparkling air of a 7,500-foot altitude. The comfortable housing was originally built by the University of Wisconsin for its summer sessions. The moderate enrollment fee covers lodging, meals, field trips, instruction. Morning and afternoon field trips, in groups of not more than 14, take the camper into this unspoiled mountain country for close acquaintance with its plant and animal life and its geological formations, under the guidance of specialist leaders. The age limit is from 18 upward. Sessions are for 12 days each, beginning the last week in June and ending the third week in August. For information:

> Audubon Camp of the West
> P. O. Box 3666
> El Monte, Calif. 91733

PARKLAND TRAILS

Probably the simplest way for a newcomer to the mountains to sample the experience is in one of the great or smaller national parks. We are listing them by states, north to south and east to west.

Montana: GLACIER NATIONAL PARK, in the true Rocky Mountains; superb glacier-sculptured scenery, waterfalls, clear-running streams, alpine meadows, evergreen forests. Also some 60 glaciers, 200 lakes, 1,000 miles of trails. Glacier and its Canadian twin, Waterton, form the Waterton-Glacier International Peace Park. Some trails are steep and many portions are too wild for a casual walk, but the visitor will find plentiful guidance to easier trails. The season is June 15 to September 10. Bus and air service to the park is from nearby cities and there is bus service within the park. Hotels, motels, chalets with meals, cabins, provide variety of accommodations. Guided nature trips and talks. Mail: West Glacier, Mont. 59936.

Montana-Wyoming-Idaho: YELLOWSTONE NATIONAL PARK. More than 1,000 miles of hiking trails in this wonderland of geysers; also the largest mountain lake in North America, spectacular waterfalls, a wide variety of wildlife including some 240 species of birds in a vast wilderness spreading around the canyon of the Yellowstone River. The season is from about June 20 to September 10. Bus and special car service to and from the park entrances, a variety of accommodations. Park rangers conduct guided walks; many trails are suited to the tenderfoot hiker. For accommodations, write:

Yellowstone National Park Co.,
Yellowstone National Park, Wyo. 83020

For park information: Yellowstone National Park, Wyo.

Wyoming: GRAND TETON NATIONAL PARK, in one of the world's boldest mountain ranges, the Tetons of the Rocky Mountains. Of 225 miles of trails, some gentle ones are around String, Leigh, and Jenny Lakes; some challenging hikes for experienced trail walkers go up the Cascade or Indian Paintbrush Canyons. There are also beautiful walks in the lush, game-rich valley of Jackson Hole, carpeted with sagebrush, the northern part of which is within the park. Guided nature hikes and climbs. Accommodations include cabins, lodges, guest ranches. Mail: Moose, Wyo. 83012.

Idaho: CRATERS OF THE MOON NATIONAL MONUMENT, a natural field museum of volcanic phenomena. Hiking trails, conducted tours of caves and lava flows. Campground. Mail: Box 29, Arco, Idaho 83213.

Utah: BRYCE CANYON NATIONAL PARK, amphitheaters of brilliantly colored spires, pinnacles, walls carved by erosion. Hiking trails, guided nature walks and trips to the canyon floor. Mail: Bryce Canyon, Utah 84717.

ZION NATIONAL PARK, striking canyon and mesa landscapes, with Zion Canyon, a chasm of vertical walls but easily accessible. Trails, guided nature walks and trips to canyon rims. Lodge, cabins, campgrounds. Mail: Springdale, Utah 84767.

Utah-Colorado: DINOSAUR NATIONAL MONUMENT, a semi-arid wilderness plateau cut by deep gorges, revealing rich deposits of dinosaur fossils. Self-guided nature trails, also boat trips through the canyons. Ask locally about road conditions to the park. Address: 91 West Main St., Vernal, Utah 84078.

Colorado: ROCKY MOUNTAIN NATIONAL PARK, in the scenic portion of the Front Range of the Rockies, with 95 peaks of 10,000-foot elevation and above. Many hiking trails in this dramatic setting; guided hikes and nature walks. (Skiing in winter.) Accommodations in hotels, lodges, and camps are on private lands within the camp or nearby; for information on these, write to the Chamber of Commerce of Estes Park and Grand Lake. Mail: Box 1080, Estes Park, Colo. 80517.

Pacific States

On the map, the Pacific coast looks like one long, continuous, magnificent walk. Indeed much of it has been walked continuously, by John Muir who strode a thousand miles of it, and by others since. There is even a great trail that runs its length, the Western mate to the East's Appalachian. Fortunately the great walking of the West coast can be savored also in smaller bites. Deep forests, majestic mountains, lakes, rivers, seashore, even beautiful city walking—the Pacific states have them all. The Guide here has tried to assemble from this treasure a mixed bag of walks large and small.

GREAT TRAIL:

The Pacific Crest Trail, 2,156 miles from Canada to Mexico, on a two-foot-wide path, winds peacefully through Washington and Oregon forests, climbs to meet the John Muir Trail in Yosemite and is a mountaineer's trail from there onward for most of the way to its southern end, 15 miles from Los Angeles, before it dips to the Mexican border. It is on the Department of the Interior list for restoration. Local walk explorers may know what its condition is at any given point.

PARKLAND TRAILS

Washington: OLYMPIC NATIONAL PARK, a mountain wilderness and the finest bit of the once spreading rain forest of the Pacific Northwest, a cathedral-like woodland teeming with an unbelievable variety of flora. It is also the only national park that has snow-capped peaks, ocean beaches, alpine flowers, hot springs, active glaciers, and the rare Roosevelt elk: all this within 1,400 square miles. It is open all year, except occasionally in times of heavy snow, and has 600 miles of trails (also ski trails). For accommodations within the park, write to the superintendent. Mail: 600 East Park Ave., Port Angeles, Wash. 98362.

MOUNT RAINIER NATIONAL PARK, a single-peak glacial system radiating from an ancient volcano (in the National Park Service description). To the visitor it is a glorious mountain whose hospitable slopes support deep forests and fresh flowering meadows. The park is open all year, but the comfortable season begins May 1. Around the mountain is a 95-mile Wonderland trail, a week-long trip for seasoned hikers. But Sunday walkers can start from Sunrise or Paradise and see, in a day's walk, alpine meadows, glaciers, sometimes black bears or mountain goats. There are also other trails (including ski trails). For hotel or lodge accommodations:

Rainier National Park Co.
776 Commerce
Tacoma, Wash. 98402

For park information: Longmire, Wash. 98397.

Oregon: CRATER LAKE NATIONAL PARK, at Medford. The park surrounds an incredibly deep blue lake that fills the crater of a long-extinct volcano; around it are many-colored lava walls up to 2,000 feet high. Trails and guided nature walks. Hotel and cabin accommodations. Mail: Box 672, Medford, Ore. 97501.

California: SEQUOIA NATIONAL PARK, in the High Sierras, including Mt. Whitney, the second-highest in the country (Alaska has the highest). But walk-seekers can drive into Grant Grove, one of the park's 24 stands of sequoias, and walk on level ground in the forest of giant trees. Other, more challenging walks, also guided nature hikes and high-country pack trips during the summer. Park season for most facilities is about May 24 to October 1. Cabins, lodge accommodations. Mail: Three Rivers, Calif. 93271.

YOSEMITE NATIONAL PARK, where San Franciscans go each spring to see the Yosemite Valley floor carpeted in wildflowers. The valley, Wawona, and Mariposa Grove are open all year, but Glacier and all points north of Yosemite Valley proper only in summer. A bus goes to the park all year from Merced; from Fresno and Lake Tahoe in the summer only. The visitor sees mountain vistas of great beauty, gorges, waterfalls, as well as groves of giant sequoias. Many trails, graded for short and long hikes, hard or easy. John Muir's favorite trails can be taken by neophytes downhill, with transportation to bring them back up. Rain gear is advised for the "mist trail" to Vernal Fall and Nevada Fall. Hotels, lodges, cabins, housekeeping camps, some all year, some summer only. Skiing and ice skating in winter. Mail: Box 577, Yosemite National Park, Calif. 95389.

HAPPY ISLES NATURE CENTER is in Yosemite. Also, the Pacific Crest Trail joins the John Muir Trail here. Both are for good climbers.

LASSEN VOLCANIC NATIONAL PARK, in northwestern California. The park surrounds the largest plug dome volcano in the world, active as recently as 1914–1917. Trails, guided and self-guided trips. Season: June 10 to September 20. A wilderness with interesting volcanic phenomena. Cabins, campgrounds. Mail: Mineral, Calif. 96063.

MT. TAMALPAIS, in Marin County north of San Francisco, is honeycombed with hundreds of trails. MUIR WOODS, a 510-acre stand of glorious giant redwoods. STINSON'S BEACH, also in Marin County, a long beach walk beside the Pacific. Hardy souls also swim there.

TILDEN PARK, on the hillside above Berkeley, has 50 miles of woodland trails, good for family excursions. WILDCAT CANYON NATURE LODGE is in the area. Also good walking is the extensive University of California campus.

LAKESIDE PARK, Oakland. The Rotary Nature Science Center is in the park.

GOLDEN GATE PARK, in San Francisco, limitless beautiful walks. Also, the walk across Golden Gate Bridge: Time it to see the sunset or, alternatively, to see the salt fog roll in. Other famous walks in San Francisco: the Embarcadero; Telegraph Hill; Chinatown on the flank of Nob Hill; Russian Hill and down its side on Lombard Street, winding and full of flowers; Sutro's Gardens.

Some claim it is possible to walk in downtown Los Angeles; *Sunset Magazine* once mapped a walking tour. Angelenos find other walking places: around the reservoir, in the Hollywood hills and canyons, along the beach at Santa Monica. UCLA campus is a fine walk. Or go 14 miles to El Monte, the AUDUBON CENTER OF SOUTHERN CALIFORNIA (1000 No. Durfee Avenue), where there are 5 miles of trails on acres of river-bottom land.

Alaska:

MOUNT MCKINLEY NATIONAL PARK, surrounding North America's towering 20,300-foot king of mountains. The huge park has large glaciers of the Alaska range, caribou, and its own species of mountain sheep and grizzly bears among its wildlife. Season is June 1 to September 15. Transportation is by bus, Alaska Railroad, or air: Anchorage is the nearest city in Alaska but Seattle is not far by air. Accommodations: McKinley Park Hotel. Guided and self-guiding trail trips, climbs (also winter sports). Mail: Mount McKinley National Park, Alaska 99755.

CAMP DENALI, near Mount McKinley National Park, has wilderness programs recommended by the Wilderness Society. For information, before June 1:

Mrs. Ginny Wood
Camp Denali
Box D
College, Alaska 99735

From June 1 to September 10: at Mount McKinley National Park.

EAGLE TRAIL, a remnant of the old gold-rush mail route, is reached by driving from Girdwood up Crow Creek Road. The path zigzags easily to the top, where there is a view of glaciers.

Hawaii

Hawaii has two national parks:

HAWAII VOLCANOES NATIONAL PARK, on the island of Hawaii. Within the park are two world-famous active volcanoes, Kilauea and Mauna Loa. Lava formations are fantastic; trails also go through rain forests, lush tropical plant life, dazzling bird life. Access is from Hilo or Kailua-Kona. Accommodations at Volcano House; also campgrounds and picnic areas. Mail: Hawaii Volcanoes National Park, Hawaii 96718.

HALEAKALA NATIONAL PARK, on the island of Maui. The dormant volcano Haleakala, 10,023 feet high, has a famous crater, one of the largest and most colorful, with rare vegetation and interesting bird life. Cabins and campground. Hikes and self-guided nature trails. Access is from Kahului or Wailuku. Mail: Box 456, Kahului, Maui, Hawaii 96732.

Virgin Islands

Virgin Islands has two unusual national Parks:

BUCK ISLAND REEF NATIONAL MONUMENT, about 5 miles offshore from Christiansted, St. Croix. Mainly for underwater walking in one of the Caribbean's finest marine gardens, but the island is a rookery of pelicans and the great black man-o'-war or frigate bird.

VIRGIN ISLANDS NATIONAL PARK, on St. John. Tropical vegetation, beautiful views, beach walks.

The Walker's Checklist (U.S.A.)

This is a list of public agencies and private organizations that can furnish further information. Some are national, some regional; many have local chapters and will send their addresses on request. *Note:* Guidebook and other prices given here are subject to change.

> Adirondack Mountain Club
> Gabriels, N.Y. 12939

For Eastern New York State and the Adirondacks. Has many local chapters; many fine trails in the region. Sponsors *Guide to Adirondack Trails* ($3.25), with maps and text describing 150 trails.

> American Youth Hostels
> 14 West 8th St.
> New York, N.Y. 10011

A guide to hostels around the world.

> Appalachian Mountain Club
> 5 Joy St.
> Boston, Mass. 02108

Sells guidebooks and maps of the Appalachian Trail, especially the New England section of this 2,050-mile footpath from Maine to Georgia, the longest continuously marked walking trail in the world. Also available: *Massachusetts and Rhode Island Trail Guide* ($3.75), with maps and text for 1,000 miles of trails in these states.

> Applachian Trail Conference
> 1916 Sunderland Place N.W.
> Washington, D.C. 20036

A central source of information on the great eastern trail. Maps, trail guides, lectures, group walks, pamphlets on hiking clothes and equipment, knapsack food, list of suppliers (outfitters). Local member clubs. Potomac Appalachian Club, at the same address, for regional information.

Audubon Camps: see National Audubon Society.

> Boy Scouts of America
> Route 1
> New Brunswick, N. J. 08903

Will supply a nation-wide list of approved trails, many of them rehabilitated historical trails.

> Connecticut Forest and Park Association
> 15 Lewis St.
> Hartford, Conn. 06103

Trail information for the state.
Sponsors *Connecticut Walk Book* ($3.50), guidebook with maps.

> Federation of Western Outdoor Clubs
> 201 South Ashdale St.
> West Covina, Calif. 91790.

Can provide addresses of 36 member clubs for regional and local information.

Finger Lakes Trail Conference
Mrs. Korby Wade, Secretary
2783 Brighton-Henrietta Town Line Road
Rochester, N.Y. 14623

For Finger Lakes Trail and western New York trails. Many local member clubs; many fine trails in the region.

Green Mountain Club
108 Merchants' Row
Rutland, Vt. 05701

Trail information, especially on the Long Trail, which this club maintains. Sponsors *Long Trail Guide* ($1.95), with maps and text for this famous trail.

Horse-Shoe Trail Club
1600 Three Penn Center Plaza
Philadelphia, Pa. 19102

Specialists in the Horse-Shoe Trail. *Horse-Shoe Trail Guide* ($1).

Izaac Walton League of America
1326 Waukegan Road
Glenview, Ill. 60025

Originally for fishermen, now a conservation society. State and local chapters.

Keystone Trails Association
P.O. Box 144
Concordsville, Pa. 19331

Local clubs and trail information for Pennsylvania, southern New Jersey, also Baltimore, Md., and Wilmington, Del. Pamphlet: *Pennsylvania Hiking Trails* (50¢) lists trails and sources of maps and guides.

(For Pennsylvania, see also: Horse-Shoe Trail Club)

Mazamas
909 N.W. 19th Ave.
Portland, Ore. 97209

Famous private mountaineering club conducts weekend and summer-outing trail trips, climbs, climbing school. Climbing a qualifying snow peak with glacier is requirement for membership.

National Audubon Society
1130 Fifth Ave.
New York, N.Y. 10028

This great conservation society has long been expanding its activities to include natural science study for adult amateurs, teachers and group leaders, children. Its Nature Center Division aids in establishing community nature centers, often with extensive walking trails; write for local addresses. For walkers who wish to enrich their walking pleasures by deepening their amateur nature interests, the summer Audubon Camps offer two-week sessions through the summer season in beautiful settings with expert instruction and field trips. For information:

Audubon Camp in Maine
Audubon Camp in Wisconsin
Audubon Field Workshops in Connecticut
  (1-week sessions)
Audubon Camp of the West
  in Wind River Mountains, Wyoming

Audubon Camp Dept.
613 Riversville Road
Greenwich, Conn. 06833

Audubon Camp of the West
P.O. Box 3666
El Monte, Calif. 91733

National Parks Association
1300 New Hampshire Ave. N.W.
Washington, D.C. 20036

Private organization for the protection of national parks. Publishes *National Parks Magazine*.

National Wildlife Federation
1412 16th St. N.W.
Washington, D.C. 20002

Famous conservation organization. Publishes *National Wildlife Magazine*.

New England Trail Conference
Hope Packard, Secretary
P.O. Box 153
Ashfield, Mass. 01330

Lists of member clubs and trails in all states of the region. Pamphlet: *Hiking Trails of New England* (25¢), map of major trails and list of guidebooks and further sources. (For New England, see also: Appalachian Mountain Club, Connecticut Forest and Park Assn., Green Mountain Club.)

New Jersey Department of Conservation and Economic Development
Trenton, N.J. 08625

Folder: *New Jersey State Parks and Forests*

New York-New Jersey Trail Conference, Inc.
G.P.O. Box 2250
New York, N.Y. 10001
George M. Zoebelein, President

Federation of hiking clubs in the New York metropolitan area, maintains nearly 500 miles of trails in northern New Jersey, southeastern New York, including this portion of the Appalachian Trail. Will send lists of member clubs for regional and local information. Sponsors *New York Walk Book*. Publishes *The Trail Walker:* list of hikes, other walkers' news. (For New York, see also: Adirondack Mountain Club, Finger Lakes Trail Conference.)

New York State Conservation Department
Division of Conservation Education
Albany, N.Y. 12226

For trail and campsite information on Catskill and Adirondack state parks. Also a folder: *New York State Parks.*

Sierra Club
1050 Mills Tower
220 Bush St.
San Francisco, Calif. 94104

Its Atlantic Chapter:

Biltmore Hotel
Madison Ave. at 43rd St.
New York, N.Y. 10017

Its Great Lakes Chapter:

1614 Sherwin
Chicago, Ill. 61626

Founded in 1892 by the great American naturalist John Muir "to help people explore, enjoy, and protect parks, wilderness, waters, forests, and wildlife," the Sierra Club has become one of the great national influences for conservation and enjoyment of the country's treasure of outdoor beauty. The club and its many local branches provide information on trails, maintain them, conduct outstanding wilderness trips in the West for groups ranging from experienced trail walkers to families with very young children. Also the publisher of a distinguished list of trail-background books and guidebooks and handsome photographic art books of wilderness regions.

Ski Touring Council,
444 Madison Ave.
New York, N.Y. 10022
R. F. Mattesich, President

For trail walking on skis, ask for the booklet ($1) giving information on trail and cross-country skiing, organized trips, learning workshops, all without fee except for the participant's own expenses. The booklet also lists regional councils for similar information in the Middle West, Mountain, and Pacific states; the New York council covers New York, Pennsylvania, and New England.

Wilderness Society
729 15th St. N.W.
Washington, D.C. 20005

Western Regional Office
2422 South Downing St.
Denver, Colo. 80209

Specializes in riding trips on wilderness trails but also conducts 8-day hiking trips, some to include the whole family, in Western mountain wilderness areas. Also some backpacking trips for hardy trail walkers.

And these Federal agencies:

> U.S. Geological Survey
> Washington, D.C. 20242

For Geological Survey maps, indispensable for unguided wilderness trail walks and country rambles. Give exact location of the area desired.

> Bureau of Sport Fisheries and Wildlife
> Department of the Interior
> Washington, D.C. 20240

For information on wilderness areas and trails in national wildlife refuges and ranges.

> National Park Service
> Department of the Interior
> Washington, D.C. 20240

For information on national parks and monuments.

> U.S. Forest Service
> Washington, D.C. 20250

For maps and information on national forests.

Walks Abroad

Canada

North Americans move so comfortably back and forth across the Canada–United States boundary that they scarcely apply the word "abroad" to their sojourns on the farther side, whichever it may be. Yet the cultural and even language diversities between the two lands are sufficient to give a visitor from each side a sense of novelty in the other. When it comes to walkers, nature abets culture by providing a treasure of surprises in plants, birds, and beasts, and especially in scenic splendors. A walker from the United States soon discovers that our shared North American continent continues to have wonder and beauty in new forms as he explores northward.

Canada's beauties for the walker are most readily accessible in her superb parklands. Some are already known and loved by United States visitors. Others deserve a better acquaintance than they have.

Most familiar are these in the Canadian Rockies, north of the line that separates Montana from Canada's two western provinces, Alberta and British Columbia:

BANFF NATIONAL PARK, embracing Lake Louise and considered one of the seven scenic wonders of the world.

JASPER NATIONAL PARK, north of Banff in this all but continuous string of mountain wilderness parklands. Jasper has 4,200 square miles for the walking explorer.

WATERTON LAKES NATIONAL PARK, just across the border and continuous with Glacier National Park. Waterton is Canada's arm of the International Peace Park.

KOOTENAY, YOHO, and MOUNT REVELSTOKE, northward in that order, three national parks in British Columbia, which is Canada's Pacific province and a land rich in magnificent lakes on the western slope of the Rockies.

WOOD BUFFALO NATIONAL PARK, spreading across the northern edge of Alberta into Canada's Northwest Territory. This is a vast and splendid preserve where the great prairie land of Canada extends into forests as it approaches subarctic latitudes.

RIDING MOUNTAIN NATIONAL PARK, in Manitoba, in the heart of the rolling prairies, a thick green woodland with many lovely lakes, habitat of a wide variety of wildlife. Elevations are not great in the Canada plains any more than in those of the United States. Riding Mountain, despite its lofty designation, is for walkers, not mountain climbers.

FUNDY NATIONAL PARK, clear across the country eastward to the Atlantic coast, in the maritime province of New Brunswick. The park borders the Bay of Fundy, looking across it to the Nova Scotia peninsula; the bay itself is just above Maine and continuous with the Maine coast. We remember it from school geographies, which never failed to mention its high tides. The park will be memorable to walkers who have explored its trails and its beaches nestled in coves along a beautiful shore.

Canada has 18 national parks in all, and more than 20 regional parks, some more and some less rugged, all inviting to the walker. There is also city walking of great charm, for example in Quebec. The central source of information on them all is:

The Canadian Government Travel Bureau
Ottawa, Ontario, Canada

The bureau has these branch offices in the United States:

680 Fifth Ave., New York, N.Y. 10019
102 West Monroe St., Chicago, Ill. 60603
124 South 7th St., Minneapolis, Minn., 55402
1 Second St., San Francisco, Calif. 94105

British Isles

If a special heaven were designed for walkers to go to when they die, it would have to be modeled on the British Isles. Here we have everything; here nature and man have lived together for centuries in such gentle harmony that to American eyes, at least, it seems that no violence has been done to either. This is not, of course, strictly true. England has its industrial wastelands, and in some places the Welsh and other hills have been ravaged for their mineral wealth no less brutally than portions of the hills of Pennsylvania and West Virginia. But for the most part the land and the way it is lived in have kept their quality.

Most striking is the way they have resisted the careless adolescent destructiveness of the automobile. Put this down to history, geography, or British national character; whatever the reason, up to the second half of the twentieth century the high-octane revolution that has devastated so much of the United States has had in this countryside only a limited success. A few adequate superhighways cut across the land to take people quickly from one place to another, and they have not become lined with the neon-lighted strip morasses of an automobile culture. Even the automobile traveler can see the well-loved, well-tended, green land through which he rides. Once off the highway, the walker finds winding roads to walk, villages and countryside that invite him at the leisurely pace of human beings afoot.

In these islands the walker chooses or mixes his own blend of walking pleasures: the ruggedness of Scottish or Welsh highlands or the Derbyshire Peaks, the gentler lowlands, the meandering Cotswold lanes, soft Cornwall, soft or rugged Ireland of the south or the north. History and prehistory merge with the land in thatched cottages, Brontë-esque moors, Roman walls, ruined castles, the legendary seats of King Arthur and the high kings of Tara, the manor houses and gardens of a more spacious era and their parklike woods and meadows. And at the end of the walk there is a pub or pleasant country inn, with a fire going against the damp, a hot dinner and a mug of good country ale.

England

The English writers have been walkers; their poetry and flowing prose have been our common heritage. These are the lands that inspired them. The Guide offers a few specifics and sources for finding more. We begin with the walking places nearest London.

HORSHAM, close to London. Nearby woods filled with primroses in the spring.

THE COTSWOLDS, among the best-preserved rural areas, dotted with steep thatched roofs. Gentle hills slope to the Thames, with charming towns such as Chipping Camden, Stow-on-the-Wold, Oxford itself. The White Horse Hill in Berkshire is famous as far back as Saxon times. Blenheim Castle, the ducal seat of the Marlboroughs, Sir Winston Churchill's family, has a superb expanse of park, open to the public at stated times. Walk Oxford's university lanes, quadrangles, fields and meadows bordering the Cherwell River.

KENT, still within easy reach of London. This is Dickens country; stop at the Leather Bottle Inn in Cobham where he wrote the last part of *The Pickwick Papers.*

CORNWALL, the peninsula pointing westward into the Atlantic. The Cornish coast is famous for its climate, so much gentler than that of the rest of England, soft and sunny even in winter, with sea mists in spring and fall. Vegetation is surprisingly southern and luxuriant although trees on the coast are dwarfed by sea winds. Dolmens and megalithic monuments of the early Britons are plentiful on the Cornish moors and those of Devon, the next county eastward. In Cornwall there are walks around Land's End, Tintagel which is the legendary site of King Arthur's castle, and the beaches along the sunny southern shore. Investigate Penzance, St. Ives, both near the peninsula's tip.

EXMOOR FOREST, straddling the Somerset-Devon county line, and DARTMOOR FOREST, southward in Devon, are both famous walking places in southern England.

CHARNWOOD FOREST, in the Midlands, a miniature mountain wilderness with some of the oldest rocks in England, the remains of a primeval forest, herds of deer.

NEEDLEWOOD FOREST, near Lichfield in Staffordshire, once a royal hunting preserve. Close by is Cannock Chase, a broad moor.

HEREFORDSHIRE, also in the Midlands, lovely parklike countryside sprinkled with charming villages. Herds of the famous native Hereford cattle browse on the meadows.

COLCHESTER, in northeastern Essex, for town walking. It was founded in 49 A.D. and is believed the oldest town in England.

SUFFOLK and NORFOLK, continuing northward above London along the east. These two counties in East Anglia are sparsely populated rural areas that have changed little with time. In central Suffolk are peaceful country villages with old thatch-roof cottages. Visit Cambridge and then head eastward for good country walking.

LINCOLNSHIRE, the next county northward, with rolling hills and large level fields of tulips that attract thousands of visitors in the spring.

DERBYSHIRE, a north-central county, as striking for its natural beauty as it was when Jane Austen described it in *Pride and Prejudice*. Dovedale, in North Derbyshire, is one of England's famous beauty spots and must be visited on foot. Its trout stream, one of the finest in England, was fished by Izaak Walton and its lush green fields are still unspoiled. Near Buxton in the uplands is the celebrated Cat and Fiddle Inn where the walker can find rest and refreshment after tramping the windswept plateau. For the Peaks in Derbyshire, choose late summer when the reddish-purple heather is in bloom. At Edale, in the PEAK DISTRICT NATIONAL PARK, begins the Pennine Way, longest and toughest footpath in Britain (250 miles).

LANCASHIRE, another good walking county, still two-thirds rural. Some of Lancashire is embraced in the Lake District.

THE LAKE DISTRICT, which Gray explored and Wordsworth and Coleridge walked. Wordsworth made it unforgettable for lovers of English poetry. It spreads across the counties of Cumberland, Westmoreland and the Furness district of Lancashire, and embraces in its 700 square miles the principal lakes of England and some of its most romantic scenery. The modern walker can take long, uninterrupted but not always sunny walks: statisticians say the region has 250 rainy days a year. Sixteen lakes of the region are within the bounds of the national park, along with many historic houses and delightful old inns.

YORKSHIRE DALES, in the northeast county of York. Famous walking in beautiful country with numerous romantic old castle ruins.

Ireland

Green land, soft air, in places rugged and mountainous, with antiquities, natural beauty, and the atmosphere of mystery and magic that inspired Yeats, Synge and all the Irish poets. The countryside is still touched with faërie. Some tempting walks:

NORTH DONEGAL, on the northwest coast, with sheltered valleys and lonely lakes.

ANTRIM, in northern Ireland. The coast road here passes the Giant's Causeway, a promontory of great basalt columns, one of the dramatic scenic spots of Ireland, with ancient castle ruins perched on the crags.

FERMANAGH, also a northerly county, with seventh-century stone carvings to see.

THE MOURNE WALL WALK, along the Mourne Mountains in County Down. Some peaks rise above 2,000 feet in this relatively rugged part of Ireland. Cairns, stone pillars and similar Stonehenge-like megaliths mark the ancient culture that still lives in Irish legend and poetry. The Youth Hostels Association conducts a summer walk here.

THE BOYNE VALLEY, not far northward from Dublin. Rich in antiquities and embracing Tara, the seat of the ancient kings.

DUBLIN, a great walking city, whether or not we have read Joyce's *Ulysses* or *Dubliners* or seen Sean O'Casey's plays. If we have, the walking is all the richer.

CORK, the city and county, on Ireland's south coast.

KERRY, west of County Cork, on the Atlantic. The Lakes of Killarney are in County Kerry.

Scotland

THE HIGHLANDS, fine climbing for hardy mountain walkers, and a good network of hostels.

ABERDEEN, a start for walks north of the city where there are long stretches of heath and sand.

BERWICKSHIRE, east of Edinburgh on the North Sea, invigorating walks along the sea cliffs.

EDINBURGH, a lovely walking city, in its unique way a rival to London.

Wales

THE BLACK MOUNTAINS and the BRECON BEACONS are favorites with walkers who like long tramps in wild mountain settings.

JERSEY, "Queen of the Channel." The island has a warmer climate than the mainland, with luxuriant southern greenery and a Continental air and cuisine. Outside of St. Helier are secluded seaward coves and beautiful lush scenery for walkers to explore.

For more information. Central sources for Great Britain and Ireland in the United States are:

British Information Services
845 Third Ave.
New York, N.Y. 10022

Literature, all kinds, alluring and useful. Ask about walking in particular.

Irish Tourist Board
33 East 50th St.
New York, N.Y. 10022

City walking guides for Dublin and Cork, specific information on the Mourne Wall Walk, abundant literature on good walking throughout Ireland.

Also these transatlantic sources, London and elsewhere:

The Camping Club of Great Britain and Ireland
38 Grosvenor Gardens
London, S.W. 1

Good walking places for those interested in a long tramp.

Wales Tourist and Holiday Association
7 Park Place
Cardiff, Wales

For good tramping in Wales.

Ramblers' Association Services Ltd.
124 Finchley Road
London N.W. 3

Varied walking activities. Ask about the Hassness Hotel which the association runs in the Lake District.

Holiday Fellowship
142 North Way
London N.W. 4

Information about its Youth Guest Houses, for young people between 17 and 29.

Youth Hostels Association
Trevelyan House
St. Albans, Hertfordshire

English youth hostels are for anybody over the age of five and are usually in areas good for walking.

Country-Wide Holidays Association
Drummond St.
London N.W. 1

and

Birch Keys, Cromwell Range
Manchester 14

The C.H.A., as it is known, conducts walking excursions.

Royal Camping Club
35 Old Kent Road
London S.E. 1

Primarily interested in camping but can provide information on good walking areas.

> Publishers Ltd.
> 69 Victoria St.
> London S.W. 1

For information about 400 great houses that have opened their doors for sight-seeing and their gardens and parks for walking, write for the publication: *Historic Houses, Castles, and Gardens in Great Britain and Ireland.* Enclose 70¢.

Country Walks, a London Transport booklet, is on sale at London Underground stations.

For London walking:

> British Travel Association
> 64/65 St. James St.
> London S.W. 1

Has an excellent 56-page booklet with a fine map of the city and two walking tours.

> M. C. Pike
> 49 Lynette Ave.
> London S.W. 4

Organized walking tours of London, for those who would like to join a group walk.

Austria

Famous walking, as well as mountain climbing, in the Austrian Alps. For information on those and other walks:

> Austrian State Tourist Department
> 444 Madison Ave.
> New York, N.Y. 10022

And in Austria:

> Austrian Travel Agency
> Friedrichstrasse 7
> Vienna 1

> Stadtsverkehrsbuero
> Makartplatz 9
> Salzburg

and

> Burggraben 3
> Innsbruck

Belgium

Belgium's old Gothic cities are interesting walking. For both city and country walking:

> Belgian Tourist Bureau
> 589 Fifth Ave.
> New York, N.Y. 10017

And in Belgium:

> Official Belgian Tourist Bureau
> Brouckere
> Brussels

and

> St. Baafsplein 10
> Ghent

Denmark

The Danes are a nation of walkers and eagerly recommend their own favorite walking places. Here are some:

FYN: In this island, you can stroll through the towns of Kerteminde and Fåborg, picturesquely situated on fjords, through Odense where Hans Christian Andersen was born, through Marstal with its narrow winding streets, a town famous for its sailing ships. Fyn has its own Tourist Association, to give particulars for its own and the many surrounding islands.

BORNHOLM, a holiday island for Danes. It has more sunshine than the rest of Denmark; nightingales sing in its trees, which include cherry, mulberry, and fig. A large forest and fine white beaches invite walking.

JYLLAND (Jutland), Denmark's large rural peninsula. Lovely hills and valleys, plentiful sandy wagon roads through a still rural land.

COPENHAGEN, where everybody walks. A pocket-size brochure, *Welcome to Wonderful Copenhagen,* maps three suggested strolls through the city.

For more information:

> Danish National Travel Office
> 505 Fifth Ave.
> New York, N.Y. 10017

And in Denmark:

> National Travel Association of Denmark
> 5–7 Banegårdspladsen
> Copenhagen

The Danish National Camping Committee lists 155 authorized campsites.

Finland

Beautiful small cities, deep northern forest wildernesses. For hardy trampers, about 160 youth hostels scattered through the country provide accommodations, mostly in school buildings. For information·

> Finnish National Travel Office
> 505 Fifth Ave.
> New York, N.Y. 10017

And in Finland:

> Finnish Travel Association
> Mikonkatu 15A
> Helsinki

France

Although the French are not typically walkers, they know their country's beautiful walking places. They suggest:

PARIS, where visitors walk even if the Parisians rarely do. Air France has a good little brochure, *Paris à Pied*. Recommended for walking and picnicking in the environs are St.-Germain-en-Laye, Marly, Île-Adam, Chantilly, Ermenonville, Montmorency, Rambouillet, Fontainebleau. The Commissariat Général de Tourisme has a folder, *Île de France*, with an excellent map of forest areas.

THE CHAMPAGNE DISTRICT, a varied landscape of valleys, forests, chalk plains; vineyards of course. For the speleologist walker, caves are as much as 15 miles deep. For the archeologist walker, there are old Roman roads crisscrossing the beautiful countryside.

BURGUNDY, called "a walker's paradise," and very good wine at the inns.

ALSACE-LORRAINE provides a scenic Route du Vin, which winds through villages and vineyards between Mulhouse and Strasbourg. In Lorraine one can walk the countryside where Joan of Arc roamed as a child.

THE JURA MOUNTAINS, French foothills of the Alps, for long tramps along winding forest roads, rushing streams, quiet lakes.

CHAMONIX, in the French Alps, the center for real mountain climbing. The Club Alpin Français and the Union International des Centres de Montagne give beginners' courses.

BRITTANY, walks in old Breton towns and along the rough, rocky coast.

THE LOIRE VALLEY, lovely walking particularly in the autumn when the grapes are harvested for the château country's light white wines. Stop at one of the châteaux that now take guests (see below for information). Or at one of the permitted campsites in the forests of Chinon, Loches, Blois (list supplied by the Touring Club de France; see also below).

THE RHONE VALLEY, especially Avignon with its narrow ancient streets. Nearby is Vaison-la-Romaine where archeologist walkers can stroll on the streets (excavated) of a Roman town of the second century B.C.

THE DORDOGNE, famous valley of the prehistoric caves with their paleolithic paintings. The nearby Auvergne countryside offers gentle mountain slopes, extinct volcanoes, extensive ancient lava beds, deep forests and lakes.

CAP FERRAT, on the Riviera. One of the loveliest promenades in the world follows the west coast and is reserved to walkers (cars are barred).

For further information:

French Government Tourist Office
610 Fifth Ave.
New York, N.Y. 10020

Air France
683 Fifth Ave.
New York, N.Y. 10022

For the walking guide to Paris, *Paris à Pied*.

And in France:

French Official Tourist Organization
8 Ave. de l'Opéra
Paris

Ask for brochures of châteaux-hotels and country houses that accommodate guests. Also for the folder *Île de France*, put out by the Commissariat Général de Tourisme.

La Société Mycologique de France
16 Rue Claude Bernard
Paris

For conducted mushroom hunts, from April to November, combining walks in the woods with instruction about France's 5,000 different species of mushrooms.

Fédération Française de Camping et de Caravaning
22 Ave. Victoria
Paris

and

Centre de Documentation au Service des Campeurs
62 Ave. Parmentier
Paris

Both these offices have free information for foreign campers and walkers. The Fédération has an excellent map indicating special landscape features, castles, spas, and Gallo-Roman remains.

Fédération Unie des Auberges de la Jeunesse
11-bis Rue de Milan
Paris

The French youth hostel association. France has about 200 hostels for hikers and cyclists.

Touring Club de France
65 Ave. de la Grande Armée
Paris 16

For a list of sites where camping is permitted throughout France.

Germany

West Germany has 60,000 miles of marked trails. Paths in the Black Forest go through woods where deer graze and Alpine flowers grow amid the rocks. At Herrenalb, trails are graded according to the degree of challenge, and are marked with hearts in four different colors. In North Bavaria are the Fichtel Mountains, which Goethe called "nature's dispensary" because of their healthfulness, and the Spessart Hills where hikers may sometimes see wild boars. Germany also has hotels made over from or on the site of old castles. For information:

German Tourist Information Office
500 Fifth Ave.
New York, N.Y. 10036

General walking information, also information on castle hotels.

German Travel Advisors
500 Fifth Ave.
New York, N.Y. 10036

and

11 South La Salle St.
Chicago, Ill. 60603

And in Germany:

Verkehrsamt
2 Bahnhofplatz
Munich

and

Hauptbahnhof
Frankfurt a/Main

Camping and campsites. Most of West Germany's 250 camps are good.

Holland

Camping is very popular in Holland, but cycling is more to the Dutch taste than walking. Dutch cities are pleasant walking. For more information on city and country:

Netherlands National Tourist Office
605 Fifth Ave.
New York, N.Y. 10017

And in Holland:

V.V.V.
5 Rokin
Amsterdam

and

19 Stadhuisplein
Rotterdam

Italy

ROME, on foot: *Roma a Piedi,* a leaflet put out by the Bettoja Hotels, has 11 walking tours, one specifically for antique hunters. For more adventurous walking:

The Italian Government Tourist Office
626 Fifth Ave.
New York, N.Y. 10020

Information on youth and student hostels, the International Tourist Camping Ground at Castelfusano at Lido di Ostia, the Pine Woods of Rome and other camping sites. Ask also about walks and accommodations around Florence and in the Tuscan and Umbrian hills.

Norway

Great forest and mountain walking in Norway, with a string of hostels spaced a day's walking apart. The Norwegians recommend warm clothing, assure us that their marked trails are suitable even for inexperienced walkers and that beautiful scenic walks are within a short distance of most railway stations through their country. Information:

> Norwegian National Travel Office
> 505 Fifth Ave.
> New York, N.Y. 10017

And in Norway:

> Norway Travel Association
> 1 H. Heyerdahlsgate
> Oslo

and

> Raadhusgaten
> Oslo

An inexpensive guidebook, *Mountain Holidays in Norway*, with information on the network of lodges and trails, is sold by the Sjellanger Bookstore, 6005 Eighth Ave., Brooklyn, N.Y. 11220.

Portugal

The Government-run inns or *pousadas* are very good, clean and inexpensive. (*Note:* Slacks and shorts are not permitted for women in Portugal.) Information:

> Portuguese Government Tourist Office
> (Casa de Portugal)
> 570 Fifth Ave.
> New York, N.Y. 10036

And in Portugal:

> Comissariado do Turismo
> Palacio Foz
> Praça dos Restauradores 21
> Lisbon

and

> S.N.I.
> Praça Dom João I 25
> Oporto

Spain

The Government-run inns, here called *paradores,* are good stopping places
for walkers. Some were old castles or monasteries. (*Note:* Slacks and shorts
are not permitted for women in Spain.) Information:

> Spanish National Tourist Office
> 589 Fifth Ave.
> New York, N.Y. 10022

And in Spain:

> Dirección General del Turismo
> Princesa 1
> Madrid

and

> Duque de Medinaceli 2
> Madrid

and

> Av. José Antonio 658
> Barcelona

Sweden

More than half of Sweden is covered with forest and woodland. In the
château country are hundreds of castles, and in sunny southern Sweden the
walker can see rock carvings of the Bronze Age. Sweden's cities are also old,
interesting, beautifully situated, and highly walkable. For information about
city, country, and mountain tramping:

> Swedish National Travel Office
> 505 Fifth Ave.
> New York, N.Y. 10017

And in Sweden:

> Turisttrafiksörbundet
> Klara Västra Kyrkogatan 6
> Stockholm

and

> Drottningtorget
> Göteborg C

and

> Lilla Nygatan 9
> Malmö

Switzerland

You do not have to be a mountaineer to enjoy Switzerland. The valleys, too, are inviting to walkers and the pleasant hotels and guest houses provide Swiss-quality rest and refreshment. For information:

Swiss National Tourist Office
608 Fifth Ave.
New York, N.Y. 10020

And in Switzerland:

Verkehrsbureau
20 Bundesgasse
Bern

and

Bahnhofplatz
Zurich

SHOPPING GUIDE

Casual walkers for pleasure are often unaware of the many kinds of walking clothes, shoes, and rough-weather wear available today that could make even a day's ramble more comfortable, let alone a weekend or a week's walking vacation. Trail walkers, backpackers, mountain climbers and all the outdoorsmen who take their nature sports seriously know the sources for sturdy, lightweight, hard-wearing clothes and equipment which the ordinary city shop or department store is not usually equipped to carry. A catalogue from an experienced outdoors outfitter or supplier is likely to be a revelation to the innocent Sunday walker (for an advance look at what a catalogue can reveal, see Chapter 9, "Comfort Is the Fashion," in this book).

The Guide has therefore assembled a list of suppliers, recommended and used by members of such knowledgeable organizations as the Sierra Club and the Wilderness Society. All the firms listed here send catalogues on request and sell by mail. (Companies that do not send catalogues are omitted for that reason, although they may be equally worthy of investigation.)

Names marked with an asterisk also supply lightweight foods for knapsack carrying and camp cooking. *Note:* The Sierra Club's new paperback book, *Food for Knapsackers and Other Trail Travelers,* is an indispensable pack item; see the Walker's Bookshelf in later pages herein.

New England States:

L. L. Bean
Freeport, Maine 04032

Stow-A-Way Products
Cohasset, Mass. 02025

Corcoran, Inc.
Stoughton, Mass. 02072

Peter Limmer and Sons
Intervale, N.H. 03845

Middle Atlantic States:

Abercrombie and Fitch Co.
Madison Ave. and 45th St.
New York, N.Y. 10017

Camp and Trail
112 Chambers St.
New York, N.Y. 10007

Thomas Black and Sons
Ogdensburg, N.Y. 13669

Southern States:

*H & H Surplus Center
1104 West Baltimore St.
Baltimore, Md. 21223

Trailblazer
P.O. Box 1
Highlands, N.C. 28741

Middle West:

Abercrombie and Fitch Co.
9 North Wabash Ave.
Chicago, Ill. 60602

Downs and Company, Dept. 666
(for pedometer)
1014 Davis St.
Evanston, Ill. 60204

Gokey Co.
94 East 4th St.
St. Paul, Minn. 55101

Herter's, Inc.
Waseca, Minn. 56093

Laacke and Joys Co.
1433 North Water St.
Milwaukee, Wis. 53202

Southwest:

*Army and Navy Surplus
Roswell, N. Mex. 88201

Mountain States:

Gerry Mountaineering Equipment Co.
Box 910
Boulder, Colo. 80302

*Holubar
1215 Grandview (or Box 7)
Boulder, Colo. 80302

*Ace Sporting Goods
5300 West 44th Ave.
Denver, Colo. 80216

*Gerry Mountaineering Equipment Co.
Ward, Colo. 80481

Pacific States:

Eddie Bauer, Expedition Outfitters
417 East Pine St.
Seattle, Wash. 98122

*Recreational Equipment
523 Pike St.
Seattle, Wash. 98101

Norm Thompson
1815 N.W. Thurman
Portland, Ore. 97209

Abercrombie and Fitch Co.
220 Post St.
San Francisco, Calif. 94108

*Gerry Mountain Sports of San Francisco Inc.
315 Sutter St.
San Francisco, Calif. 94108

*The Smilie Co.
536 Mission St.
San Francisco, Calif. 94105

*The Ski Hut
1615 University Ave.
Berkeley, Calif. 94703

A. I. Kelty Manufacturing Co.
P.O. Box 3453
Glendale, Calif. 91201

Highland Outfitters
P.O. Box 121
Riverside, Calif. 92502

Part III

THE COMPANY
OF WALKERS

A peripatetic ramble through the literature of walking, to which is added THE WALKER'S BOOKSHELF.

THE OPEN ROAD

by Walt Whitman

Afoot and light-hearted I take to the open road,
Healthy, free, the world before me,
The long brown path before me leading wherever I choose.

Henceforth I ask not good-fortune, I myself am good-fortune,
Henceforth I whimper no more, postpone no more, need nothing,
Done with indoor complaints, libraries, querulous criticisms,
Strong and content I travel the open road.

—Leaves of Grass

ON GOING A JOURNEY

by William Hazlitt

When William Hazlitt was twenty-one, he found it difficult to express himself . . . a terrible burden to a young man who was trying to make a living as a writer. He turned to painting, an enterprise for which he showed considerable talent. It was not until he met Charles Lamb, and had painted the portrait of Lamb that now hangs in the National Portrait Gallery in London, that his interest in writing was rekindled. When his idol, Napoleon, was defeated at Waterloo, he had a nervous breakdown. But he recovered, to write The Life of Napoleon Buonaparte *in four volumes and the series of essays published under the titles* Table Talk, Plain Speaker, *and* The Round Table. *He died at the age of fifty-two, in the presence of Charles Lamb, his own son, and a few other loyal friends. His last words were, "Well, I've had a happy life."*

ONE OF THE PLEASANTEST things in the world is going a journey; but I like to go by myself. I can enjoy society in a room; but out of doors, nature is company enough for me. I am then never less alone than when alone.

"The fields his study, nature was his book."

I cannot see the wit of walking and talking at the same time. When I am in the country I wish to vegetate like the country. . . . I go out of town in order to forget the town and all that is in it. . . . I like more elbow-room and fewer incumbrances. I like solitude, when I give myself up to it, for the sake of solitude; nor do I ask for

"a friend in my retreat,
Whom I may whisper solitude is sweet."

The soul of a journey is liberty, perfect liberty, to think, feel, do, just as one pleases. We go a journey chiefly to be free of all impediments and of all inconveniences; to leave ourselves behind, much more to get rid of others. . . . For once let me have a truce with impertinence. Give me the clear blue sky over my head, and the green turf beneath my feet, a winding road before me, and a three hours' march to dinner—and then to thinking! It is hard if I cannot start some game on these lone heaths. I laugh, I run, I leap, I sing for joy. From the point of yonder rolling cloud I plunge into my past being, and revel there. . . . Then long-forgotten things, like "sunken wrack and sumless treasuries," burst upon my eager sight, and I begin to feel, think, and be myself again. Instead of an awkward silence, broken by attempts at wit or dull common-places, mine is that undisturbed silence of the heart which alone is perfect eloquence. No one likes puns, alliterations, antitheses, argument, and analysis better than I do; but I sometimes had rather be without them. . . . Is not this wild rose sweet without a comment? Does not this daisy leap to my heart set in its coat of emerald? Yet if I were to explain to you the circumstance that has so endeared it to me, you would only smile. Had I not better then keep it to myself, and let it serve me to brood over, from here to yonder craggy point, and from thence onward to the far-distant horizon? I should be but bad company all that way, and therefore prefer being alone. I have heard it said that you may, when the moody fit comes on, walk or ride on by yourself, and indulge your reveries. But this looks like a breach of manners, a neglect of others, and you are thinking all the time that you ought to rejoin your party. "Out upon such half-faced fellowship," say I. I like to be either entirely to myself, or entirely at the disposal of others; to talk or be silent, to walk or sit still, to be sociable or solitary. . . . "Let me have a companion of my way," says Sterne, "were it but to remark how the shadows lengthen as the sun declines." It is beautifully said; but, in my opinion, this continual comparing of notes interferes with the involuntary impression of things upon the mind, and hurts the sentiment. If you only hint what you feel in a kind of dumb show, it is insipid: if you have to explain it, it is making a toil of a pleasure. You cannot read the book of nature without being perpetually put to the trouble of translating it for the benefit of others. I am for this synthetical method on a journey in preference to the analytical. I am content to lay in a stock of ideas then, and to examine and anatomise them afterwards. I want to see my vague notions float like the down of the thistle before the breeze, and not to have them entangled in the briars and thorns of controversy. For once, I like to have it all my own way; and this is impossible unless you are alone. . . . I have no objection to argue a point with any one for twenty miles of measured road, but not for pleasure. If you remark the scent of a bean-field crossing the road, perhaps your fellow-traveller has no smell. If you point to a distant object, perhaps he is short-sighted, and has to take out his glass to look at it. . . . Now I never quarrel with myself, and take all my own conclusions for granted till I find it necessary to defend them against objections. It is not merely that you may not be of accord on the objects and circumstances that present themselves before you—these may recall a number of objects, and lead to associations too delicate and refined to be possibly communicated to others. Yet these I love to cherish, and sometimes still fondly clutch them, when I can escape from the throng to do so. To give way to our feelings before company seems extravagance or affectation; and, on the other hand, to have to unravel this mystery of our being at every turn, and to make others take an equal interest in it (otherwise the end is not answered), is a task to which few are competent. We must "give it an understanding, but no tongue." My old friend Coleridge, however, could do both. He could go on in the most delightful explanatory way over hill and dale a summer's day, and convert a landscape into a didactic poem or a Pindaric ode. "He talked far above singing." If I could so clothe my ideas in sounding and flowing words, I might perhaps wish to have some one with me to admire the swelling theme; or I could be more content, were it possible for me still to hear his echoing voice in the woods of All-Foxden. They had "that fine madness in them which our first poets had"; and if they could have been caught by some rare instrument, would have breathed such strains as the following:—

> "Here be woods as green
> As any, air likewise as fresh and sweet
> As when smooth Zephyrus plays on the fleet
> Face of the curled streams, with flow'rs as many
> As the young spring gives, and as choice as any;
> Here be all new delights, cool streams and wells,
> Arbours o'ergrown with woodbine, caves and dells;
> Choose where thou wilt, whilst I sit by and sing,
> Or gather rushes to make many a ring
> For thy long fingers; tell thee tales of love,
> How the pale Phœbe, hunting in a grove,
> First saw the boy Endymion, from whose eyes
> She took eternal fire that never dies;

> How she convey'd him softly in a sleep,
> His temples bound with poppy, to the steep
> Head of old Latmos, where she stoops each night,
> Gilding the mountain with her brother's light,
> To kiss her sweetest."

Fletcher's *Faithful Shepherdess.*

Had I words and images at command like these, I would attempt to wake the thoughts that lie slumbering on golden ridges in the evening clouds: but at the sight of nature my fancy, poor as it is, droops and closes up its leaves, like flowers at sunset. I can make nothing out on the spot:—I must have time to collect myself. . . .

I grant, there is one subject on which it is pleasant to talk on a journey; and that is, what one shall have for supper when we get to our inn at night. The open air improves this sort of conversation or friendly altercation, by setting a keener edge on appetite. . . . How fine it is to enter some old town, walled and turreted, just at approach of night-fall, or to come to some straggling village, with the lights streaming through the surrounding gloom; and then, after inquiring for the best entertainment that the place affords, to "take one's ease at one's inn"! These eventful moments in our lives' history are too precious, too full of solid, heart-felt happiness to be frittered and dribbled away in imperfect sympathy. I would have them all to myself, and drain them to the last drop: they will do to talk of or to write about afterwards. What a delicate speculation it is, after drinking whole goblets of tea—

"The cups that cheer, but not inebriate,"

and letting the fumes ascend into the brain, to sit considering what we shall have for supper—eggs and a rasher, a rabbit smothered in onions, or an excellent veal-cutlet! . . . Then, in the intervals of pictured scenery and Shandean contemplation, to catch the preparation and the stir in the kitchen. . . . These hours are sacred to silence and to musing, to be treasured up in the memory, and to feed the source of smiling thoughts hereafter. . . . I associate nothing with my travelling companion but present objects and passing events. In his ignorance of me and my affairs, I in a manner forget myself. But a friend reminds one of other things, rips up old grievances, and destroys the abstraction of the scene. He comes in ungraciously between us and our imaginary character. . . . The *incognito* of an inn is one of its striking privileges—"lord of one's self, uncumber'd with a name." Oh! it is great to shake off the trammels of the world and of public opinion—to lose our importunate, tormenting, everlasting personal identity in the elements of nature, and become the creature of the moment, clear of all ties—to hold to the universe only by a dish of sweet-breads, and to owe nothing but the score of the evening—and no longer seeking for applause and meeting with contempt, to be known by no other title than *the Gentleman in the parlour!* . . . We baffle prejudice and disappoint conjecture; and from being so to others, begin to be objects of curiosity and wonder even to ourselves. . . . I have certainly spent some enviable hours at inns—sometimes when I have been left entirely to myself, and have tried to solve some metaphysical problem, as once at Witham-common, where I found out the proof that likeness is not a case of the association of ideas . . . —at other times I might mention luxuriating in books, with a peculiar interest in this way, as I remember sitting up half the night to read *Paul and Virginia,* which I picked up at an inn at Bridgewater, after being drenched in the rain all day. . . . It was on the tenth of April, 1798, that I sat down to a volume of the *New Eloise,* at the inn at Llangollen, over a bottle of sherry and a cold chicken. The letter I chose was that in which St. Preux describes his feelings as he first caught a glimpse from the heights of the Jura of the Pays de Vaud, which I had brought with me as a *bon bouche* to crown the evening with. It was my birth-day, and I had for the first time come from a place in the neighbourhood to visit this delightful spot. The road to Llangollen turns off between Chirk and Wrexham; and on passing a certain point you come all at once upon the valley, which opens like an amphitheatre, broad, barren hills rising in majestic state on either side, with "green upland swells that echo to the bleat of flocks" below, and the river Dee babbling over its stony bed in the midst of them. The valley at this time "glittered green with sunny showers," and a budding ash-tree dipped its tender branches in the chiding stream. How proud, how glad I was to walk along the high road that overlooks the delicious prospect, repeating the lines which I have just quoted from Mr. Coleridge's poems! But besides the prospect which opened beneath my feet, another also opened to my inward sight, a heavenly vision, on which were written, in letters large as Hope could make them, these four words, LIBERTY, GENIUS, LOVE, VIRTUE; which have since faded into the light of common day, or mock my idle gaze.

"The beautiful is vanished, and returns not."

Still I would return some time or other to this enchanted spot; but I would return to it alone. What other self could I find to share that influx of thoughts, of regret, and delight, the fragments of which I could hardly conjure up to myself, so much have they been broken and defaced. I could stand on some tall rock, and overlook the precipice of years that separates me from what I then was. I was at that time going shortly to visit the poet whom I have above named. Where is he now? Not only I myself have changed; the world which was then new to me, has become old and incorrigible. . . .

There is hardly anything that shows the short-sightedness or capriciousness of the imagination more than travelling does. With change of place we change our ideas; nay, our opinions and feelings. We can by an effort indeed transport ourselves to old and long-forgotten scenes, and then the picture of the mind revives again; but we forget those that we have just left. It seems that we can think but of one place at a time. The canvas of the fancy is but of a certain extent, and if we paint one set of objects upon it, they immediately efface every other. We cannot enlarge our conceptions, we only shift our point of view. The landscape bares its bosom to the enraptured eye, we take our fill of it, and seem as if we could form no other image of beauty or grandeur. We pass on, and think no more of it: the horizon that shuts it from our sight, also blots it from our memory like a dream. In travelling through a wild barren country I can form no idea of a woody and cultivated one. It appears to me that all the world must be barren, like what I see of it. In the country we forget the town, and in town we despise the country. . . . All that part of the map that we do not see before us is a blank. The world in our conceit of it is not much bigger than a nutshell. It is not one prospect expanded into another, county joined to county, kingdom to kingdom, lands to seas, making an image voluminous and vast;—the mind can form no larger idea of space than the eye can take in at a single glance. The rest is a name written in a map, a calculation of arithmetic. For instance, what is the true signification of that immense mass of territory and population known by the name of China to us? An inch of pasteboard on a wooden globe, of no more account than a China orange! Things near us are seen of the size of life: things at a distance are diminished to the size of the understanding. We measure the universe by ourselves, and even comprehend the texture of our being only piece-meal. In this way, however, we remember an infinity of things and places. The mind is like a mechanical instrument that plays a great variety of tunes, but it must play them in succession. One idea recalls another, but it at the same time excludes all others. In trying to renew old recollections, we cannot as it were unfold the whole web of our existence; we must pick out the single threads. So in coming to a place where we have formerly lived, and with which we have intimate associations, every one must have found that the feeling grows more vivid the nearer we approach the spot, from the mere anticipation of the actual impression: we remember circumstances, feelings, persons, faces, names that we had not thought of for years; but for the time all the rest of the world is forgotten! . . .

I have no objection to go to see ruins, aqueducts, pictures, in company with a friend or a party, but rather the contrary, for the former reason reversed. They are intelligible matters, and will bear talking about. The sentiment here is not tacit, but communicable and overt. Salisbury Plain is barren of criticism, but Stonehenge will bear a discussion antiquarian, picturesque, and philosophical. In setting out on a party pf pleasure, the first consideration always is where we shall go to: in taking a solitary ramble, the question is what we shall meet with by the way. "The mind is its own place"; nor are we anxious to arrive at the end of our journey. I can myself do the honours indifferently well to works of art and curiosity. I once took a party to Oxford with no mean *éclat*—shewed them that seat of the Muses at a distance,

"With glistering spires and pinnacles adorn'd—"

descanted on the learned air that breathes from the grassy quadrangles and stone walls of halls and colleges—was at home in the Bodleian; and at Blenheim quite superseded the powdered Cicerone that attended us, and that pointed in vain with his wand to commonplace beauties in matchless pictures. As another exception to the above reasoning, I should not feel confident in venturing on a journey in a foreign country without a companion. I should want at intervals to hear the sound of my own language. There is an involuntary antipathy in the mind of an Englishman to foreign manners and notions that requires the assistance of social sympathy to carry it off. As the distance from home increases, this relief, which was at first a luxury, becomes a passion and an appetite. A person would almost feel stifled to find himself in the deserts of Arabia without friends and countrymen: there must be allowed to be something in the view of Athens or old Rome that claims the utterance of speech; and I own that the Pyramids are too mighty for any single contemplation. In such situations, so opposite to all one's ordinary train of ideas, one seems a species by one's-self, a limb torn off from society, unless one can meet with instant fellowship and support.—Yet I did not feel this want or craving very pressing once, when I first set my foot on the laughing shores of France. Calais was peopled with novelty and delight. The confused, busy murmur of the place was like oil and wine poured into my ears; nor did the mariners' hymn, which was sung from the top of an old crazy vessel in the harbour, as the sun went down, send an alien sound into my soul. I only breathed the air of general humanity. I walked over "the vine-covered hills and gay regions of France," erect and satisfied; for the image of man was not cast down and chained to the foot of arbitrary thrones: I was at no loss for language, for that of all the great schools of painting was open to me. The whole is vanished like a shade. Pictures, heroes, glory, freedom, all are fled: nothing remains but the Bourbons and the French people!—There is undoubtedly a sensation in travelling into foreign parts that is to be had nowhere else; but it is more pleasing at the time than lasting. It is too remote from our habitual associations to be a common topic of discourse or reference, and, like a dream or another state of existence, does not piece into our daily modes of life. It is an animated but a momentary hallucination. It demands an effort to exchange our actual for our ideal identity; and to feel the pulse of our old transports revive very keenly, we must "jump" all our present comforts and connexions. Our romantic and itinerant character is not to be domesticated. Dr. Johnson remarked how little foreign travel added to the facilities of conversation in those who had been abroad. In fact, the time we have spent there is both delightful, and in one sense instructive; but it appears to be cut out of our substantial, downright existence, and never to join kindly on to it. We are not the same, but another, and perhaps more enviable individual, all the time we are out of our own country. We are lost to ourselves, as well as our friends. So the poet somewhat quaintly sings,

> "Out of my country and myself I go."

Those who wish to forget painful thoughts, do well to absent themselves for a while from the ties and objects that recall them; but we can be said only to fulfil our destiny in the place that gave us birth. I should on this account like well enough to spend the whole of my life in travelling abroad, if I could anywhere borrow another life to spend afterwards at home!

—New Monthly Magazine, January, 1822

WALKING TOURS

by Robert Louis Stevenson

It is hard to imagine that the author of Treasure Island *and* Virginibus Puerisque *started out in life to be an engineer and then a lawyer. It was only by a wrinkle of fate that he began to write, subsequently producing* Kidnapped, The Strange Case of Dr. Jekyll and Mr. Hyde *and* A Child's Garden of Verses. *He was born in Edinburgh, lived in Monterey, died in Samoa.*

IT MUST not be imagined that a walking tour, as some would have us fancy, is merely a better or worse way of seeing the country. There are many ways of seeing landscape quite as good; and none more vivid, in spite of canting dilettantes, than from a railway train. But landscape on a walking tour is quite accessory. He who is indeed of the brotherhood does not voyage in quest of the picturesque, but of certain jolly humours—of the hope and spirit with which the march begins at morning, and the peace and spiritual repletion of the evening's rest. He cannot tell whether he puts his knapsack on, or takes it off, with more delight. The excitement of the departure puts him in key for that of the arrival. Whatever he does is not only a reward in itself, but will be further rewarded in the sequel; and so pleasure leads on to pleasure in an endless chain. It is this that so few can understand; they will either be always lounging or always at five miles an hour; they do not play off the one against the other, prepare all day for the evening, and all evening for the next day. And, above all, it is here that your overwalker fails of comprehension. His heart rises against those who drink their curaçoa in liqueur glasses, when he himself can swill it in a brown john. He will not believe that the flavour is more delicate in the smaller dose. He will not believe that to walk this unconscionable distance is merely to stupefy and brutalise himself, and come to his inn, at night, with a sort of frost on his five wits, and a starless night of darkness in his spirit. Not for him the mild luminous evening of the temperate walker! He has nothing left of man but a physical need for bedtime and a double nightcap; and even his pipe, if he be a smoker, will be savourless and disenchanted. It is the fate of such an one to take twice as much trouble as is needed to obtain happiness, and miss the happiness in the end; he is the man of the proverb, in short, who goes farther and fares worse.

Now, to be properly enjoyed, a walking tour should be gone upon alone. If you go in a company, or even in pairs, it is no longer a walking tour in anything but name; it is something else, and more in the nature of a picnic. A walking tour should be gone upon alone, because freedom is of the essence; because you should be able to stop and go on, and follow this way or that, as the freak takes you; and because you must have your own pace, and neither trot alongside a champion walker, nor mince in time with a girl. And then you must be open to all impressions, and let your thoughts take colour from what you see. You should be as a pipe for any wind to play upon. "I cannot see the wit," says Hazlitt, "of walking and talking at the same time. When I am in the country I wish to vegetate like the country," which is the gist of all that can be said upon the matter. There should be no cackle of voices at your elbow, to jar on the meditative silence of the morning. And so long as a man is reasoning he cannot surrender himself to that fine intoxication that comes of much motion in the open air, that begins in a sort of a dazzle and sluggishness of the brain, and ends in a peace that passes comprehension.

During the first day or so of any tour there are moments of bitterness, when the traveler feels more than coldly towards his knapsack, when he is half in a mind to throw it bodily over the hedge, and, like Christian on a similar occasion, "give three leaps and go on singing." And yet it soon acquires a property of easiness. It becomes magnetic; the spirit of the journey enters into it. And no sooner have you passed the straps over your shoulder than the lees of sleep are cleared from you, you pull yourself together with a shake, and fall at once into your stride. And surely, of all possible moods, this, in which a man takes the road, is the best. Of course, if he *will* keep thinking of his anxieties, if he *will* open the merchant Abudah's chest and walk arm-in-arm with the hag—why, wherever he is, and whether he walk fast or slow, the chances are that he will not be happy. And so much the more shame to himself! There are perhaps thirty men setting forth at that same hour, and I would lay a large

wager there is not another dull face among the thirty. It would be a fine
thing to follow, in a coat of darkness, one after another of these wayfarers, some summer morning, for the first few miles upon the road. This
one, who walks fast, with a keen look in his eyes, is all concentrated in his
own mind; he is up at his loom, weaving and weaving, to set the landscape to words. This one peers about, as he goes, among the grasses; he
waits by the canal to watch the dragon-flies; he leans on the gate of the
pasture, and cannot look enough upon the complacent kine. And here
comes another, talking, laughing, and gesticulating to himself. His face
changes from time to time, as indignation flashes from his eyes or anger
clouds his forehead. He is composing articles, delivering orations, and
conducting the most impassioned interviews, by the way. A little farther
on, and it is as like as not he will begin to sing. And well for him,
supposing him to be no great master in that art, if he stumble across no
stolid peasant at a corner; for on such an occasion, I scarcely know which
is the more troubled, or whether it is worse to suffer the confusion of your
troubadour or the unfeigned alarm of your clown. A sedentary population, accustomed, besides, to the strange mechanical bearing of the
common tramp, can in no wise explain to itself the gaiety of these passers-
by. I knew one man who was arrested as a runaway lunatic, because,
although a full-grown person with a red beard, he skipped as he went like
a child. And you would be astonished if I were to tell you all the grave
and learned heads who have confessed to me that, when on walking tours,
they sang—and sang very ill—and had a pair of red ears when, as
described above, the inauspicious peasant plumped into their arms from
round a corner. And here, lest you should think I am exaggerating, is
Hazlitt's own confession, from his essay "On Going a Journey," which is
so good that there should be a tax levied on all who have not read it:—

"Give me the clear blue sky over my head," says he, "and the green
turf beneath my feet, a winding road before me, and a three hours' march
to dinner—and then to thinking! It is hard if I cannot start some game on
these lone heaths. I laugh, I run, I leap, I sing for joy."

Bravo! After that adventure of my friend with the policeman, you
would not have cared, would you, to publish that in the first person? But
we have no bravery nowadays, and, even in books, must all pretend to be
as dull and foolish as our neighbours. It was not so with Hazlitt. And
notice how learned he is (as, indeed, throughout the essay) in the theory
of walking tours. He is none of your athletic men in purple stockings, who
walk their fifty miles a day: three hours' march is his ideal. And then he
must have a winding road, the epicure!

Yet there is one thing I object to in these words of his, one thing in the great master's practice that seems to me not wholly wise. I do not approve of that leaping and running. Both of these hurry the respiration; they both shake up the brain out of its glorious open-air confusion; and they both break the pace. Uneven walking is not so agreeable to the body, and it distracts and irritates the mind. Whereas, when once you have fallen into an equable stride, it requires no conscious thought from you to keep it up, and yet it prevents you from thinking earnestly of anything else. Like knitting, like the work of a copying clerk, it gradually neutralises and sets to sleep the serious activity of the mind. We can think of this or that, lightly and laughingly, as a child thinks, or as we think in a morning doze; we can make puns or puzzle out acrostics, and trifle in a thousand ways with words and rhymes; but when it comes to honest work, when we come to gather ourselves together for an effort, we may sound the trumpet as loud and long as we please; the great barons of the mind will not rally to the standard, but sit, each one, at home, warming his hands over his own fire, and brooding on his own private thought!

In the course of a day's walk, you see, there is much variance in the mood. From the exhilaration of the start, to the happy phlegm of the arrival, the change is certainly great. As the day goes on, the traveller moves from the one extreme end towards the other. He becomes more and more incorporated with the material landscape, and the open-air drunkenness grows upon him with great strides, until he posts along the road, and sees everything about him, as in a cheerful dream. The first is certainly brighter, but the second stage is the more peaceful. A man does not make so many articles towards the end, nor does he laugh aloud; but the purely animal pleasures, the sense of physical well-being, the delight of every inhalation, of every time the muscles tighten down the thigh, console him for the absence of the others, and bring him to his destination still content.

Nor must I forget to say a word on bivouacs. You come to a milestone on a hill, or some place where deep ways meet under trees; and off goes the knapsack, and down you sit to smoke a pipe in the shade. You sink into yourself, and the birds come round and look at you; and your smoke dissipates upon the afternoon under the blue dome of heaven; and the sun lies warm upon your feet, and the cool air visits your neck and turns aside your open shirt. If you are not happy, you must have an evil conscience. You may dally as long as you like by the roadside. It is almost as if the millennium were arrived, when we shall throw our clocks and watches over the house-top, and remember time and seasons no more. Not to keep hours for a lifetime is, I was going to say, to live for ever. You have no idea, unless you have tried it, how endlessly long is a summer's day that you measure out only by hunger, and bring to an end only when you are drowsy. I know a village where there are hardly any clocks, where no one knows more of the days of the week than by a sort of instinct for the *fête* on Sundays, and where only one person can tell you the day of the month, and she is generally wrong; and if people were aware how slow Time journeyed in that village, and what armfuls of spare hours he gives, over and above the bargain, to its wise inhabitants, I believe there would be a stampede out of London, Liverpool, Paris, and a variety of large towns, where the clocks lose their heads, and shake the hours out each one faster than the other, as though they were all in a wager. And all these foolish pilgrims would each bring his own misery along with him, in a watch-pocket! It is to be noticed there were no clocks and watches in the much-vaunted days before the flood. It follows, of course, there were no appointments, and punctuality was not yet thought upon. "Though ye take from a covetous man all his treasure," says Milton, "he has yet one jewel left; ye cannot deprive him of his covetousness." And so I would say of a modern man of business, you may do what you will for him, put him in Eden, give him the elixir of life—he has still a flaw at heart, he still has his business habits. Now, there is no time when business habits are more mitigated than on a walking tour. And so during these halts, as I say, you will feel almost free.

But it is at night, and after dinner, that the best hour comes. There are no such pipes to be smoked as those that follow a good day's march; the flavour of the tobacco is a thing to be remembered, it is so dry and aromatic, so full and so fine. If you wind up the evening with grog, you will own there was never such grog; at every sip a jocund tranquillity spreads about your limbs, and sits easily in your heart. If you read a book—and you will never do so save by fits and starts—you find the language strangely racy and harmonious; words take a new meaning; single sentences possess the ear for half an hour together; and the writer endears himself to you, at every page, by the nicest coincidence of sentiment. It seems as if it were a book you had written yourself in a dream. To all we have read on such occasions we look back with special favour. "It was on the 10th of April, 1798," says Hazlitt, with amorous precision, "that I sat down to a volume of the new 'Héloïse,' at the Inn at Llangollen, over a bottle of sherry and a cold chicken." I should wish to quote more, for though we are mighty fine fellows nowadays, we cannot write like Hazlitt. And, talking of that, a volume of Hazlitt's essays would be a capital pocket-book on such a journey; so would a volume of Heine's songs; and for "Tristram Shandy" I can pledge a fair experience.

If the evening be fine and warm, there is nothing better in life than to lounge before the inn door in the sunset, or lean over the parapet of the bridge, to watch the weeds and the quick fishes. It is then, if ever, that you taste Joviality to the full significance of that audacious word. Your muscles are so agreeably slack, you feel so clean and so strong and so idle, that whether you move or sit still, whatever you do is done with pride and a kingly sort of pleasure. You fall in talk with any one, wise or foolish, drunk or sober. And it seems as if a hot walk purged you, more than of anything else, of all narrowness and pride, and left curiosity to play its part freely, as in a child or a man of science. You lay aside all your own hobbies, to watch provincial humours develop themselves before you, now as a laughable farce, and now grave and beautiful like an old tale.

Or perhaps you are left to your own company for the night, and surly weather imprisons you by the fire. You may remember how Burns, numbering past pleasures, dwells upon the hours when he has been "happy thinking." It is a phrase that may well perplex a poor modern, girt about on every side by clocks and chimes, and haunted, even at night, by flaming dial-plates. For we are all so busy, and have so many far-off projects to realise, and castles in the fire to turn into solid habitable mansions on a gravel soil, that we can find no time for pleasure trips into the Land of Thought and among the Hills of Vanity. Changed times, indeed, when we must sit all night, beside the fire, with folded hands; and a changed world for most of us, when we find we can pass the hours without discontent, and be happy thinking. We are in such haste to be doing, to be writing, to be gathering gear, to make our voice audible a moment in the derisive silence of eternity, that we forget that one thing, of which these are but the parts—namely, to live. We fall in love, we drink hard, we run to and fro upon the earth like frightened sheep. And now you are to ask yourself if, when all is done, you would not have been better to sit by the fire at home, and be happy thinking. To sit still and contemplate,—to remember the faces of women without desire, to be pleased by the great deeds of men without envy, to be everything and everywhere in sympathy, and yet content to remain where and what you are—is not this to know both wisdom and virtue, and to dwell with happiness? After all, it is not they who carry flags, but they who look upon it from a private chamber, who have the fun of the procession. And once you are at that, you are in the very humour of all social heresy. It is no time for shuffling, or for big empty words. If you ask yourself what you mean by fame, riches, or learning, the answer is far to seek; and you go back into that kingdom of light imaginations, which seem so vain in the eyes of Philistines perspiring after wealth, and so momentous to those who are stricken with the disproportions of the world, and, in the face of the gigantic stars, cannot stop to split differences between two degrees of the infinitesimally small, such as a tobacco pipe or the Roman Empire, a million of money or a fiddlestick's end.

You lean from the window, your last pipe reeking whitely into the darkness, your body full of delicious pains, your mind enthroned in the seventh circle of content; when suddenly the mood changes, the weather-cock goes about, and you ask yourself one question more: whether, for the interval, you have been the wisest philosopher or the most egregious of donkeys? Human experience is not yet able to reply; but at least you have had a fine moment, and looked down upon all the kingdoms of the earth. And whether it was wise or foolish, to-morrow's travel will carry you, body and mind, into some different parish of the infinite.

—*Virginibus Puerisque*

A WALK WITH THOREAU

by Ralph Waldo Emerson

Emerson was thirty-four and Thoreau but twenty when they went to the Cliff together on April 25, 1838. Twenty-seven years later Emerson, as "serene as a sequoia," was to meet John Muir in Yosemite.

YESTERDAY AFTERNOON I went to the Cliff with Henry Thoreau. Warm, pleasant, misty weather, which the great mountain amphitheatre seemed to drink in with gladness. A crow's voice filled all the miles of air with sound. A bird's voice, even a piping frog, enlivens a solitude and makes world enough for us. At night I went out into the dark and saw a glimmering star and heard a frog, and Nature seemed to say, Well do not these suffice? Here is a new scene, a new experience. Ponder it, Emerson, and not like the foolish world, hanker after thunders and multitudes and vast landscapes, the sea or Niagara.

—The Heart of Emerson's Journals

WALKING

by Henry David Thoreau

Borrowing some land from Emerson and an ax from Bronson Alcott, and accepting a suggestion from Ellery Channing, Thoreau went to Walden Pond in 1845 "to begin the grand process of devouring himself alive." The result was an imperishable classic. Robert Louis Stevenson describes Thoreau as a man with a thin, penetrating, big-nosed face . . . "a man shockingly devoid of weaknesses." There were few things Thoreau could not do. He could make a house, a boat, a pencil or a book. And he baked his own bread. It was typical of Thoreau that he proudly returned Alcott's ax "sharper than when I borrowed it." If Thoreau had been a man, according to Stevenson, instead of a manner of elm tree, he might have seen his friends more often, and perhaps even married. This essay was first published in the Atlantic Monthly *in June 1862.*

I WISH to speak a word for Nature, for absolute freedom and wildness, as contrasted with a freedom and culture merely civil,—to regard man as an inhabitant, or a part and parcel of Nature, rather than a member of society. I wish to make an extreme statement, if so I may make an emphatic one, for there are enough champions of civilization: the minister and the school-committee and every one of you will take care of that.

I have met with but one or two persons in the course of my life who understood the art of Walking, that is, of taking walks,—who had a genius, so to speak, for *sauntering:* which word is beautifully derived "from idle people who roved about the country, in the Middle Ages, and asked charity, under pretense of going *à la Sainte Terre,*" to the Holy Land, till the children exclaimed, "There goes a *Sainte-Terrer,*" a Saunterer, a Holy-Lander. They who never go to the Holy Land in their walks, as they pretend, are indeed mere idlers and vagabonds; but they who do go there are saunterers in the good sense, such as I mean. . . .

I think that I cannot preserve my health and spirits, unless I spend four hours a day at least,—and it is commonly more than that,—sauntering through the woods and over the hills and fields, absolutely free from all worldly engagements. You may safely say, A penny for your thoughts, or a thousand pounds. When sometimes I am reminded that the mechanics and shopkeepers stay in their shops not only all the forenoon, but all the afternoon too, sitting with crossed legs, so many of them,—as if the legs were made to sit upon, and not to stand or walk upon,—I think that they deserve some credit for not having all committed suicide long ago. . . .

No doubt temperament, and, above all, age, have a good deal to do with it. As a man grows older, his ability to sit still and follow indoor occupations increases. He grows vespertinal in his habits as the evening of life approaches, till at last he comes forth only just before sundown, and gets all the walk that he requires in half an hour.

But the walking of which I speak has nothing in it akin to taking exercise, as it is called, as the sick take medicine at stated hours,—as the swinging of dumb-bells or chairs; but is itself the enterprise and adventure of the day. If you would get exercise, go in search of the springs of life. Think of a man's swinging dumb-bells for his health, when those springs are bubbling up in far-off pastures unsought by him!

Moreover, you must walk like a camel, which is said to be the only beast which ruminates when walking. When a traveler asked Wordsworth's servant to show him her master's study, she answered, "Here is his library, but his study is out of doors." . . .

My vicinity affords many good walks; and though for so many years I have walked almost every day, and sometimes for several days together, I have not yet exhausted them. An absolutely new prospect is a great happiness, and I can still get this any afternoon. Two or three hours' walking will carry me to as strange a country as I expect ever to see. A single farm-house which I had not seen before is sometimes as good as the dominions of the King of Dahomey. There is in fact a sort of harmony discoverable between the capabilities of the landscape within a circle of ten miles' radius, or the limits of an afternoon walk, and the threescore years and ten of human life. It will never become quite familiar to you. . . .

I can easily walk ten, fifteen, twenty, any number of miles, commencing at my own door, without going by any house, without crossing a road except where the fox and the mink do: first along by the river, and then the brook, and then the meadow and the woodside. There are square miles in my vicinity which have no inhabitant. From many a hill I can see civilization and the abodes of man afar. The farmers and their works are scarcely more obvious than woodchucks and their burrows. Man and his affairs, church and state and school, trade and commerce, and manufactures and agriculture, even politics, the most alarming of them all,—I am pleased to see how little space they occupy in the landscape. . . .

When I go out of the house for a walk, uncertain as yet whither I will bend my steps, and submit myself to my instinct to decide for me, I find, strange and whimsical as it may seem, that I finally and inevitably settle southwest, toward some particular wood or meadow or deserted pasture or hill in that direction. My needle is slow to settle,—varies a few degrees, and does not always point due southwest, it is true, and it has good authority for this variation, but it always settles between west and south-southwest. The future lies that way to me, and the earth seems more unexhausted and richer on that side. . . . Eastward I go only by force; but westward I go free. Thither no business leads me. It is hard for me to believe that I shall find fair landscapes or sufficient wildness and freedom behind the eastern horizon. I am not excited by the prospect of a walk thither; but I believe that the forest which I see in the western horizon stretches uninterruptedly toward the setting sun, and there are no towns nor cities in it of enough consequence to disturb me. Let me live where I will, on this side is the city, on that the wilderness, and ever I am leaving the city more and more, and withdrawing into the wilderness. I should not lay so much stress on this fact, if I did not believe that something like this is the prevailing tendency of my countrymen. I must walk toward Oregon, and not toward Europe. And that way the nation is moving, and I may say that mankind progress from east to west. . . .

We go eastward to realize history and study the works of art and literature, retracing the steps of the race; we go westward as into the future, with a spirit of enterprise and adventure. The Atlantic is a Lethean stream, in our passage over which we have had an opportunity to forget the Old World and its institutions. If we do not succeed this time, there is perhaps one more chance for the race left before it arrives on the banks of the Styx; and that is in the Lethe of the Pacific, which is three times as wide. . . .

Every sunset which I witness inspires me with the desire to go to a West as distant and as fair as that into which the sun goes down. He appears to migrate westward daily, and tempt us to follow him. He is the Great Western Pioneer whom the nations follow. . . .

Columbus felt the westward tendency more strongly than any before. He obeyed it, and found a New World for Castile and Leon. The herd of men in those days scented fresh pastures from afar. . . .

Where on the globe can there be found an area of equal extent with that occupied by the bulk of our States, so fertile and so rich and varied in its productions, and at the same time so habitable by the European, as this is? Michaux, who knew but part of them, says that "the species of large trees are much more numerous in North America than in Europe; in the United States there are more than one hundred and forty species that exceed thirty feet in height; in France there are but thirty that attain this size." Later botanists more than confirm his observations. Humboldt came to America to realize his youthful dreams of a tropical vegetation, and he beheld it in its greatest perfection in the primitive forests of the Amazon, the most gigantic wilderness on the earth, which he has so eloquently described. . . .

Sir Francis Head, an English traveler and a Governor-General of Canada, tells us that "in both the northern and southern hemispheres of the New World, Nature has not only outlined her works on a larger scale, but has painted the whole picture with brighter and more costly colors than she used in delineating and in beautifying the Old World. . . . The heavens of America appear infinitely higher, the sky is bluer, the air is fresher, the cold is intenser, the moon looks larger, the stars are brighter, the thunder is louder, the lightning is vivider, the wind is stronger, the rain is heavier, the mountains are higher, the rivers longer, the forests bigger, the plains broader." This statement will do at least to set against Buffon's account of this part of the world and its productions. . . .

To Americans I hardly need to say,—

"Westward the star of empire takes its way."

As a true patriot, I should be ashamed to think that Adam in paradise was more favorably situated on the whole than the backwoodsman in this country.

Our sympathies in Massachusetts are not confined to New England; though we may be estranged from the South, we sympathize with the West. There is the home of the younger sons, as among the Scandinavians they took to the sea for their inheritance. . . .

The West of which I speak is but another name for the Wild; and what I have been preparing to say is, that in Wildness is the preservation of the World. Every tree sends its fibres forth in search of the Wild. The cities import it at any price. Men plough and sail for it. From the forest and wilderness come the tonics and barks which brace mankind. Our ancestors were savages. The story of Romulus and Remus being suckled by a wolf is not a meaningless fable. The founders of every state which has risen to eminence have drawn their nourishment and vigor from a similar wild source. It was because the children of the Empire were not suckled by the wolf that they were conquered and displaced by the children of the northern forests who were.

I believe in the forest, and in the meadow, and in the night in which the corn grows. . . .

A tanned skin is something more than respectable, and perhaps olive is a fitter color than white for a man,—a denizen of the woods. "The pale white man!" I do not wonder that the African pitied him. Darwin the naturalist says, "A white man bathing by the side of a Tahitian was like a plant bleached by the gardener's art, compared with a fine, dark green one, growing vigorously in the open fields."

Ben Jonson exclaims,—

"How near to good is what is fair!"

So I would say,—

How near to good is what is *wild!*

Life consists with wildness. The most alive is the wildest. Not yet subdued to man, its presence refreshes him. One who pressed forward incessantly and never rested from his labors, who grew fast and made infinite demands on life, would always find himself in a new country or wilderness, and surrounded by the raw material of life. He would be climbing over the prostrate stems of primitive forest-trees.

Hope and the future for me are not in lawns and cultivated fields, not in towns and cities, but in the impervious and quaking swamps. When, formerly, I have analyzed my partiality for some farm which I had contemplated purchasing, I have frequently found that I was attracted solely by a few square rods of impermeable and unfathomable bog,—a natural sink in one corner of it. That was the jewel which dazzled me. I derive more of my subsistence from the swamps which surround my native town than from the cultivated gardens in the village. . . .

When I would recreate myself, I seek the darkest wood, the thickest and most interminable and, to the citizen, most dismal swamp. I enter a swamp as a sacred place,—a *sanctum sanctorum*. There is the strength, the marrow of Nature. The wild-wood covers the virgin-mould,—and the same soil is good for men and for trees. A man's health requires as many acres of meadow to his prospect as his farm does loads of muck. These are the strong meats on which he feeds. A town is saved, not more by the righteous men in it than by the woods and swamps that surround it. A township where one primitive forest waves above while another primitive forest rots below,—such a town is fitted to raise not only corn and potatoes, but poets and philosophers for the coming ages. In such a soil grew Homer and Confucius and the rest, and out of such a wilderness comes the Reformer eating locusts and wild honey. . . .

The civilized nations—Greece, Rome, England—have been sustained by the primitive forests which anciently rotted where they stand. They survive as long as the soil is not exhausted. Alas for human culture! little is to be expected of a nation, when the vegetable mould is exhausted, and it is compelled to make manure of the bones of its fathers. There the poet sustains himself merely by his own superfluous fat, and the philosopher comes down on his marrow-bones.

It is said to be the task of the American "to work the virgin soil," and that "agriculture here already assumes proportions unknown everywhere else." I think that the farmer displaces the Indian even because he redeems the meadow, and so makes himself stronger and in some respects more natural. I was surveying for a man the other day a single straight line one hundred and thirty-two rods long, through a swamp, at whose entrance might have been written the words which Dante read over the entrance to the infernal regions,—"Leave all hope, ye that enter,"—that is, of ever getting out again; where at one time I saw my employer actually up to his neck and swimming for his life in his property, though it was still winter. He had another similar swamp which I could not survey at all, because it was completely under water, and nevertheless, with regard to a third swamp, which I did *survey* from a distance, he remarked to me, true to his instincts, that he would not part with it for any consideration, on account of the mud which it contained. And that man intends to put a girdling ditch round the whole in the course of forty months, and so redeem it by the magic of his spade. . . .

In literature it is only the wild that attracts us. Dullness is but another name for tameness. It is the uncivilized free and wild thinking in "Hamlet" and the "Iliad," in all the Scriptures and Mythologies, not learned in the schools, that delights us. . . . A truly good book is something as natural, and as unexpectedly and unaccountably fair and perfect, as a wild flower discovered on the prairies of the West or in the jungles of the East. Genius is a light which makes the darkness visible, like the lightning's flash, which perchance shatters the temple of knowledge itself,—and not a taper lighted at the hearth-stone of the race, which pales before the light of common day.

We hug the earth,—how rarely we mount! Methinks we might elevate ourselves a little more. We might climb a tree, at least. I found my account in climbing a tree once. It was a tall white-pine, on the top of a hill; and though I got well pitched, I was well paid for it, for I discovered new mountains in the horizon which I had never seen before,—so much more of the earth and the heavens. I might have walked about the foot of the tree for three-score years and ten, and yet I certainly should never have seen them. But, above all, I discovered around me,—it was near the end of June,—on the ends of the topmost branches only, a few minute and delicate red cone-like blossoms, the fertile flower of the white pine looking heavenward. I carried straightway to the village the topmost spire, and showed it to stranger jurymen who walked the streets,—for it was court-week,—and the farmers and lumber-dealers and wood-choppers and hunters, and not one had ever seen the like before, but they wondered as at a star dropped down. . . . We see only the flowers that are under our feet in the meadows. The pines have developed their delicate blossoms on the highest twigs of the wood every summer for ages, as well over the heads of Nature's red children as of her white ones; yet scarcely a farmer or hunter in the land has ever seen them.

We had a remarkable sunset one day last November. I was walking in a meadow, the source of a small brook, when the sun at last, just before setting, after a cold gray day, reached a clear stratum in the horizon, and the softest, brightest morning sunlight fell on the dry grass and on the stems of the trees in the opposite horizon and on the leaves of the shrub-oaks on the hillside, while our shadows stretched long over the meadow eastward, as if we were the only motes in its beams. It was such a light as we could not have imagined a moment before, and the air also was so warm and serene that nothing was wanting to make a paradise of that meadow. When we reflected that this was not a solitary phenomenon, never to happen again, but that it would happen forever and ever an infinite number of evenings, and cheer and reassure the latest child that walked there, it was more glorious still.

The sun sets on some retired meadow, where no house is visible, with all the glory and splendor that it lavishes on cities, and perchance as it has never set before,—where there is but a solitary marsh-hawk to have his wings gilded by it, or only a musquash looks out from his cabin, and there is some little black-veined brook in the midst of the marsh, just beginning to meander, winding slowly round a decaying stump. We walked in so pure and bright a light, gilding the withered grass and leaves, so softly and serenely bright, I thought I had never bathed in such a golden flood, without a ripple or a murmur to it. The west side of every wood and rising ground gleamed like the boundary of Elysium, and the sun on our backs seemed like a gentle herdsman driving us home at evening.

So we saunter toward the Holy Land, till one day the sun shall shine more brightly than ever he has done, shall perchance shine into our minds and hearts, and light up our whole lives with a great awakening light, as warm and serene and golden as on a bankside in autumn.

—Excursions

THE PLEASURE
OF WALKING

by Oliver Wendell Holmes

*If reading these beguiling paragraphs by the magnificent "Autocrat"
does nothing more than send you back to the original from which
they came, you will owe us a large debt of thanks. Our edition,
published in 1887, and rescued from the shelf of a rare-book dealer,
bears this charming, handwritten inscription: "May you enjoy this
as I have. I should like to recommend you to read it in the Royal
Hotel of Honolulu or under the pines of Monterey—I fancy it could
not seem quite so good anywhere else."*

1.

YOU THINK you know all about *walking,*—don't you, now? Well,
how do you suppose your lower limbs are held to your body? They are
sucked up by two cupping vessels, ("cotyloid"—cup-like—cavities,) and
held there as long as you live, and longer. At any rate, you think you
move them backward and forward at such a rate as your will determines,
don't you? On the contrary, they swing just as any other pendulums
swing, at a fixed rate, determined by their length. You can alter this by
muscular power, as you can take hold of the pendulum of a clock and
make it move faster or slower; but your ordinary gait is timed by the same
mechanism as the movements of the solar system.

2.

I do not deny the attraction of walking. I have bored this ancient city
through and through in my daily travels, until I know it as an old inhabitant of a Cheshire knows his cheese. Why, it was I who, in the course of

these rambles, discovered that remarkable avenue called *Myrtle Street,* stretching in one long line from east of the Reservoir to a precipitous and rudely paved cliff which looks down on the grim abode of Science, and beyond it to the far hills; a promenade so delicious in its repose, so cheerfully varied with glimpses down the northern slope into busy Cambridge Street, with its iron river of the horse-railroad, and wheeled barges gliding backward and forward over it,—so delightfully closing at its western extremity in sunny courts and passages where I know peace, and beauty, and virtue, and serene old age must be perpetual tenants,—so alluring to all who desire to take their daily stroll, in the words of Dr. Watts,—

> "Alike unknowing and unknown,"—

that nothing but a sense of duty would have prompted me to reveal the secret of its existence. I concede, therefore, that walking is an immeasurably fine invention, of which old age ought constantly to avail itself. . . .

3.

The pleasure of exercise is due first to a purely physical impression, and secondly to a sense of power in action. The first source of pleasure varies of course with our condition and the state of the surrounding circumstances; the second with the amount and kind of power, and the extent and kind of action. In all forms of active exercise there are three powers simultaneously in action,—the will, the muscles, and the intellect. Each of these predominates in different kinds of exercise. In walking, the will and muscles are so accustomed to work together and perform their task with so little expenditure of force, that the intellect is left comparatively free. The mental pleasure in walking, as such, is in the sense of power over all our moving machinery.

—*The Autocrat of the Breakfast Table*

THE ART OF WALKING

by Christopher Morley

The art of the essay, shaped by such masters as Addison, Steele, Johnson, Chesterton, Montaigne, Hazlitt, Huneker and Lamb, has begun to disappear from the literary scene. Christopher Morley was one of its most skillful practitioners, and his essays on walking and sauntering were among his best. This one was first published in 1917. It is a source of great satisfaction to those who loved the work of this American mandarin that there is now a park dedicated to him on Long Island, New York.

"THERE WAS fine walking on the hills in the direction of the sea."

This heart-stirring statement, which I find in an account of the life of William and Dorothy Wordsworth when they inhabited a quiet cottage near Crewkerne in Dorset, reminds me how often the word "walking" occurs in any description of Wordsworth's existence. De Quincey assures us that the poet's props were very ill shapen—"they were pointedly condemned by all female connoisseurs in legs"—but none the less he was *princeps arte ambulandi*. Even had he lived today, when all our roads are barbarized by exploding gasoline vapours, I do not think Wordsworth would have flivvered. Of him the Opium Eater made the classic pronouncement: "I calculate that with these identical legs W. must have traversed a distance of 175,000 to 180,000 English miles—a mode of exertion which, to him, stood in the stead of alcohol and all other stimulants whatsoever to the animal spirits; to which, indeed, he was indebted for a life of unclouded happiness, and we for much of what is most excellent in his writings."

A book that says anything about walking has a ready passage to my inmost heart. The best books are always those that set down with "amorous precision" the satisfying details of human pilgrimage. How one sympathizes with poor Pepys in his outburst (April 30, 1663) about a gentleman who seems to have been "Always Taking the Joy Out of Life."

Lord! what a stir Stankes makes, with his being crowded in the streets, and wearied in walking in London, and would not be wooed to go to a play, nor to Whitehall, or to see the lions, though he was carried in a coach. I never could have thought there had been upon earth a man so little curious in the world as he is.

Now your true walker is mightily "curious in the world," and he goes upon his way zealous to sate himself with a thousand quaintnesses. When he writes a book he fills it full of food, drink, tobacco, the scent of sawmills on sunny afternoons, and arrivals at inns late at night. He writes what Mr. Mosher calls a book-a-bosom. Diaries and letters are often best of all because they abound in these matters. And because walking can never again be what it was—the motor-cars will see to that—it is our duty to pay it greater reverence and honor.

Wordsworth and Coleridge come first to mind in any talk about walking. The first time they met was in 1797 when Coleridge tramped from Nether Stowey to Racedown (thirty miles in an air-line, and full forty by road) to make the acquaintance of William and Dorothy. That is practically from the Bristol Channel to the English ditto, a rousing stretch. It was Wordsworth's pamphlet describing a walk across France to the Alps that spurred Coleridge on to this expedition. The trio became fast friends, and William and Dorothy moved to Alfoxden (near Nether Stowey) to enjoy the companionship. What one would give for some adequate account of their walks and talks together over the Quantocks. They planned a little walking trip into Devonshire that autumn (1797) and "The Ancient Mariner" was written in the hope of defraying the expenses of the adventure.

De Quincey himself, who tells us so much jovial gossip about Wordsworth and Coleridge, was no mean pedestrian. He describes a forty-mile all-night walk from Bridgewater to Bristol, on the evening after first meeting Coleridge. He could not sleep after the intellectual excitement of the day, and through a summer night "divinely calm" he busied himself with meditation on the sad spectacle he had witnessed: a great mind hastening to decay.

I have always fancied that walking as a fine art was not much practiced before the Eighteenth Century. We know from Ambassador Jusserand's famous book how many wayfarers were on the roads in the Fourteenth Century, but none of these were abroad for the pleasures of moving meditation and scenery. We can gather from Mr. Tristram's *Coaching Days and Coaching Ways* that the highroads were by no means safe for solitary travellers even so late as 1750. In *Joseph Andrews* (1742) whenever any of the characters proceed afoot they are almost certain to be held up. Mr. Isaac Walton, it is true, was a considerable rambler a century earlier than this, and in his Derbyshire hills must have passed many lonely gullies; but footpads were more likely to ambush the main roads. It would be a hard-hearted bandit who would despoil the gentle angler of his basket of trouts. Goldsmith, too, was a lusty walker, and tramped it over the Continent for two years (1754–56) with little more baggage than a flute; he might have written *The Handy Guide for Beggars* long before Vachel Lindsay. But generally speaking, it is true that cross-country walks for the pure delight of rhythmically placing one foot before the other were rare before Wordsworth. I always think of him as one of the first to employ his legs as an instrument of philosophy.

After Wordsworth they come thick and fast. Hazlitt, of course—have you paid the tax that R.L.S. imposes on all who have not read Hazlitt's "On Going a Journey"? Then Keats: never was there more fruitful walk than the early morning stroll from Clerkenwell to the Poultry in October, 1816, that produced "Much have I travelled in the realms of gold." He must have set out early enough, for the manuscript of the sonnet was on Cowden Clarke's table by breakfast time. And by the way, did you know that the copy of Chapman's Homer which inspired it belonged to the financial editor of the *Times?* Never did financial editor live to better purpose!

There are many words of Keats that are a joyful viaticum for the walker: get these by rote in some membrane of memory:

The great Elements we know of are no mean comforters: the open sky sits upon our senses like a sapphire crown—the Air is our robe of state— the Earth is our throne, and the sea a mighty minstrel playing before it.

The Victorians were great walkers. Railways were but striplings; inns were at their prime. Hark to the great names in the walker's Hall of Fame: Tennyson, FitzGerald, Matthew Arnold, Carlyle, Kingsley, Meredith, Richard Jefferies. What walker can ever forget the day when he first read *The Story of My Heart?* In my case it was the 24th of August, 1912, on a train from London to Cambridge. Then there were George Borrow, Emily Brontë on her Yorkshire moors, and Leslie Stephen, one of the princes of the clan and founder of the famous Sunday Tramps of whom Meredith was one. Walt Whitman would have made a notable addition to that posse of philosophic walkers, save that I fear the garrulous half-baked old barbarian would have been disappointed that he could not dominate the conversation.

There have been stout walkers in our own day. Mr. W. H. Davies (the Super-Tramp), G. M. Trevelyan, Hilaire Belloc, Edward Thomas who died on the field of honor in April, 1917, and Francis Ledwidge, who was killed in Flanders. Who can forget his noble words, "I have taken up arms for the fields along the Boyne, for the birds and the blue sky over them." There is Walter Prichard Eaton, the Jefferies of our own Berkshires. One could extend the list almost without end. Sometimes it seems as though literature were a co-product of legs and head.

Charles Lamb and Leigh Hunt were great city ramblers, followed in due course by Dickens, R. L. S., Edward Lucas, Holbrook Jackson, and Pearsall Smith. Mr. Thomas Burke is another, whose *Nights in Town* will delight the lover of the greatest of all cities. But urban wanderings, delicious as they are, are not quite what we mean by walking. On pavements one goes by fit and start, halting to see, to hear, and to speculate. In the country one captures the true ecstasy of the long, unbroken swing, the harmonious glow of mind and body, eyes fed, soul feasted, brain and muscle exercised alike.

Meredith is perhaps the Supreme Pontiff of modern country walkers: no soft lover of drowsy golden weather, but master of the stiffer breed who salute frost and lashing rain and roaring southwest wind, who leap to grapple with the dissolving riddles of destiny. February and March are his months:

> For love we Earth, then serve we all;
>   Her mystic secret then is ours:
> We fall, or view our treasures fall,
>   Unclouded, as beholds her flowers
>
> Earth, from a night of frosty wreck,
>   Enrobed in morning's mounted fire,

When lowly, with a broken neck,
The crocus lays her cheek to mire.

I suppose every walker collects a few precious books which form the bible of his chosen art. I have long been collecting a Walker's Breviary of my own. It includes Stevenson's *Walking Tours,* G. M. Trevelyan's *Walking,* Leslie Stephen's *In Praise of Walking,* shards and crystals from all the others I have mentioned. Michael Fairless, Vachel Lindsay, and Frank Sidgwick have place in it. On my private shelf stands *Journeys to Bagdad* by Mr. Charles Brooks, who has good pleasantry to utter on this topic; and a manly little volume, *Walking as Education,* by the Rev. A. N. Cooper, "the walking parson," published in England in 1910. On that same shelf there will soon stand a volume of delicious essays by one of the most accomplished of American walkers, Mr. Robert Cortes Holliday, the American Belloc, who, in his *Walking Stick Papers,* has bravely stated why so few of the fair sex are able to participate in walking tours:

No one, though (this is the first article to be observed), should ever go a journey with any other than him with whom one walks arm in arm, in the evening, the twilight, and, talking (let us suppose) of men's given names, agrees that if either should have a son he shall be named after the other. Walking in the gathering dusk, two and two, since the world began, there have always been young men who have thus to one another plighted their troth. If one is not still one of these, then, in the sense here used, journeys are over for him. What is left to him of life he may enjoy, but not journeys. Mention should be made in passing that some have been found so ignorant of the nature of journeys as to suppose that they might be taken in company with members, or a member, of the other sex. Now one who writes of journeys would cheerfully be burned at the stake before he would knowingly under-estimate women. But it must be confessed that it is another season in the life of man that they fill.

They are too personal for the high enjoyment of going a journey. They must forever be thinking about you or about themselves; with them everything in the world is somehow tangled up in these matters; and when you are with them (you cannot help it, or if you could they would not allow it) you must forever be thinking about them or yourself. Nothing on either side can be seen detached. They cannot rise to that philosophic plane of mind which is the very marrow of going a journey. One reason for this is that they can never escape from the idea of society: You are in their society, they are in yours; and the multitudinous personal ties which connect you all to that great order called society that you have for a period got away from physically are present. Like the business man who goes on a vacation from his business and takes his business habits along with him, so on a journey they would bring society along, and all sort of etiquette.

He that goes a journey shakes off the trammels of the world; he has fled all impediments and inconveniences; he belongs, for the moment, to no time or place. He is neither rich nor poor, but in that which he thinks and sees. There is not such another Arcadia for this on earth as in going a journey. He that goes a journey escapes, for a breath of air, from all conventions; without which, though, of course, society would go to pot; and which are the very natural instinct of women.

Mr. Holliday has other goodly matter upon the philosophy and art of locomotion, and those who are wise and have a lively faith may be admitted to great and surpassing delights if they will here and now make memorandum to buy his book. . . .

Speaking of Vachel Lindsay, his *Handy Guide for Beggars* will bring an itch along the shanks of those who love shoe-leather and a knobbed stick. Vachel sets out for a walk in no mean and pettifogging spirit: he proceeds as an army with banners: he intends that the world shall know he is afoot: the Great Khan of Springfield is unleashed—let alewives and deacons tremble!

Ungenerous hosts have cozened Vachel by begging him to recite his poems at the beginning of each course, in the meantime getting on with their eating; but despite the naïveté of his eagerness to sing, there is a plain and manly simplicity about Vachel that delights us all. We like to know that here is a poet who has wrestled with poverty, who never wrote a Class Day poem at Harvard, who has worn frayed collars or none at all, and who lets the barber shave the back of his neck. We like to know that he has tramped the ties in Georgia, harvested in Kansas, been fumigated in New Jersey, and lives contented in Illinois. Four weeks a year he lives as the darling of the cisalleghany Browning Societies, but he is always glad to get back to Springfield and resume his robes as the local Rabin-dranath. If he ever buys an automobile I am positive it will be a Ford. Here is *homo americanus,* one of ourselves, who never wore spats in his life.

But even the plain man may see visions. Walking on crowded city streets at night, watching the lighted windows, delicatessen shops, peanut carts, bakeries, fish stalls, free lunch counters piled with crackers and saloon cheese, and minor poets struggling home with the Saturday night marketing—he feels the thrill of being one, or at least two-thirds, with this various, grotesque, pathetic, and surprising humanity. The sense of fellowship with every other walking biped, the full-blooded understanding that Whitman and O. Henry knew in brimming measure, comes by gulps and twinges to almost all. That is the essence of Lindsay's feeling about life. He loves crowds, companionship, plenty of sirloin and onions, and seeing his name in print. He sings and celebrates the great symbols of our hodge-podge democracy: ice-cream soda, electrical sky-signs, Sunday-school picnics, the movies, Mark Twain. In the teeming ooze and ocean bottoms of our atlantic humanity he finds rich corals and rainbow shells, hospitality, reverence, love, and beauty.

This is the sentiment that makes a merry pedestrian, and Vachel has scrutineered and scuffled through a dozen states, lightening larders and puzzling the worldly. Afoot and penniless is his technique—"stopping when he had a mind to, singing when he felt inclined to"—and begging his meals and bed. I suppose he has had as many free meals as any American citizen; and this is how he does it, copied from his little pamphlet used on many a road:

RHYMES TO BE TRADED FOR BREAD

Being new verses by Nicholas Vachel Lindsay, Springfield, Illinois, June, 1912, printed expressly as a substitute for money.

This book is to be used in exchange for the necessities of life on a tramp-journey from the author's home town, through the West and back, during which he will observe the following rules:

(1) Keep away from the cities.
(2) Keep away from the railroads.
(3) Have nothing to do with money. Carry no baggage.
(4) Ask for dinner about quarter after eleven.
(5) Ask for supper, lodging, and breakfast about quarter of five.
(6) Travel alone.
(7) Be neat, truthful, civil, and on the square.
(8) Preach the Gospel of Beauty.

In order to carry out the last rule there will be three exceptions to the rule against baggage. (1) The author will carry a brief printed statement, called "The Gospel of Beauty." (2) He will carry this book of rhymes for distribution. (3) Also he will carry a small portfolio with pictures, etc., chosen to give an outline of his view of the history of art, especially as it applies to America.

Perhaps I have tarried too long over Vachel; but I have set down his theories of vagabonding because many walkers will find them interesting. *The Handy Guide for Beggars* will leave you footsore but better for the exercise. And when the fascinating story of American literature in this decade (1910–20) is finally written, there will be a happy and well-merited corner in it for a dusty but "neat, truthful, and civil" figure from Springfield, Illinois.

A good pipeful of prose to solace yourself withal, about sunset on a lonely road, is that passage on "Lying Awake at Night" to be found in *The Forest* by Stewart Edward White.

The motors have done this for us at least, that as they have made the highways their own beyond dispute, walking will remain the mystic and private pleasure of the secret and humble few. For us the byways, the footpaths, and the pastures will be sanctified and sweet. Thank heaven there are still gentle souls uncorrupted by the victrola and the limousine. In our old trousers and our easy shoes, with pipe and stick, we can do our fifteen miles between lunch and dinner, and glorify the ways of God to man.

And sometimes, about two o'clock of an afternoon (these spells come most often about half an hour after lunch), the old angel of peregrination lifts himself up in me, and I yearn and wamble for a season afoot. When a blue air is moving keenly through bare boughs this angel is most vociferous. I gape wanly round the lofty citadel where I am pretending to earn the Monday afternoon envelope. The filing case, thermostat, card index, typewriter, automatic telephone: these ingenious anodynes avail me not. Even the visits of golden nymphs, sweet ambassadors of commerce, who rustle in and out of my room with memoranda, mail, manuscripts, aye, even these lightfoot figures fail to charm. And the mind goes out to the endless vistas of streets, roads, fields, and rivers that summon the wanderer with laughing voice. Somewhere a great wind is scouring the hillsides; and once upon a time a man set out along the Great North Road to walk to Royston in the rain. . . .

Grant us, O Zeus! the tingling tremor of thigh and shank that comes of a dozen sturdy miles laid underheel. Grant us "fine walking on the hills in the direction of the sea"; or a winding road that tumbles down to some Cotswold village. Let an inn parlor lie behind red curtains, and a table be drawn toward the fire. Let there be a loin of cold beef, an elbow of yellow cheese, a tankard of dog's nose. Then may we prop our Bacon's Essays against the pewter and study those mellow words: "Certainly it is heaven upon earth to have a man's mind move in charity, rest in providence, and turn upon the poles of truth."

—Essays

THE ENDS OF THE EARTH

by G. K. Chesterton

Any man who could sensibly claim that Satan fell through the force of gravity, write an essay on "Tremendous Trifles," argue for "The Advantages of Having One Leg," and title a novel The Man Who Was Thursday *is obviously a member in good standing of the company of walkers. Chesterton is that man.*

I AM a bad traveller, or at least a bad tourist. My weakness as a traveller is that the world seems to me so amusing everywhere that it is hardly worth while to travel. When I start out for the ends of the earth, I am stopped on the road by an entertaining lamp post or a wildly signalling window-blind; and have not even sufficient sense of the scale of difference between these passing questions and the Quest.

—Alarms and Discursions

PENANG

by Winfield Townley Scott

1

I knew a man who wanted to see Penang
Because of the sound of its name when he was a boy.
And when he was a man he went to Penang
And found it an enchanting, a Malayan place.
He was not at all disappointed, he told me.

2

I myself, who originally came from
Plymouth, Massachusetts,—where people visit—
Have once with a most definite satisfaction
Walked in the streets of Springfield, Illinois.
More than names, then? No. Nothing is more than names.

—*Poetry,* December, 1962

THE EXHILARATIONS
OF THE ROAD

by John Burroughs

The lesson in running brooks, John Burroughs once pointed out, is that motion is a great purifier and health producer. Born April 3, 1837, he became a friend to Walt Whitman, Thomas Edison, Henry Ford and John Muir. He admired Emerson so much that his own writing began to have the inspired quality of Emerson's prose. According to Donald Culross Peattie, Burroughs looked and spoke like the prophet Elijah. He despised nature study as taught in the schools. He summed up his reaction to nature with the words "We have walked together."

OCCASIONALLY on the sidewalk, amid the dapper, swiftly moving, high-heeled boots and gaiters, I catch a glimpse of the naked human foot Nimbly it scuffs along, the toes spread, the sides flatten, the heel protrudes; it grasps the curbing, or bends to the form of the uneven surfaces,—a thing sensuous and alive, that seems to take cognizance of whatever it touches or passes. How primitive and uncivil it looks in such company,—a real barbarian in the parlor! We are so unused to the human anatomy, to simple, unadorned nature, that it looks a little repulsive; but it is beautiful for all that. Though it be a black foot and an unwashed foot, it shall be exalted. It is a thing of life amid leather, a free spirit amid cramped, a wild bird amid caged, an athlete amid consumptives. It is the symbol of my order, the Order of Walkers. That unhampered, vitally playing piece of anatomy is the type of the pedestrian, man returned to first principles, in direct contact and intercourse with the earth and the elements, his faculties unsheathed, his mind plastic, his body toughened, his heart light, his soul dilated; while those cramped and distorted members in the calf and kid are the unfortunate wretches doomed to carriages and cushions.

I am not going to advocate the disuse of boots and shoes, or the abandoning of the improved modes of travel; but I am going to brag as lustily as I can on behalf of the pedestrian, and show how all the shining angels second and accompany the man who goes afoot, while all the dark spirits are ever looking out for a chance to ride.

When I see the discomforts that able-bodied American men will put up with rather than go a mile or half a mile on foot, the abuses they will tolerate and encourage, crowding the street car on a little fall in the temperature or the appearance of an inch or two of snow, packing up to overflowing, dangling to the straps, treading on each other's toes, breathing each other's breaths, crushing the women and children, hanging by tooth and nail to a square inch of the platform, imperiling their limbs and killing the horses,—I think the commonest tramp in the street has good reason to felicitate himself on his rare privilege of going afoot. Indeed, a race that neglects or despises this primitive gift, that fears the touch of the soil, that has no footpaths, no community of ownership in the land which they imply, that warns off the walker as a trespasser, that knows no way but the highway, the carriage-way, that forgets the stile, the foot-bridge, that even ignores the rights of the pedestrian in the public road, providing no escape for him but in the ditch or up the bank, is in a fair way to far more serious degeneracy.

Shakespeare makes the chief qualification of the walker a merry heart:—

> "Jog on, jog on, the footpath way,
>   And merrily hent the stile-a;
> A merry heart goes all the day,
>   Your sad tires in a mile-a."

The human body is a steed that goes freest and longest under a light rider, and the lightest of all riders is a cheerful heart. Your sad, or morose, or embittered, or preoccupied heart settles heavily into the saddle, and the poor beast, the body, breaks down the first mile. Indeed, the heaviest thing in the world is a heavy heart. Next to that, the most burdensome to the walker is a heart not in perfect sympathy and accord with the body,— a reluctant or unwilling heart. The horse and rider must not only both be willing to go the same way, but the rider must lead the way and infuse his own lightness and eagerness into the steed. Herein is no doubt our trouble, and one reason of the decay of the noble art in this country. We

are unwilling walkers. We are not innocent and simple-hearted enough to
enjoy a walk. We have fallen from that state of grace which capacity to
enjoy a walk implies. . . .

A man must invest himself near at hand and in common things, and be
content with a steady and moderate return, if he would know the blessedness of a cheerful heart and the sweetness of a walk over the round earth.
This is a lesson the American has yet to learn,—capability of amusement
on a low key. He expects rapid and extraordinary returns. He would
make the very elemental laws pay usury. He has nothing to invest in a
walk; it is too slow, too cheap. We crave the astonishing, the exciting, the
far away, and do not know the highways of the gods when we see them,—
always a sign of the decay of the faith and simplicity of man.

If I say to my neighbor, "Come with me, I have great wonders to show
you," he pricks up his ears and comes forthwith; but when I take him on
the hills under the full blaze of the sun, or along the country road, our
footsteps lighted by the moon and stars, and say to him, "Behold, these
are the wonders, these are the circuits of the gods, this we now tread is a
morning star," he feels defrauded, and as if I had played him a trick. And
yet nothing less than dilatation and enthusiasm like this is the badge of the
master walker.

If we are not sad, we are careworn, hurried, discontented, mortgaging
the present for the promise of the future. If we take a walk, it is as we
take a prescription, with about the same relish and with about the same
purpose; and the more the fatigue, the greater our faith in the virtue of the
medicine.

Of those gleesome saunters over the hills in spring, or those sallies of
the body in winter, those excursions into space when the foot strikes fire
at every step, when the air tastes like a new and finer mixture, when we
accumulate force and gladness as we go along, when the sight of objects
by the roadside and of the fields and woods pleases more than pictures or
than all the art in the world,—those ten or twelve mile dashes that are but
the wit and effluence of the corporeal powers,—of such diversion and
open road entertainment, I say, most of us know very little.

I notice with astonishment that at our fashionable watering-places
nobody walks; that, of all those vast crowds of health-seekers and lovers
of country air, you can never catch one in the fields or woods, or guilty of
trudging along the country road with dust on his shoes and sun-tan on his
hands and face. The sole amusement seems to be to eat and dress and sit
about the hotels and glare at each other. The men look bored, the women

look tired, and all seem to sigh, "O Lord! what shall we do to be happy and not be vulgar?" Quite different from our British cousins across the water.

It is indeed astonishing with what ease and hilarity the English walk. To an American it seems a kind of infatuation. When Dickens was in this country, I imagine the aspirants to the honor of a walk with him were not numerous.

I fear, also, the American is becoming disqualified for the manly art of walking by a falling off in the size of his foot. He cherishes and cultivates this part of his anatomy, and apparently thinks his taste and good breeding are to be inferred from its diminutive size. A small, trim foot, well booted or gaitered, is the national vanity. How we stare at the big feet of foreigners, and wonder what may be the price of leather in those countries, and where all the aristocratic blood is, that these plebeian extremities so predominate! If we were admitted to the confidences of the shoemaker to Her Majesty or to His Royal Highness, no doubt we should modify our views upon this latter point, for a truly large and royal nature is never stunted in the extremities; a little foot never yet supported a great character.

It is said that Englishmen, when they first come to this country, are for some time under the impression that American women all have deformed feet, they are so coy of them and so studiously careful to keep them hid. That there is an astonishing difference between the women of the two countries in this respect, every traveler can testify; and that there is a difference equally astonishing between the pedestrian habits and capabilities of the rival sisters, is also certain.

The English pedestrian, no doubt, has the advantage of us in the matter of climate; for, notwithstanding the traditional gloom and moroseness of English skies, they have in that country none of those relaxing, sinking, enervating days, of which we have so many here, and which seem especially trying to the female constitution,—days which withdraw all support from the back and loins, and render walking of all things burdensome. Theirs is a climate of which it has been said that "it invites men abroad more days in the year and more hours in the day than that of any other country."

Then their land is threaded with paths which invite the walker, and which are scarcely less important than the highways. I heard of a surly nobleman near London who took it into his head to close a footpath that passed through his estate near his house, and open another a little farther off. The pedestrians objected; the matter got into the courts, and after protracted litigation the aristocrat was beaten. The path could not be closed or moved. The memory of man ran not to the time when there was not a footpath there, and every pedestrian should have the right of way there still.

I remember the pleasure I had in the path that connects Stratford-on-Avon with Shottery, Shakespeare's path when he went courting Anne Hathaway. By the king's highway the distance is some farther, so there is a well-worn path along the hedgerows and through the meadows and turnip patches. The traveler in it has the privilege of crossing the railroad track, an unusual privilege in England, and one denied to the lord in his carriage, who must either go over or under it. (It is a privilege, is it not, to be allowed the forbidden, even if it be the privilege of being run over by the engine?) In strolling over the South Downs, too, I was delighted to find that where the hill was steepest some benefactor of the order of walkers had made notches in the sward, so that the foot could bite the better and firmer; the path became a kind of stairway, which I have no doubt the plowman respected.

When you see an English country church withdrawn, secluded, out of the reach of wheels, standing amid grassy graves and surrounded by noble trees, approached by paths and shaded lanes, you appreciate more than ever this beautiful habit of the people. Only a race that knows how to use its feet, and holds footpaths sacred, could put such a charm of privacy and humility into such a structure. I think I should be tempted to go to church myself if I saw all my neighbors starting off across the fields or along paths that led to such charmed spots, and were sure I should not be jostled or run over by the rival chariots of the worshipers at the temple doors. I think that is what ails our religion; humility and devoutness of heart leave one when he lays by his walking shoes and walking clothes, and sets out for church drawn by something.

Indeed, I think it would be tantamount to an astonishing revival of religion if the people would all walk to church on Sunday and walk home again. . . . They would walk away from their *ennui,* their worldly cares, their uncharitableness, their pride of dress; for these devils always want to ride, while the simple virtues are never so happy as when on foot. Let us walk by all means; but if we will ride, get an ass.

Then the English claim that they are a more hearty and robust people than we are. It is certain they are a plainer people, have plainer tastes, dress plainer, build plainer, speak plainer, keep closer to facts, wear broader shoes and coarser clothes, and place a lower estimate on themselves,—all of which traits favor pedestrian habits. The English grandee is not confined to his carriage; but if the American aristocrat leaves his, he is ruined. Oh the weariness, the emptiness, the plotting, the seeking rest and finding none, that go by in the carriages! while your pedestrian is always cheerful, alert, refreshed, with his heart in his hand and his hand free to all. He looks down upon nobody; he is on the common level. His pores are all open, his circulation is active, his digestion good. His heart is not cold, nor are his faculties asleep. He is the only real traveler; he alone tastes the "gay, fresh sentiment of the road." He is not isolated, but is at one with things, with the farms and the industries on either hand. The vital, universal currents play through him. He knows the ground is alive; he feels the pulses of the wind, and reads the mute language of things. His sympathies are all aroused; his senses are continually reporting messages to his mind. Wind, frost, rain, heat, cold, are something to him. He is not merely a spectator of the panorama of nature, but a participator in it. . . . The walker does not need a large territory. When you get into a railway car you want a continent, the man in his carriage requires a township; but a walker like Thoreau finds as much and more along the shores of Walden Pond. The former, as it were, has merely time to glance at the headings of the chapters, while the latter need not miss a line, and Thoreau reads between the lines. Then the walker has the privilege of the fields, the woods, the hills, the byways. The apples by the roadside are for him, and the berries, and the spring of water, and the friendly shelter; and if the weather is cold, he eats the frost grapes and the persimmons, or even the white-meated turnip, snatched from the field he passed through, with incredible relish.

Afoot and in the open road, one has a fair start in life at last. There is no hindrance now. Let him put his best foot forward. He is on the broadest human plane. This is on the level of all the great laws and heroic deeds. From this platform he is eligible to any good fortune. He was sighing for the golden age; let him walk to it. Every step brings him nearer. The youth of the world is but a few days' journey distant. . . .

I think if I could walk through a country, I should not only see many things and have adventures that I should otherwise miss, but that I should come into relations with that country at first hand, and with the men and women in it, in a way that would afford the deepest satisfaction. Hence I envy the good fortune of all walkers, and feel like joining myself to every tramp that comes along. . . . I think how much richer and firmer-grained life would be to me if I could journey afoot through Florida and Texas, or follow the windings of the Platte or the Yellowstone, or stroll through Oregon, or browse for a season about Canada. In the bright, inspiring days of autumn I only want the time and the companion to walk back to the natal spot, the family nest, across two States and into the mountains of a third. What adventures we would have by the way . . . what spectacles we would behold . . . what characters we should fall in with, and how seasoned and hardy we should arrive at our destination!

It is another proof of how walking brings out the true character of a man. The devil never yet asked his victims to take a walk with him. You will not be long in finding your companion out. All disguises will fall away from him. As his pores open his character is laid bare. His deepest and most private self will come to the top. It matters little with whom you ride, so he be not a pickpocket; for both of you will, very likely, settle down closer and firmer in your reserve, shaken down like a measure of corn by the jolting as the journey proceeds. But walking is a more vital copartnership; the relation is a closer and more sympathetic one, and you do not feel like walking ten paces with a stranger without speaking to him.

Hence the fastidiousness of the professional walker in choosing or admitting a companion, and hence the truth of a remark of Emerson, that you will generally fare better to take your dog than to invite your neighbor. Your cur-dog is a true pedestrian, and your neighbor is very likely a small politician. The dog enters thoroughly into the spirit of the enterprise; he is not indifferent or preoccupied; he is constantly sniffing adventure, laps at every spring, looks upon every field and wood as a new world to be explored, is ever on some fresh trail, knows something important will happen a little farther on, gazes with the true wonder-seeing eyes, whatever the spot or whatever the road finds it good to be there,—in short, is just that happy, delicious, excursive vagabond that touches one at so many points, and whose human prototype in a companion robs miles and leagues of half their power to fatigue.

Persons who find themselves spent in a short walk to the market or the post-office, or to do a little shopping, wonder how it is that their pedestrian friends can compass so many weary miles and not fall down from sheer exhaustion; ignorant of the fact that the walker is a kind of projectile that drops far or near according to the expansive force of the motive that set it in motion, and that it is easy enough to regulate the charge according to the distance to be traversed. If I am loaded to carry only one mile and am compelled to walk three, I generally feel more fatigue than if I had walked six under the proper impetus of pre-adjusted resolution. In other words, the will or corporeal mainspring, whatever it be, is capable of being wound up to different degrees of tension, so that one may walk all day nearly as easy as half that time, if he is prepared beforehand. . . . It is for this reason that an unknown road is always a long road. We cannot cast the mental eye along it and see the end from the beginning. . . .

Then, again, how annoying to be told it is only five miles to the next place when it is really eight or ten! We fall short nearly half the distance, and are compelled to urge and roll the spent ball the rest of the way. In such a case walking degenerates from a fine art to a mechanic art; we walk merely; to get over the ground becomes the one serious and engrossing thought; whereas success in walking is not to let your right foot know what your left foot doeth. Your heart must furnish such music that in keeping time to it your feet will carry you around the globe without knowing it. The walker I would describe takes no note of distance; his walk is a sally, a *bonmot,* an unspoken *jeu d'esprit;* the ground is his butt, his provocation; it furnishes him the resistance his body craves; he rebounds upon it, he glances off and returns again, and uses it gayly as his tool.

I do not think I exaggerate the importance or the charms of pedestrianism, or our need as a people to cultivate the art. I think it would tend to soften the national manners, to teach us the meaning of leisure, to acquaint us with the charms of the open air, to strengthen and foster the tie between the race and the land. No one else looks out upon the world so kindly and charitably as the pedestrian; no one else gives and takes so much from the country he passes through. . . .

Man takes root at his feet, and at best he is no more than a potted plant in his house or carriage till he has established communication with the soil by the loving and magnetic touch of his soles to it. . . .

The roads and paths you have walked along in summer and winter weather, the fields and hills which you have looked upon in lightness and gladness of heart, where fresh thoughts have come into your mind, or some noble prospect has opened before you, and especially the quiet ways where you have walked in sweet converse with your friend, pausing under the trees, drinking at the spring,—henceforth they are not the same; a new charm is added; those thoughts spring there perennial, your friend walks there forever.

We have produced some good walkers and saunterers, and some noted climbers; but as a staple recreation, as a daily practice, the mass of the people dislike and despise walking. Thoreau said he was a good horse, but a poor roadster. I chant the virtues of the roadster as well. I sing of the sweetness of gravel, good sharp quartz-grit. It is the proper condiment for the sterner seasons, and many a human gizzard would be cured of half its ills by a suitable daily allowance of it. I think Thoreau himself would have profited immensely by it. His diet was too exclusively vegetable. A man cannot live on grass alone. If one has been a lotus-eater all summer, he must turn gravel-eater in the fall and winter. Those who have tried it know that gravel possesses an equal though an opposite charm. It spurs to action. The foot tastes it and henceforth rests not. The joy of moving and surmounting, of attrition and progression, the thirst for space, for miles and leagues of distance, for sights and prospects, to cross mountains and thread rivers, and defy frost, heat, snow, danger, difficulties, seizes it; and from that day forth its possessor is enrolled in the noble army of walkers.

—Winter Sunshine

DEPARTURE

by Edna St. Vincent Millay

It's little I care what path I take,
And where it leads it's little I care; . . .

I wish I could walk for a day and a night,
And find me at dawn in a desolate place
With never the rut of a road in sight,
Nor the roof of a house, nor the eyes of a face.

—*Collected Poems*

EMERSON AT YOSEMITE

by John Muir

Iohn Muir was born in Scotland, where he developed an insatiable appetite for moors and lakes and rugged landscapes. We remember him as the daring young man who walked a thousand miles to the Gulf, laid out the trails we are still using in Yosemite and the red woods of California, and was host at his campfires in the Sierras to Emerson and Burroughs and to Theodore Roosevelt, who was President of the United States at the time. His meeting with Emerson was recounted in the Atlantic Monthly *in an article called "The Forests of Yosemite Park."*

DURING my first years in the Sierra I was ever calling on everybody within reach to admire the vast, billowy forests of conifers, but I found no one half warm enough until Emerson came. I had read his essays and felt sure that of all men he would best interpret the sayings of these noble mountains and trees. Nor was my faith weakened when I met him in Yosemite. He seemed as serene as a sequoia, his head in the empyrean; and forgetting his age, plans, duties, ties of every sort, I proposed a camping trip back in the heart of the mountains.

He seemed anxious to go, but considerately mentioned his party. I said: "Never mind. The mountains are calling; run away, and let plans and parties and dragging lowland duties all 'gang tap-sal-teerie.' We'll go up a cañon singing your own song, 'Good-by, proud world! I'm going home,' in divine earnest. Up there lies a new heaven and a new earth; let us go to the show." But alas, it was too late, too near the sundown of his life. The shadows were growing long, and he leaned on his friends. His party, full of indoor philosophy, failed to see the natural beauty and fullness of promise of my wild plan and laughed at it in good-natured ignorance, as if it were necessarily amusing to imagine that Boston people might be led to accept Sierra manifestations of God at the price of rough camping. Anyhow, they would have none of it and held Mr. Emerson to the hotels and trails.

After spending only five tourist days in Yosemite he was led away, but I saw him two days more; for I was kindly invited to go with the party as far as the Mariposa Big Trees. I told Mr. Emerson that I would gladly go to the sequoias with him, if he would camp in the grove. He consented heartily, and I felt sure that we would have at least one good wild memorable night round a sequoia campfire. Next day we rode through the magnificent forests of the Merced basin, and I kept calling his attention to the sugar pines, quoting his wood notes, "Come listen what the pine tree saith," and so forth, pointing out the noblest as kings and high priests, the most eloquent and commanding preachers of all the mountain forests, stretching forth their century-old arms in benediction over the congregations crowded about them. He gazed in devout admiration, saying but little, while his fine smile faded away.

Early in the afternoon, when we reached Clark's Station, I was surprised to see the party dismount. And when I asked if we were not going up into the grove to camp, they said: "No, it would never do to lie out in the night air. Mr. Emerson might take cold; and you know, Mr. Muir, that would be a dreadful thing." In vain I urged that only in homes and hotels were colds caught, that nobody ever was known to take cold camping in these woods, that there was not a single cough or sneeze in all the Sierra. Then I pictured the big climate-changing, inspiring fire I would make, praised the beauty and fragrance of sequoia flame, told how the great trees would stand about us transfigured in the purple light while the stars looked down between the great domes, ending by urging them to come on and make an immortal Emerson night of it. But the house habit was not to be overcome, nor the strange dread of pure night air, though it is only cooled day air with a little pure dew in it. So the carpet dust and unknowable reeks were preferred. And to think of this being a Boston choice! Sad commentary on culture and the glorious transcendentalism.

Accustomed to reach whatever place I started for, I was going up the mountain alone to camp and wait the coming of the party next day. But since Emerson was so soon to vanish, I concluded to stop with him. He hardly spoke a word all the evening, yet it was a great pleasure simply to be near him, warming in the light of his face as at a fire. In the morning we rode up the trail through a noble forest of pine and fir into the

Mariposa Grove and stayed an hour or two, mostly in ordinary tourist fashion—looking at the biggest giants, measuring them with a tape line, riding through prostrate fire-bored trunks, and so forth, though Mr. Emerson was alone occasionally, sauntering about as if under a spell. As we walked through a fine group, he quoted, "There were giants in those days," recognizing the antiquity of the race. To commemorate his visit, Galen Clark, the guardian of the grove, selected the finest of the unnamed trees and requested him to give it a name. He named it Samoset, after the New England sachem, as the best that occurred to him.

The poor bit of measured time was soon spent, and while the saddles were being adjusted I again urged Emerson to stay. "You are yourself a sequoia," I said. "Stop and get acquainted with your big brethren." But he was past his prime and was now as a child in the hands of his affectionate but sadly civilized friends, who seemed as full of old-fashioned conformity as of bold intellectual independence. It was the afternoon of the day and the afternoon of his life, and his course was now westward down all the mountains into the sunset. The party mounted and rode away in wondrous contentment, apparently. I followed to the edge of the grove. Emerson lingered in the rear of the train, and when he reached the top of the ridge, after all the rest of the party were over and out of sight, he turned his horse, took off his hat, and waved me a last good-by.

I felt lonely, so sure had I been that Emerson of all men would be the quickest to see the mountains and sing them. Gazing awhile on the spot where he vanished, I sauntered back into the heart of the grove, made a bed of sequoia plumes and ferns by the side of a stream, gathered a store of firewood, and then walked about until sundown. The birds, robins, thrushes, and warblers that had kept out of sight came about me, now that all was quiet, and made cheer. After sundown I built a great fire, and as usual had it all to myself. And though lonesome for the first time in these forests, I quickly took heart again—the trees had not gone to Boston, nor the birds; and as I sat by the fire, Emerson was still with me in spirit, though I never again saw him in the flesh. He sent books and wrote, cheering me on; advised me not to stay too long in solitude. Soon he hoped my guardian angel would intimate that my probation was at a close. Then I was to roll up my herbariums, sketches, and poems (though I never knew I had any poems), and come to his house; and when I tired of him and his humble surroundings, he would show me to better people.

But there remained many a forest to wander through, many a mountain and glacier to cross, before I was to see his Wachusett and Monadnock, Boston and Concord. It was seventeen years after our parting on the Wawona Ridge that I stood beside his grave under a pine tree on the hill above Sleepy Hollow. He had gone to higher Sierras, and, as I fancied, was again waving his hand in friendly recognition.

—*Atlantic Monthly,* April, 1900

NIGHT WALKS

by Charles Dickens

One would have expected the author of David Copperfield *and* The Pickwick Papers *to be a great walker. This essay by a self-cured insomniac proves that he was also a good doctor. His prescription: "If you can't sleep, try walking."*

SOME YEARS AGO, a temporary inability to sleep, referable to a distressing impression, caused me to walk about the streets all night, for a series of several nights. The disorder might have taken a long time to conquer, if it had been faintly experimented on in bed; but it was soon defeated by the brisk treatment of getting up directly, after lying down, and going out, and coming home tired at sunrise.

In the course of those nights, I finished my education in a fair amateur experience of houselessness. My principal object being to get through the night, the pursuit of it brought me into sympathetic relations with people who have no other object every night in the year.

The month was March, and the weather damp, cloudy, and cold. The sun not rising before half-past five, the night perspective looked sufficiently long at half-past twelve; which was about my time for confronting it.

The restlessness of a great city, and the way in which it tumbles and tosses before it can get to sleep, formed one of the first entertainments offered to the contemplation of us houseless people. It lasted about two hours. We lost a great deal of companionship when the late public-houses turned their lamps out, and when the potmen thrust the last brawling drunkards into the street; but stray vehicles and stray people were left us, after that. If we were very lucky, a policeman's rattle sprang and a fray turned up; but, in general, surprisingly little of this diversion was provided. Except in the Haymarket, which is the worst kept part of London, and about Kent-street in the Borough, and along a portion of the line of the Old Kent-road, the peace was seldom violently broken. But, it was always the case that London, as if in imitation of individual citizens belonging to it, had expiring fits and starts of restlessness. After all seemed quiet, if one cab rattled by, half-a-dozen would surely follow; and Houselessness even observed that intoxicated people appeared to be magnetically attracted towards each other; so that we knew when we saw one drunken object staggering against the shutters of a shop, that another drunken object would stagger up before five minutes were out, to frater-nise or fight with it. When we made a divergence from the regular species of drunkard, the thin-armed, puff-faced, leaden-lipped gin-drinker, and encountered a rarer specimen of a more decent appearance, fifty to one but that specimen was dressed in soiled mourning. As the street experi-ence in the night, so the street experience in the day; the common folk who come unexpectedly into a little property come unexpectedly into a deal of liquor.

At length these flickering sparks would die away, worn out—the last veritable sparks of waking life trailed from some late pieman or hot-potato man—and London would sink to rest. And then the yearning of the houseless mind would be for any sign of company, any lighted place, any movement, anything suggestive of any one being up—nay, even so much as awake, for the houseless eye looked out for lights in windows.

Walking the streets under the pattering rain, Houselessness would walk and walk and walk, seeing nothing but the interminable tangle of streets, save at a corner, here and there, two policemen in conversation, or the sergeant or inspector looking after his men. Now and then in the night—but rarely—Houselessness would become aware of a furtive head peering out of a doorway a few yards before him, and, coming up with the head, would find a man standing bolt upright to keep within the doorway's shadow, and evidently intent upon no particular service to society. Under a kind of fascination, and in a ghostly silence suitable to the time, Houselessness and this gentleman would eye one another from head to foot, and so, without exchange of speech, part, mutually suspicious. Drip, drip, drip, from ledge and coping, splash from pipes and water-spouts, and by-and-by the houseless shadow would fall upon the stones that pave the way to Waterloo-bridge; it being in the houseless mind to have a halfpenny worth of excuse for saying "Good-night" to the toll-keeper, and catching a glimpse of his fire. A good fire and a good great-coat and a good woollen neck-shawl, were comfortable things to see in conjunction with the toll-keeper; also his brisk wakefulness was excellent company when he rattled the change of halfpence down upon that metal table of his, like a man who defied the night, with all its sorrowful thoughts, and didn't care for the coming of dawn. . . . The wild moon and clouds were as restless as an evil conscience in a tumbled bed, and the very shadow of the immensity of London seemed to lie oppressively upon the river. . . .

When a church clock strikes, on houseless ears in the dead of the night, it may be at first mistaken for company and hailed as such. But, as the spreading circles of vibration, which you may perceive at such a time with great clearness, go opening out, for ever and ever afterwards widening perhaps (as the philosopher has suggested) in eternal space, the mistake is rectified and the sense of loneliness is profounder. . . .

There was early coffee to be got about Covent-garden Market, and that was more company—warm company, too, which was better. Toast of a very substantial quality, was likewise procurable; though the towzled-headed man who made it, in an inner chamber within the coffee-room, hadn't got his coat on yet, and was so heavy with sleep that in every interval of toast and coffee he went off anew behind the partition into complicated cross-roads of choke and snore, and lost his way directly. Into one of these establishments (among the earliest) near Bow-street, there came one morning as I sat over my houseless cup, pondering where to go next, a man in a high and long snuff-coloured coat, and shoes, and, to the best of my belief, nothing else but a hat, who took out of his hat a large cold meat pudding; a meat pudding so large that it was a very tight fit, and brought the lining of the hat out with it. This mysterious man was known by his pudding, for on his entering, the man of sleep brought him a pint of hot tea, a small loaf, and a large knife and fork and plate. Left to himself in his box, he stood the pudding on the bare table, and, instead of cutting it, stabbed it, overhand, with the knife, like a mortal enemy; then took the knife out, wiped it on his sleeve, tore the pudding asunder with his fingers, and ate it all up. The remembrance of this man with the pudding remains with me as the remembrance of the most spectral person my houselessness encountered. . . .

When there was no market, or when I wanted variety, a railway terminus with the morning mails coming in, was remunerative company. But like most of the company to be had in this world, it lasted only a very short time. The station lamps would burst out ablaze, the porters would emerge from places of concealment, the cabs and trucks would rattle to their places (the post-office carts were already in theirs), and, finally, the bell would strike up, and the train would come banging in. But there were few passengers and little luggage, and everything scuttled away with the greatest expedition. The locomotive post-offices, with their great nets—as if they had been dragging the country for bodies—would fly open as to their doors, and would disgorge a smell of lamp, an exhausted clerk, a guard in a red coat, and their bags of letters; the engine would blow and heave and perspire, like an engine wiping its forehead and saying what a run it had had; and within ten minutes the lamps were out, and I was houseless and alone again. . . .

And so by faster and faster degrees, until the last degrees were very fast, the day came, and I was tired and could sleep.

—*The Uncommercial Traveller*

A SPRING WALK

by John Kieran

In an amusing footnote to the Foreword of his Treasury *of* Great
Nature Writing, *John Kieran wrote, "The insertion of verse in this
volume is all my fault. I am incorrigibly fond of poetry. I managed
to get it in over the dead bodies of several publishing executives who
threw themselves out of various windows when I insisted." Which is
a better portrait of the man than any we could paint. Some of you
may still remember him as one of that amazing panel of witty experts
(along with Clifton Fadiman and F.P.A.) who made the* Information
Please *radio and television program a delight for millions. Edwin
Way Teale once said of his nature writing, "He has made a recreation
of a recreation."*

SIMPLE HONESTY compels the warning that reading these words
may possibly do you good and, therefore, you had better give some
thought to the matter of dropping it right here. From this point you
continue reading only at your own risk and peril.

Henry Thoreau, the American essayist and philosopher, once said: "If
I knew for a certainty that a man was coming to my house with the
conscious design of doing me good, I should run for my life." Quite right,
too, but don't start running immediately because I herewith disclaim any
conscious design of doing anybody any good.

I am merely setting down some reflections on a habit I have formed of
walking at least two miles, if possible, every day. However, walking has
been highly spoken of as a healthful exercise. In fact, many sedentary
physicians prescribe it for patients, alleging that "a walk will do you
good." Now, I view the matter in an entirely different light. I walk
because I like to walk. I enjoy the exercise and I am entertained by what I
see and hear along the way. It may be that the doctors are right in saying

that "walking is good for you," but the only opinion I have to offer from a medical standpoint is that I have been taking daily walks for some thirty years and I conclude that, though habit-forming, the practice is not quickly fatal. If amiable mention of some of the enjoyments of walking stirs a reader to going for a walk which, as the weight of medical opinion has it, "will do him good," the blame lies on his own head and I wash my hands of it.

One thing about walking is that it costs practically nothing, which is an important item these days. It is also a highly respectable diversion—especially in the springtime—and often looked upon with admiration if the walker wears tweeds and carries a blackthorn stick, though that isn't the way I take to the road myself. Old clothes and a pair of field glasses with which to spy on birds are my equipment.

Walking is time-honored, hallowed by footprints famous in history. Plato expounded his philosophy while walking up and down an olive grove in an Athens park some 2,300 years ago. Peter the Hermit went on a walking tour of France and Germany in 1095 A.D. and stirred up the First Crusade, which eventually led to the others and a vast amount of long-distance walking.

There is no reason for boasting of walking as though it were a special talent or virtue possessed by an endowed few. Everybody who isn't bedridden walks to some extent every day. But to set out deliberately for a walk is another matter, and any discussion of it must include mention of relevant matters such as time, place, distance and weather conditions. Edward Payson Weston walked all the way across the United States. Dr. Livingstone walked across Africa. Admiral Peary finally reached the North Pole on foot, and Roald Amundsen arrived at the South Pole in similar plodding fashion which, I think, was going to extremes. I merely hope to get in my modest two miles or more a day, preferably over open and friendly country.

Often it takes me some hours because I so frequently stand around watching birds through my field glasses or stop to peer through a pocket magnifying glass at buds, leaves, flowers, seed pods, insects or other interesting items encountered en route. If it is good country, I never tire of going over the same ground and heartily concur in the opinion of the naturalist John Burroughs: "To learn something new, take the path today that you took yesterday."

There is a neighborhood swamp that I have been visiting since boyhood, and it still keeps turning up something new for me. There the skunk cabbages, brazenly poking their noses up through the snow and frozen ground in January, start the spring push. There the early birds from the South arrive in late February and the spring "peepers" sound off in March. It's in the swamp that the fresh greenery of the young year first catches the eye. Here is the home of the wood duck and the bittern, the spicebush and the marsh marigold, the speckled alder and the red maple.

Since I walk at all seasons, I encounter all sorts of weather, some of which I do not approve. I like walking in the spring rain when I am properly dressed for the occasion, but I never met a man, woman or beast who really enjoyed walking in a drenching downpour. Personally, I'm against high winds, too, by land or sea, especially at low temperatures when they cut like a knife. Tennyson moodily mentions "blasts that blow the poplar white" and such strong winds that "rooks are blown about the skies." Picturesque and poetical, to be sure, but Aeolus can put those winds back in the bag so far as I am concerned. Rain needn't bother a walker unless it is overdone, in which case it makes hard going. A curious thing that soon becomes apparent to one who is not easily balked of a daily walk is that, whether it is raining or blowing, the weather is never as bad outside as it looks through a living-room window.

I have good friends who share my liking for cross-country work and they double the enjoyment of a fine walk. But even if I start out alone, I meet many friends along the way. Eyebrows may be raised, or there may be some significant tapping of the forehead, when I mention some of these friends. One is a red-tailed hawk that I have come to know because it has several primary feathers permanently missing from its right wing.

Other friends are an assortment of painted turtles that sun themselves on a half-submerged log in my favorite swamp. Before we became well acquainted they would slide off into the water at my approach, but now that we know one another they acknowledge the friendship by remaining undisturbed as I go by. On several occasions, indeed, one or two have winked at me. Other firm friends are three tall tulip trees that stand on a roadside above a river, their great trunks looming up like Greek columns. Every time I meet these trees I feel the better for it.

Comfortable footwear is at the bottom of every enjoyable step along the road. If the shoe doesn't fit, no sensible walker would think of wearing it. Woolen socks are best. Dress optional, depending upon the weather. When in doubt, play it safe.

Take to the woods on windy days. It's quieter there. Keep your ears open. You can always hear more birds than you can see. Keep your eyes open. There are flowers in bloom through most months of the year, and trees are as interesting even in early spring as they are in summer. These are not sinister suggestions to stir up nonwalkers but merely my own rules of conduct. I have a few more. Take the sun over your shoulder for the best views. Avoid slippery footing as you would the plague, and don't sit on damp ground. Keep walking.

—*Collier's,* April 18, 1953

ON GOING ABOUT AND SEEING THINGS

by Lin Yutang

This admirable essay on travel as seen through the eyes of Lin Yutang appeared in a book of his published in 1937. Time has only mellowed its gentle Oriental wisdom.

TRAVEL used to be a pleasure, now it has become an industry. No doubt there are greater facilities for traveling today than a hundred years ago, and governments with their official travel bureaus have exploited the tourist trade, with the result that the modern man travels on the whole much more than his grandfather. Nevertheless travel seems to have become a lost art. In order to understand the art of travel, one should first of all beware of the different types of false travel, which is no travel at all.

The first kind of false travel is travel to improve one's mind. This matter of improving one's mind has undoubtedly been overdone. I doubt very much whether one's mind can be so easily improved. Anyway there is very little evidence of it at clubs and lectures. But if we are usually so serious as to be bent upon improving our minds, we should at least during a vacation let the mind lie fallow, and give it a holiday. . . .

The second kind of false travel is travel for conversation, in order that one may talk about it afterwards. I have seen visitors at Hup'ao of Hangchow, a place famous for its tea and spring water, having their picture taken in the act of lifting tea cups to their lips. To be sure, it is a highly poetic sentiment to show friends a picture of themselves drinking tea at Hup'ao. The danger is that one spends less thought on the actual taste of the tea than on the photograph itself. This sort of thing can become an obsession, especially with travelers provided with cameras, as we so often see on sight-seeing buses in Paris and London. The tourists are so busy with their cameras that they have no time to look at the places themselves. Of course they have the privilege of looking at them in the pictures afterwards when they go home, but it is obvious that pictures of Trafalgar Square or the Champs Elysees can be bought in New York or in Peiping. As these historical places become places to be talked about afterwards instead of places to be looked at, it is natural that the more places one visits, the richer the memory will be, and the more places there will be to talk about. This urge for learning and scholarship therefore impels the tourist to cover as many points as possible in a day. He has in his hand a program of places to visit, and as he comes to a place, he checks it off with a pencil on the program. I suspect such travelers are trying to be efficient even on their holiday.

This sort of foolish travel necessarily produces the third type of false travelers, who travel by schedule, knowing beforehand exactly how many hours they are going to spend in Vienna or Budapest. Before such a traveler departs, he makes a perfect schedule for himself and religiously adheres to it. Bound by the clock and run by the calendar as he is at home, he is still bound by the clock and run by the calendar while abroad.

In place of these false types of travel, I propose that the true motives of travel are, or should be, otherwise. In the first place, the true motive of travel should be travel to become lost and unknown. . . .

A true traveler is always a vagabond, with the joys, temptations and sense of adventure of the vagabond. Either travel is "vagabonding" or it is no travel at all. The essence of travel is to have no duties, no fixed hours, no mail, no inquisitive neighbors, no receiving delegations, and no destination. A good traveler is one who does not know where he is going to, and a perfect traveler does not know where he came from. He does not even know his own name and surname. . . . Probably he hasn't got a single friend in a strange land, but as a Chinese nun expressed it, "Not to care for anybody in particular is to care for mankind in general." Having no particular friend is having everybody as one's friend. Loving mankind in general, he mixes with them and goes about observing the charms of people and their customs. . . .

The spirit of vagabondage makes it possible for people taking a vacation to get closer to Nature. Travelers of this kind will therefore insist on going to the summer resorts where there are the fewest people and one can have some sort of real solitude and communion with Nature. Travelers of this sort, therefore, do not in their preparation for journeys go into a department store and take a lot of time to select a pink or a blue bathing suit. Lipstick is still allowable because a vacationist, being a follower of Jean Jacques Rousseau, wants to be natural, and no lady can be quite natural without a good lipstick. But that is due to the fact that one goes to the summer resorts and beaches where everybody goes, and the entire benefit of a closer association with Nature is lost or forgotten. . . .

I may suggest that there is a different kind of travel, travel to see nothing and to see nobody, but the squirrels and muskrats and woodchucks and clouds and trees. A friend of mine, an American lady, described for me how she went with some Chinese friends to a hill in the neighborhood of Hangchow, *in order to see nothing.* It was a misty day in the morning, and as they went up, the mist became heavier and heavier. One could hear the soft beat of drops of moisture on the leaves of grass. There was nothing to be seen but fog. The American lady was discouraged. "But you must come along; there's a wonderful sight on top," insisted her Chinese friends. She went up with them and after a while saw an ugly rock in the distance enveloped by the clouds, which had been heralded as a great sight. "What is there?" she asked. "That is the Inverted Lotus," her friends replied. Somewhat mortified, she was ready to go down. "But there is a still more wonderful sight on top," they said. Her dress was already half damp with the moisture, but she had given up the fight already and went on with them. Finally they reached the summit. All about them was an expanse of mists and fogs, with the outline of distant hills barely visible on the horizon. "But there is nothing to see here," my American friend protested. "That is exactly the point. We come up to see nothing," her Chinese friends replied.

There is all the difference between seeing things and seeing nothing. Many travelers who see things really see nothing, and many who see nothing see a great deal. I am always amused at hearing of an author going to a foreign country to "get material for his new book," as if he had exhausted all there was to see in humanity in his own town or country and as if the theme could ever be exhausted. "Thrums" must be unromantic and the Island of Guernsey too dull to build a great novel upon! We come therefore to the *philosophy of travel as consisting of the capacity to see things,* which abolishes the distinction between travel to a distant country and going about the fields of an afternoon.

The two become the same thing, as Chin Shengt'an insisted. The most necessary outfit a traveler has to carry along with him is "a special talent in his breast and a special vision below his eyebrows," as the Chinese dramatic critic expressed it in his famous running comment on the drama *Western Chamber*. The point is whether one has got the heart to feel and the eyes to see. If he hasn't, his visits to the mountains are a pure waste of time and money; on the other hand, if he has got "a special talent in his breast and a special vision below his eyebrows," he can get the greatest joy of travel even without going to the mountains, by staying at home and watching and going about the field to watch a sailing cloud, or a dog, or a hedge, or a lonely tree.

—*The Importance of Living*

WALKING MOODS

by George Gissing

One of our perennial rereading *books is that golden repository of mellow moods and dark wisdom,* The Private Papers of Henry Ryecroft. *Here, brought together for our "walker's reader," are the nostalgic paragraphs that deal with our favorite subjects, books and walking.*

TO-DAY I have walked afar, and at the end of my walk I found the little white-flowered woodruff. It grew in a copse of young ash. When I had looked long at the flower, I delighted myself with the grace of the slim trees about it—their shining smoothness, their olive hue. Hard by stood a bush of wych elm; its tettered bark, overlined as if with the character of some unknown tongue, made the young ashes yet more beautiful. It matters not how long I wander. There is no task to bring me back; no one will be vexed or uneasy, linger I ever so late. Spring is shining upon these lanes and meadows; I feel as if I must follow every winding track that opens by my way. Spring has restored to me something of the long-forgotten vigour of youth; I walk without weariness; I sing to myself like a boy, and the song is one I knew in boyhood.

For more than six years I trod the pavement, never stepping once upon mother earth—for the parks are but pavement disguised with a growth of grass.

Sometimes I added the labour of a porter to my fasting endured for the sake of books. At the little shop near Portland Road Station I came upon a first edition of Gibbon, the price an absurdity—I think it was a shilling a volume. To possess those clean-paged quartos I would have sold my coat. As it happened, I had not money enough with me, but sufficient at home. I was living at Islington. Having spoken with the bookseller, I walked home, took the cash, walked back again, and—carried the tomes from the west end of Euston Road to a street in Islington far beyond the *Angel*. I did it in two journeys—this being the only time in my life when I thought of Gibbon in avoirdupois. Twice—three times reckoning the walk for the money—did I descend on Euston Road and climb Pentonville on that occasion. Of the season and the weather I have no recollection; my joy in the purchase I had made drove out every other thought. Except, indeed, of the weight. I had infinite energy, but not much muscular strength, and the end of the last journey saw me upon a chair, perspiring, flaccid, aching—exultant!

Morning after morning, of late, I have taken my walk in the same direction, my purpose being to look at a plantation of young larches. There is no lovelier colour on earth than that in which they are now clad; it seems to refresh as well as gladden my eyes, and its influence sinks deep into my heart. Too soon it will change; already I think the first radiant verdure has begun to pass into summer's soberness. The larch has its moment of unmatched beauty—and well for him whose chance permits him to enjoy it, spring after spring.

Could anything be more wonderful than the fact that here am I, day by day, not only at leisure to walk forth and gaze at the larches, but blessed with the tranquillity of mind needful for such enjoyment? On any morning of spring sunshine, how many mortals find themselves so much at peace that they are able to give themselves wholly to delight in the glory of heaven and of earth? Is it the case with one man in every fifty thousand? Consider what extraordinary kindness of fate must tend upon one, that not a care, not a preoccupation, should interfere with his contemplative thought for five or six days successively! So rooted in the human mind (and so reasonably rooted) is the belief in an Envious Power, that I ask myself whether I shall not have to pay, by some disaster, for this period of sacred calm. For a week or so I have been one of a small number, chosen out of the whole human race by fate's supreme benediction. It may be that this comes to every one in turn; to most, it can only be once in a lifetime, and so briefly. That my own lot seems so much better than that of ordinary men sometimes makes me fearful.

In this hot weather I like to walk at times amid the full glow of the sun. Our island sun is never hot beyond endurance, and there is a magnificence in the triumph of high summer which exalts one's mind. Among streets it is hard to bear, yet even there, for those who have eyes to see it, the splendour of the sky lends beauty to things in themselves mean or hideous. I remember an August bank-holiday, when, having for some reason to walk across London, I unexpectedly found myself enjoying the strange desertion of great streets, and from that passed to surprise in the sense of something beautiful, a charm in the vulgar vista, in the dull architecture which I had never known. Deep and clear-marked shadows, such as one only sees on a few days of summer, are in themselves very impressive, and become more so when they fall upon highways devoid of folk. I remember observing, as something new, the shape of familiar edifices, of spires, monuments. And when at length I sat down somewhere on the Embankment, it was rather to gaze at leisure than to rest, for I felt no weariness, and the sun, still pouring upon me its noontide radiance, seemed to fill my veins with life.

That sense I shall never know again. For me Nature has comforts, raptures, but no more invigoration. The sun keeps me alive, but cannot, as in the old days, renew my being. I would fain learn to enjoy without reflecting.

My walk in the golden hours leads me to a great horse-chestnut, whose root offers a convenient seat in the shadow of its foliage. At that resting-place I have no wide view before me, but what I see is enough—a corner of waste-land, over-flowered with poppies and charlock, on the edge of a field of corn. The brilliant red and yellow harmonize with the glory of the day. Near by, too, is a hedge covered with great white blooms of the bindweed. My eyes do not soon grow weary.

A whole day's walk yesterday with no plan; just a long ramble of hour after hour, entirely enjoyable. It ended at Topsham, where I sat on the little churchyard terrace, and watched the evening tide come up the broad estuary. I have a great liking for Topsham, and that churchyard, over-looking what is not quite sea, yet more than river, is one of the most restful spots I know. Of course, the association with old Chaucer, who speaks of Topsham sailors, helps my mood. I came home very tired; but I am not yet decrepit, and for that I must be thankful.

The unspeakable blessedness of having a *home!* Much as my imagina-tion has dwelt upon it for thirty years, I never knew how deep and exquisite a joy could lie in the assurance that one is at *home* for ever. Again and again I come back upon this thought; nothing but Death can oust me from my abiding place. And death I would fain learn to regard as a friend, who will but intensify the peace I now relish.

When one is at home, how one's affections grow about everything in the neighbourhood! I always thought with fondness of this corner of Devon, but what was that compared with the love which now strengthens in me day by day! Beginning with my house, every stick and stone of it is dear to me as my heart's blood; I find myself laying an affectionate hand on the door-post, giving a pat, as I go by, to the garden gate. Every tree and shrub in the garden is my beloved friend; I touch them, when need is, very tenderly, as though carelessness might pain, or roughness injure them. If I pull up a weed in the walk, I look at it with a certain sadness before throwing it away; it belongs to my home. And all the country round about. These villages, how delightful are their names to my ear! I find myself reading with interest all the local news in the Exeter paper. Not that I care about the people; with barely one or two exceptions, the people are nothing to me, and the less I see of them the better I am pleased. But the *places* grow ever more dear to me. I like to know of anything that has happened at Heavitree, or Brampford Speke, or Newton St. Cyres. I begin to pride myself on knowing every road and lane, every bridle path and foot-way for miles about. I like to learn the names of farms and of fields. And all this because here is my abiding place, because I am home for ever.

It seems to me that the very clouds that pass above my house are more interesting and beautiful than clouds elsewhere.

How the mood for a book sometimes rushes upon one, either one knows not why, or in consequence, perhaps, of some most trifling suggestion. Yesterday I was walking at dusk. I came to an old farmhouse; at the garden gate a vehicle stood waiting, and I saw it was our doctor's gig. Having passed, I turned to look back. There was a faint afterglow in the sky beyond the chimneys; a light twinkled at one of the upper windows. I said to myself *"Tristram Shandy,"* and hurried home to plunge into a book which I had not opened for I dare say twenty years.

Not long ago, I awoke one morning and suddenly thought of the Correspondence between Goethe and Schiller; and so impatient did I become to open the book that I got up an hour earlier than usual. A book worth rising for; much better worth than old Burton, who pulled Johnson out of bed. A book which helps one to forget the idle or venomous chatter going on everywhere about us, and bids us cherish hope for a world "which has such people in't."

These volumes I had at hand; I could reach them down from my shelves at the moment when I hungered for them. But it often happens that the book which comes into my mind could only be procured with trouble and delay; I breathe regretfully and put aside the thought. Ah! the books that one will never read again. They gave delight, perchance something more; they left a perfume in the memory; but life has passed them by for ever. I have but to muse, and one after another they rise before me. Books gentle and quieting; books noble and inspiring; books that well merit to be pored over, not once but many a time. Yet never again shall I hold them in my hand; the years fly too quickly, and are too few. Perhaps when I lie waiting for the end, some of those lost books will come into my wandering thoughts, and I shall remember them as friends to whom I owed a kindness—friends passed upon the way. What regret in that last farewell!

One of the shining moments of my day is that when, having returned a little weary from an afternoon walk, I exchange boots for slippers, out-of-doors coat for easy, familiar, shabby jacket, and, in my deep, soft-elbowed chair, await the tea-tray. Perhaps it is while drinking tea that I most of all enjoy the sense of leisure. In days gone by, I could but gulp down the refreshment, hurried, often harassed, by the thought of the work I had before me; often I was quite insensible of the aroma, the flavour, of what I drank. Now, how delicious is the soft yet penetrating odour which floats into my study with the appearance of the teapot! What solace in the first cup, what deliberate sipping of that which follows! What a glow does it bring after a walk in chilly rain! The while, I look around at my books and pictures, tasting the happiness of their tranquil possession. I cast an eye towards my pipe; perhaps I prepare it, with seeming thoughtfulness, for the reception of tobacco. And never, surely, is tobacco more soothing, more suggestive of humane thoughts, than when it comes just after tea—itself a bland inspirer.

—*The Private Papers of Henry Ryecroft*

THE JOY OF WALKING

by Donald Culross Peattie

Donald Culross Peattie first attracted attention in 1935 with An Almanac for Moderns, *a diary of the iridescent thoughts, like butterflies, which gently brush the pages of a true scientist's notebook. In this essay he is writing about an America that was rediscovering its feet in 1942 because of wartime gasoline rationing.*

AMERICA, land of the motor car, land of the rubber tire, is going off wheels and learning to walk.

Of this I sing.

If ever you complained of a speed-mad America and extolled the charms of the horse-and-buggy age, if ever you jeered that wheels had made us a nation of tenderfeet and groaned that our highways kill more than the bombing of London, your prayers are answered and your fears made groundless. For America is finding its feet again.

Yesterday I moved from a house eleven miles from my children's school to a new home, where, by walking three-quarters of a mile, they can board the school bus. So I save rubber. But this morning I discovered that to get the morning mail I must also go down to the highway, making a mile-and-a-half round trip during which I climb back up a 300-foot hill.

I set out, my mind full of the usual Monday morning humdrums and problems, complaining to myself that in this way I missed the morning news broadcast and consumed a valuable half-hour of my freshest energies, in order to get the post. I was even "noble" about it, assuring myself that it was just one of countless inconveniences that we were all facing.

But I came back to my desk with my blood tingling, with every stale and mundane concern washed out of my head and all self-pity jeered out of me by jays and crows, frisking, scolding squirrels and errant Spring winds.

I had heard the titmouse calling his merry song of peet-o, peet-o, and song sparrows tuning up on the alder bushes where the catkins were hanging out all pollen-dusty and fertile. I had heard the brook gurgling among its boulders, and smelled fresh loam, lichen wet with dew, spawn of toadstool. I had seen the mountains in long shafts of early light and a flight of band-tailed pigeons flashing white wings as they crossed a little valley on important pigeon business. The oats were shooting, pale green and tender, out of the fine black earth in the fields, and I heard a plowman shout at his old white horse as he turned at the end of the velvety furrow and set the blade in the next row.

Had I taken my car to run down to the mailbox I should have had only a fleeting glimpse, or none, of all these fine sights. Of all these fragrances I should have caught not a whiff, but only gasoline fumes. Above the noise of the wheels how should I have heard the sea-dirge of the pines, or the chuckling of the linnets, or the jolly scampering of lizards on old leaves?

True, I should have "saved" about twenty-five minutes of my priceless time. For what? For the sake of a more sluggish digestion, of a wider girth beneath my belt, staler air in my lungs, duller thoughts in my head, a posture grown by that much older. I should have lopped off half an hour of fresh and living experience. For, after all, time is not money; time is an opportunity to live before you die. So a man who walks, and lives and sees and thinks as he walks, has lengthened his life.

It was Thoreau, himself one of the most inveterate of walkers, who insisted that if you took the train from Concord to Fitchburg, and he took shanks' mare, he would arrive first. For, he reasoned, you would have to stop and work till you had earned the price of a ticket. While you were doing that he would be in Scotland afore ye. And have seen enough sights and had enough encounters to write another immortal chapter.

All the great naturalists have been habitual walkers, for no laboratory, no book, car, train or plane takes the place of honest footwork for this calling, be it amateur's or professional's. Gilbert White and Izaak Walton were devotees of the art and tireless exponents of its charms. W. H. Hudson in England was practically a tramp, and so was John Muir in this country. John thought nothing of walking from one end of the Sierra to the other, just to see a tree or a flower; he once walked from Wisconsin to the Gulf of Mexico! Asked what preparations he made for these famous treks, he replied: "I throw a loaf of bread and a pound of tea in an old sack and jump over the back fence."

There spake the true walker, as contrasted with those persons with overdeveloped thyroids who walk to set records, who add stones to their packs when climbing mountains and count their steps to calculate how far they have come. Not thus did John Burroughs walk, or Richard Jefferies or Alexander Wilson. John James Audubon could and often did walk a hundred miles in two days. It sounds like a startling record, but on one of my own walks, along the old Roman Road from Canterbury to London, I was overtaken by a little Welsh soldier, though I was walking fast; he had come thirty-five miles that day, and hoped to make it fifty before he slept—in some hedge. He slowed to my pace for ten miles, while he told me his adventures in many parts of the world. Then he had to leave me because he could not wait.

He was quite a philosopher, that fellow, and indeed all walkers become philosophers. Didn't Plato and Socrates pace up and down in the stoas of the Acropolis while they pulled their beards and unriddled the universe? Robert Louis Stevenson and Ralph Waldo Emerson were Peripatetics too, as you can easily tell by the kind of philosophy they expounded, one peculiarly kindly, reasonable, hopeful, cheerful and refreshing.

Something happens to the walker who knows how to think and observe as he goes. In the first place he is physically prevented from wasting his time and cluttering his mind in a great many ways that, we get to imagining, are inevitable or even pleasant or important. While you are walking you cannot be reached by telephone or telegraph, and you cannot reach anybody in those ways. That in itself is a great blessing. You cannot put out a hand, as you do even in an automobile, and twiddle the radio and so let in the war and the stock market, a flood of soda-pop and chewing-gum spiels, and all the quizzes and jazzes that wrangle on the innocent airs. You cannot play bridge or consult an astrologer, bet on a horse or go to a movie. In the compensation for these keen deprivations, walking offers you health, happiness and an escape from civilization's many madnesses.

I have often started off on a walk in the state called mad—mad in the sense of sore-headed, or mad with tedium or confusion; I have set forth dull, null and even thoroughly discouraged. But I never came back in such a frame of mind, and I never met a human being whose humor was not the better for a walk. It is the sovereign remedy for the hot-tempered and the low-spirited—provided, of course, that you know how to walk.

When I was about 8 years old I was actually taught to walk by an elderly man who was a master of the art. He showed me how to carry that good companion, a stick, without tiring of it; how to climb without getting winded, slanting your body forward, going on the balls of your feet and respecting the hill ahead of you. From him I learned that you should never take a highroad if you can find a byroad or a footpath. He taught me not to chatter; he instructed me to quench thirst well before I started out, to go stoutly shod and lightly clad.

True, that was country walking. Later I learned, by myself, the joys of circumambulating city streets—at their most magical in the dusk and early in the morning. No American city, with its checkerboard street plan, is the equal in fascination, for the pedestrian, of London and Paris. Yet New York, Boston, Washington and San Francisco, to mention only some cities I know, have their charms for the foot passenger. To enjoy city walking to the utmost you have to throw yourself into a mood of loving humanity. For a whistling boy must be your bird song, girls' faces your wayside flowers, the flow and roar of the street your clattering, swirling streams, and tall buildings your sun-smitten crags. And by night you have the spattered office lights above for your winking constellations.

But alas, as our rubber heels wear off and cannot be replaced, curb-trotting is going to jar and tire us more than in the past. And so I think we shall for pleasure be riding out again to the end of the bus or trolley line or taking the old plush-and-varnish suburban trains to some outlying point, and there we'll alight and step forth amid country sights and sounds. We shall smell again the bittersweet reek of leaf fires where people on the edge of the village are raking their lawns and watching for the first crocuses. We shall hunt again for spicebush, and set our teeth in the thin sweet bark just to taste and smell again that tingling aromatic principle.

We shall be carrying bird glasses and cameras (light ones in both cases, if we are wise) and snacks of lunch. Personally, I'm down on sandwiches. Far rather would I take a mixture of shelled pecans and sweet dried currants, with dark chocolate for dessert, and in warm weather, cider preferred or apple juice, since they are refreshing even if not iced. But rather than carry too much heavy liquid, I'd chance buttermilk from some old springhouse, or just nice, wet, well-water, tasting a little, with a cool astringent tang, of iron from the pump and tin from the dipper.

So, good luck to you fellow-hiker, wherever you go! May you never run out of tobacco or songs; may the trees be great and old and the girls young and comely. May the sun shine upon your cheek and the shade lie upon the back of your neck. May you find wood and strawberries and sassafras. But he who flingeth away the bottle and hindereth not the picnic paper, he that carveth the beech bole and she that expects others to carry her coat, camera and pack, may their socks be lumpy, and farm dogs bite their calves!

—*The New York Times Magazine*, April 5, 1942

"WHAT A LOVELY WALK!"

by Henri Frédéric Amiel

"One needs to love and be loved every day," confessed this awkward, solitary and unworldly Swiss professor. His three loves were his books, his walks, and the tender, adoring women who sought him out. He summed up what he had put into the 14,000 pages of his journal with the memorable words: "It is never too late to be wise."

April 2, 1851.—What a lovely walk! Clear sky, rising sun, all the tints vivid, all the contours distinct, save the softly misty and infinite lake. A sheen of hoar-frost powdered the meadows, gave the green box-hedges a charming vivacity and all the countryside a tone of vigorous health, youth and freshness.—"Bathe, O disciple, your earthly breast in the flush of dawn!" Faust tells us, and he is right. Every dawn signs a new contract with existence; the morning air breathes a new and joyous energy into the veins and marrow; every day is a microscopic repetition of life. All is fresh, flowing, light in the morning as in childhood. Like the atmosphere, spiritual truth is more transparent. Like the young leaves, the organs absorb the light more eagerly, breathe in more ether and less of the terrestrial elements.

To the contemplative soul, the night and the starry sky speak of God, eternity, infinity. Dawn is the time for projects, for the will, for budding actions. The sap of nature is diffused in the soul and urges it to live, as silence and the "morne sérénité de la voûte azurée" incline it to collect itself.—Spring is here. Primroses and violets have celebrated its arrival. The peach-trees are opening their imprudent corollas; the swelling buds of the pear-trees and the lilacs announce the burst of bloom that is to come; the honeysuckle is already green. Sing, poets, for nature is singing already her song of resurrection. Through all the leaves she is murmuring a hymn of gladness, and the birds must not be the only ones to raise a clearer voice.

Lancy, October 31, 1852.—A half hour's walk in the garden in a fine rain.—Autumnal landscape. The sky hung with various shades of gray, mists trailing over the mountains on the horizon; nature melancholy; leaves falling on all sides like the last illusions of youth under the tears of incurable sorrows. A flock of chirping birds pursued one another in the thickets, sporting among the branches like schoolboys huddled together and hiding in some pavilion. The ground strewn with leaves, brown, yellow and reddish; the trees half stripped, some more, some less, with patches of russet, lemon-yellow, amaranth (the order of spoliation: first the catalpas, then the mulberries, acacias, planes, walnuts, lindens, elms and lilacs); clumps and shrubbery turning red; a few flowers still, roses, nasturtiums, red, white, yellow and streaked dahlias, shedding their petals, withered petunias, mesembrianthemums of a deep carnation, eclipsing the mignonettes with their crown-like leafage in tints of mauve and rose; dried maize, bare fields, impoverished hedges.—The fir, alone vigorous, green, stoical in the midst of this universal sickliness, eternal youth braving the decline.—All these countless and marvellous symbols, which the forms and colours, the vegetation, which all living things, the earth and the sky offer every moment to the eye that can see them, charmed and thrilled me. I held the wand of poetry and had only to touch one of these objects for it to tell me its moral significance. I had a scientific curiosity also. I took notes and I asked questions. Why does the red dominate? What makes one kind of leaf last longer than another? Etc., etc.

Every landscape is a state of the soul, and he who reads in both marvels at the likeness in every detail. True poetry is truer than science, because it is synthetic and grasps at once what the combination of all the sciences can only attain at best some day in the future. The poet divines the soul of nature, the scientist only serves to accumulate the materials for its demonstration. The one rests in the whole, the other lives in a particular region. The one is concrete, the other abstract.

The soul of the world is more open and intelligible than the individual soul; it has more space, time and strength to manifest itself.

January 31, 1854.—A walk: the air incredibly pure, delights for the eye, a warm and gently caressing sunlight, one's whole being joyous. A spring-like charm. Felt to my marrow this purifying, moving influence, laden with poetry and tenderness; had a strong religious feeling of gratitude and wonder. Seated motionless on a bench in the Tranchées, beside the ditches with their garb of moss, carpeted with grass, I felt intensely, delightfully alive. . . .

Mornex, April 6, 1869 (8 a.m.).—Magnificent weather. The Alps are dazzling in their gauze of silver. Sensations of every kind have flooded me: the soft pleasure of a good bed, the delights of a walk at sunrise, the charms of a wonderful view, the enjoyment of an excellent breakfast, a longing for travel, as I glanced over pictures of Spain (by Vivian) and Scottish pasture-lands (by Cooper), a thirst for joy, a hunger for work, emotions and life, dreams of happiness, musings of love; the need for being, an ardour still to feel and launch myself into life stirred in the depths of my heart. A sudden reawakening of youth, a welling up of poetry, a spring-tide of the soul, a sprouting forth again of the wings of desire. Yearnings to conquer, wander, adventure. A forgetting of age, ties, duties, cares; outbursts of youth, as if life were beginning anew. It is as if the fire had reached the powder, as if our soul were blown to the four winds. One longs to devour the world, to try everything, see everything. The ambition of Faust; lust for the universe; the horror of one's cell; one throws off the cowl, and one longs to press all nature in one's arms and against one's heart. O passions, one beam of the sun is enough to kindle all of you together! The cold, black mountain becomes a volcano again and its crown of snow evaporates under a single blast of its burning breath. The spring brings on these sudden, impossible resurrections. By making the vital juices thrill and bubble, it produces impetuous longings, terrible inclinations, frenzies of life that are unforeseen and inextinguishable. It bursts the rigid bark of the trees and the iron mask of all the austerities. It makes the monk tremble in the shadow of his monastery, the virgin behind the curtains of her chamber, the child on his bench at school, the old man in the toils of his rheumatism.

> *O Hymen, Hymenæe!*
> *Notusque calor per membra cucurrit.*

All these stirrings are only the infinite variations of the great instinct of nature; they sing the same thing in every tongue; they are the hymn to Venus, the yearning for the infinite. They witness the exaltation of the being who longs to die to the individual life and absorb the universe into himself or be dissolved in it. . . .

Charnex, September 22, 1871 (4 p.m.).—A rift in the rainy vault lets through a white beam that breaks in my room like a sardonic laugh and passes more quickly than it came.

After dinner, a walk as far as Chailly, between two showers . . . The landscape grey but vast, a handful of sunbeams falling on the lake, far vistas, mountains bedimmed with mist, and, in spite of everything, the beauty of the country. One cannot weary of this picturesque and soothing view. I find a charm in rainy prospects; the dull colours are more velvety, the flat tones grow more tender. The landscape is like a face that has been weeping; it is less beautiful, certainly, but more expressive.

Behind the superficial beauty, joyous, shining, palpable, the aesthetic sense discovers a whole order of beauty that is hidden, veiled, secret, mysterious, akin to moral beauty. This latter beauty reveals itself only to the initiate, and it is all the sweeter for this. It is a little like the refined joy of sacrifice, like the madness of faith, like the pleasure of tears; it is not within the reach of everyone. Its attraction is a curious thing and gives one the impression of a strange perfume or a bizarre melody. Once one has acquired the taste for it, one delights in it, one becomes enamoured of it, for one finds in it

Son bien premièrement, puis le dédain d'autrui,

and it is so agreeable not to be of the same mind as the fools. And that is not possible with the obvious things and the incontestable beauties. Charm is the name of this esoteric and paradoxical beauty that escapes the vulgar and sets one adream. This is why the ugly, when it has charm, does not charm us half-way. A sphinx that pleases enchants its lover, for it has two philtres instead of one. . . .

Clarens, September 23, 1877.—Beautiful, bluish morning, poetically misty. Wandered a long hour on the Belmont road, a gracious belvedere reproducing on a small scale the terrace-road to Charnex . . . With eyes, ears and lungs I breathed in the pure air, the sensations of every kind that arise from this sweet morning countryside. Slanting sheets of sunlight, the Dent du Midi, sheer white, emerging from a vast collar of mists; wooded, rolling slopes, the lake glittering and full of motion, mountains of emerald and amethyst, lacy effect of walnut-trees, trailing shadows, ripening vines, red apples, butterflies, a few couples on their way to church, a few sails on the water, trains creeping shyly along with their plumes of smoke, the Oasis with its roses, its cypresses and weeping willows, all in that magic circle bounded by the Pléiades, the Cubly, the Caux, the Sonchoz, the Arvel, the Dent du Midi and the Grammont. The whole country seemed to me like a censer, and the morning was a prayer. It is good to meditate here, to live, dream and die.

A light breeze stirs the fringe of the striped cloth awning that shelters my balcony. The songs of a few birds, the pounding of wheels, a few women's voices rise to my open chamber. But one feels the Sabbath repose of some vaster silence, enveloping these little nearby sounds. . . .

—*The Private Journal of Henri Frédéric Amiel,* translated by
Van Wyck Brooks and Charles Van Wyck Brooks

WALKING DOWN A RIVER

by Edwin Way Teale

Naturalist, photographer, essayist, Pulitzer Prize winner Edwin Way Teale has won deserved recognition in all these fields. He was awarded the John Burroughs Medal for distinguished nature writing, was made an Associate of the Royal Photographic Society of Great Britain for his photographic work, and a Fellow of the New York Academy of Sciences for his contributions to botany and zoology. His books have been published in France, Spain, Sweden, Finland, and in Braille editions. His masterwork is the four-volume record of his seasonal journey across the North American countryside, of which Journey into Summer *is the volume from which this essay was taken. The others in the series are* North with the Spring, Autumn Across America, *and* Wandering Through Winter.

EDEN PHILLPOTTS, the English author who has spent most of his life writing about lonely Dartmoor, tells of meeting a stranger at a luncheon in London. The man asked him if he knew Dartmoor.

"Not as well as I could wish," Phillpotts answered.

It developed that his companion had once motored across the sparsely settled tableland.

"Hardly a thing you would do twice, certainly."

Phillpotts suggested the next time he try walking across it. The man was greatly amused by this advice.

"Surely," he said, "no sane man would waste his time like that."

Yet Phillpotts knew that the way to become acquainted with an area intimately, to appreciate it best, is to walk over it. And the slower the walk the better. For a naturalist, the most productive pace is a snail's pace. A large part of his walk is often spent standing still. A mile an hour may well be fast enough. For his goal is different from that of the pedestrian. It is not how far he goes that counts; it is not how fast he goes; it is how much he sees.

And, in deeper truth, it is not *just* how much he sees. It is how much he appreciates, how much he feels. Nature affects our minds as light affects the photographic emulsion on a film. Some films are more sensitive than others; some minds are more receptive. To one observer a thing means much; to another the same thing means almost nothing. As the poet William Blake wrote in one of his letters: "The Tree which moves some to tears of joy is in the Eyes of others only a Green thing that stands in the way."

Under the morning sun of the second day of summer, Nellie and I began walking down wild Sunday River. A side road, first hardtop, then gravel, then dirt, then, at last, little more than wheeltracks leading on, had carried us to the upper reaches of the tumbling stream.

As we changed into rubber-soled sneakers that would cling to rocks and let us wade through shallows, we looked about us. On all sides, green-clad mountains gazed down upon us. Hardly four miles to the west the Appalachian Trail swung sharply north toward Goose Eye and Old Speck mountains. Eight miles or so to the east flowed the beautiful Andros-coggin. And only twenty miles to the north Lake Umbagog straddled the Maine–New Hampshire line. . . .

To the lost man, to the pioneer penetrating new country, to the naturalist who wishes to see wild land at its wildest, the advice is always the same—follow a stream. The river is the original forest highway. It is nature's own Wilderness Road.

Long past now were the torrents of spring, and Sunday River rushed and gurgled down only half its rocky bed. Without haste, we followed its course as it flowed, plunging down little waterfalls, cascading among granite boulders, sliding over tilting ledges, fanning out into quiet pools. Once the whole river fell over a brink in a plunge of foaming water. Again the stream slowed into long, lazy stretches sparkling in the sun. We advanced mainly from rock to rock, soon learning to avoid wet patches of moss, as slippery as ice. Steppingstones down a river—this was the story of much of our travels that day. We progressed slowly, stopping often. We had no schedule. We had no goal except our own enjoyment of this alder-bordered north-country stream flowing through a land of singing birds.

They were everywhere around us, these birds of the forest water-course—parula and Nashville and chestnut-sided warblers, redstarts and yellowthroats, chickadees and phoebes, blue jays sounding a raucous alarm, and robins, a few still nesting, singing in the higher trees. Always with us was the monologue of the red-eyed vireo and the endlessly repeated "Chebec!" of the tireless least flycatcher. Bluebirds called over us, and once a flock of goldfinches went roller-coastering by above the treetops. Time after time, clear above the rush of the stream, we heard the ovenbird set the forests ringing. But predominant among all this music of early summer there was that sweet, minor, infinitely moving lament, that voice of the north woods, the unhurried song of the little white-throated sparrow.

Somewhere, far up this forest stream, we came upon an old farmhouse —low, lonely, huddled in a tiny valley within sound of the water. Under its roof, living in these primitive surroundings, Kenneth Roberts, twenty years before, had written some of the finest pages of his *Northwest Passage*.

Half a mile or so downstream, I remember, we sat for a long time beside a diminutive waterfall only a foot or two high, delighting in the low music that filled the air. The water gurgled and hissed, lisped and murmured. Never before had we appreciated quite so clearly how many rushing, bubbling, liquid sounds combine to form the music of falling water. All down the river, all through the day, all through the night, the song of the running water went on and on. Light and dark are the same to a flowing stream. For it, only gravity matters.

Where a shelving rock of gray granite slanted down above another little waterfall, we ate our lunch that noon, a lunch of buns and cheese, small ripe tomatoes and sweet red grapes. Our extra dessert was the finest imaginable, handfuls of wintergreen berries picked on the mossy slope of the bank above. As we sat there little keys of moosewood came whirling down around us. Across the river, a redstart, a parula and a magnolia warbler sang, the parula repeating over and over its whirling upward trill that concluded in a kind of trip or turnover at the end; the magnolia, like the redstart, short and explosive, but with notes more rounded and whistled. Above the lower trees of this farther bank, an ash leaned out over the stream. From its dead top, a cedar waxwing over and over darted out, snapped up a flying insect and returned to its perch again. Its curving course cut through the air like the swing of a scythe. It was engaged in its own aerial mowing, gathering in its own harvest of summer.

Working downstream that afternoon, we came to turns where all the young birches and alders were tilted in the same direction, bent by the high waters of spring. At times we skirted rapids, pushing our way among

the streamside alders. Again we clambered over great tangles of driftwood, flood-wrack caught among the trees and bushes. . . .

At times a remembrance will be hard and solid like an artifact, a piece
of pottery or an arrowhead found in the sand. At other times a memory
will be quicksilver. We can never quite grasp it or hold it. It slides
through our fingers when we try to squeeze it tight. One recollection of
our wandering along the river comes back as clear-cut as the imprint we
found in the hardening mud of a streamside puddle. Here a wildcat had
set its foot, leaving behind a track as delicately defined as a plaster
mold.

At the top of the bank nearby, above the green mats of the bunchberry
starred with white, a cranberry tree spread its broad, three-pointed
leaves. . . . Across its top, like clots of river foam, ran the white masses
of its flowers. In the autumn they would be replaced by the red fruit, sour
and translucent, that provided the pioneers with a substitute for cran-
berries and a jelly that, while tart, was less bitter than that of the related
wayfaring tree. Each fall, like the pioneers of old, the ruffed grouse
harvest the acid berries.

Past undercut forest floor, past rocks overlaid with moss, past shaded
banks shaggy with reindeer lichen, past the slide of water down some long
chute of tilted rock we followed the stream in its windings. In many
places we stopped to examine depressions like bowls or basins worn into
the ledges and larger rocks. Each contained smooth, rounded pieces of
granite. They ranged from pebbles to balls the size of grapefruit. The
larger the depression the larger were these hard grinding stones that,
whirled in the grip of the flood torrents, abraded deeper into the rock
below. One huge boulder rose out of the river bed with three potholes like
steps ascending its downstream side. Water striders skated on the surface
film of the largest basin.

Several times we climbed the bank and stood in little forest openings.
Once a snowshoe rabbit bolted away. Another time a raven, flying
overhead, croaked and veered aside. Many of the openings were strewn
with spikenard and meadow rue and star flowers in bloom. Witch hobble
lifted its paired foliage like opposing wings and the yellow stars of the
Clintonia nodded above the shining green of the leaves outspread below.
Small and sweet, wild strawberries had ripened in the sun. We gathered a
handful and followed the stream once more, eating the wild fruit as we
went and nibbling on the terminal twigs of the black birch, rich with the
flavor of wintergreen.

The largest opening we encountered along the upper stream spread away for sixty acres or more. Farmed long ago, now abandoned for half a century, with the forest creeping back across the land, it spoke of pioneer homesteads that once extended far up this forest river. In earlier days, this whole valley was famous bear country. One Maine trapper, who died only a decade or so ago, caught fifteen black bears along the Sunday River.

Now the most arresting feature of the opening was an apple orchard gone wild. It ran for twenty or thirty acres across the clearing. Some of the trees were seedlings, some had sprouted from old stumps, some might well have been a century old. Their trunks were richly robed in lichens. We stopped, at one point, within ten feet of a yellow-bellied sapsucker hammering away in perfect silence. Its strikes, cushioned by the soft, muffling layers of lichen, fell as though on sponge rubber. But sap was still running in the old tree and the sapsucker was there to tap it.

We were sitting at the edge of this wild orchard—making its last stand with the encompassing forest pressing closer year by year—listening to the whitethroats of the apple trees, some singing in one key, others in another, a few going down the scale instead of up as most do, when we noticed the deer. It was gazing at us from behind a clump of Canada plums, odd-appearing bushes with elongated fruit already forming amid the spiny branches. For minutes we sat perfectly still. Then the doe, relatively unafraid, immensely curious, began stalking in a slow half-circle around us.

It stretched out its neck, sniffed the air, thrust forward its great ears, lifted high its dainty hoofs as it advanced step by step, flipping up in a flash of white from time to time its fluffy tail. At times it was hardly more than thirty feet away. First with one forefoot, then with the other, it pawed the ground, then bent and picked up some special delicacy. Wandering about, browsing here and there, it lifted its head several times and looked around holding a bouquet of red clover blossoms in its mouth. Its slow movements, viewed closely, appeared somewhat stiff and mechanical. It is speed that brings out the grace of the deer family. Now in summer, with the blood-lust of the hunting season lulled by law, the wild creatures grew less wild. At last, still unalarmed and unafraid, the doe wandered away among the apple trees.

Night came slowly on this next to the longest day of the year. Going back upstream in the sunset and the twilight, we tarried along the way. Beside the reach of a quiet pool between two waterfalls, we rubbed on insect repellant and sat for a time watching the leap of trout and the ripple-rings that ran and met and overlapped on the tinted surface of the still water. Minute by minute in the evening air the parade of the insects increased. Frail, flying creatures, born of the rushing water, were on the wing.

Endlessly turning, endlessly followed in every curve and convolution by their reflections, mothlike caddis flies drifted low above the stream. Submerged throughout their early life, the aquatic larvae of these insects inhabit little houses of their own devising, tubes thatched with bits of debris or minute stones or fragments of twigs. Some even spin tiny nets among the rocks of the rapids within which they catch their microscopic forms of food. Considering the bizarre and adventurous days of these small creatures as we sat there in the twilight, we reflected on how odd it is that human beings who can hardly wait to discover life on Mars have so little curiosity about life on Earth.

Whitethroats along the riverside now were giving their single-note, crepuscular calls, a sharp chinking sound like the striking of little chisels in the dusk. Slowly darkness enveloped the forest. It settled over the stream. The light-colored boulders and the foam of the river—these were the last to disappear. . . .

—Journey into Summer

TO OWN THE STREETS AND FIELDS

by Hal Borland

Hal Borland, novelist, essayist and naturalist, has written over twenty books, all to some degree concerned with the outdoors. Among his recent ones are Beyond Your Doorstep, Sundial of the Seasons, Countryman, *and* Hill Country Harvest. *For many years he has written the nature editorials for* The New York Times. *He lives in the lower Berkshires of northwestern Connecticut.*

HE WAS about 10 years old, sandy-haired, stocky, deeply tanned. A car stopped and offered him a ride, but he declined and went on walking resolutely up the country road. So I quickened my step and caught up with him. We exchanged greetings. We discussed the weather. He spoke his mind, diplomatically. Obviously, he was a possibility for the campaign of 1988 or '92, so I asked, "Are you walking, by any chance, to fit yourself for the Presidency?"

"What?" he asked.

"Do you expect to be President of the United States? President Truman is quite a walker, you know."

He looked at me with a suspicious smile. "Are you kiddin'?" He picked up a stone and shied it at a tree, and I asked, "Just why are you walking then?"

He became very serious. "To get tough," he said. "I want to be quarterback on our team, and I got to get tough."

A few minutes later he left me and took a short cut through the orchard to his house, singing "Sioux City Sue" at the top of his lungs. And I continued my walk, down past the hollow where the cattails were turning brown and over the ridge where scarlet mottled the sumac. I didn't care to play quarterback; I merely wanted to walk.

Quarterback or President, we are scarcely out of the cradle before we try to walk; some instinct lies there within us to get up on our hind legs and take one step after another. We learn to talk largely by imitation; but we learn to walk, to stand and move from one place to another, because of that inner compulsion to get up off all-fours and assert our manhood. We stand, and a new world is spread before us. We walk, and we can explore that world. The more we walk, the more we learn.

You can rate a man's curiosity about his world and his fellow men by his walking habits. Certainly the one who walks isn't the kind that expects all things to come to him. I suspect that it would be possible, if one were to study the matter systematically, to gauge a man's mental breadth and depth by examining his attitude toward walking; whether he likes to walk, and where he walks, and how, and why.

Is it possible to walk without some stimulus to thought? I doubt it. The very movement seems to stir the mind into action. The jolt of even the smoothest gait tends to loosen ideas, give them a chance to rub against each other and mingle and find new proportion and arrangement. The physiologist, of course, will explain this by saying that exercise and fresh air improve the circulation and stimulate the brain by feeding it more oxygen. But I doubt the sufficiency of that explanation. It reduces walking to the status of premeditated exercise; and whoever generated a great thought, or even an enduring one, by doing calisthenics in front of an open window?

Half the benefit, and even more of the satisfaction, of walking comes from the leisurely change of scene. It may be only from one city block to another, or it may be from one hilltop to the next, but it is change, and it is stimulating. Even if you walk substantially the same route day after day, there is change in the familiar things you see. This is more noticeable in the country, where the wind, the clouds, the light, the growing things are never twice the same. But there is change, too, even in a city street, in the shop windows and the dooryards, in the people you meet.

And there is a leisure about walking, no matter what pace you set, that lets down the tension. It is your own pace, be it an amble, a saunter, a stroll, a promenade, a jog, a hike or a trot. If you have set yourself a distance you can take it fast or slow, and if you have set yourself a time you can hurry or dawdle. The decision is yours, and so is the world for a little while.

Some prefer to walk alone, aloof with their thoughts, or open to passing companionship. I am one who prefers to walk with a companion whose ways and words are mine, who is in step with me and I with her.

But any walker's companion should be his own choice. As a general rule, the chatterer should be left behind. One needs a walking companion who understands economy of words as well as of energy. I suspect that at least some of those who prefer a dog's company on a walk have walked once too often with a person who must keep up a continuous rattle of conversation. Such a talker is no walker; he—or she—is a perambulating egotist afraid to let the world's immensity shrink him to his proper size.

Walking can shrink the biggest of us, give us that sense of proportion which we all need on occasion. In an automobile you feel that miles are of no consequence and that all hills are low. In an airplane you lose your sense of both time and distance. In both cases you feel that you, not the machine, have altered reality. But on foot you soon learn how high is a hill and how long is a mile. And when you have walked the same road through all the seasons, you know how certain is change and how gradual.

Walkers acquire a special ownership of roads and streets and parks and fields. I shall forever own certain parts of a dozen cities, because I walked their streets, a stranger, and became familiar with their sights and sounds and smells and knew their people, even though they did not know me. Even though I met those people later and they showed me the city that they knew, my ownership was in no way changed. I had made my own discoveries.

All walking is discovery. On foot we take the time to see things whole. We see trees as well as forests, people as well as crowds. When the mood is right—and walking provokes such a mood when we are most in need of it—we can even see ourselves with particular clarity. We get our feet back on the ground.

The man on horseback may be a symbol of leadership in a particular cause, but I prefer the man afoot for my leader—at least the man who has not forgotten the virtues of walking. He has a sense of time and proportion, and if he lacks patience he can and will quickly acquire or renew it. He knows, from experience afoot, that if he hurries beyond need or reason he will wear himself out before he has reached his destination; that if he travels at a steady pace he will arrive where he is headed and get there fit for whatever awaits him. So doing, he will also have had an intimate look at the world around him. He will have had time for discovery and appraisal.

It is all very well to know the whole world, but breadth of knowledge calls for depth of understanding. He knows most about the world who knows best that world which is within reach of his own footsteps. Not all hills and valleys are alike, but unless a man knows his own hills and valleys he is not likely to understand those of another man a thousand miles away. And I am not at all sure that he even understands himself.

He who walks may see and understand. You can study all America from one hilltop, if your eyes are open and your mind is willing to reach. But first you must walk to that hill.

—*The New York Times Magazine,* October 6, 1946

IS WALKING THE NEW STATUS SYMBOL?

by Joseph Wood Krutch

Joseph Wood Krutch has had a multiplicity of brilliant careers: as teacher, as drama critic, as biographer, and as naturalist. Among his best-loved books are Samuel Johnson, Henry David Thoreau, The Twelve Seasons, The Desert Year, *and* Grand Canyon.

THE MODERN MALE lost interest in his own legs about the time that he developed an ardent concern with those of his female companions. Then skirts went up, and until the most recent revolution in taste transferred his attentions to certain other conspicuous secondary sex characteristics, he was so absorbed in an aesthetic contemplation of the now obvious fact that ladies did have legs that he naturally forgot even the practical uses he could make of his own. Now, after a generation or two, the novelty has worn off, and walking is coming back into fashion.

I am aware, of course, that there are rival theories to explain the decline of pedestrianism for pleasure or as a means of getting from one place to another. Followers of Thorstein Veblen attribute this to the alleged fact that members of the leisure class refused to use their legs in order to demonstrate that they did not have to. In China, the deformed feet of female aristocrats were a status symbol proudly exhibited by those who wished to make it evident that if they wanted to go anywhere there would always be someone to carry them. In the West, high-heeled shoes served the same purpose, although the fact that they could be taken off indicated a less absolute confidence. Senior executives can't very well wear crippling shoes but many of them now play routine golf by riding from shot to shot in motorized carts just to avoid the exercise once supposed to be the excuse for the game.

There is no doubt that the tide is turning. Notice this novel phenomenon. A group of young executives bound for lunch has spent ten minutes trying to get a taxi which would carry them at a snail's pace across town. One says to the other, "Let's save time by walking." And once the astonishment at the novel suggestion has worn off, there is a general agreement with this original idea. Our young executives are learning an important lesson. Laborsaving devices sometimes increase labor, and rapid transit is often the slowest way of getting somewhere.

This is only a minor example of a cultural revolution. We have a Secretary of the Interior who not only walks but climbs and a justice of the Supreme Court who writes books shamelessly describing his pedestrian exploits. It looks as though walking, not riding, is about to become a status symbol.

Notoriously, Americans tend to extremes. They have been more exuberantly committed than any other people to whatever is thought of as modern—whether it be gadgets, clothes or even social manners. And walking tended to be more completely outmoded here than anywhere else. In England, on the other hand, country walking never went completely out of fashion, and the public right-of-way along traditional paths across private property is jealously protected to this day.

The German student's *Wanderjahr* never completely ceased to be a respectable tradition, and within the last decade the youth hostels have become increasingly familiar all over Europe. American college youths have discovered them, and the European tour conducted at least partly on foot has become increasingly popular. The significant fact is that such partly pedestrian tours are not merely for those who cannot afford anything else—their advantages as well as their economy have come to be what count.

We have begun to recover just a bit from our obsession with the automobile and the airplane and to realize that the motorcar (and, of course, the airplane) are methods of locomotion rather than ends in themselves—that if you travel for the sake of seeing something rather than simply to get from one place to another, you might almost as well stay at home. From a jet flying at forty thousand feet you see so little that luxury consists in watching a movie while traversing India or Japan, and from an automobile you see little except superhighways and cloverleaves which are the same everywhere.

Another recent phenomenon operates positively in the same direction. Americans have rediscovered nature. Books about animals, plants, mountains and oceans are being bought in unprecedented numbers. Bird-watchers, once eccentric figures of fun, are now too numerous to be laughed at. The Audubon Society estimates that there are some ten million of them in the United States. The head of one of our largest corporations has published a splendid book about hummingbirds and it has even been suggested that on a fine weekend there are more people out with binoculars than in the football or baseball stadia.

But you can't observe nature from an automobile. You may ride out of the city but once you get into the country, there is no substitute for legs. And that is equally true whether your taste is for the ambitious hike or merely for what I like to call window-shopping in nature, which means strolling about in no matter how leisurely a fashion but keeping your eyes open for the violet by the mossy stone or for one of the little creatures who share the earth with us. Thoreau is more widely read today than ever before and one of the things we are learning from him is that nature is as wonderful in the small and the near at home as in the grandiose and the remote.

Even those who are uncomfortable as soon as they leave what an ultra-urbanized acquaintance of mine used to call "God's concrete" will find that city walking also affords delight. You can't get the best of a city from a taxi or a bus (to say nothing of a subway) because much of it, like much of the best in the country, is made up of little things. Two hundred and fifty years ago the London poet John Gay wrote a descriptive poem subtitled "The Art of Walking the Streets of London," and he knew something that is equally true today—you learn a city only by walking it.

Whether you walk in the city or the country the motion of the legs stimulates both the tongue and the brain. Precious little good talk is ever originated in any rapidly moving vehicle. The *New Yorker* magazine often reports absurd fragments overheard on a bus or in the subway, but it has never, as far as I can recall, recorded anything wise. Advertising slogans are thought up by men sitting at desks in offices they rode to, and the gobbledygook of sociologists and bureaucrats originates in the same way.

"The road," said Cervantes, "is always better than the inn." That is profoundly true and implies the most fundamental of all reasons why it is better to walk than to ride. We walk in order to enjoy what the road has to offer. We ride in order to get quickly to the inn. If walking were a recent technological marvel and legs a new invention, we would realize that they are more remarkable than the automobile or even the wheel.

They can negotiate a wider variety of terrain than any vehicle. They can go places even a jeep can't. And they last much longer. Hurrah for what our fathers used to call shank's mare! Nowadays "the man who has everything" is using his legs.

—*The American Scholar,* Autumn, 1964

THE PEDESTRIAN

by Ray Bradbury

A policeman once stopped Ray Bradbury for walking at night, and in anger, as he explains in the introduction to the new edition of his novel Fahrenheit 451, *he "wrote a story carrying the entire ridiculous episode one step further into a future where all pedestrians are suspect and criminal." Here is the story, which first appeared in* The Golden Apples of the Sun, *and it is not as farfetched as it seems, especially if you live in or around Los Angeles.*

TO ENTER out into that silence that was the city at eight o'clock of a misty evening in November, to put your feet upon that buckling concrete walk, to step over grassy seams and make your way, hands in pockets, through the silences, that was what Mr. Leonard Mead most dearly loved to do. He would stand upon the corner of an intersection and peer down long moonlit avenues of sidewalk in four directions, deciding which way to go, but it really made no difference; he was alone in this world of 2052 A.D., or as good as alone, and with a final decision made, a path selected, he would stride off, sending patterns of frosty air before him like the smoke of a cigar.

Sometimes he would walk for hours and miles and return only at midnight to his house. And on his way he would see the cottages and homes with their dark windows, and it was not unequal to walking through a graveyard where only the faintest glimmers of firefly light appeared in flickers behind the windows. Sudden gray phantoms seemed to manifest upon inner room walls where a curtain was still undrawn against the night, or there were whisperings and murmurs where a window in a tomblike building was still open.

Mr. Leonard Mead would pause, cock his head, listen, look, and march on, his feet making no noise on the lumpy walk. For long ago he had wisely changed to sneakers when strolling at night, because the dogs in intermittent squads would parallel his journey with barkings if he wore hard heels, and lights might click on and faces appear and an entire street be startled by the passing of a lone figure, himself, in the early November evening.

On this particular evening he began his journey in a westerly direction, toward the hidden sea. There was a good crystal frost in the air; it cut the nose and made the lungs blaze like a Christmas tree inside; you could feel the cold light going on and off, all the branches filled with invisible snow. He listened to the faint push of his soft shoes through autumn leaves with satisfaction, and whistled a cold quiet whistle between his teeth, occasionally picking up a leaf as he passed, examining its skeletal pattern in the infrequent lamplights as he went on, smelling its rusty smell.

"Hello, in there," he whispered to every house on every side as he moved. "What's up tonight on Channel 4, Channel 7, Channel 9? Where are the cowboys rushing, and do I see the United States Cavalry over the next hill to the rescue?"

The street was silent and long and empty, with only his shadow moving like the shadow of a hawk in mid-country. If he closed his eyes and stood very still, frozen, he could imagine himself upon the center of a plain, a wintry, windless Arizona desert with no house in a thousand miles, and only dry river beds, the streets, for company.

"What is it now?" he asked the houses, noticing his wrist watch. "Eight-thirty P.M.? Time for a dozen assorted murders? A quiz? A revue? A comedian falling off the stage?"

Was that a murmur of laughter from within a moon-white house? He hesitated, but went on when nothing more happened. He stumbled over a particularly uneven section of sidewalk. The cement was vanishing under flowers and grass. In ten years of walking by night or day, for thousands of miles, he had never met another person walking, not one in all that time.

He came to a cloverleaf intersection which stood silent where two main highways crossed the town. During the day it was a thunderous surge of cars, the gas stations open, a great insect rustling and a ceaseless jockeying for position as the scarab-beetles, a faint incense puttering from their exhausts, skimmed homeward to the far directions. But now these highways, too, were like streams in a dry season, all stone and bed and moon radiance.

He turned back on a side street, circling around toward his home. He was within a block of his destination when the lone car turned a corner quite suddenly and flashed a fierce white cone of light upon him. He stood entranced, not unlike a night moth, stunned by the illumination, and then drawn toward it.

A metallic voice called to him:

"Stand still. Stay where you are! Don't move!"

He halted.

"Put up your hands!"

"But—" he said.

"Your hands up! Or we'll shoot!"

The police, of course, but what a rare, incredible thing; in a city of three million, there was only *one* police car left, wasn't that correct? Ever since a year ago, 2052, the election year, the force had been cut down from three cars to one. Crime was ebbing; there was no need now for the police, save for this one lone car wandering and wandering the empty streets.

"Your name?" said the police car in a metallic whisper. He couldn't see the men in it for the bright light in his eyes.

"Leonard Mead," he said.

"Speak up!"

"Leonard Mead!"

"Business or profession?"

"I guess you'd call me a writer."

"No profession," said the police car, as if talking to itself. The light held him fixed, like a museum specimen, needle thrust through chest.

"You might say that," said Mr. Mead. He hadn't written in years. Magazines and books didn't sell any more. Everything went on in the tomblike houses at night now, he thought, continuing his fancy. The tombs, ill-lit by television light, where the people sat like the dead, the gray or multicolored lights touching their faces, but never really touching *them*.

"No profession," said the phonograph voice, hissing. "What are you doing out?"

"Walking," said Leonard Mead.

"Walking!"

"Just walking," he said simply, but his face felt cold.

"Walking, just walking, walking?"

"Yes, sir."

"Walking where? For what?"

"Walking for air. Walking to *see.*"

"Your address!"

"Eleven South Saint James Street."

"And there is air *in* your house, you have an air *conditioner,* Mr. Mead?"

"Yes."

"And you have a viewing screen in your house to see with?"

"No."

"No?" There was a crackling quiet that in itself was an accusation.

"Are you married, Mr. Mead?"

"No."

"Not married," said the police voice behind the fiery beam. The moon was high and clear among the stars and the houses were gray and silent.

"Nobody wanted me," said Leonard Mead with a smile.

"Don't speak unless you're spoken to!"

Leonard Mead waited in the cold night.

"Just *walking,* Mr. Mead?"

"Yes."

"But you haven't explained for what purpose."

"I explained; for air, and to see, and just to walk."

"Have you done this often?"

"Every night for years."

The police car sat in the center of the street with its radio throat faintly humming.

"Well, Mr. Mead," it said.

"Is that all?" he asked politely.

"Yes," said the voice. "Here." There was a sigh, a pop. The back door of the police car sprang wide. "Get in."

"Wait a minute, I haven't done anything!"

"Get in."

"I protest!"

"Mr. Mead."

He walked like a man suddenly drunk. As he passed the front window of the car he looked in. As he had expected, there was no one in the front seat, no one in the car at all.

"Get in."

He put his hand to the door and peered into the back seat, which was a little cell, a little black jail with bars. It smelled of riveted steel. It smelled of harsh antiseptic; it smelled too clean and hard and metallic. There was nothing soft there.

"Now if you had a wife to give you an alibi," said the iron voice. "But——"

"Where are you taking me?"

The car hesitated, or rather gave a faint whirring click, as if information, somewhere, was dropping card by punch-slotted card under electric eyes. "To the Psychiatric Center for Research on Regressive Tendencies."

He got in. The door shut with a soft thud. The police car rolled through the night avenues, flashing its dim lights ahead.

They passed one house on one street a moment later, one house in an entire city of houses that were dark, but this one particular house had all of its electric lights brightly lit, every window a loud yellow illumination, square and warm in the cool darkness.

"That's *my* house," said Leonard Mead.

No one answered him.

The car moved down the empty river-bed streets and off away, leaving the empty streets with the empty sidewalks, and no sound and no motion all the rest of the chill November night.

—Twice 22

THE GENTLE ART
OF WALKING

by H. I. Brock

*Henry Irving Brock was born in Virginia in 1876 and died there in
1961. He was at one time an editor of the New York* Post. *He was
also a reporter, commentator, and feature writer for* The New York
Times, *and a contributor to its editorial page as well as to* The New
York Times Magazine, *in which this essay first appeared.*

WHEN man became man and a biped he learned to use shanks'
mare to go places. Still his first step on his own is his first accomplishment
toward independence. On his two legs he performed all his land journeys
for centuries. He kept on walking most of the time even when he had
tamed a four-footed fellow-creature to carry him on his longer and
speedier journeys. He invented wheels—and still he walked on most of
his affairs. Only when he mounted those wheels on air cushions and
hitched them to a gas engine did he get the notion in his head that he
could not get anywhere by walking.

Now that war, which used to depend on foot soldiers, has gone in for
tanks and airplanes, the civilian finds himself grounded—more or less—
with the prospect that, as the days pass, it will be rather more than less.

Whether more or less, he's got to make the best of it. Very well.
Because the centuries have formed the human body for walking, the
doctors agree that, take it all in all, to use the body for walking is one of
the best ways to keep it fit. The natural play of the muscles and the joints
promotes a healthy circulation of the blood, is good for the nerves, assists
the brain and dissipates humors—or eliminates poisons, if you prefer the
modern way of putting it. You get much better exercise swinging along on

your two feet than you do sitting on the back of your lap behind the steering wheel of a motor car.

Poets have gone tramping time out of mind to invoke the muse. Statesmen have used that simple method of getting down to earth and escaping the welter of words which is politics. Philosophers have been peripatetics —walkers about. Einstein pursued relativity afoot across the rolling country around Princeton. Which means that you can walk while you think—and, if the thinking you do while you walk seems more like ruminating, the conclusion that comes out of the proceeding is sometimes all the clearer. Dr. John Huston Finley, apostle of pedestrianism, said that "the land of our better selves is most surely reached by walking."

People who have continued to walk from choice include other notable persons of our time: college presidents, authors, editors, critics of the drama and doctors of divinity. Some of them treat walking as a sport— walk for the glory of walking and the record of mileage covered; some of them go walking to explore the world or the city or the neighborhood. Explorers generally, when they do not go upon ocean voyages, have gone on foot—witness the encounter between Stanley and Dr. Livingstone in the heart of Africa.

Sentimental journeys have been made on the legs that God gave us, and pilgrimages by treading the highways and byways with the staff that is the comforter. But walking for its own sake, like riding on a horse for its own sake—not merely to ketch a fox or to fly fences, or to get where you are going—is what counts with many walkers. There is the feel of the thing— the way you get into the swing of it after you have fallen into your stride and the rhythm of the movement gets into you the way, one long-legged footman said, it does when you dance. This chap, who writes for a living, said he liked a four-mile gait and ten or fifteen miles to go, but he could do a day's journey and climb mountains as well.

Naturally he was interested in the "technique" of walking—the body forward, the shoulders back, the free swing of the legs from the hips with the swing of the arms to help. He had been doing some civilian drill and he noticed that the doughboys' stride, posture and rhythm, as the drill sergeant's manual was applied, produced a tonic effect. He illustrated his point by marching up and down in cadence.

As a matter of fact, each fighting nation has developed a marching technique of its own. The British on the march are looser-jointed than we are, with freer knee action, and the French go at a long loping swing that seems to use the shoulders to push ahead with. It is a technique, anyway, that uses the whole body and carries you over the ground at a great pace—on the level particularly. Perhaps it is not so good for hill climbing. . . .

Generally speaking—aside from hikers who go across country singly or in packs, and mountain climbers who have an itch to get to the top of high places the hard way—the principle holds good of dividing into two kinds the people who make a serious business or recreation of walking. They are those who walk to be walking and those who walk to look at things.

The first kind take up walking, in the beginning, perhaps, for the sake of the exercise and then fall in love with walking and pursue it as a passion. They are prone to carry machines that clock their miles for them and to accumulate "centuries"—hundred-mile credits. They talk about walking as horsy folk talk about riding.

The other sort are really explorers—curious people who love the scenery of the country: woods, fields and streams, the road over the hill, lanes winding among farmsteads, mountain trails, either tame land or wild; or who love the sights of the city and like an intimate view of the goings-on, and the habitations of men packed together. Some walkers combine the passion for walking with the curiosity of the sight-seer.

I know a critic of the drama who says he walks to lose himself, to become (as he puts it) one of the missing men of a great city, and thus capture freedom. Nobody can find him at home, or in the office, or get him on the telephone. At heart this man is no less an explorer than Amundsen. Part of the kick of going off to the ends of the earth is getting away from things gone stale and drab through custom.

Our critic, playing truant, has poked around the waterfront of New York for years. He knows the North River roustabouts, the loafers on the East River piers. He knows the Jersey shores where the ships are berthed, the harbor front under Staten Island's hills, the docks and shipyards and yacht basins that fringe Brooklyn's long and smudgy reach along the river and the bay. One of the great advantages of walking here in New York is that you can take ferries at small expense, rest while you cross the water, watch the panorama of the port and have the sense of disembarking in a strange country. Each of our islands is strange to the other. And many parts of this big town are strange to every other part of it.

Like the wise Ulysses, though your ship is only a ferryboat, you are a seafarer and a collector of men and cities. The prescription for that sort of walking, our modern Ulysses says (and he has seen many strange places scattered around the globe), is to put on old clothes, from shoes to hat, and leave your everyday self behind you with your white-collar suit.

Unfortunately the waterfront is not, in these days, for inquisitive strangers or amateur vagrants, the happy hunting ground it used to be. The Coast Guard has taken over. But New York remains a city which holds within it many cities. And some of them are interior cities. Even in walking through Central Park you can visit in effect three continents—Europe, Africa and South America—besides encountering the soldiers of all the United Nations.

If you stroll through the lovely gardens where the park faces the Jeffersonian façade of the Museum of the City of New York you will be in the West Indies and hear little but Spanish spoken. And, though strolling is not walking, if you have walked all the way up there from the Plaza, you have had a walk not beneath the contempt of any but the most fanatical pedestrian.

Our 22,000-odd acres of parks, it may be noted, offer admirable walking terrain whether for exercise or exploration, with the problem of getting to the distant ones by subway or bus an additional challenge to the spirit of adventure. If you are not adventurous the nearest park will serve perfectly well.

However, the subways and the ferries and the trains take you out of the city not inconveniently. There is rough country on the Palisades right across the Hudson, with climbing effects if your taste runs to clambering over rocks—pedestrian steeplechasing instead of flat walking. The path on top of the Croton Aqueduct is good going for those who choose the country but had liefer follow the open trail than emulate the mountain goat.

But above all, if you have mastered the art of walking pavements without pain to your feet, there are all the streets of New York open to you. If you have never walked the streets of New York except in the beaten track of your affairs they offer ample room for exercise and clocking records and a field of exploration that is matched by hardly any city in the world. If you have walked the streets of New York in days gone by and think you know the little old town, do not let that stop you. So many parts of it have been so changed in a decade that the men who think they know the city best will find almost any walk a voyage of discovery.

—*The New York Times Magazine,* July 12, 1942

THE ROAD NOT TAKEN

by Robert Frost

Two roads diverged in a yellow wood,
And sorry I could not travel both
And be one traveler, long I stood
And looked down one as far as I could
To where it bent in the undergrowth;

Then took the other, as just as fair,
And having perhaps the better claim,
Because it was grassy and wanted wear;
Though as for that the passing there
Had worn them really about the same,

And both that morning equally lay
In leaves no step had trodden black.
Oh, I kept the first for another day!
Yet knowing how way leads on to way,
I doubted if I should ever come back.

I shall be telling this with a sigh
Somewhere ages and ages hence:
Two roads diverged in a wood, and I—
I took the one less traveled by,
And that has made all the difference.

—Collected Poems

A MORNING WALK
WITH BASHAN

by Thomas Mann

Thomas Mann won the Nobel Prize in 1929. His Buddenbrooks, The
Magic Mountain, *and* Joseph and His Brothers *deserve Clifton Fadiman's prediction that "in the year 1999 there is at least a fair chance
that Thomas Mann will be awarded the palm as the century's greatest
writer of imaginative prose." But we doubt that anything he ever
wrote will charm as many readers as will this affectionate piece
about his dog.*

WHEN SPRING, which all men agree is the fairest season of the
year, comes round again and happens to do honor to its name, I love to
go for half an hour's stroll in the open air before breakfast. I take this
stroll whenever the early chorus of the birds has succeeded in rousing me
betimes—because I had been wise enough to terminate the preceding day
at a seemly hour. And then I go walking—hatless—in the spacious
avenue in front of my house, and sometimes in the parks which are more
distant. Before I capitulate to the day's work, I long to draw a few
draughts of young morning air and to taste the joy of the pure early
freshness of things. Standing on the steps which lead down from my front
door, I give a whistle. This whistle consists of two tones, a base tone and
a deeper quarter-tone—as though I were beginning the first notes of the
second phrase of Schubert's Unfinished Symphony, a signal which may be
regarded as equal in tonal value to a name of two syllables.

The very next moment, as I go on towards the garden gate, a sound is
heard in the distance, a sound at first almost inaudible, then growing
rapidly nearer and clearer—a sound such as might ensue if a metal tag
were to be set clinking against the brass trimmings of a leather collar.
Then, as I turn round, I see Bashan curving in swift career around the

corner of the house and heading for me full tilt as though he intended to knock me over. His efforts cause him to shorten his underlip a bit, so that two or three of his lower front teeth are laid bare. How splendidly they gleam in the early sun!

Bashan comes straight from his kennel. This is situated behind the house under the floor of the veranda, which is supported on pillars. It is probable that, after a night of divers and unknown adventures, he had been enjoying a short morning doze in his kennel, until my two-syllabic whistle roused him to swift activity. This kennel or miniature hut is equipped with curtains made of coarse material, and is lined with straw. Thus it chances that a stray straw or two may be clinging to Bashan's coat—already rather ruffled up from his lying and stretching—or that one of these refractory straws may even be left sticking between his toes. This is a vision which always reminds me of the old Count Moor in Schiller's *Robbers*—as I once saw him in a most vivid and imaginative production, coming out of the Hunger Tower, with a straw between two of his toes.

Involuntarily I take up a flank position to the charging Bashan as he comes storming onward—an attitude of defence—for his apparent intention of lunging himself between my feet and laying me low is most amazingly deceptive. But always at the last moment and just before the collision, he manages to put on the brakes and to bring himself to— something which testifies to his physical as well as his mental self-control. And now—without uttering a sound—for Bashan makes but scant use of his sonorous and expressive voice—he begins to carry out a confused dance of welcome and salutation all about me, a dance consisting of rapid tramplings, of prodigious waggings—waggings which are not limited to that member which is intended for their proper expression—but which demand tribute of his entire hindquarters up to his very ribs, furthermore an annular contraction of his body, as well as darting, far-flung leaps into the air, also rotations about his own axis—performances which, strange to say, he endeavors to hide from my gaze, for whenever I turn towards him, he tranfers them to the other side. The very moment, however, I bend down and stretch out my hand, he is brought suddenly with a single leap to my side. There he stands, like a statue, with his shoulder-blade pressing against my shin-bone. He stands aslant, with his strong paws braced against the ground, his face uplifted towards mine, so that he peers into my eyes from below and in a reversed direction. . . .

It is good thus to go walking in the morning, the senses rejuvenated, the spirit purged by the healing bath and long Lethean draught of the night. You look upon the day that lies before you, regard it with strong, serene confidence, but you hesitate lazily to begin it—you are master of an unusually free and unburdened span of time lying between the dream and the day, your reward for the good use you have made of your time. The illusion that you are leading a life that is constant, simple, undissipated and benignly introspective, the illusion that you belong utterly to yourself, renders you happy. Man is disposed to regard his case or condition of the moment, be this glad or troubled, peaceful or passionate, for the true, essential, and permanent aspect of his life, and above all is in fancy inclined to elevate every happy *ex tempore* to a radiant rule and an unbreakable habit, whereas he is really condemned to live by improvisation, from hand to mouth, so to speak.

So, drawing in deep breaths of the morning air, you believe in your freedom and in your worth, though you ought to be aware, and at heart *are* aware, that the world is holding its snares ready to entangle you in them, and that in all probability you will again be lying in bed until nine tomorrow morning, because you had got into it at two the night before, heated, befogged, and full of passionate debate. . . . Well, so be it. To-day you are the man of sobriety and the dew-clad early hour, the right royal lord of that mad hunter yonder who is just making another jump across the fence out of sheer joy that you are apparently content to live this day with him and not waste it upon the world you have left behind you.

We follow the tree-lined avenue for about five minutes, to that point where it ceases to be a road and becomes a coarse desert of gravel parallel to the course of the river. We turn our backs upon this and strike into a broad, finely gravelled street which, like the poplar-lined road, is equipped with a cycle-path, but is still void of houses. This leads to the right, between low-lying allotments of wooded land, towards the declivity which bounds our river-banks—Bashan's field of action towards the east. . . .

I have a great love for brooks, as I have for all bodies of water—from the ocean to the smallest, scum-covered puddle. When I happen to be in the mountains during the summer and chance to hear the secret splashing and gossip of such a streamlet, then I must follow the liquid call, even though it be distant, and I cannot rest until I have found its hiding-place. Then, face to face, I make acquaintance with the talkative child of the crags and the heights. Beautiful are the proud torrential brooks which come down in crystalline thunder between pines and steep terraces of stone, form green, ice-cold pools in rocky baths and basins, and then go plunging to the next step in a dissolution of snowy foam. But I am also fond of looking upon the brooks of the flatland, whether they be shallow, so as scarcely to cover the polished, silvery, and slippery pebbles of their beds, or as deep as little rivers which—protected on both banks by low, overhanging willows—go shouldering themselves forward with a vigorous thrust, flowing more swiftly in the middle than at the sides. . . .

It is good to walk here, lightly assailed by the warm summer wind. The weather is warm, so it is probable that Bashan will go wading into the brook to cool his belly—only his belly, for he has a distinct aversion to bringing the more elevated parts of his anatomy in contact with the water. There he stands, with his ears laid back and an expression of piety and alertness upon his face, and lets the water swirl around him and past him. After this he comes sidling up to me in order to shake himself—an operation which, according to his own conviction, must occur in my immediate vicinity. The vigor with which he shakes himself causes a thin spray of water and mud to fly my way. It is no use warding him off with flourished stick and intense objurgations. Under no conditions will he tolerate any interference with anything that appears to him natural, inevitable, and according to the fitness of things. . . .

It is possible that visitors have been to call on me, and I have been left behind, stranded, as it were, within my own four walls, crushed by conversation, and with the breath of the strangers apparently still hanging in the air. It is good then to go at once and loaf for a little along the Heine or Schiller Street, to draw a breath of fresh air and to anoint myself with nature.

I look up to the heavens, peer into the green depths of the world of tender and delicate leaves, my nerves recover themselves and grow quiet—peace and serenity return to my spirit.

Bashan is always with me on such forays. He had not been able to prevent an invasion of the house by the outer world in the shape of the visitors, even though he had lifted up his voice in loud and terrible protest. But that had done no good, and so he had stepped aside. And now he is jubilant that he and I are once more together in the hunting-grounds. With one ear turned carelessly inside out, and loping obliquely, as is the common habit of dogs—that is, with his hind legs moving not directly behind his front legs, but somewhat to the side, he goes trotting on the gravel in front of me. And suddenly I see that some tremendous emotion has seized him, body and soul. His short bobbed tail begins to wave furiously. His head lunges forward and to one side, his body stretches and extends itself. He jumps hither and thither, and the next moment, with his nose still glued to the ground, he goes darting off. He has struck a scent. He is on the spoor of a rabbit.

—*A Man and His Dog,*
translated by Herman George Scheffauer

COUNTRY WALKS

by Walter Teller

Walter Teller endeared himself to us when we reached that prismatic sentence in his book which sums up life, regardless of any area code: "You do not complain to a beautiful morning." He was born in New Orleans, was educated at Haverford and Columbia University. The book from which these segments were taken, Area Code 215, *is a celebration of life in Bucks County. He now lives with his wife Jane and four children in Princeton, New Jersey.*

VIRTUALLY all of our township roads, at this date, have been stoned and paved the better to drive on. Few are still fit for walking. When you walk, you walk against traffic, wary, adapting, on the alert, keeping step with a fast-wheeling evolution, for the test of successful pedestrianism is, after all, survival. In the scheme of contemporary reversal such pleasures as walking—the time and the space to walk in— these become the new luxuries. And naturally. For where many are riding few will be able to walk. Only those who feel rich can afford it—or those who are, or feel poor. . . .

February 19. On a cold but clear and sunshiny day I walked over the same old faded-green, simply trussed bridge that trembles from New Hope to Lambertville. A bridge is to walking as flying to transportation— one of the great routes by which to go. You are up and the view is below, as well as around and aloft. This day the river was shore to shore frozen and ice lay under a blanket of snow. To port side and starboard the course stretched broad, white and dazzling. As I say, the day though sunny was cold. Going across I met no one. The uniformed interstate bridge police, sitting in glass-plated stations at either end of the bridge, checked the weights of the trucks rolling by. . . .

A warm afternoon, just a little warmer than perfect—perfection is rare but days sometimes have it—and I wanted to walk, but where it was shady and where I could get away from automobiles. To accomplish that I would first have to use my own; that's how it is in Lahaska. . . .

Carversville, one-time home of both the Excelsior Normal Institute and the Baconian Literary Society, lies at an intersection of country roads about four miles north-northeast of Lahaska. From here to there one travels through some of the better lands in the country, checkerboarded with winter wheat which now looks like fresh young grass, and with ground plowed or harrowed, or planted to corn. Though a few farmers practice strip cropping and contour farming, most of Bucks still is farmed in accord with the ancient pattern of right-angled fields. After skirting the east edge of Carversville village, I turned onto Fleecy Dale Road and followed it east through the winding valley of the Paunacussing Creek. On my left, rocky cliff-like hills rose abruptly; on my right flowed the stream. At the first chance, I turned right and crossed the creek. I was then on Old Carversville Road. A few hundred yards up ahead the macadam ends and the walking part of the road begins, eastward toward Lumberville on the river, seven miles north of New Hope.

A free-breathing day, easy and spotlessly fair. I had forgotten a little how good a dirt road feels under the soles of one's shoes. Up the southern bank of the valley I went, on both sides woods in which all young growth showed the same fresh green. Presently I came to a clearing where an old man, working beside the road, was cutting wood for next winter. Using a bucksaw and sawbuck, he nibbled at an untidy pile, reducing it piece by piece to proper lengths for his stove. On the hillside below and facing the creek stood his little stone house, reroofed with galvanized iron and surrounded by overgrown fields. I spoke to him. He replied with a smile like a travesty of an advertisement. Displaying a few multicolored teeth he announced that he no longer farmed. Then after scanning the sky, he added he thought it would be a wet summer.

—Area Code 215

BUTTERFLY WALKS

by Vladimir Nabokov

The success of Vladimir Nabokov's bestseller Lolita *has unfortunately distorted his substantial reputation as a writer of poems, novels and translations. Like Conrad, he began to write in English rather late in life and did so with brilliance, subtlety and beauty. His first book in English,* The Real Life of Sebastian Knight, *was published when he was forty-two.* Lolita, *which* The New Yorker *called a "shocking but major work . . . the conjunction of a sense of humor with a sense of horror," was first printed in Paris. It came to New York in 1958. Young Nabokov was seven when he joined the distinguished company of lepidopterists. He has since walked thousands of rugged miles pursuing butterflies. A swallowtail that escaped him in the Russian garden of his childhood he captured forty years later under an aspen near Boulder. "Butterfly Walks" is from his evocative autobiography,* Speak, Memory.

ON a summer morning, in the legendary Russia of my boyhood, my first glance upon awakening was for the chink between the white inner shutters. If it disclosed a watery pallor, one had better not open them at all, and so be spared the sight of a sullen day sitting for its picture in a puddle. How resentfully one would deduce, from a line of dull light, the leaden sky, the sodden sand, the gruel-like mess of broken brown blossoms under the lilacs—and that flat, fallow leaf (the first casualty of the season) pasted upon a wet garden bench!

But if the chink was a long glint of dewy brilliancy, then I made haste to have the window yield its treasure. With one blow, the room would be cleft into light and shade. The foliage of birches moving in the sun had the translucent green tone of grapes, and in contrast to this there was the dark velvet of fir trees against a blue of extraordinary intensity, the like of which I rediscovered only many years later, in the montane zone of Colorado.

From the age of seven, everything I felt in connection with a rectangle of framed sunlight was dominated by a single passion. If my first glance of the morning was for the sun, my first thought was for the butterflies it would engender. . . .

I have hunted butterflies in various climes and disguises: as a pretty boy in knickerbockers and sailor cap; as a lanky cosmopolitan expatriate in flannel bags and beret; as a fat hatless old man in shorts. . . . Incredibly happy memories, quite comparable, in fact, to those of my Russian boyhood, are associated with my research work at the Museum of Comparative Zoology, Cambridge, Massachusetts (1941–1948). No less happy have been the many collecting trips taken almost every summer, during twenty years, through most of the states of my adopted country.

In Jackson Hole and in the Grand Canyon, on the mountain slopes above Telluride, Colorado, and on a celebrated pine barren near Albany, New York, dwell, and will dwell, in generations more numerous than editions, the butterflies I have described as new. Several of my finds have been dealt with by other workers; some have been named after me . . .

Few things indeed have I known in the way of emotion or appetite, ambition or achievement, that could surpass in richness and strength the excitement of entomological exploration. From the very first it had a great many intertwinkling facets. One of them was the acute desire to be alone, since any companion, no matter how quiet, interfered with the concentrated enjoyment of my mania. Its gratification admitted of no compromise or exception. Already when I was ten, tutors and governesses knew that the morning was mine and cautiously kept away.

In this connection, I remember the visit of a schoolmate, a boy of whom I was very fond and with whom I had excellent fun. He arrived one summer night—in 1913, I think—from a town some twenty-five miles away. His father had recently perished in an accident, the family was ruined and the stouthearted lad, not being able to afford the price of a railway ticket, had bicycled all those miles to spend a few days with me.

On the morning following his arrival, I did everything I could to get out of the house for my morning hike without his knowing where I had gone. Breakfastless, with hysterical haste, I gathered my net, pill boxes, killing jar, and escaped through the window. Once in the forest, I was safe; but still I walked on, my calves quaking, my eyes full of scalding tears, the whole of me twitching with shame and self-disgust, as I visualized my poor friend, with his long pale face and black tie, moping in the hot garden—patting the panting dogs for want of something better to do, and trying hard to justify my absence to himself.

Let me look at my demon objectively. With the exception of my parents, no one really understood my obsession, and it was many years before I met a fellow sufferer . . .

It is astounding how little the ordinary person notices butterflies. "None," calmly replied that sturdy Swiss hiker with Camus in his rucksack when purposely asked by me for the benefit of my incredulous companion if he had seen any butterflies while descending the trail where, a moment before, you and I had been delighting in swarms of them. It is also true that when I call up the image of a particular path remembered in minute detail but pertaining to a summer before that of 1906, preceding, that is, the date on my first locality label, and never revisited, I fail to make out one wing, one wingbeat, one azure flash, one moth-gemmed flower, as if an evil spell had been cast on the Adriatic coast making all its "leps" (as the slangier among us say) invisible. Exactly thus an entomologist may feel some day when plodding beside a jubilant, and already helmetless botanist amid the hideous flora of a parallel planet, with not a single insect in sight; and thus (in odd proof of the odd fact that whenever possible the scenery of our infancy is used by an economically minded producer as a ready-made setting for our adult dreams) the seaside hilltop of a certain recurrent nightmare of mine, whereinto I smuggle a collapsible net from my waking state, is gay with thyme and melilot, but incomprehensibly devoid of all the butterflies that should be there.

I also found out very soon that a "lepist" indulging in his quiet quest was apt to provoke strange reactions in other creatures . . . On a path above the Black Sea, in the Crimea, among shrubs in waxy bloom, in March 1918, a bow-legged Bolshevik sentry attempted to arrest me for signaling (with my net, he said) to a British warship. In the summer of 1929, every time I walked through a village in the Eastern Pyrenees, and happened to look back, I would see in my wake the villagers frozen in the various attitudes my passage had caught them in, as if I were Sodom and they Lot's wife. A decade later, in the Maritime Alps, I once noticed the grass undulate in a serpentine way behind me because a fat rural policeman was wriggling after me on his belly to find out if I were not trapping songbirds. America has shown even more of this morbid interest in my retiary activities than other countries have—perhaps because I was in my forties when I came there to live, and the older the man, the queerer he looks with a butterfly net in his hand. Stern farmers have drawn my attention to NO FISHING signs; from cars passing me on the highway have come wild howls of derision; sleepy dogs, though unmindful of the worst bum, have perked up and come at me, snarling; tiny tots have pointed me out to their puzzled mamas; broad-minded vacationists have asked me whether I was catching bugs for bait; and one morning on a wasteland, lit by tall yuccas in bloom, near Santa Fe, a big black mare followed me for more than a mile.

When, having shaken off all pursuers, I took the rough, red road that ran from our Vyra house toward field and forest, the animation and luster of the day seemed like a tremor of sympathy around me.

Very fresh, very dark Arran Browns, which emerged only every second year (conveniently, retrospection has fallen here into line), flitted among the firs or revealed their red markings and checkered fringes as they sunned themselves on the roadside bracken. Hopping above the grass, a diminutive Ringlet called Hero dodged my net. Several moths, too, were flying—gaudy sun lovers that sail from flower to flower like painted flies, or male insomniacs in search of hidden females, such as that rust-colored Oak Eggar hurtling across the shrubbery. I noticed (one of the major mysteries of my childhood) a soft pale green wing caught in a spider's web (by then I knew what it was: part of a Large Emerald). The tremendous larva of the Goat Moth, ostentatiously segmented, flat-headed, flesh-colored and glossily flushed, a strange creature "as naked as a worm" to use a French comparison, crossed my path in frantic search for a place to pupate (the awful pressure of metamorphosis, the aura of a disgraceful fit in a public place). On the bark of that birch tree, the stout one near the park wicket, I had found last spring a dark aberration of Sievers' Carmelite (just another gray moth to the reader). In the ditch, under the bridgelet, a bright-yellow Silvius Skipper hobnobbed with a dragonfly (just a blue libellula to me). From a flower head two male Coppers rose to a tremendous height, fighting all the way up—and then, after a while, came the downward flash of one of them returning to his thistle. These were familiar insects, but at any moment something better might cause me to stop with a quick intake of breath. . . .

Let me also evoke the hawkmoths, the jets of my boyhood! Colors would die a long death on June evenings. The lilac shrubs in full bloom before which I stood, net in hand, displayed clusters of a fluffy gray in the dusk—the ghost of purple. A moist young moon hung above the mist of a neighboring meadow. In many a garden have I stood thus in later years— in Athens, Antibes, Atlanta—but never have I waited with such a keen desire as before those darkening lilacs. And suddenly it would come, the low buzz passing from flower to flower, the vibrational halo around the streamlined body of an olive and pink Hummingbird moth poised in the air above the corolla into which it had dipped its long tongue. Its handsome black larva (resembling a diminutive cobra when it puffed out its ocellated front segments) could be found on dank willow herb two months later. Thus every hour and season had its delights. And, finally, on cold, or even frosty, autumn nights, one could sugar for moths by painting tree trunks with a mixture of molasses, beer, and rum. Through the gusty blackness, one's lantern would illumine the stickily glistening furrows of the bark and two or three large moths upon it imbibing the sweets, their nervous wings half open butterfly fashion, the lower ones exhibiting their incredible crimson silk from beneath the lichen-gray primaries. *"Catocala adultera!"* I would triumphantly shriek in the direction of the lighted windows of the house as I stumbled home to show my captures to my father.

The "English" park that separated our house from the hayfields was an extensive and elaborate affair with labyrinthine paths, Turgenevian benches, and imported oaks among the endemic firs and birches . . . On a picturesque boulder, a little mountain ash and a still smaller aspen had climbed, holding hands, like two clumsy, shy children. Other, more elusive trespassers—lost picnickers or merry villagers—would drive our hoary gamekeeper Ivan crazy by scrawling ribald words on the benches and gates. The disintegrating process continues still, in a different sense, for when, nowadays, I attempt to follow in memory the winding paths from one given point to another, I notice with alarm that there are many gaps, due to oblivion or ignorance, akin to the terra-incognita blanks map makers of old used to call "sleeping beauties."

Beyond the park, there were fields, with a continuous shimmer of butterfly wings over a shimmer of flowers—daisies, bluebells, scabious, and others—which now rapidly pass by me in a kind of colored haze like those lovely, lush meadows, never to be explored, that one sees from the diner on a transcontinental journey. At the end of this grassy wonderland, the forest rose like a wall. There I roamed, scanning the tree trunks (the enchanted, the silent part of a tree) for certain tiny moths, called Pugs in England—delicate little creatures that cling in the daytime to speckled surfaces, with which their flat wings and turned-up abdomens blend. There, at the bottom of that sea of sunshot greenery, I slowly spun round the great boles. Nothing in the world would have seemed sweeter to me than to be able to add, by a stroke of luck, some remarkable new species to the long list of Pugs already named by others. . . .

On my butterfly hunts I always preferred hiking to any other form of locomotion (except, naturally, a flying seat gliding leisurely over the plant mats and rocks of an unexplored mountain, or hovering just above the flowery roof of a rain forest); for when you walk, especially in a region you have studied well, there is an exquisite pleasure in departing from one's itinerary to visit, here and there by the wayside, this glade, that glen, this or that combination of soil and flora—to drop in, as it were, on a familiar butterfly in his particular habitat, in order to see if he has emerged, and if so, how he is doing.

There came a July day—around 1910, I suppose—when I felt the urge to explore the vast marshland beyond the Oredezh. After skirting the river for three or four miles, I found a rickety footbridge. While crossing over, I could see the huts of a hamlet on my left, apple trees, rows of tawny pine logs lying on a green bank, and the bright patches made on the turf by the scattered clothes of peasant girls, who, stark naked in shallow water, romped and yelled, heeding me as little as if I were the discarnate carrier of my present reminiscences.

On the other side of the river, a dense crowd of small, bright blue male butterflies that had been tippling on the rich, trampled mud and cow dung through which I trudged rose all together into the spangled air and settled again as soon as I had passed.

After making my way through some pine groves and alder scrub I came to the bog. No sooner had my ear caught the hum of diptera around me, the guttural cry of a snipe overhead, the gulping sound of the morass under my foot, than I knew I would find here quite special arctic butter-flies, whose pictures, or, still better, nonillustrated descriptions I had worshiped for several seasons. And the next moment I was among them. Over the small shrubs of bog bilberry with fruit of a dim, dreamy blue, over the brown eye of stagnant water, over moss and mire, over the flower spikes of the fragrant bog orchid (the *nochnaya fialka* of Russian poets), a dusky little Fritillary bearing the name of a Norse goddess passed in low, skimming flight. Pretty Cordigera, a gemlike moth, buzzed all over its uliginose food plant. I pursued rose-margined Sulphurs, gray-marbled Satyrs. Unmindful of the mosquitoes that furred my forearms, I stooped with a grunt of delight to snuff out the life of some silver-studded lepidopteron throbbing in the folds of my net. Through the smells of the bog, I caught the subtle perfume of butterfly wings on my fingers, a perfume which varies with the species—vanilla, or lemon, or musk, or a musty, sweetish odor difficult to define. Still unsated, I pressed forward. At last I saw I had come to the end of the marsh. The rising ground beyond was a paradise of lupines, columbines, and pentstemons. Mariposa lilies bloomed under Ponderosa pines. In the distance, fleeting cloud shadows dappled the dull green of slopes above timber line, and the gray and white of Longs Peak.

I confess I do not believe in time. I like to fold my magic carpet, after use, in such a way as to superimpose one part of the pattern upon another. Let visitors trip. And the highest enjoyment of timelessness—in a landscape selected at random—is when I stand among rare butterflies and their food plants. This is ecstasy, and behind the ecstasy is something else, which is hard to explain. It is like a momentary vacuum into which rushes all that I love. A sense of oneness with sun and stone. A thrill of gratitude to whom it may concern—to the contrapuntal genius of human fate or to tender ghosts humoring a lucky mortal.

—Speak, Memory

AN INLAND STROLL
IN SPRING

by Henry Beston

The Outermost House, *from which this essay has been taken, is the chronicle of a solitary year spent at Eastham on Cape Cod. There in a tiny house, the Fo'castle, with two rooms, ten windows and a fireplace, Henry Beston spent a contemplative year with the dunes, the birds and the sea. The result, written on the oilcloth-covered kitchen table, was published in 1928. It has become an international classic that may one day rival* Walden. *In 1964, the house itself was officially designated a* National Literary Landmark.

I DEVOTED the entire day yesterday to an adventure I have long had in mind, a walk across the Cape from outer ocean to Cape Cod Bay. As the crow flies, the distance from the Fo'castle to the west shore is about four and a half miles; afoot and by the road, it is nearer seven and a half, for one must follow roads lying north of the great lagoon. The day was pleasant; cool, easterly winds blew across the moors, and it was warm enough when I found both shelter and the sun.

I walked to Nauset Station close along the landward edge of the dunes, out of sight and sound of the sea. All up and down these western gradients of grass and sand the plant life of the region is pushing through the surface drifts and sandy overflowings which crept eastward during winter; green leaves of the beach pea are thrusting up; sand crumbs still lodged in their unfolded crevices; the dune goldenrod is shouldering the bright particles aside. Against the new olive colouring of the dunes, the compact thickets of beach plum are as charred-looking as ever, but when I stroll over to a thicket I find its buds tipped with a tiny show of green.

Arriving at Nauset, I found my coast guard neighbours airing their bedding and cleaning house. Andrew Wetherbee hailed me from the tower; we shouted pleasantries and passed the time of day. Then down Nauset road I went, turning my back on ocean and a rising tide.

The first mile of the road from Nauset to Eastham village winds through a singular country. It is a belt of wild, rolling, and treeless sand moorland which follows along the rim of the earth cliff for two thirds of its length and runs inland for something like a mile. Nauset Station, with its tiny floor of man-made greenery, lies at the frontier between my dune world and this sea-girt waste. Coast guard paths and the low, serried poles of the coast guard telephone are the only clues to the neighbourhood of man.

Desolate and half desert as it is, this borderland of the Cape has an extraordinary beauty, and for me the double attraction of mystery and wide horizons. Just to the north of the station, the grass turns starveling and thin, and the floor of the border waste becomes a thick carpet of poverty grass, *Hudsonia tomentosa,* variegated with channels and starry openings of whitish sand. All winter long this plant has been a kind of a rag grey; it has had a clothlike look and feel, but now it wears one of the rarest and loveliest greens in nature. I shall have to use the term "sage green" in telling of it, but the colour is not so simply ticketed; it is sage green, yes, but of an unequalled richness and sable depth. All along the waste, the increasing light is transmuting the grey sand of winter to a mellowness of grey-white touched with silver; the moor blanches, the plant puts on the dark. To my mind this wild region is at its best in twilight, for its dun floor gathers the dark long before the sunset colour has faded from the flattened sky, and one may then walk there in the peace of the earth gloom and hear from far below the great reverberation of the sea.

West of this treeless waste the Nauset road mounts to the upland floor of the Cape and to the inhabited lands.

When Henry Thoreau walked through Eastham in 1849, warding off a drenching autumnal rain with his Concord umbrella, he found this region practically treeless, and the inhabitants gathering their firewood on the beach. Nowadays, people on the outer Cape have their wood lots as well as inlanders. The tree that has rooted itself into the wind-swept bar is the pitch pine, *Pinus rigida,* the familiar tree of the outer Long Island wastes and the Jersey barrens. *Rigida* has no particular interest or beauty—one writer on trees calls it "rough and scraggly"—yet let me say no harm of it, for it is of value here: it furnishes firewood, holds down the earth and sand, and shelters the ploughed fields. In favourable situations, the pine reaches a height of between forty and fifty feet; on these windy sands, trees of the oldest growth struggle to reach between twenty-five and thirty. The trunk of this pine is brownish, with an overtone of violet, and seldom grows straight to its top; its leaves occur in a cluster of three, and its dry cones have a way of adhering for years to its branches.

They are forever burning up, these pitch-pine woods. A recent great fire in Wellfleet burned four days, and at one time seemed about to descend upon the town. Coast guard crews were sent to help the villagers. Many deer, they tell me, were seen running about in the burning woods, terror-stricken by the smoke and the oncoming crackle of the crest of flame. Encircled by the fire, one man jumped into a pond; scarce had he plunged when he heard a plunge close by and found a deer swimming by his side.

The thickets were rusty yesterday, for the tree thins out its winter-worn foliage in the spring. As I paused to study a group of particularly dead-looking trees, I scared up a large bird from the wood north of the road; it was a marsh hawk, *Circus Hudsonius*. Out of the withered tops flew this shape of warm, living brown, flapped, sailed on, and sank in the thickets by the marsh. I was glad to see this bird and to have some hint of its residence, because a female bird of this species makes a regular daily visit to the dunes. She comes from somewhere on the mainland north of the marsh, crosses the northeast corner of the flats, and on reaching the dunes aligns her flight with the long five miles of the great wall. Down the wall she comes, this great brown bird, flying fifteen or twenty feet above the awakening green. Now she hovers a second as if about to swoop, now she sinks as if about to snatch a prey—and all the time advancing. I have seen her flutter by the west windows of the Fo'castle so near that I could have touched her with a stick. Apparently, she is on the watch for beach mice, though I have as yet seen no mouse tracks on the dunes. She arrives between ten and eleven o'clock on practically all fair weather mornings, and occasionally I see her search the dunes again late in the afternoon. *Circus Hudsonius* is a migrant, but some birds spend the winter in southern New England, and I have a notion that this female has wintered in Nauset woods.

Once Nauset road approaches Eastham village the thickets of pitch pines to the eastward fall behind, the fields south of the road widen into superb treeless moorlands rolling down to the shores of the great lagoon, orchard tops become visible in hollows, and a few houses sit upon the moors like stranded ships. Eastham village itself, however, is not treeless, for there are shade trees near many houses and trees along the road.

All trees on the outer Cape are of interest to me, for they are the outermost of trees—trees with the roar of breakers in their leaves—but I find one group of especial interest. As one goes south along the main highway, one encounters a straggle of authentic western cottonwoods, *Populus deltoides.* The tree is rare in the northeast; indeed, these trees are the only ones of their kind I have ever chanced to find in Massachusetts. They were planted long ago, the village declares, by Cape Codders who emigrated to Kansas, and then returned, homesick for the sea. The trees grow close by the roadside, and there is a particularly fine group at the turn of the road near Mr. Austin Cole's. In this part of the Cape, an aërial fungus paints the trunks of deciduous trees an odd mustard-orange, and as I passed yesterday by the cottonwoods I saw that the group was particularly overspread with this picturesque stain. The growth seems to do no harm of any kind.

At a boulder commemorative of the men of Eastham who served in the Great War, I turned south on the main highway and presently reached the town hall and the western top of the moorland country. There I left the road and walked east into the moors to enjoy the incomparable view of the great Eastham marshes and the dunes. Viewed from the seaward scarp of the moors, the marsh takes form as the greener floor of a great encirclement of rolling, tawny, and treeless land. From a marsh just below, the vast flat islands and winding rivers of the marsh run level to the yellow bulwark of the dunes, and at the end of the vista the eye escapes through valleys in the wall to the cold April blue of the North Atlantic plain. The floor of ocean there seems higher than the floor of the marsh, and sailing vessels often have an air of sailing past the dunes low along the sky. A faint green colours the sky line of the dunes, and on the wide flanks of the empty moorlands stains of springtime greenness well from the old tawniness of earth. Yesterday I heard no ocean sound.

So beautiful was the spacious and elemental scene that I lingered a while on the top of the moor cliff shelving to the marsh. The tide was rising in the creeks and channels, and the gulls remaining in the region had been floated off their banks and shoals. The great levels seemed, for the moment, empty of their winged and silvery life.

During the winter, one bird has made this moorland region all his own, and that bird the English starling. The birds apparently spend the winter on these hills. I have crossed the open country during a northeast gale just to watch them wheeling in the snow. Scarce had one flock settled ere another was up; I saw them here and there and far away. I find these Eastham birds of particular interest, for they are the first American starlings I have seen to recover their ancestral and European mode of life. In Europe, the bird is given to congregating in vast flocks—there are river lowlands in England where such starling flocks gather in crowded thousands—and once this starling army has established itself in a region it is theirs completely and forever.

Are the flocks at Eastham the beginning of one of those European mobs? Will the various flocks now inhabiting the moors ultimately mingle to form one enormous and tyrannous confederacy? The separate winter swarms already consist of fifty to seventy-five birds, and I imagine that, if the stray members of each flock were to return to their congregations, these bands might be found to contain well over a hundred individuals. Such a mingling as I speak of may possibly take place; again, it may be that the resources of the region are already taxed to support the present birds; let us hope that this last is the truth. The presence of these rabble blackbirds disturbs the entire natural economy of the region, for they strip every autumnal bush and plant bare of its last seed and berry and leave nothing for our native birds to feed on when they return in the spring.

With spring, the birds desert the moors, pair off, and retire to the village barns and the chimneys of unopened summer cottages.

The hour of flood tide approaching, I left the moors behind and went to the west shore to see what I could of the strangest of all regional migrations.

—The Outermost House

THE VAGABOND

by Robert Louis Stevenson

Give to me the life I love,
   Let the lave go by me,
Give the jolly heaven above
   And the byway nigh me.

Bed in the bush with stars to see,
   Bread I dip in the river—
There's the life for a man like me,
   There's the life for ever.

Let the blow fall soon or late,
   Let what will be o'er me;
Give the face of earth around,
   And the road before me.

Wealth I ask not, hope nor love,
   Nor a friend to know me;
All I ask, the heaven above
   And the road below me.

—Songs of Travel

THE GENTLE ART OF TRAMPING

by Stephen Graham

Stephen Graham wrote most of his books in the open air, sitting on logs in the pine forests or on bridges over mountain streams, by the side of a morning fire or on the sea sand after a morning dip . . . which may explain why his books, like Emerson's, "smell of pines and resound with the hum of insects." The zigzag walk, *which you will find in Part 4, was his secret and his invention.*

1.

IT IS A GENTLE ART; know how to tramp and you know how to live. Manners makyth man, and tramping makyth manners. Know how to meet your fellow wanderer, how to be passive to the beauty of Nature and how to be active to its wildness and its rigor. Tramping brings one to reality.

If you would have a portrait of Man you must not depict him in high hat and carrying in one hand a small shiny bag, nor would one draw him in gnarled corduroys and with red handkerchief about his neck, nor with lined brow on a high bench watching a hand that is pushing a pen, nor with pick and shovel on the road. You cannot show him carrying a rifle, you dare not put him in priest's garb with conventional cross on breast. You will not point to King or Bishop with crown or miter. But most fittingly you will show a man with staff in hand and burden on his shoulders, striving onward from light to darkness upon an upward road, shading his eyes with his hand as he seeks his way. You will show a figure something like that posthumous picture of Tolstoy, called "Tolstoy pilgrimaging toward eternity."

So when you put on your old clothes and take to the road, you make at least a right gesture. You get into your right place in the world in the right way. Even if your tramping expedition is a mere jest, a jaunt, a spree, you are apt to feel the benefits of getting into a right relation toward God, Nature, and your fellow man. You get into an air that is refreshing and free. You liberate yourself from the tacit assumption of your everyday life.

What a relief to escape from being voter, taxpayer, authority on old brass, brother of man who is an authority on old brass, author of best seller, uncle of author of best seller. . . .

Tramping is a way of approach, to Nature, to your fellow man, to a nation, to a foreign nation, to beauty, to life itself. And it is an art, because you do not get into the spirit of it directly you leave your back door and make for the distant hill. There is much to learn, there are illusions to be overcome. There are prejudices and habits to be shaken off.

First of all there is the physical side: you need to study equipment, care of health, how to sleep out of doors, what to eat, how to cook on the camp fire. These things you teach yourself. For the rest Nature becomes your teacher, and from her you will learn what is beautiful and who you are and what is your special quest in life and whither you should go. You relax in the presence of the great healer and teacher, you turn your back on civilization and most of what you learned in schools, museums, theaters, galleries. You live on manna vouchsafed to you daily, miraculously. You stretch out arms for hidden gifts, you yearn toward the moonbeams and the stars, you listen with new ears to bird's song and the murmurs of trees and streams. If ever you were proud or quarrelsome or restless, the inflammation goes down, fanned by the coolness of humility and simplicity. From day to day you keep your log, your day-book of the soul, and you may think at first that it is a mere record of travel and of facts; but something else will be entering into it, poetry, the new poetry of your life, and it will be evident to a seeing eye that you are gradually becoming an artist in life, you are learning the gentle art of tramping, and it is giving you an artist's joy in creation.

2.

The principal motive of the wander-spirit is curiosity—the desire to know what is beyond the next turning of the road, and to probe for oneself the mystery of the names of the places in maps. In a subconscious way the born wanderer is always expecting to come on something very wonderful—beyond the horizon's rim. The joys of wandering are often balanced by the pains; but there is something which is neither joy nor pain which makes the desire to wander or explore almost incurable in many human beings.

The child experiences his first wander-thrill when he is taken to places where he has never been before. I remember from the age of nine a barefoot walk with my mother along the Lincolnshire sands from Sutton to Skegness, and the romantic and strange sights on the way. What did we not build out of that adventure? And who does not remember the pleasurable thrill, the pleasure that's all but pain, of being lost in a wood, or in a strange countryside, and meeting some crazy individual who humored the idea by apostrophizing a little brook in this style: "I am now marching upon the banks of the mighty Congo"? The imagination wishes to be stirred with the romance of places, and is stirred. In a great city like London or New York, even though living there, certainly I for one am homesick; not for a home and an armchair, but for a rolling road and a stout pair of boots, and my own stick fire by the roadside at dawn, and the old pot which is slow to boil.

3.

Going tramping is at first an act of rebellion; only afterwards do you get free from rebelliousness as Nature sweetens your mind. Town makes men contentious; the country smooths out their souls.

4.

I have mentioned the "zigzag" walk. Did you ever make one? Probably not, for it is my secret. I invented it. A frequent wish of the traveler and wanderer is to obtain genuinely chance impressions of cities and countries. He would trust neither his own choice of road, nor the guide's choice, nor the map. But if he goes forth aimlessly he inevitably finds himself either making for the gayer and better-lighted places, or returning to his own door. The problem is to let chance and the town take charge of you, for the world we travel in is more wonderful than human plan or idle hearts desire.

One day in New York, wishing to explore that great city in a truly haphazard way I hit on the following device—a zigzag walk. The first turning to the left is the way of the heart. Take it at random and you are sure to find something pleasant and diverting. Take the left again and the piquancy may be repeated. But reason must come to the rescue, and you must turn to the right in order to save yourself from a mere uninteresting circle. To make a zigzag walk you take the first turning to the left, the first to the right, then the first to the left again, and so on.

I had a wonderful night's walking thus in New York, taking cross sections of that marvelous cosmopolitan city. And many were the surprises and delights and curiosities that the city unfolded to me in its purlieus and alleys and highways and quays. That was several years ago. After New York I saw Paris for the first time, and wandered that way there. . . . I saw more of Paris in a night than many may do in a month. After Paris I tried the experiment in Cologne. . . . I explored the city in that way. How unusual and real and satisfactory were the impressions obtained by going—not the crowd's way, but the way of the zigzag, the diagonal between heart and reason.

However, the most charming and delightful associations of my zigzag walk are not those of the great foreign cities which I have known, but of our mysterious and crooked-streeted capital, London herself.

It was Christmas time and I said to my wife: "Let us do our shopping on the zigzag way." . . .

Our steps took us along various grand crescents of pathway, and the intention of the city with regard to our ultimate destination began to seem very obscure. There were several knotty points as to which was a turning and which was not, and when I made an artful decision the companion of my way said to me, "You want to shape things to your own ends."

"No," said I. "I want to be faithful and just."

A stiff discussion set in and we could not get the matter straight. However, we eventually found ourselves in St. James' Park, and there was an issue for us into Birdcage Walk where, in the barracks beyond, we saw the soldiers at drill. . . .

Thus ended the first lap of our zigzag walk through London, and we promised ourselves to return to the point where we had left off and continue this way of chance as soon as a convenient moment came. . . .

A friend to whom we had communicated the secret of our street adventure had warned us that if in the near future we should disappear from London life he would come in search of us to the Maze at Hampton Court, from which, he was afraid, once entered, we should never extricate ourselves. So we made a rule: No parks, no mazes. Incidentally, however, we spent a remarkable and amusing hour in that artificial wilderness of

Battersea. If zigzagging should ever become fashionable I am afraid that most people will consider it *de rigueur* to follow out the mazes and labyrinths to the last intricacy and the correct issue, and that they will not have the courage to cut the Gordian knot as we did. . . .

This is distinctly not a walk on which to embark with one's wife. It reveals points of difference. It brings out the hidden crookedness of character, confirms all obstinacies and predeterminations. It is possible to get more excited over a trivial turning (mark you, trivial, a place where three ways meet) than over the most portentous decision in real life. I imagine it is always so. . . .

You can put no destination label on your rucksack, and if any one asks where you are going, you may tell him in confidence, whisper the dreadful fact in his ear—"honestly, you do not know." The adventure is not getting there, it's the on-the-way. It is not the expected; it is the surprise; not the fulfillment of prophecy, but the providence of something better than that prophesied. You are not choosing what you shall see in the world, but are giving the world an even chance to see you.

I am still on that zigzag way, pursuing the diagonal between the reason and the heart; the chart could be made by drawing lines from star to star in the night sky, not forgetting many dim, shy, fitfully glimmering out-of-the-way stars, which one would not purpose visiting. I said we would not enter a maze, but we have made one and are in one, a maze of Andalusia and Dalmatia, of Anahuac and Anatolia, of Seven Rivers Land and Seven Kings. The first to the left, the next to the right! No blind alleys. A long way. *Beaucoup zigzag, eh!*

—*The Gentle Art of Tramping*

ANYWHERE OUT OF THE WORLD

by Charles Baudelaire

*Baudelaire used to blame his parents for the strangeness of his char-
acter (his father was sixty-two and his mother twenty-eight when
they were married). He translated Edgar Allan Poe's macabre tales
into haunting French and was thus responsible for Poe's great
European reputation. This is one of his* Petits Poèmes en Prose, *little
masterpieces which he called "experiments and confessions."*

LIFE IS A HOSPITAL, in which every patient is possessed by the
desire to change his bed. This one would prefer to suffer in front of the
stove, and that one believes he would get well if he were placed by the
window.

It seems to me that I should always be happier elsewhere than where I
happen to be, and this question of moving is one that I am continually
talking over with my soul.

"Tell me, my soul, poor chilled soul, what do you say to living in
Lisbon? It must be very warm there, and you would bask merrily, like a
lizard. It is by the sea; they say that it is built of marble, and that the
people have such a horror of vegetation that they uproot all the trees.
There is a landscape that would suit you,—made out of light and
minerals, with water to reflect them."

My soul does not answer.

"Since you love tranquillity, and the sight of moving things, will you
come and live in Holland, that heavenly land? Perhaps you could be
happy in that country, for you have often admired pictures of Dutch life.
What do you say to Rotterdam, you who love forests of masts, and ships
anchored at the doors of houses?"

My soul remains silent.

"Perhaps Batavia seems more attractive to you? There we would find the intellect of Europe married to the beauty of the tropics."

Not a word. Can my soul be dead?

"Have you sunk into so deep a stupor that only your own torment gives you pleasure? If that be so, let us flee to those lands constituted in the likeness of Death. I know just the place for us, poor soul! We will leave for Torneo. Or let us go even farther, to the last limits of the Baltic; and if possible, still farther from life. Let us go to the Pole. There the sun obliquely grazes the earth, and the slow alternations of light and obscurity make variety impossible, and increase that monotony which is almost death. There we shall be able to take baths of darkness, and for our diversion, from time to time the Aurora Borealis shall scatter its rosy sheaves before us, like reflections of the fireworks of Hell!"

At last my soul bursts into speech, and wisely cries to me: "Anywhere, anywhere, as long as it be out of this world!"

—*Petits Poèmes en Prose,*
translated by Arthur Symons

COLERIDGE WALKS AND TALKS

by John Keats

Samuel Taylor Coleridge has been described by John Stuart Mill as one of the "great seminal minds" of his age (1772–1834). Though his writings, particularly "The Rime of the Ancient Mariner," are well-known to students, he gave the best of himself to talk with friends. A unique reflection of this golden flow of his eloquence and erudition is John Keats's letter to George and Georgiana Keats reporting on his meeting with Coleridge in April 1819, near Highgate.

LAST SUNDAY I took a Walk towards highgate and in the lane that winds by the side of Lord Mansfield's park I met Mr. Green our Demonstrator at Guy's in conversation with Coleridge—I joined them, after enquiring by a look whether it would be agreeable—I walked with him at his alderman-after-dinner pace for near two miles I suppose. In those two Miles he broached a thousand things—let me see if I can give you a list—Nightingales, Poetry—on Poetical Sensation—Metaphysics— Different genera and species of Dreams—Nightmare—a dream accompanied by a sense of touch—single and double touch—A dream related— First and second consciousness—the difference explained between will and Volition—so many metaphysicians from a want of smoking the second consciousness—Monsters—the Kraken—Mermaids—Southey believes in them—Southey's belief too much diluted—A Ghost story— Good morning—I heard his voice as he came towards me—I heard it as he moved away—I had heard it all the interval—if it may be called so.

—The Letters of John Keats

NOTES ON WALKING

by Ralph Waldo Emerson

Could Emerson have been thinking of himself when he wrote, "A man is a golden impossibility"? Surely a thoughtful reading of his Essays *must prove that so formidable a man could never exist. But neither could Bach, Mozart, Shakespeare, nor Montaigne. How rich we all are for these magnificent accidents.*

WALKING has the best value as gymnastics for the mind. "You shall never break down in a speech," said Sydney Smith, "on the day on which you have walked twelve miles." . . . "Walking," said Rousseau, "has something which animates and vivifies my ideas." And Plato said of exercise that "it would almost cure a guilty conscience." . . .

Few men know how to take a walk. The qualifications . . . are endurance, plain clothes, old shoes, an eye for Nature, good humor, vast curiosity, good speech, good silence and nothing too much. If a man tells me that he has an intense love of Nature, I know, of course, that he has none. Good observers have the manners of trees and animals, their patient good sense, and if they add words, 't is only when words are better than silence. But a loud singer, or a story-teller, or a vain talker profanes the river and the forest, and is nothing like so good company as a dog. . . .

When Nero advertised for a new luxury, a walk in the woods should have been offered. 'T is one of the secrets for dodging old age. For Nature makes a like impression on age as on youth. Then I recommend it to people who are growing old, against their will. A man in that predicament, if he stands before a mirror, or among young people, is made quite too sensible of the fact; but the forest awakes in him the same feeling it did when he was a boy, and he may draw a moral from the fact that 't is the old trees that have all the beauty and grandeur. I admire the taste which makes the avenue to a house, were the house never so small, through a wood; besides the beauty, it has a positive effect on manners, as it disposes the mind of the inhabitant and of his guests to the deference due to each. Some English reformers thought the cattle made all this wide space necessary between house and house, and that, if there were no cows to pasture, less land would suffice. But a cow does not need so much land as the owner's eyes require between him and his neighbor. . . .

I think 't is the best of humanity that goes out to walk. In happy hours, I think all affairs may be wisely postponed for this walking. Can you hear what the morning says to you, and believe *that?* Can you bring home the summits of Wachusett, Greylock, and the New Hampshire hills? the Savin groves of Middlesex? the sedgy ripples of the old Colony ponds? the sunny shores of your own bay, and the low Indian hills of Rhode Island? the savageness of pinc-woods? Can you bottle the efflux of a June noon, and bring home the tops of Uncanoonuc? The landscape is vast, complete, alive. We step about, dibble and dot, and attempt in poor linear ways to hobble after those angelic radiations. The gulf between our seeing and our doing is a symbol of that between faith and experience. . . .

No man is suddenly a good walker. Many men begin with good resolution, but they do not hold out, and I have sometimes thought it would be well to publish an Art of Walking, with Easy Lessons for Beginners. These we call apprentices. Those who persist from year to year, and obtain at last an intimacy with the country, and know all the good points within ten miles, with the seasons for visiting each, know the lakes, the hills, where grapes, berries and nuts, where the rare plants are; where the best botanic ground; and where the noblest landscapes are seen, and are learning all the time;—these we call professors.

—Country Life

When I bought my farm, I did not know what a bargain I had in the bluebirds, bobolinks and thrushes, which were not charged in the bill; as little did I guess what sublime mornings and sunsets I was buying—what reaches of landscape, and what fields and lanes for a tramp. Neither did I fully consider what an indescribable luxury is our Indian river, the Musketaquid,—which runs parallel with the village street and to which every house on that long street has a back door, which leads down through the garden to the riverbank, when a skiff, or a dory, gives you, all summer, access to enchantments, new every day, and all winter, to miles of ice for the skater. And because our river is no Hudson or Mississippi I have a problem long waiting for an engineer,—this,—to what height I must build a tower in my garden that shall show me the Atlantic Ocean from its top—the ocean twenty miles away.

Still less did I know what good and true neighbors I was buying, men of thought and virtue, some of them now known the country through for their learning, or subtlety, or active or patriotic power, but whom I had the pleasure of knowing long before the Country did; and of other men not known widely but known at home, farmers,—not doctors of laws but doctors of land, skilled in turning a swamp or a sandbank into a fruitful field, and, when witch-grass and nettles grew, causing a forest of apple-trees or miles of corn and rye to thrive. . . .

There are two companions, with one or other of whom 't is desirable to go out on a tramp. One is an artist, that is, who has an eye for beauty. If you use a good and skilful companion, you shall see through his eyes; and, if they be of great discernment, you will learn wonderful secrets. In walking with Allston, you shall see what was never before shown to the eye of man. And as the perception of beauty always exhilarates, if one is so happy as to find the company of a true artist, he is a perpetual holiday and benefactor, and ought only to be used like an oriflame or a garland, for feasts and May-days, and parliaments of wit and love.

The other is a naturalist, for the reason that it is much better to learn the elements of geology, of botany, or ornithology and astronomy by word of mouth from a companion than dully from a book. There is so much, too, which a book cannot teach which an old friend can. A man should carry Nature in his head—should know the hour of the day or night, and the time of the year, by the sun and stars; should know the solstice and the equinox, the quarter of the moon and the daily tides. . . .

But the countryman, as I said, has more than he paid for; the landscape is his. I am sorry to say the farmers seldom walk for pleasure. It is a fine art;—there are degrees of proficiency, and we distinguish the professors of that science from the apprentices. But there is a manifest increase in the taste for it. 'T is the consolation of mortal men. It is an old saying that physicians or naturalists are the only professional men who continue their tasks out of study-hours; and the naturalist has no barren places, no winter, and no night, pursuing his researches in the sea, in the ground, in barren moors, in the night even, because the woods exhibit a whole new world of nocturnal animals; in winter, because, remove the snow a little, a multitude of plants live and grow, and there is a perpetual push of buds, so that it is impossible to say when vegetation begins. I think no pursuit has more breath of immortality in it.

—*Concord Walks*

WHERE THE FOREST MURMURS

by Fiona Macleod

The talented Celtic lady, Fiona Macleod, who wrote about "the still ecstasy of nature" and a "beauty so great and complex that the imagination is stilled into an aching hush," turned out to be, on the death of William Sharp in 1905, the Scottish gentleman who wrote literary biographies, novels and poems under the name of Sharp. No one remembers the work of William Sharp; the work of Fiona Macleod is still collected and cherished.

IT IS when the trees are leafless, or when the last withered leaves rustle in the wintry air, creeping along the bare boughs like tremulous mice, or fluttering from the branches like the tired and starving swallows left behind in the ebbing tides of migration, that the secret of the forest is most likely to be surprised. Mystery is always there. Silence and whispers, still glooms, sudden radiances, the passage of wind and idle airs, all these inhabit the forest at every season. But it is not in their amplitude that great woodlands reveal their secret life. In the first vernal weeks the wave of green creates a mist or shimmering veil of delicate beauty, through which the missel-thrush calls, and the loud screech of the jay is heard like a savage trumpet-cry. The woods then are full of a virginal beauty. There is intoxication in the light air. The cold azure among the beech-spaces or where the tall elms sway in the east wind, is, like the sea, exquisitely desirable, exquisitely unfamiliar, inhuman, of another world. Then follow the days when the violets creep through the mosses at the base of great oaks, when the dust of snow-bloom on the blackthorn gives way to the trailing dog-rose, when myriads of bees among the chestnut-blossoms fill the air with a continuous drowsy unrest, when the cushat calls from the heart of the fir, when beyond the green billowy roof of elm and horn-beam, of oak and beech, of sycamore and lime and tardy ash, the mysterious bells of the South fall through leagues of warm air, as the unseen cuckoo sails on the long tides of the wind. Then, in truth, is there magic in the woods. The forest is alive in its divine youth. Every bough is a vast plume of joy: on every branch a sunray falls, or a thrush sways in song, or the gauzy ephemeridae dance in rising and falling aerial cones. The wind moves with the feet of a fawn, with the wings of a dove, with the passing breath of the white owl at dusk. There is not a spot where is neither fragrance nor beauty nor life. From the tiniest arch of grass and twig the shrew-mouse will peep: above the shallowest rainpool the dragon-fly will hang in miraculous suspense, like one of the faery javelins of Midir which in a moment could be withheld in mid-flight. The squirrel swings from branch to branch: the leveret shakes the dew from the shadowed grass: the rabbits flitter to and fro like brown beams of life: the robin, the chaffinch, the ousel, call through the warm green-glooms: on the bramble-spray and from the fern-garth the yellowhammer reiterates his gladsome single song: in the cloudless blue fields of the sky the swifts weave a maze of shadow, the rooks rise and fall in giddy ascents and descents like black galleys surmounting measureless waves and sinking into incalculable gulfs.

Then the forest wearies of this interminable exuberance, this daily and nightly charm of exultant life. It desires another spell, the enchantment of silence, of dreams. One day the songs cease: the nests are cold. In the lush meadows the hare sleeps, the corncrake calls. By the brook the cattle stand, motionless, or with long tails rhythmically a-swing and ears a-twitch above the moist amber-violet dreamless eyes. The columnar trees are like phantom-smoke of secret invisible fires. In the green-glooms of the forest a sigh is heard. A troubled and furtive moan is audible in waste indiscoverable places. The thunder-time is come. Now in the woods may be seen and heard and felt that secret presence which in the spring months hid behind songs and blossom, and later clothed itself in dense veils of green and all the magic of June. Something is now evident, that was not evident: somewhat is entered into the forest. The leaves know it: the bracken knows it: the secret is in every copse, in every thicket, is palpable in every glade, is abroad in every shadow-thridden avenue, is common to the spreading bough and the leaning branch. It is not a rumour; for that might be the wind stealthily lifting his long wings from glade to glade. It is not a whisper; for that might be the secret passage of unquiet airs, furtive heralds of the unloosening thunder. It is not a sigh; for that might be the breath of branch and bough, of fern-frond and grass, obvious in the great suspense. It is an ineffable communication. It comes along the ways of silence; along the ways of sound: its light feet are on sunrays and on shadows. Like dew, one knows not whether it is mysteriously gathered from below or secretly come from on high: simply it is there, above, around, beneath.

But the hush is dispelled at last. The long lances of the rain come slanting through the branches; they break, as against invisible barriers, and fall in a myriad pattering rush. The hoarse mutterings and sudden crashing roar of the thunder possess the whole forest. There are no more privacies, the secrecies are violated. From that moment the woods are renewed, and with the renewal the secret spirit that dwells within them withdraws, is not to be surprised, is inaudible, indefinitely recedes, is become remote, obscure, ineffable, incommunicable. And so, through veils of silence, and hot noons and husht warm midnights, the long weeks of July and August go by.

In the woods of September surely the forest-soul may be surprised, will be the thought of many. In that month the sweet incessant business of bird and beast lessens or is at an end. The woodpecker may still tap at the boles of gnarled oaks and chestnuts; the squirrel is more than ever mischievously gay; on frosty mornings, when the gossamer webs are woven across every bramble, and from frond to frond of the bronze-stained bracken, the redbreast tries and retries the poignant new song he has somehow learned since first he flaunted his bright canticles of March and April from the meadow-hedge or the sunned greenness of the beech-covert. But there is a general silence, a present suspense, while the lime yellows, and the birch takes on her pale gold, and oak and sycamore and ash slowly transmute their green multitudes into a new throng clad in russet or dull red or sunset-orange. The forest is full of loveliness: in her dusky ways faint azure mists gather. When the fawn leaps through the fern it is no longer soundlessly: there is a thin dry rustle, as of a dove brushing swiftly from its fastness in an ancient yew. One may pass from covert to covert, from glade to glade, and find the Secret just about to be revealed . . . somewhere beyond the group of birches, beside that oak it may be, just behind that isolated thorn. But it is never quite overtaken. It is as evasive as moonlight in the hollows of waves. When present, it is already gone. When approached, it has the unhasting but irretrievable withdrawal of the shadow. In October this bewildering evasion is still more obvious, because the continual disclosure is more near and intimate. When, after autumns of rain and wind, or the sudden stealthy advent of nocturnal frosts, a multitude of leaves becomes sere and wan, and then the leaves strew every billow of wind like clots of driven foam, or fall in still wavering flight like flakes of windless snow, then, it is surely then that the great surprise is imminent, that the secret and furtive whisper will become a voice. And yet there is something withheld. In November itself there are days, weeks even, when a rich autumn survives. The oaks and ashes will often keep their red and orange till after St. Luke's Peace; in sheltered parts of the forest even the plane, the sycamore, and the chestnut will flaunt their thin leopard-spotted yellow bannerets. I remember coming upon a Spanish chestnut in the centre of a group of all but leafless hornbeams. There seemed to be not a leaf missing from that splendid congregation of scarlet and amber and luminous saffron. A few yards on and even the hardy beeches and oaks were denuded of all but a scattered and defeated company of brown or withered stragglers. Why should that single tree have kept its early October loveliness unchanged through those weeks of rain and wind and frosts of midnight and dawn? There was not one of its immediate company but was in desolate ruin, showing the bare nests high among the stark boughs. Through the whole forest the great unloosening had gone. Even the oaks in hollow places which had kept greenness like a continual wave suspended among dull masses of seaweed, had begun to yield to the vanishing call of the last voices of summer. Day by day their scattered tribes, then whole clans, broke up the tents of home and departed on the long mysterious exile. Yet this sentinel at the Gate of the North stood undaunted, splendid in warrior array. The same instinct that impels the soul from its outward home into the incalculable void moves the leaf with the imperious desire of the grey wind. But as, in human life, there are some who retain a splendid youth far into the failing regions of grey hair and broken years, so in the forest life there are trees which seem able to defy wind and rain and the consuming feet of frost.

The most subtle charm of the woods in November is in those blue spaces which lie at so brief a distance in every avenue of meeting boughs, under every enclosing branch. This azure mist which gathers like still faint smoke has the spell of silent waters, of moonlight, of the pale rose of serene dawns. It has a light that is its own, as unique as that unnameable flame which burns in the core of the rainbow. The earth breathes it; it is

the breath of the fallen leaves, the moss, the tangled fern, the undergrowth, the trees; it is the breath also of the windless grey-blue sky that
leans so low. Surely, also, it is the breath of that other-world of which our
songs and legends are so full. It has that mysteriousness, that spell, with
which in imagination we endow the noon silences, the eves and dawns of
faery twilights.

Still, the silence and the witchery of the forest solitudes in November
are of the spell of autumn. The last enchantment of mid-winter is not yet
come.

It is in "the dead months" that the forest permits the last disguises to
fall away. The forest-soul is no longer an incommunicable mystery. It is
abroad. It is a communicable dream. In that magnificent nakedness it
knows its safety. For the first time it stands like a soul that has mastered
all material things and is fearless in face of the immaterial things which
are the only life of the spirit.

In these "dead months" of December and January the forest lives its
own life. It is not asleep as the poets feign. Sleep has entered into the
forest, has made the deep silence its habitation: but the forest itself is
awake, mysterious, omnipresent, a creature seen at last in its naked
majesty.

One says lightly, there is no green thing left. That, of course, is a mere
phrase of relativity. There is always green fern somewhere, even in the
garths of tangled yellow-brown bracken. There is always moss somewhere, hidden among the great serpentine roots of the beeches. The ilex
will keep its dusty green through the harvest winter: the yew, the cypress,
the holly, have no need of the continual invasion of the winds and rains
and snows. On the ash and elm the wood-ivy will hang her spiked leaves.
On many of the oaks the lovely dull green of the mistletoe will droop in
graceful clusters, the cream-white berries glistening like innumerable
pleiads of pearls. But these are lost in the immense uniformity of
desolation. They are accidents, interludes. The wilderness knows them, as
the grey wastes of tempestuous seas know a wave here and there that lifts
a huge rampart of jade crowned with snow, or the long resiliency of
gigantic billows which reveal smooth falling precipices of azure. The
waste itself is one vast desolation, the more grey and terrible because in
the mass invariable.

To go through those winter-aisles of the forest is to know an elation
foreign to the melancholy of November or to the first fall of the leaf. It is
not the elation of certain days in February, when the storm-cock tosses

his song among the wild reefs of naked bough and branch. It is not the elation of March, when a blueness haunts the myriad unburst buds, and the throstle builds her nest and calls to the South. It is not the elation of April, when the virginal green is like exquisite music of life in miraculous suspense, nor the elation of May, when the wild rose moves in soft flame upon the thickets and the returned magic of the cuckoo is an intoxication, nor the elation of June, when the merle above the honeysuckle and the cushat in the green-glooms fill the hot noons with joy, and when the long fragrant twilights are thrilled with the passion of the nightjar. It has not this rapture nor that delight; but its elation is an ecstasy that is its own. It is then that one understands as one has never understood. It is then that one loves the mystery one has but fugitively divined. Where the forest murmurs there is music: ancient, everlasting. Go to the winter woods: listen there, look, watch, and "the dead months" will give you a subtler secret than any you have yet found in the forest. Then there is always one possible superb fortune. You may see the woods in snow. There is nothing in the world more beautiful than the forest clothed to its very hollows in snow. That is a loveliness to which surely none can be insensitive. It is the still ecstasy of Nature, wherein every spray, every blade of grass, every spire of reed, every intricacy of twig, is clad with radiance, and myriad form is renewed in continual change as though in the passionate delight of the white Artificer. It is beauty so great and complex that the imagination is stilled into an aching hush. There is the same trouble in the soul as before the starry hosts of a winter night.

—*The Silence of Amor* and
Where the Forest Murmurs

ARE WALKERS PEOPLE?

by Richard G. Lillard

Richard G. Lillard lives with his wife and daughters in a canyon of the Hollywood Hills. From this vantage point he has watched and worried about what man is doing to destroy his own environment, especially in southern California. He is the author of Desert Challenge *and* The Great Forest. *This essay is from* Eden in Jeopardy.

JUST as the pleasure of driving has disappeared, so has the pleasure of walking, for the car replaces the pedestrian and the hiker in Southern California. Human beings continue to walk gladly in Paris or London or even New York, but in San Diego or Pasadena, in Bakersfield or Los Angeles, or in new, widespread desert tracts like Apple Valley or Desert Hot Springs, men take to the car, as do the cowboy and the prospector. Though better protected by law than in most nations, the pedestrian ceases to be a respectable or desirable individual. Like the bicyclist, he is prohibited the use of any freeway and receives a ticket if he tries to use one. In Beverly Hills and rich subdivisions like Bel-Air, pedestrians are suspects per se and are questioned or frisked by policemen in patrol cars. To have no car is to be poor and vagrant and criminally inclined. Virtually gone as custom or habit is walking in parks, walking in open country, walking to shop or to window-shop along city streets, especially such touted sights, such wide boulevards as Wilshire, the "Champs-Elysees of Los Angeles," or the "roadside business" streets paralleling Camino del Rio at "Fashionable Mission Valley Center." Automobilized Southern California typically offers the spacious, paved new Civic Center in Santa Monica, bare of pedestrians, or the artificial "old-time" street inside the gates of Disneyland, crowded by people who leave their cars outside and pay to walk in.

Southern California cities are places where foot walkers are not people, where human legs are largely useless, where walking to buy food is impossible, where a man is helpless without his car—as much lost as an old-time cowboy on a cattle drive without his horse. More and more, Old World and American critics of Los Angeles ignore the old jests about a crackpot population in a pasteboard setting and stress instead its "inhumane" traffic on a sterile wasteland of cement. The single solution to transportation—the private automobile—is making Los Angeles "a horrible example" of the modern city.

—Eden in Jeopardy

THE LOOK-OFF

by Robert L. Dickinson

The first edition of the New York Walk Book *was published by the American Geographical Society in 1923. About a third of it (text, maps and drawings) was the work of Dr. Robert L. Dickinson, who died in his ninetieth year in 1950. This was his introduction to that edition, which has been reprinted in subsequent editions.*

Soil that ever was Indian can never lose all of that impress. Our Island of Islands, borne down at one end by the world's biggest burden of steel and stone and pressure of haste and material gain, still holds, on the primitive sweep of its further free tip, the Redman's cave and the beached canoe, tall trees, steep cliffs, and airs of the Great Spirit. The magic of the moccasin still makes good medicine. Fortunate are we that in civilization lurks the antidote to civilization—that strain in the blood of all of us, of caveman and treeman, of nomad and seaman, of chopper and digger, of fisher and trailer, crying out to this call of the earth, to this tug of freefoot up-and-over, to the clamor for out-and-beyond. Happy are we, in our day, harking back to this call, to be part of an ozone revival toward lucky finds in this wide fair wilderness and toward breakaway into Everyman's Out-of-doors.

The order and fashion of the revival were somewhat in this wise. Our seniors remember the days of swift expansion, when the sole concern was the building site. "Blast the scenery," said the seventies and proceeded to do it. Railroads and roads and money returns from quarries and lumber had full right of way. Into our towns one came, through ugly suburbs, into uglier urbs. And then, when hope was least, a messenger of the new-old freedom appeared. The bicycle swung us, a generation now white-haired, round a wide radius of country roads, and gave back to us the calves and the leg gear of our patroon saint, Father Knickerbocker, and with the legs two eyes for environs. When the time came for supplanting tandem tires by a rubber quartette, and a touch of the toe leapt past all two legs could do, a motor radius that swept a circle almost infinitely wide gave new concepts of the countrysides. Still attention was focussed on the roadway, and the new driver saw even less over wheel than over handlebar. Next golf arose, and the well-to-do strolled upon greenswards, ever watching a ball. Then scout training arrived to set the young generation on its feet and to teach it to see what it saw and to care for itself in the open. With it came nature study to fill the woods and fields with life and growth. And then the fashion for walking was upon us—walking, with its leisure to observe the detail of beauty; walking, organized and planned, imparting impetus to safeguard and preserve the best of the countryside: walking, the only simple exercise, at once democratic, open-air, wide-eyed, year-round.

It has been amusing to watch New York, which is hardly in other ways hesitant, waken by degrees to the idea that as a center for exercise on foot she may claim variety and advantage and adventure surpassed by few cities. You can choose your walk along the sweep of the beaches of the Atlantic, or the deep hill bays of Long Island, or the rocky coves of Connecticut; over ridges showing fair silhouettes of the citadels and cathedrals of commerce—or where beavers build; on the looped, mile-long bridges that span an estuary—or across a canal lock; above precipices overhanging a mighty river and through noble community forests between lonely peaks and little lakes—or just in lovely common country, rolling and wooded, meadowed and elm-dotted, interlaced with chuckling brooks. To and from these multitudinous footways and camp sites transportation is provided with an expedition and diversity possible only to a large city. And, last of all, the chance at this will be under the variegated stimulus of our particular climate and around the only great capital that is within easy reach of the second color wonder of the world—Indian summer in steep-hill country.

—New York Walk Book

THE WOODS, MY FRIENDS

by William Wordsworth

The woods, my Friends, are round you roaring,
Rocking and roaring like a sea; . . .

Away we go—and what care we
For treasons, tumults and for wars?
We are as calm in our delight
As is the crescent-moon so bright
Among the scattered stars.

—Peter Bell

FOLLOW YOUR NOSE!

by David Grayson

David Grayson was the pen name used by Ray Stannard Baker, an intimate of President Woodrow Wilson and Director of the Press at the Versailles Conference. He was the 1940 winner of the Pulitzer Prize in American History, for the eight-volume biography of Wilson, and the author of Adventures in Contentment, The Friendly Road, *and a host of other books recording his escape to the country.*

ON A SPRING MORNING one has only to step out into the open country, lift his head to the sky—and follow his nose. . . .

It was a big and golden morning, and Sunday to boot, and I walked down the lane to the lower edge of the field, where the wood and the marsh begin. The sun was just coming up over the hills and all the air was fresh and clear and cool. High in the heavens a few fleecy clouds were drifting, and the air was just enough astir to waken the hemlocks into faint and sleepy exchanges of confidence.

It seemed to me that morning that the world was never before so high, so airy, so golden. All filled to the brim with the essence of sunshine and spring morning—so that one's spirit dissolved in it, became a part of it. Such a morning! Such a morning!

From that place and just as I was I set off across the open land.

It was the time of all times for good odours—soon after sunrise—before the heat of the day had drawn off the rich distillations of the night.

In that keen moment I caught, drifting, a faint but wild fragrance upon the air, and veered northward full into the way of the wind. I could not at first tell what this particular odour was, nor separate it from the general good odour of the earth; but I followed it intently across the moor-like open land. Once I thought I had lost it entirely, or that the faint northern airs had shifted, but I soon caught it clearly again, and just as I was saying to myself, "I've got it, I've got it!"—for it is a great pleasure to identify a friendly odour in the fields—I saw, near the bank of the brook, among ferns and raspberry bushes, a thorn-apple tree in full bloom.

"So there you are!" I said.

I hastened toward it, now in the full current and glory of its fragrance. The sun, looking over the taller trees to the east, had crowned the top of it with gold, so that it was beautiful to see; and it was full of honey bees as excited as I.

A score of feet onward toward the wind, beyond the thorn-apple tree, I passed wholly out of the range of its fragrance into another world, and began trying for some new odour. After one or two false scents, for this pursuit has all the hazards known to the hunter, I caught an odour long known to me, not strong, nor yet very wonderful, but distinctive. It led me still a little distance northward to a sunny slope just beyond a bit of marsh, and, sure enough, I found an old friend, the wild sweet geranium, a world of it, in full bloom, and I sat down there for some time to enjoy it fully.

Beyond that, and across a field wild with tangles of huckleberry bushes and sheep laurel where the bluets and buttercups were blooming, and in shady spots the shy white violet, I searched for the odour of a certain clump of pine trees I discovered long ago. I knew that I must come upon it soon, but could not tell just when or where. I held up a moistened finger to make sure of the exact direction of the wind, and bearing, then, a little eastward, soon came full upon it—as a hunter might surprise a deer in the forest. I crossed the brook a second time and through a little marsh, making it the rule of the game never to lose for an instant the scent I was following—even though I stopped in a low spot to admire a mass of thrifty blue flags, now beginning to bloom—and came thus to the pines I was seeking. They are not great trees, nor noble, but gnarled and angular and stunted, for the soil in that place is poor and thin, and the winds in winter keen; but the brown blanket of needles they spread and the shade they offer the traveller are not less hospitable; nor the fragrance they give off less enchanting. The odour of the pines is one I love.

I sat down there in a place I chose long ago—a place already as familiar with pleasing memories as a favourite room—so that I wonder that some of the notes I have written there do not of themselves exhale the very odour of the pines.

And all about was hung a fair tapestry of green, and the earthy floor was cleanly carpeted with brown, and the roof above was in arched mosaic, the deep, deep blue of the sky seen through the gnarled and knotted branches of the pines. Through a little opening among the trees, as through a window, I could see the cattle feeding in the wide meadows, all headed alike, and yellow butterflies drifted across the open spaces, and there were bumblebees and dragonflies. And presently I heard someone tapping, tapping, at the door of the wood and glancing up quickly I saw my early visitor. There he was, as neighbourly as you please, and not in the least awed by my intrusion; there he was, far out on the limb of a dead tree, stepping energetically up and down, like a sailor reefing a sail, and rapping and tapping as he worked—a downy woodpecker.

"Good morning, sir," I said.

He stopped for scarcely a second, cocked one eye at me, and went back to his work again. Who was I that I should interrupt his breakfast?

And I was glad I was there, and I began enumerating, as though I were the accredited reporter for the *Woodland Gazette,* all the good news of the day.

"The beech trees," I said aloud, "have come at last to full leafage. The wild blackberries are ready to bloom, the swamp roses are budded. Brown planted fields I see, and drooping elms, and the young crows cry from their nests on the knoll. . . . I know now that, whoever I am, whatever I do, I am welcome here; the meadows are as green this spring for Tom the drunkard, and for Jim the thief, as for Jonathan the parson, or for Walt the poet: the wild cherry blossoms as richly, and the odour of the pine is as sweet—"

At that moment, like a flame for clearness, I understood some of the deep and simple things of life, as that we are to be like the friendly pines, and the elm trees, and the open fields, and reject no man and judge no man. Once, a long time ago, I read a sober treatise by one who tried to prove with elaborate knowledge that, upon the whole, good was triumphant in this world, and that probably there was a God, and I remember going out dully afterward upon the hill, for I was weighed down with a strange depression, and the world seemed to me a hard, cold, narrow place where good must be heavily demonstrated in books. And as I sat there the evening fell, a star or two came out in the clear blue of the sky, and suddenly it became all simple to me, so that I laughed aloud at that laborious big-wig for spending so many futile years in seeking doubtful proof of what he might have learned in one rare hour upon my hill. And far more than he could prove—far more. . . .

As I came away from that place I knew I should never again be quite the same person I was before.

—Great Possessions

IN DEFENSE OF
THE FOOTWALKER

by Lewis Mumford

*Lewis Mumford holds no academic degrees, but he has held pro-
fessorships and lectureships in some of our great universities. He was
the first American to receive a Royal Gold Medal for architecture
from Queen Elizabeth in 1961. Like his Scottish mentor Patrick
Geddes, Mumford has devoted much of his intellectual life to devising
plans for us to untangle the mess we have made of our cities. A
"Renaissance man" in the true sense, he has made impressive contributions to the fields of art, literature, history, architecture, and city
planning. Among his earlier books are* The Story of Utopias, Sticks
and Stones, Herman Melville, *and* Technics and Civilization. *In 1962
he won the National Book Award for* The City in History. *Also in
1962 he received the Award of Merit of the American Institute of
Architects; all the more remarkable since he is neither a professional
architect nor a city planner.*

IN OUR entrancement with the motorcar, we have forgotten how
much more efficient and how much more flexible the footwalker is. Before
there was any public transportation in London, something like fifty
thousand people an hour used to pass over London Bridge on their way to
work; a single artery. Railroad transportation can bring from forty to
sixty thousand people per hour, along a single route, whereas our best
expressways, using far more space, cannot move more than four to six
thousand cars: even if the average occupancy were more than one and a
half passengers, as at present, this is obviously the most costly and
inefficient means of handling the peak hours of traffic. As for the
pedestrian, one could move a hundred thousand people, by the existing

streets, from, say, downtown Boston to the Common, in something like half an hour, and find plenty of room for them to stand. But how many weary hours would it take to move them in cars over these same streets? And what would one do with the cars after they had reached the Common? Or where, for that matter, could one assemble these cars in the first place? For open spaces, long distances, and low population densities, the car is now essential; for urban space, short distances, and high densities, the pedestrian.

Every urban transportation plan should, accordingly, put the pedestrian at the center of all its proposals, if only to facilitate wheeled traffic. But to bring the pedestrian back into the picture, one must treat him with the respect and honor we now accord only to the automobile: we should provide him with pleasant walks, insulated from traffic, to take him to his destination, once he enters a business precinct or residential quarter. Every city should heed the example of Rotterdam in creating the Lijnbaan, or of Coventry in creating its new shopping area. It is nonsense to say that this cannot be done in America, because no one wants to walk.

Where walking is exciting and visually stimulating, whether it is in a Detroit shopping center or along Fifth Avenue, Americans are perfectly ready to walk. The legs will come into their own again, as the ideal means of neighborhood transportation, once some provision is made for their exercise, as Philadelphia is now doing, both in its Independence Hall area, and in Penn Center. But if we are to make walking attractive, we must not only provide trees and wide pavements and benches, beds of flowers and outdoor cafés, as they do in Rotterdam: we must also scrap the monotonous uniformities of American zoning practice, which turns vast areas, too spread out for pedestrian movement, into single-district zones, for commerce, industry, or residential purposes. (As a result, only the mixed zones are architecturally interesting today despite their disorder.)

Why should anyone have to take a car and drive a couple of miles to get a package of cigarettes or a loaf of bread, as one must often do in a suburb? Why, on the other hand, should a growing minority of people not be able again to walk to work, by living in the interior of the city, or, for that matter, be able to walk home from the theatre or the concert hall? Where urban facilities are compact, walking still delights the American: does he not travel many thousands of miles just to enjoy this privilege in the historic urban cores of Europe? And do not people now travel for miles, of an evening, from the outskirts of Pittsburgh, just for the pleasure of a stroll in Mellon Square? Nothing would do more to give life back to our blighted urban cores than to re-instate the pedestrian, in malls and pleasances designed to make circulation a delight. And what an opportunity for architecture!

—The Highway and the City

ABOUT ROADS

by Madge Jenison

Madge Jenison was a bookseller before she became the author of a book about her shop, The Sunwise Turn. *Her curious, provocative work on roads, from which this was taken, is as heavily laden with wisdom as a bee with honey at the end of a long day away from its hive.*

ALL IS ROADS, even the way we think. It is not possible to minimize roads. They are a root fact, the keyhole, the key, the way we get into and go out of our lives. The very form and pressure of the time. It is a road civilization we live in. The truest things about roads is that they are so important. Building roads where there ought to be roads may be a greater deed than those of generals with gilded shoulders. They may have an importance eclipsing governments. "The future is stored in thee and the past is stored in thee."

Who says so? A wind through a cut says so. The river, in its channel in the soil. Glittering Venus, going down among the cedars.

> *It is heavenly borne and cannot die,*
> *Being a parcell of the skie.*

It will rise again.

The ceaseless pattern of the cage says so. The "broad-distributing blood." The differential, clicking on the rail of the little fresh-water local, puffing up the slope at the north of Valley Cottage. The mysterious vitality that runs along the vestibuled corridors of transcontinental trains. . . .

The battle of Burma says so. Emerson says so. "He who builds a great road earns a place in the story." The Panama Canal says so. The Embarcadero, the elevators on thousands of little sidings in North

Dakota, the multitude of rough transport drivers that filled all the lanes of England by night for four years. The silken creeping of cars on eight-lane highways. . . . James Truslow Adams, in 1931, feared for America with its retreating frontier. When America had reached its last frontier and could go no farther, what would she do? Where would the American go? . . . He took to the air, and engaged to explore the summits above space. There is no such thing to man as a frontier.

It is like looking at civilization through a new keyhole to begin to think about roads. All is roads, even the way we think. A curious similarity is in all roads. A thought is so extraordinarily like a cow path, and then Watling Street, and then 9W, that sometimes in the company of a thought we seem to be in the swift-running rush of the courier from Marathon, and sometimes at one of those dead ends upon which we come in the back country of California.

Routing is the boon of the intelligence. Experience with all its confusion tends to become a road. Pythagoras found that out. "Even God geometrizes," he said. A reason is a road. A law is a road. Codes of behavior, and canons of taste and art, and habits are roads that go on while we forget. The body has these roads. Even money is a road, and by sheer force of momentum, when Rockefeller had ceased for thirty years to work, it continued to go on in a torrent of wealth, so that he made four times as much money after he retired as when he was active.

To learn to draw is a road. Love is a road. Traits become roads. Even character seems to be only a road where the grades, overpasses, easements, direction, are especially well engineered for a maximum of traffic with a minimum of accidents. "Nothing so cheers the heart and delights the eyes as to look back over a stretch of difficult road."

Death itself may be perhaps only a road, more comprehensible and with a new kind of distance. "It may be," Spinoza says, "that immortality is not the reward of clear thinking. It is clear thinking itself."

Half the world's books take you out on roads. The Bible, so full of matter, is full of roads. Amos the cowherd, and Isaiah, who is said to have been a prince, and Daniel and Samuel and David, and Jeremiah were all haunted by roads.

"Thus saith the Lord. Stand ye in the ways, and see, and ask for the old paths, where is the good way; and walk in it; and ye shall find rest for your souls. But they said, we will not walk in it."

One of those ingenious people with a taste for long, quiet tasks that go rambling down the years has counted how many times the word "way" occurs in the Bible. It is six hundred times in the Old Testament, one hundred in the New.

Jesus and the Apostles Twelve and Paul walked the great, many-gated roads. "At midday, O King, as I came nigh unto Damascus, I saw in the way a light from Heaven. And I heard the voice of the Lord which said unto me, I am Jesus of Nazareth. Arise. . . . Why tarriest thou? Make haste. Depart. I have appeared to this purpose, to make thee a minister and a witness. Now I send thee."

Jesus, preaching the landlessness of the soul, had not where to lay his head. "I am the Way," he said.

"Blind Homer, singing, wrote two books, and one was a travel book." Odysseus wandered much on the sea-bright roads and saw the abodes of men and learned their minds; and his son Telemachus went after him. The red-haired Menelaus looked into many hearts.

The whole earth is only a sepulcher of those who have gone on roads. Caesar and his Larks, and the meek, famous Tenth Legion. Arthur, who "rode freshly and with great royalty"; and Launcelot du Lac, "doing his deeds full actual"; and Dame Guinevere; Sir Miles of the Launds, "passing true to his promise"; and Gawain and Gaheris his brother. All fairy tales have roads in them.

That lodestar, "venerable mighty Chaucer"; Dante, wandering in the bitter landscape of burning sepulchers; the lean and foolish knight, forever pricking on the plain, on the steed like a great comic poem, with Sancho, that early riser, who was always remembering that it was dinner time, and looking about for an island that he might be governor of it. Here is "the wisest and most splendid book in the world," to be taken in the wallet, and looked into on the road.

Great Rabelais, and that great and honest worker, Montaigne. And the rascally, sweet young Prince Hal, the good, sweet-smelling lord; and Sir John Sack-and-Sugar, Sir John Paunch, the round man, the ton of flesh, sitting unbuttoned in his buff-leather jerkin before an inn fire, with a fair hot wench in flame-colored taffeta on his knee. Villon, the Parisian poet; Christian the pilgrim; Laurence Sterne, in his old *disobligéant* with the lady with the widowed look. If you love a road, you will look into them all. . . .

Whitman, Mr. Pickwick, Captain Ahab, Doughty—all these and many more have embraced the world and walked on roads, which begin and bring to an end.

What are they, these ubiquitous, overwhelming roads, going forever up and down? Every road is a wish gone out to work, carried to its market, stated on the earth, "affirming its worth." It is the nature of roads that they are fever, even folly. Roads begin in excess. They are overflow and good measure. Extra moments open roads. A road is always a way out. We are all tendencies, and none of us is complete. When you begin to think, and when you begin to act, you go on a road. We know faith actively on a road.

Every road is an accumulation of persistence. It is a conjecture persisted in. Repeated use makes a road. The *Tao* means "trodden into the earth." When you go out and come back, it is a road. Persistence was a finding of extreme value. This is one of the profoundest factors in being alive. "Nothing that is done on earth has much power, but when it is done over and over." The nature of roads is to sustain and go forward. They are continuity.

"The path to my fixed purpose is laid with iron rails, where my soul is grooved to rise."

There is great peril in roads. They are sacrifice, and they are also danger. Order is dangerous, and straightness is dangerous. "Straight roads for some minds, crooked for those who wish to go places, not a place." An old English usage of this word is "to be in one's road, to be in one's way, so as to cause obstruction and inconvenience." There are great risks in habits, the deep grooves of established schemes. There is security in roads and habits, and there is freedom in roads and habits. They form regular lanes so that we go on them without scouting all the way, leaving the brain on part time, released for "the higher branches." But many a good thing may be found by going off the road. Advance is likely to depart from the road. All origins of new species and all sports and mutations and evolutions have had to go off a road. The ruddy and lusty old dame occupies new territory through "discontinuous events." There is no such thing as a straight line in evolution.

Something there is that does not like a road. Lowes Dickinson suggests that it is imagination. "Usage which is reasonable generates usage which is unreasonable." A genius is able to get away from his habits. Blood is not streaming that can go off the road, but Cézanne can. Whitehead says that those societies must decay which do not combine reverence for the symbols they have set up—with liberty of revision. And now modern theory in physics wipes out cause and effect and the "inevitability of gradualness." "The uncertainty principle is thoroughly established as a definite probability. We are no longer confined within certainties. A phenomenon may start as a divergent event and degenerate into a convergent. The science of logic itself is challenged by the illusory character of certainty." It is clear that we must accustom ourselves to be surprised. The variants in us and without us have forever to be built up against the determinants.

Roads tend to be long. They cannot afford to be short. Thoreau was surprised by this truth in the Maine woods.

"I suspect that if you went to the end of the world, you would find someone going farther."

To go as far as you can go and then farther than you can go. This is our way. Roads gain significance through this: that you can get back on them. One of the greatest strengths of roads is that they are always so strangely shorter coming back than going out.

What do they mean, these roads? They are the most highly consolidated and interlocking system of action we have except the state and church. A structural block of concerted, articulated power. They are made of more than crushed stone and creosoted wood blocks, shoulders, fills, cambers, culverts. They are going somewhere besides Popham Pines, Vermont, and the Galle-Face Hotel looking on the Indian Sea. They exist for reasons of vast importance and long reach, connected with the "doings of the miraculous spirit of life." Distribution is the nature of things. Exchange, transfer, currency, traffic, communication. Communication is the child of the road. The race is absorbed in this matter. We have always been trying to get communication; on the installment plan if it must be so. Men have shouted it by relays; wigwagged it with flags; signaled it by waving blankets, by laying them on the ground; sent it by arrow, by puffs of smoke, by drums, by carrier birds, in writing, on streaks of lightning.

Battle couriers traversed the roads of Peru at full speed. Alexander tried to carry fire signals to a high perfection, but he found them ineffectual, because you could deal only with the simplest ideas. You could say only that the emperor had died, or the enemy was approaching on the left. Chin, the good son of Han, could signal along a chain of a thousand brick towers, set on the peaks of hills. From these signal stations, sometimes three stories high, news could be passed by fire over as much as a thousand miles a day. Indications in the brickwork of the Great Wall make it seem probable that the towers were finished before the wall itself, as if communication were felt to be more important than defcnsc. The African drummer approached an understanding of airways, so that Livingstone and Stanley found themselves expected days ahead, when they arrived at a village. . . .

Civilization is a road. In a world trying to see what it is, consciousness is a road, warm and shut in, the sweet, secret place where the flesh and the seed leaf of a lived life meet. Old Aristotle told us that man wants to know. He who wants to know must look upon his destiny as a road. "Pilgrim, pilgrimage; and the Road was but myself toward myself." Consciousness is stimulated to the extreme degree by change and what is strange. Men began as a part of things. Then they began to be aware of themselves, gathering surface, collecting more and more differences and emerging connections, little trans-highways coming in, divergences in themselves from the world outside.

Then they began to be conscious of the reality of other people. It is surely of great moment that exchange and communication have begun with gift-giving and friendliness. "All evidence among primitive people is that the forerunner of trade has been voyages for adventure and sociability. Voyages taken for these reasons turn into trading voyages. The manifest advantage of receiving goods from outside sources, without the necessity of war, always came late. Early European traders in Africa have been much harassed by the excessive amount of singing and talking and ceremonial necessary for trade exchange." From the "walk-about" on the Andaman islands, down to the great medieval European fairs; down to the peddler in Kansas in the seventies and eighties with a copy of *Harper's* under the seat cushion of his buggy; and down to the Irish fairs today, where everybody goes to market, whether he has anything to sell or not, where everybody talks and nobody listens—the background of roads has been social.

"It is not the shilling but the warmth it carries with it from your hand" which accounts for early travel.

Ouspensky declares his belief that there "exists in the world now, for the first time, without a habitation or a name, having no outward sign or symbol, no officers, constitution, bylaws, dues, or any of the things considered essential to the corporate life of a human group," a fraternity, an organization, an order. And he affirms that at various times and in divers places he has encountered members of this order, to which he feels that he himself belongs, and that they recognize one another at sight, with no differences of race, language, color, or class acting as a barrier to their mutual understanding and communion; not even—the relation once established and cemented—silence, or distance, or any of the things which restrict human intercourse of the ordinary sort.

Road is a cold word. There must be in language a word with the sound of steadily rolling, great rivers. In it, the voice of Pericles, high on the Acropolis, a little faint above the din of history, but the cadence of it left, and the movement of the hand. In it the smooth, continuous movement, the fearless sweep of the Oregon coast-line highway. That growth on jungle roads is in this word, which almost obliterates them, devours them, so that you hasten your step to keep it from overcoming you as you pass. In it, the soft, warm, long reverberation of temple bells in Tibet which do not hit the air, but the air takes it within; and it rolls on, as if you looked down a long road where you had not gone, and unlocks a door at the end.

Sounds are roads. Smells are roads. Roads are light, shade, spirit, distance, challenge, enchanted seas, growth, "that upon which the inevitable comes to pass," and "the free conception of what is posssible." Road is not a word; it is every word.

A queer idea is about, that roads are something in the National Automobile Association Blue Book, or in a folded paper called a timetable. They exist to pile oranges and pomegranates on tables in icy little New England parlors; to show you rivers and harbors; to furnish you with starts for journeys; to bring up your blood pressure; to melt your heart with the horns on them, as you sit through your first night in Cairo on a little balcony under a desert moon, and try to be perfectly mature and perfectly calm, and not go completely off the beam.

Such are the living aspects of roads.

"Not that I have already obtained, but I press on," Paul wrote to the Corinthians.

—Roads

THERE IS A PLEASURE
IN THE PATHLESS WOODS

by Lord Byron

There is a pleasure in the pathless woods,
There is a rapture on the lonely shore,
There is society where none intrudes,
By the deep Sea, and Music in its roar:
I love not Man the less, but Nature more,
From these our interviews, in which I steal
From all I may be or have been before,
To mingle with the Universe, and feel
What I can ne'er express, yet can not all conceal.

—Childe Harold's Pilgrimage,
Canto the Fourth, CLXXVIII

GOING OUT FOR A WALK

by Max Beerbohm

Max Beerbohm's "Happy Hypocrite" boasted that he hadn't seen a buttercup in over twenty years. (Charles Lamb, in the same spirit, confessed that he didn't much care if he never saw a mountain in his life.) It seems only fitting, therefore, that the "incomparable Max," suave master of paradox, should have the last word on walking in this book. He wrote it in 1918.

IT IS A FACT that not once in all my life have I gone out for a walk. I have been taken out for walks; but that is another matter. Even while I trotted prattling by my nurse's side I regretted the good old days when I had, and wasn't, a perambulator. When I grew up it seemed to me that the one advantage of living in London was that nobody ever wanted me to come out for a walk. London's very drawbacks—its endless noise and hustle, its smoky air, the squalor ambushed everywhere in it—assured this one immunity. Whenever I was with friends in the country, I knew that at any moment, unless rain were actually falling, some man might suddenly say, "Come out for a walk!" in that sharp imperative tone which he would not dream of using in any other connection. People seem to think there is something inherently noble and virtuous in the desire to go for a walk. Any one thus desirous feels that he has a right to impose his will on whomever he sees comfortably settled in an arm-chair, reading. It is easy to say simply "No" to an old friend. In the case of a mere acquaintance one wants some excuse. "I wish I could, but"—nothing ever occurs to me except "I have some letters to write." This formula is unsatisfactory in three ways. (1) It isn't believed. (2) It compels you to rise from your chair, go to the writing-table, and sit improvising a letter to somebody until the walkmonger (just not daring to call you liar and hypocrite) shall have lumbered out of the room. (3) It won't operate on Sunday mornings. "There's no post out till this evening" clinches the matter; and you may as well go quietly.

Walking for walking's sake may be as highly laudable and exemplary a thing as it is held to be by those who practise it. My objection to it is that it stops the brain. Many a man has professed to me that his brain never works so well as when he is swinging along the high road or over hill and dale. This boast is not confirmed by my memory of anybody who on a Sunday morning has forced me to partake of his adventure. Experience teaches me that whatever a fellow-guest may have of power to instruct or to amuse when he is sitting on a chair, or standing on a hearth-rug, quickly leaves him when he takes one out for a walk. The ideas that came so thick and fast to him in any room, where are they now? where that encyclopædic knowledge which he bore so lightly? where the kindling fancy that played like summer lightning over any topic that was started? The man's face that was so mobile is set now; gone is the light from his fine eyes. He says that A. (our host) is a thoroughly good fellow. Fifty yards further on, he adds that A. is one of the best fellows he has ever met. We tramp another furlong or so, and he says that Mrs. A. is a charming woman. Presently he adds that she is one of the most charming women he has ever known. We pass an inn. He reads vapidly aloud to me: "The King's Arms. Licensed to sell Ales and Spirits." I foresee that during the rest of the walk he will read aloud any inscription that occurs. We pass a "Uxminster. 11 Miles." We turn a sharp corner at the foot of a hill. He points at the wall, and says "Drive Slowly." I see far ahead, on the other side of the hedge bordering the high road, a small notice-board. He sees it too. He keeps his eye on it. And in due course "Trespassers," he says, "Will Be Prosecuted." Poor man!—mentally a wreck.

Luncheon at the A.'s, however, salves him and floats him in full sail. Behold him once more the life and soul of the party. Surely he will never, after the bitter lesson of this morning, go out for another walk. An hour later, I see him striding forth, with a new companion. I watch him out of sight. I know what he is saying. He is saying that I am rather a dull man to go a walk with. He will presently add that I am one of the dullest men he ever went a walk with. Then he will devote himself to reading out the inscriptions.

How comes it, this immediate deterioration in those who go walking for walking's sake? Just what happens? I take it that not by his reasoning faculties is a man urged to this enterprise. He is urged, evidently, by something in him that transcends reason; by his soul, I presume. Yes, it must be the soul that raps out the "Quick march!" to the body.—"Halt! Stand at ease!" interposes the brain, and "To what destination," it suavely asks the soul, "and on what errand, are you sending the body?"—"On no errand whatsoever," the soul makes answer, "and to no destination at all. It is just like you to be always on the look-out for some subtle ulterior motive. The body is going out because the mere fact of its doing so is a sure indication of nobility, probity, and rugged grandeur of character."—"Very well, Vagula, have your own wayula! But I," says the brain, "flatly refuse to be mixed up in this tomfoolery. I shall go to sleep till it is over." The brain then wraps itself up in its own convolutions, and falls into a dreamless slumber from which nothing can rouse it till the body has been safely deposited indoors again.

Even if you go to some definite place, for some definite purpose, the brain would rather you took a vehicle; but it does not make a point of this; it will serve you well enough unless you are going for a walk. It won't, while your legs are vying with each other, do any deep thinking for you, nor even any close thinking; but it will do any number of small odd jobs for you willingly—provided that your legs, also, are making themselves useful, not merely bandying you about to gratify the pride of the soul. Such as it is, this essay was composed in the course of a walk, this morning. I am not one of those extremists who must have a vehicle to every destination. I never go out of my way, as it were, to avoid exercise. I take it as it comes, and take it in good part. That valetudinarians are always chattering about it, and indulging in it to excess, is no reason for despising it. I am inclined to think that in moderation it is rather good for one, physically. But, pending a time when no people wish me to go and see them, and I have no wish to go and see any one, and there is nothing whatever for me to do off my own premises, I never will go out for a walk.

—And Even Now

THE WALKER'S BOOKSHELF

Some of these books give specific information on sidewalk, country, and wilderness walks. Some share with the reader their authors' walking adventures in near and far places. And some offer the armchair companionship of good walkers who are also good writers, for whom space was lacking in our own anthology. A few, published abroad or no longer in print, may entail a walk to the public library or the secondhand-book stall, thus giving double pleasure.

Armchair Companions, Classic and Contemporary

Beadle's Dime Book of Pedestrianism, 1867. A bit of antiquarian Americana, its author one H. Chadwick, published by the New York publisher of the imperishable dime novels.

Delineations of American Scenery and Character, by John James Audubon. G. A. Baker, 1926. A book of selections—made by F. H. Herrick—from the writings of the great naturalist and artist, who was also an evocative writer, published seventy-five years after his death in 1851. Good browsing also are Audubon's *Journal,* published in 1929, and his *Letters,* 1930. (*Audubon and His Journals,* edited by Maria R. Audubon, is available in paperback: two volumes—Dover.) For the walker who loves either birds or art, or both, is the history-making first edition of Audubon's original water-color paintings for *The Birds of America,* the complete collection of 431 paintings, reproduced for the first time from his original water colors, published by Houghton Mifflin in 1966 ($75). All previous editions of the Audubon paintings have been "renderings," hand-colored engravings made in England for the original publication of *The Birds of America.*

An American Year, by Hal Borland. Simon and Schuster, rev. 1957. Illustrated by Alexander Anderson. A tender journal of country life and landscapes by *The New York Times's* beloved outdoor editorialist of more than thirty years. A beautiful book, with 63 woodcuts beautifully illustrating the seasons.

The Insect World of Jean Henri Fabre. Dodd, Mead, 1949. Selections from the writings of the great entomologist, edited with commentary and biographical note by another fine naturalist and writer, Edwin Way Teale. Also available in paperback—Crowell, and a reissue by Premier. Fabre's books are generally available in good translation, and are seductive invitations to the nearby out-of-doors.

A Sand County Almanac and Sketches Here and There, by Aldo Leopold. Oxford University Press, 1949, new edition 1967. By one of the gifted modern naturalist-writers, a journal in the classic tradition.

John of the Mountains, by John Muir. Houghton Mifflin, 1938. Muir's journals. Also of interest to walkers who love the mountains and the wilds are Muir's books published during his lifetime, such as *My First Summer in the Sierra,* 1911, and *A Thousand-Mile Walk to the Gulf,* 1916. Muir's *The Mountains of California* and *Yosemite* are in pocket-size paperback (Doubleday). His *Studies in the Sierra* is one of the Sierra Club's beautiful books.

Walks and Talks of an American Farmer in England, by Frederick Law Olmsted. Putnam, 1852. Charming ambulatory chats, published during his lifetime, by the patron saint of New York City walkers, the designer of Central Park as well as of other famous parks and park systems in Brooklyn, Chicago, Montreal, Buffalo, and Boston.

Central Park, by Henry Hope Reed, Jr., and Sophia Duckworth. Clarkson N. Potter, 1966. Bringing Olmsted's masterpiece up to date, the story of the great park in a great city, with pictures, maps, descriptions of its many current goings-on from boating, bowling, baseball, and kite-flying to Shakespeare, symphonies, and dining *al fresco.* Two guided walking tours, besides rambles in the Ramble, a miniature wilderness in the park's heart beloved by bird-watchers and seekers of serenity, where the jangle of the metropolis is magically blotted out.

Journey into Summer, by Edwin Way Teale. Dodd, Mead, 1960. The contemporary naturalist-writer follows the coming of summer across the continent. Also by Teale: *North with the Spring,* 1951; *Autumn Across America,* 1956; and most recently, *Wandering Through Winter,* 1965; all published by Dodd, Mead.

Walden, by Henry David Thoreau. This best-known companion of walkers, first printed during Thoreau's lifetime, is available in several editions, including paperbacks published by Doubleday and Houghton Mifflin. Less well-known but equally rewarding are *A Week on the Concord and Merrimack Rivers* and the four posthumous selections from his journals, *The Maine Woods, Excursions, Cape Cod, A Yankee in Canada.* (All but the last-named are available in paperback.) The standard Walden Edition includes all the journals, as well as Thoreau's letters.

The River of Life, by Rutherford Platt. Simon and Schuster, 1956. Drawings by Bernarda Bryson. Also available in paperback—Simon and Schuster, 1962. About the other living things that inhabit the world around us; a book that enlarges the awe and wonder of the unity of life.

King Solomon's Ring, by Konrad Z. Lorenz. Crowell, 1952, paperback. Enchanting and revealing experiences of the distinguished naturalist and lover of animals, all kinds.

The Quiet Crisis, by Stewart L. Udall. Rinehart, 1963. Also available in paperback—Macmillan, 1964. Our walking Secretary of the Interior calls attention to beauties of our American land which may soon be as extinct as the passenger pigeon unless those who care will bestir themselves.

The American Landscape: A Critical View, by Ian Nairn. Random House, 1965. A book for city walkers and city lovers, filled with fine photographs of the many fascinating things to see in a city. This architect's proposal for a pedestrian network that can be developed out of what there is in the city *today* is the basis of our PPP proposal in Chapter 13.

Forever Wild: The Adirondacks, by Eliot Porter. The Adirondack Museum and Harper & Row, 1966. Captions by William Chapman White.

For Both Reading and Looking

A scattering of handsome picture books, publications of the Sierra Club. (Prices range generally from $15 to $25. For the complete list, write to: Sierra Club, c/o The Book Warehouse, Inc., Vreeland Avenue, Borough of Totowa, Paterson, N. J. 07512.)

In Wildness Is the Preservation of the World, by Eliot Porter. 1963. Text as well as title from Thoreau.

Not Man Apart: The Big Sur Coast. 1965. The text is from Robinson Jeffers, poet of the Big Sur.

The Place No One Knew: Glen Canyon on the Colorado, by Eliot Porter. 1963.

Summer Island: Penobscot Country, by Eliot Porter. 1966. The island off the Maine coast photographed and described by one who spent his boyhood there.

These We Inherit: The Parklands of America, by Ansel Adams. 1962.

This Is the American Earth, by Ansel Adams and Nancy Newhall. 1960.

Time and the River Flowing: Grand Canyon, by François Leydet. 1964.

Words of the Earth, by Cedric Wright. 1960.

For Seaside Walkers

The Edge of the Sea, by Rachel Carson. Houghton Mifflin, 1955. Also available in paperback—New American Library, 1959. Walking the beach with the late marine biologist opens our eyes to the mysterious border world between sea and land.

Gift from the Sea, by Anne Morrow Lindbergh. Pantheon, 1955. Also available in paperback—Random House, 1964. An introspective experience of living at the sea's edge.

The Great Beach, by John Hay. Doubleday, 1963. Another eloquent naturalist explores the 50-mile frontier between land and sea on the outer reaches of Cape Cod.

Nonsuch: Land of Water, by William Beebe. Brewer, Warren & Putnam, 1932; Putnam, 1934. Also, his *A Book of Bays,* Harcourt, Brace, 1942. The famous naturalist who went underwater in his bathysphere also explored nearer the surface.

The Outermost House, by Henry Beston. Rinehart, 1949. Also available in paperback—Viking, 1961. First published in 1928, a distinguished naturalist's record of a year on Nauset Beach. A companion piece to Thoreau's *Cape Cod* of 1865.

Mountains and Wilderness

Cache Lake Country, by John J. Rowlands. Norton, 1947. Wilderness life in the North Woods.

California's Back Country, by Dick Smith and Frank von Schaick. McNally and Loftin, 1963. An exploration of lesser-known areas of the rugged land.

Grand Canyon, by Joseph Wood Krutch. Sloane, 1958. Also available in paperback—Doubleday. A fresh view of this most dramatic walking site through the eyes of a professor of literature turned naturalist.

The Man Who Walked Through Time, by Colin Fletcher. Knopf, 1968. The story of the first trip afoot through the depths of the Grand Canyon, by the author of *The Thousand-Mile Summer.*

Great National Parks of the World, by Richard Carrington. Random House, 1968. Covers the five continents, with evocative and informative text; color and black-and-white photographs.

The Roadless Area, by Paul Brooks. Knopf, 1964. Quetico, the yet undespoiled lake country of upper Wisconsin.

Thousand Acre Marsh, by Dudley Cammett Lunt. Macmillan, 1959. On Delaware's tidal creeks, marshes, and swamplands.

The Woods and the Sea, by Dudley Cammett Lunt. Knopf, 1965. Trails and tales of Maine's rocky coast, wild woodlands and the free-running Allagash, which may become a National Waterway.

The Thousand-Mile Summer: In Desert and High Sierra, by Colin Fletcher. Howell-North, 1964. A record, with photographs, of a six-month walk along the backbone of California. A contemporary companion piece to Muir's *Thousand-Mile Walk.*

Walks Through the Past

Hawkers and Walkers in Early America, by Richardson Wright. Lippincott, 1927. A lively account of men who lived their lives afoot, the itinerant painters, peddlers, and vendors who sometimes rode but more often walked the country lanes and wilderness trails, plying their trades.

The Immense Journey, by Loren Eiseley. Random House, 1957. Also available in paperback—Random House, 1958. The eloquent evolutionist takes the reader through eons of earth's history on his walks.

The Lost Towns and Roads of America, by J. R. Humphreys. Doubleday, 1961. A cross-country jaunt over old roads and through forgotten towns, in a leisurely, nostalgic trip through the American past.

Places and People, Near and Far

Natural History of New York City, by John Kieran. Houghton Mifflin, 1959. A famous sidewalk naturalist's guide to the discovery and enjoyment of wildlife in and around a great modern city. For city dwellers everywhere.

Spring in Washington, by Louis J. Hallé, Jr. Harper, 1957. Also available in paperback—Atheneum, 1963. The nation's chief city and, for walking, its most beautiful, evoked in the season of its greatest beauty by a walker and amateur naturalist who is by profession a career diplomat.

The Silent Traveller in San Francisco, by Yee Chiang. Norton, 1964. The most recent of the charming "Silent Traveller" books, a unique series by a philosophic and observant visitor to the West from another, older culture. Also, *The Silent Traveller, in Boston; in New York;* and these abroad: *in Paris; in London; in Edinburgh; in Dublin; in Lakeland; in Oxford; in the Yorkshire Dales.*

Shanks's Pony, by Morris Marples. Dent, 1959. Adventures of an English walker.

Tramping in Arran, by Tom Hall. Gall & Inglis, Edinburgh, 1960. Walking adventures in the group of three Arran (or Aran) islands, timeless and remote, in Galway Bay off the west coast of Ireland. The Irish poet and dramatist John Millington Synge also wrote of them in *The Aran Islands* (Humphries, 1907), a journal of his retreat there. (Some readers will remember Robert Flaherty's moving documentary film of the primitive life in the islands, *Man of Aran.*)

Down the Rhone on Foot, by Clara Vyvyan. Transatlantic, 1955. This Englishwoman walker has written other books, including: *Cornish Year,* 1959; *on Timeless Shores: Journeys in Ireland,* 1957; and *Temples and Flowers: a Journey to Greece,* 1956, also published by Transatlantic.

Afoot in Portugal, by John Gibbons. Newnes, 1931. A walk through a land where many Americans now go to vacation.

Bushwalking Around Sydney, by Paddy Pallin. Angus and Robertson, Sydney, 1959. Still farther afield, a walking adventure down under.

A Walker's Treasuries of Good Reading: Some Anthologies

The Art of Walking, edited by Edwin V. Mitchell. Loring and Mussey, 1934. Good reading, from fellow walkers of other decades.

Book of Naturalists, edited by William Beebe. Knopf, 1944. A writing naturalist's own selection.

Great American Nature Writing, edited by Joseph Wood Krutch. Sloane, 1950. Decorations by Rudolph Freund. Professor Krutch, taking an editor's privilege, included some other than American writers that he could not bear to omit. A highly personal collection by a man of impeccable taste.

The Gypsy Trail, compiled by Pauline Goldmark and Mary Hopkins. Kennerley, 1922. An older collection but the writing is imperishable.

The Poetry of Earth, edited by E. D. H. Johnson. Atheneum, 1966. Great English nature writing and walking, by some of England's great walker-writers, with illustrations by their contemporaries.

Treasury of Great Nature Writing, edited by John Kieran. Doubleday, 1957. Mainly American, including some grand pieces by contemporaries better known in other literary fields.

For Practical Use: Guidebooks

America's Wonderlands: The Scenic National Parks and Monuments of the United States. National Geographic Society, 1959. Descriptive and specific.

Directory of Hiking Trails in the United States. William Hoeferlin, 1966. Lists park and forest trails by states, and describes the 18 great American trails.

The State Parks, by Tilden Freeman. Knopf, 1962. For pleasurable reading and discovery of some well- and some little-known park walking places. Also available in a pocket edition that can be carried along when exploring in person.

The Goodyear Guide to State Parks: New England and New York, by Howard N. and Lucille L. Sloane. Crown, laminated paperback, 1967. The first of a series of six regional guides which will cover the country.

Massachusetts–Rhode Island Trail Guide. Appalachian Mountain Club, 1964. Wilderness walking in New England.

New York Walk Book, by Raymond Torrey. American Geographical Society, 1951. The third edition of this famous guidebook, still useful although it is some sixteen years old. A fourth edition is projected for publication in 1969.

Pacific Crest Trails from Alaska to Cape Horn, by Joseph Hazard. Superior Publishing Co., 1948. Describes the great trail running down the Western coastal range, with its subsidiary branches.

Deepest Valley, by Genny Schumacher. Sierra Club, both hardcover and paperback, 1962. Background and guide to Owens Valley in the Sierras.

Illustrated Guide to Yosemite, by Virginia and Ansel Adams. Sierra Club, hardcover and paperback, 1964. One of the Sierra Club guidebooks, fine pictures and text at modest price.

Guide to the John Muir Trail and the High Sierra Region, by Walter A. Starr, Jr. Sierra Club, paperback, 1962. A classic wilderness trail, in an authoritative guide.

Mammoth Lakes Sierra, by Genny Schumacher and others. Sierra Club, hardcover and paperback, 1959. Another fine Sierra Club background and guidebook.

Going Light, with Backpack or Burro, edited by David R. Brower. Sierra Club, 1956. Lively reading and practical guidance, in knapsack size, to the art of wilderness traveling and camping. A classic, now in its eighth printing.

Woodall's Travel-Camping the 4 Seasons 1967–68. Simon and Schuster, paperback, 1967. Specifically a guide to trailer camps by states, with facilities and ratings. Emphasis is on active recreation, including many good walking and hiking places in all seasons.

Roads and Trails of Olympic National Park, by Frederick Leissler. University of Washington Press, 1965. A paperback guide to walking in one of the most beautiful of our national parks.

100 Hikes in Western Washington. The Mountaineers, Seattle, 1966.

Routes and Rocks: Hiker's Guide to the North Cascades. The Mountaineers, Seattle, 1965.

Exploring the Olympic Peninsula, by Ruth Kirk. University of Washington Press, paperback, 1964. Illustrated.

Food for Knapsackers and Other Trail Travelers, by Winnie Thomas and Hasse Bunnelle. Sierra Club, paperback, 1966. How to travel light and eat well. A fresh look at the knapsack commissary.

Some City Walking Guides

New York Places and Pleasures, by Kate Simon. World Publishing, 1959. A paperback written for World's Fair visitors originally but now a classic guide to the city. One chapter is devoted to walks to points of interest and through New York's many and varied ethnic neighborhoods.

Footloose in Seattle, by Janice Krenmayr. A series of slim paperbacks, with walk tours, 1961, 1962, 1963. Write to: Osborn-Warne, P.O. Box 231, Midway, Wash. 98031.

Herb Caen's Guide to San Francisco. Doubleday, 1957. The classic walking guide to one of the most walkable of American cities.

San Francisco at Your Feet, by Margot Patterson Doss. Grove, paperback, 1964. Another, for the same city, pocket size and very good.

The Dolphin Guide to San Francisco and the Bay Area, Present and Past, by Curt Gentry. Doubleday, 1962. The "Dolphin Guides" generally have walks, with maps. This one guides you on five walks within the city (and one drive), also on 10 one-day automobile tours of the Bay Area with enough information for your own choice of further walks.

American Guide Series. These guidebooks, written as WPA projects in the 1930's, were unusually fine and are still of value. They describe and locate points of interest in rural and urban areas, state by state. In some instances the specifics may need updating from current information sources before you go out to walk.

Mexico Places and Pleasures, by Kate Simon. World Publishing, 1963. Also available in paperback—Doubleday, 1965. By the author of *New York Places and Pleasures.* One chapter has charming walks in Mexico City, its shops, markets, squares with shady benches to rest and watch the life around you, and times of day for the walk.

Turn Right at the Fountain, by George W. Oakes. Holt, 1965. A famous walker's guide to London, with five planned walking tours.

London for Everyone: An Informal Guide, by Archibald G. Ogden. Doubleday, paperback, 1966. Extremely pleasant introduction to London even for those who know it, with eight guided walks, some longer, some shorter, plus two more, in the form of strolls, in Chelsea and Belgravia. Lively, literate talk as you go, good maps, timely pub stops for refreshments.

London, by Nikolaus Pevsner. Penguin, 1957. History, architecture, street by street, from Roman London through all its rich past, by a distinguished authority. This is part of a series by the same author on great buildings and houses of England.

The Dolphin Guide to Paris, by William Davenport. Doubleday, paperback, 1962. A dozen guided promenades, with maps, photographs, places to lunch, see art and antiquities, and shop en route.

Connaissance du Vieux Paris, by Jacques Hillairet. Le Club Français du Livre, 1959. For those with a reading knowledge of French and a fondness for old houses and their history, this historical, sometimes gossipy, account of Old Paris, street by street, building by building, is worth its price ($7.95) as a lively walking companion. In 3 volumes, available at the Librairie de France, 610 Fifth Avenue, N.Y.C.

Camping and Motoring Through Europe, by Paul and Grace Witte. Amity Tours, 1960. Lists recommended campsites in England and 15 countries on the Continent. Book is available with a 1965–66 camp directory. Check before walking.

For Young Walkers

First Book of Hiking, by C. William Harrison. Watts, 1964. One of the "First Book" series, for the youngest readers. If they are old enough to read, they are old enough to learn the joys of walking.

Instructions to Young Ramblers, by Ronald W. Clark. Soccer Associates, 1958. Useful guidance, encouragement and admonitions.

Use Your Legs, by Guy R. Williams. Chapman Hall, 1961. Why walk? If you can't persuade them, this may.

Pocket Guides to Nature

Note: All nature lovers are perforce walkers, but not all walkers are nature lovers. Yet a nature interest often develops out of walking. Birds are the most generally captivating, so in the categories that follow "General" we put the bird guides first. (Some of the paperback books listed below are also available in hardcover editions.)

General

Complete Field Guide to American Wildlife, by Henry Hill Collins, Jr. Harper, 1959. Excellent identification guide to birds, mammals, reptiles, amphibians, fishes, seashells. Includes animal tracks.

For the Birds

Field Guide to the Birds, by Roger Tory Peterson. Houghton Mifflin. This is the classic, first published in 1934, in continuous print and in every bird-watcher's pocket. It covers American birds east of the Rockies. Also by Peterson in Houghton Mifflin hardcover edition: *Field Guide to Western Birds,* rev. 1961; *Field Guide to Birds of Britain and Europe,* 1966.

Field Guide to Birds of the West Indies, by James Bond. Houghton Mifflin, 1961. The author is the original James Bond, but only in name, not in character. The distinguished ornithologist was a friend of the late Ian Fleming, who appropriated the name for 007, hero of his spy thrillers.

How to Know the Birds, by Roger Tory Peterson. New American Library, 1957. A simplified guide, useful for beginning and young birders.

Birds of North America, by Chandler S. Robbins, Bertel Bruun, and Herbert S. Zim. Golden Press, 1966. Illustrated by Arthur B. Singer. One volume complete, in sturdy paperback, of land and water birds from coast to coast, Canada to Mexico. Color pictures are conveniently placed opposite the matching texts; with the texts also are maps of summer and winter habitats and "sonagrams" of bird songs.

Naming the Birds at a Glance, by Lou Blachly and Randolph Jenks. Knopf, 1963. Guide drawings by Sheridan Oman. A primer for the beginning birder, covering land birds from the Rockies east. Identification is made easy; birds are classified by color markings instead of by species.

How to Know the Land Birds, by Harry E. Jaques. William C. Brown, 1947. One of a series of nature guides in paperback issued by this publisher.

Address: 135 South Locust St., Dubuque, Ia. 52001. Others in the series are listed below under their separate subjects.

Birds in Our Lives, a U.S. Government publication. Everything about birds, their own lives and their many-sided impact on ours, in 576 pages by 61 authors. Send $9 with your order to the Superintendent of Documents, Government Printing Office, Washington, D.C. 20402.

Trees and Shrubs

Field Guide to the Trees and Shrubs, by George A. Petrides. Houghton Mifflin Field Guide series, hardcover, 1958.

How to Know the Trees, by Harry E. Jaques. William C. Brown, 1946.

How to Know the Western Trees, by H. Baerg. William C. Brown, 1955.

Flowers, Ferns, Grasses, and Other Greenery

The Pictorial Encyclopedia of Plants and Flowers, by F. A. Novak. Crown, 1966.

How to Know the Wild Flowers, by Mrs. William S. Dana. Dover paperback, rev. 1963. Mrs. Dana's book was first published in 1831.

Wild Flowers of America, edited by H. W. Rickett. Crown, 1953. This book is illustrated with 400 flowers in full color painted by Mary Vaux Walcott and Dorothy Falcon Pratt.

How to Know the Spring Flowers, by Mabel J. Cuthbert. William C. Brown, 1949.

How to Know the Fall Flowers, by Mabel J. Cuthbert. William C. Brown, 1948.

Field Guide to Rocky Mountain Wildflowers, by John Craighead and others. Houghton Mifflin, 1963.

Field Guide to the Ferns, by Boughton Cobb. Houghton Mifflin, 1956.

How to Know the Ferns, by Frances T. Parsons. Dover paperback, 1961. Another classic, this book first appeared in 1899.

How to Know the Cacti, by E. Yale Dawson. William C. Brown, 1963.

How to Know the Grasses, by R. W. Pohl. William C. Brown, 1954.

How to Know the Mosses and Liverworts, by Henry S. Conard. William C. Brown, 1956.

How to Know the Economic Plants, by Harry E. Jaques. William C. Brown, 1958.

How to Know the Weeds, by Harry E. Jaques. William C. Brown, 1959.

Wild Flowers of Greece, by D. Phitos, edited by Kaity A. Argyropoulo. Athens Society of the Friends of the Trees, 1965. This little gem, in sturdy paperback, with beautiful color photographs (by Valerie Finnis, John

Buxton and Dr. H. Roessler) will be your treasured pocket companion if your visit is in the spring, when Greece and the islands burst into unimaginable profusion and variety of bloom. You may have to go to Athens to get it, as we did.

Along Fresh- and Salt-water Shores

Field Guide to the Shells of Our Atlantic and Gulf Coasts, by Percy A. Morris. Houghton Mifflin, rev. 1951.

Field Guide to the Shells of the Pacific Coast and Hawaii, by Percy A. Morris. Houghton Mifflin, 1952.

How to Know the American Marine Shells, by R. Tucker Abbott. New American Library paperback, 1961.

How to Know the Seaweeds, by E. Yale Dawson. William C. Brown, 1956.

How to Know the Freshwater Algae, by Gerald W. Prescott. William C. Brown, 1954.

The Insect World

Insect Friends, by Edwin Way Teale. Dodd Mead, 1955. And by the same author: *Junior Book of Insects,* also Dodd Mead, 1953.

How to Know the Insects, by Harry E. Jaques. William C. Brown, 1947.

Field Guide to the Butterflies, by Alexander B. Klots. Houghton Mifflin, 1951.

How to Know the Beetles, by Harry E. Jaques. William C. Brown, 1951.

How to Know the Spiders, by B. J. Kaston. William C. Brown, 1953.

Animal Life of Land and Water

The Pictorial Encyclopedia of the Animal Kingdom, by V. J. Stanek. Crown, 1963. Includes insects, also microscopic animals.

Field Guide to the Mammals, by W. H. Burt and R. P. Grossenheider. Houghton Mifflin, 1964.

How to Know the Mammals, by Ernest S. Booth. William C. Brown, 1950.

How to Know the American Mammals, by Ivan T. Sanderson. New American Library paperback, 1951.

Field Guide to Reptiles and Amphibians, by Roger Conant. Houghton Mifflin, 1958.

Field Guide to Animal Tracks, by Olaus Murie. Houghton Mifflin, 1954.

How to Know the Eastern Land Snails, by J. B. Burch. William C. Brown, 1962.

How to Know Freshwater Fishes, by Samuel Eddy. William C. Brown, 1957.

For Rock Fanciers

Field Guide to Rocks and Minerals, by Frederick H. Pough. Houghton Mifflin, 1953.

How to Know the Minerals and Rocks, by Richard M. Pearl. New American Library paperback, 1955.

And for Night Walks

Field Guide to the Stars and Planets, by Donald H. Menzel. Houghton Mifflin, 1963.

"Vest Pocket" Guides: Vest Pocket books on trees, minerals, and other nature subjects, weightless for walks, are published by Ottenheimer Publishers, 99 Paintors Mill Road, Owing Mills, Md. 21117. Write for their list.

INDEX

ABOUT THE AUTHORS

AARON SUSSMAN is the author of *The Amateur Photographer's Handbook,* a classic in its field, now in the third printing of its seventh revised edition. He started his writing career as a reporter on the Brooklyn *Eagle* and the New York *Daily News,* has contributed to *Saturday Review,* the N.Y. *Herald Tribune Book Review, Publishers' Weekly,* and *Popular Photography,* and has written introductions to many books, including *Magic and Mystery in Tibet* by Alexandra David-Neel, *The Art of Selfishness* by David Seabury, and *Five Girls* by Sam Haskins. He has also been a bookseller, a publisher and, currently, a partner in an advertising agency which specializes in book publishing. He studied chemical engineering at C.C.N.Y. and journalism at New York University. He started walking at two, and has never given it up.

MRS. RUTH GOODE is a senior staff writer on MD, a leading medical magazine, and an author or co-author of more than a score of books, mainly in the fields of medicine and psychiatry. Among them are: *Man and his Body,* written with Dr. Benjamin F. Miller, *My Love Affair with the State of Maine* with Gertrude Mackenzie, and two books on marriage which have had world-wide success, written with her husband, Gerald, who is also a medical writer and an addicted walker. A born New Yorker, Mrs. Goode acquired her taste for country walking on geology field trips at Smith College, where she was graduated *summa cum laude* and Phi Beta Kappa. She learned city walking as a reporter on a metropolitan newspaper, her first job. She has a son who writes music and a daughter who writes fiction, and both are enthusiastic walkers.